Information and Communication Overload in the Digital Age

Rui Pedro Figueiredo Marques
University of Aveiro, Portugal

Joao Carlos Lopes Batista
University of Aveiro, Portugal

A volume in the Advances in Information Quality and Management (AIQM) Book Series

www.igi-global.com

Published in the United States of America by
    IGI Global
    Information Science Reference (an imprint of IGI Global)
    701 E. Chocolate Avenue
    Hershey PA 17033
    Tel: 717-533-8845
    Fax: 717-533-8661
    E-mail: cust@igi-global.com
    Web site: http://www.igi-global.com

Library of Congress Cataloging-in-Publication Data

Names: Marques, Rui Pedro Figueiredo, editor. | Batista, Joao Carlos Lopes, 1963- editor.
Title: Information and communication overload in the digital age / Rui Pedro Figueiredo Marques and Joao Carlos Lopes Batista, editors.
Description: Hershey, PA : Information Science Reference (an imprint of IGI Global), 2017. | Includes bibliographical references and index.
Identifiers: LCCN 2016054398| ISBN 9781522520610 (hardcover) | ISBN 9781522520627 (ebook)
Subjects: LCSH: Information resources management. | Information technology--Management. | Telecommunication--Social aspects. | Media literacy. | Information behavior.
Classification: LCC T58.64 .I458 2017 | DDC 303.48/33--dc23 LC record available at https://lccn.loc.gov/2016054398

This book is published in the IGI Global book series Advances in Information Quality and Management (AIQM) (ISSN: 2331-7701; eISSN: 2331-771X)

British Cataloguing in Publication Data
A Cataloguing in Publication record for this book is available from the British Library.

All work contributed to this book is new, previously-unpublished material. The views expressed in this book are those of the authors, but not necessarily of the publisher.

Advances in Information Quality and Management (AIQM) Book Series

ISSN:2331-7701
EISSN:2331-771X

MISSION

Acquiring and managing quality information is essential to an organization's success and profitability. Innovation in information technology provides managers, researchers, and practitioners with the tools and techniques needed to create and adapt new policies, strategies, and solutions for information management.

The **Advances in Information Quality and Management (AIQM) Book Series** provides emerging research principals in knowledge society for the advancement of future technological development. This series aims to increase available research publications and emphasize the global response within the discipline and allow for audiences to benefit from the comprehensive collection of this knowledge.

COVERAGE

- IT Innovation and Diffusion
- Human and Societal Issue
- Knowledge Management
- Application of IT to Operation
- IT Management in Public Organizations
- Decision Support and Group Decision Support Systems
- Supply Chain Management
- Mobile Commerce
- Electronic Commerce Technologies
- Web services and technologies

IGI Global is currently accepting manuscripts for publication within this series. To submit a proposal for a volume in this series, please contact our Acquisition Editors at Acquisitions@igi-global.com or visit: http://www.igi-global.com/publish/.

Titles in this Series

For a list of additional titles in this series, please visit: www.igi-global.com

Handbook of Research on Information Architecture and Management in Modern Organizations
George Leal Jamil (Informações em Rede, Brazil) José Poças Rascão (Polytechnic Institute of Setúbal, Portugal) Fernanda Ribeiro (Porto University, Portugal) and Armando Malheiro da Silva (Porto University, Portugal)
Information Science Reference • copyright 2016 • 625pp • H/C (ISBN: 9781466686373) • US $325.00 (our price)

Inventive Approaches for Technology Integration and Information Resources Management
Mehdi Khosrow-Pour (Information Resources Management Association, USA)
Information Science Reference • copyright 2014 • 315pp • H/C (ISBN: 9781466662568) • US $205.00 (our price)

Quality Innovation Knowledge, Theory, and Practices
Latif Al-Hakim (University of Southern Queensland, Australia) and Chen Jin (Zhejiang University, China)
Information Science Reference • copyright 2014 • 640pp • H/C (ISBN: 9781466647695) • US $245.00 (our price)

Rethinking the Conceptual Base for New Practical Applications in Information Value and Quality
George Leal Jamil (FUMEC University, Brazil) Armando Malheiro (Universidade do Porto, Portugal) and Fernanda Ribeiro (Universidade do Porto, Portugal)
Information Science Reference • copyright 2014 • 345pp • H/C (ISBN: 9781466645622) • US $175.00 (our price)

Cases on Electronic Records and Resource Management Implementation in Diverse Environments
Janice Krueger (Clarion University of Pennsylvania, USA)
Information Science Reference • copyright 2014 • 467pp • H/C (ISBN: 9781466644663) • US $175.00 (our price)

www.igi-global.com

701 E. Chocolate Ave., Hershey, PA 17033
Order online at www.igi-global.com or call 717-533-8845 x100
To place a standing order for titles released in this series,
contact: cust@igi-global.com
Mon-Fri 8:00 am - 5:00 pm (est) or fax 24 hours a day 717-533-8661

Bernadette Kneidinger-Müller, *University of Bamberg, Germany*

Margarida Lucas, *University of Aveiro, Portugal*

António Moreira, *University of Aveiro, Portugal*

Rui Pascoal, *Lusófona University of Humanities and Technologies, Portugal*

Silvia Torsi, *University of Trento, Italy*

Table of Contents

Section 1
Overview

Chapter 1
Joao Batista, University of Aveiro, Portugal
Rui Pedro Figueiredo Marques, University of Aveiro, Portugal

Chapter 2
Ana Lúcia Terra, Polytechnic Institute of Porto, Portugal

Chapter 3
Hernando Gómez Gómez, Universidad Europea de Madrid, Spain
Enrique Corrales Crespo, Universidad Europea de Madrid, Spain

Section 2
Heterogeneous Factors of Overload

Chapter 4
S. T. Ahmed, UAE University, UAE

Section 3
Solution Proposals

Detailed Table of Contents

Section 1
Overview

Chapter 1

Joao Batista, University of Aveiro, Portugal
Rui Pedro Figueiredo Marques, University of Aveiro, Portugal

This chapter presents an overview on information and communication overload. The theme is contextualized and the main concepts are discussed based on the published literature. The individual, the organizational and the social perspectives are considered. To deepen this discussion, the authors developed a bibliometric analysis, which demonstrated the steady increase of interest in this topic, apparently enhanced by new developments in information technology. These technologies have presented solutions for some problems, but at the same time they have raised new issues of information overload. The bibliometric analysis also shows that many of these new issues are communication issues, contributing to justify our argument that, currently, the problems of information overload and communication overload are interrelated.

Chapter 2

Ana Lúcia Terra, Polytechnic Institute of Porto, Portugal

In this chapter email overload is presented as a component of information overload and some of its causes and consequences are identified. Furthermore, an analysis on the skills required to deal with information overload is made. Then, a critical literature review about the concept of email overload is realized, stressing aspects such as the amount of messages, personal characteristics and skills or technological issues. Solutions for this organizational problem are presented based on relevant case studies from the literature review. Key components to consider in email overload management are also identified, including information management techniques and technological options, training, time management and information behavior (individual and organizational).

Chapter 3

Hernando Gómez Gómez, Universidad Europea de Madrid, Spain
Enrique Corrales Crespo, Universidad Europea de Madrid, Spain

The modern society establishes a complex relationship that combines the visual overload derived from technology insertion which is adapted to the today´s needs and executed through devices swiftly embraced. In this certain sense, one of the most overloaded environments currently is, in fact, the photography. The internet and digital mass media development have promoted to get a surprising image surplus, impossible to distinguish between the real occurrence and the photographic observed event. Therefore, is necessary to contemplate a sustainable scenario in photography. It must determinate a balance between images which are produced, consumed and those which can be assumed by society. The photography evolution and the new denomination PostPhotography installs a brand new discourse initially literal, linked to words and needing a unit of speech to make exist the images.

Section 2
Heterogeneous Factors of Overload

Chapter 4

S. T. Ahmed, UAE University, UAE

One of the most crucial areas in which information and technologies need to be managed in our information-rich society is in schools. Whilst information overload is often associated with organisations or social communication, schools represent the intersection of several stakeholders for whom information and communication must be managed effectively. Using a case study of a school in a Gulf State, this chapter analyses how mismanagement and miscommunication relating to the use of ICT is hindering the educational progress of children by examining school/teacher-pupil interaction; home-school communication, and; the application of ICT in the curriculum. It presents a professional and parental perspective on how the use and management of information technologies and effective communication are critical in maintaining acceptable levels of educational achievement. It draws on the experiences of both pupils and parents and uses a framework of participant observation to illustrate the problems of information overload as mismanagement and miscommunication.

Chapter 5

Mobile communication media such as smartphones have dramatically increased the social availability of users. The perpetual contact is experienced quite ambivalently, not only as a big advantage of technological development but also as a new reason for increasing communication overload. This chapter details how people evaluate mobile availability in their everyday lives and how they cope with experiences of overload and stress. Using the transactional theory of stress and coping (Lazarus & Cohen, 1977), data from a diary study and qualitative interviews with German smartphone users are analyzed. The findings emphasize the high level of subjectivity that influences how everyday experiences of smartphone usage and mobile availability are evaluated.

Chapter 6

Time management as an important source of wellbeing is here described along with the opportunities to link this activity to physical space, contacts and mobile personal cloud. The user-centered design of a novel agenda is the theme of this chapter. Some user studies were carried on, concept design and rough evaluations followed. The fishtank paradigm of interaction is here presented. It overcomes the linear perception of time and provides a gradient of devices for attention starting from peripheral awareness to proper notification according to the urgency of the tasks to execute. The final aim of the project is to support prospective as like as autobiographical memory in order to live the present time at its' fullest.

Chapter 7

Information and communication overload have gained a new dimension in today's digital world. The exposure to the volume of information being distributed has probably never been so high due to the rapid increase of communication channels at our disposal. Facing great volumes of information (and communication channels) may cause constraints in our personal and professional lives and therefore it requires the ability to deal with and solve the problems related with them. This chapter presents the DigComp, a tool that proposes a set of knowledge, skills and attitudes that are part of digital competence, one of the eight key competences for lifelong learning and essential for participation in our increasingly digitalised society. It takes the stance that the DigComp may work as a foundation for "calculating" the boundaries of that so-called overload. The intention is to find in this tool the right ally to gauge the acquisition of competences that will make any user more critically aware and proactive towards the ways s/he deals with communication and information in her/his daily routines.

Information overload is an important issue in the digital economy. Although, information can be easily accessed and disseminated by widespread use of information and communication technologies (ICT) since 1990s; among countries, there are still significant disparities in information access and utilization as well as ICT access and usage. ICT affect economy, industries and companies holistically and have important functions like increasing economic growth and promoting development. The basic purpose of this study is to analyze the impact of ICT on economic growth and electricity consumption for a group of Balkan and Eastern European countries by using other economic variables that affect electricity consumption and growth, such as income and electricity consumption for control purposes. This study employed a panel data method on a group of Balkan and Eastern European countries to verify the effect of other economic variables, primarily electricity consumption and found that ICT had positive impacts on economic growth.

Section 3
Solution Proposals

Chapter 9

Javier Serrano-Puche, University of Navarra, Spain

In the contemporary media ecosystem, online consumption is framed and characterized by a number of general elements. These key factors are: a) the overabundance of information available to users (information overload); b) the speed of online interaction; c) the emergence of attention as currency; d) the multiplicity of different screens; and e) the socialization of consumption. This chapter, grounded on a comprehensive literature review, first provides a description of these elements. A digital diet is then proposed based on the development of three areas: knowing how to use the technological tools and applications to deal with information overload; learning how to manage attention and cognitive overload; and, finally, establishing regular periods of digital disconnection. The conclusion is that practicing these healthy habits leads to more useful and effective media consumption.

Chapter 10

Thomas Ellwart, Trier University, Germany
Conny Herbert Antoni, Trier University, Germany

This chapter discusses information overload (IO) from a team level perspective. Organizational team research underlines the importance of emergent knowledge structures in work groups, so-called team cognition. Two types of team cognition are introduced that are closely related to IO, namely shared team mental models and transactive memory systems. After a brief introduction of the concepts, empirical evidence about the impact of team cognition on dysfunctional IO as well as functional information exchange are presented. In the second part of the chapter, strategies and tools for adapting team cognition in high IO situations are introduced. The focus on team level constructs in IO research complements individual, technical, and organizational approaches to IO by underlining the importance of team knowledge structures in social systems.

Information is managed avoiding overload in Fab Labs, digital manufacturing environments. Collaborative spaces like Maker Spaces, Hacker Spaces, Tech Shops and Fab Labs are intended to stimulate innovation, through the exchange and sharing of information, knowledge, and experience among its members. They leverage innovation stimulating the creativity of its participants and enabling the creation of products and solutions based on personal projects, developed communally. With the motto "Learn, Make, Share," these spaces aim to empower its members for the realization of local and community-based sustainable solutions, using open source tools and equipment's, to allow every member the possibility of creating low cost products, with the ability to very quickly show the viability of these ideas through the acceptance by the community, that will make these solutions evolve collaboratively. It will be analyzed and described how Fab Labs manage their information to avoid information overload, maximizing the networking amongst its members.

This chapter explores the benefits and challenges of using augmented reality (AR) technology in outdoor sports environments. Questions emerge about the presentation of information more appropriate to give a user without being excessive. The aim is to assess the problems related with information overload before implementing an AR system to be used in outdoors environments. Solutions are listed to manage and interact, the best way, with the information on the mobile device of AR, and achieve social acceptance. The Solutions and Recommendations answer through an empirical research about what data are more appropriate without information overload for outdoor sports. Finally, to better understand, an AR Mockup example frame AR components of information and possible features, which represent the ideal display for sportsman, without information and communication overload.

Chapter 13

Sonja Ganguin, Leipzig University, Germany
Johannes Gemkow, Leipzig University, Germany
Rebekka Haubold, Leipzig University, Germany

This article deals with the concept of information overload as a crucial element of the changing information environment. Against this background, the authors discuss an alternative process for the conceptualisation of educational media literacy. By combining two nationally-based concepts on media literacy (German and Anglo-American), the yield of such a transnational approach will be demonstrated. The first section is dedicated to a historical overview. Based on the observation that humanity is currently dealing and always has dealt with information overload, leads to the necessity of coping with said overload. To this end, the second section will present and didactically reduce both discourses to their essentials. The third section provides a possible conceptualisation of both concepts and practical application of the combined approach for scholastic learning. The aim of this paper is to stimulate an international exchange on media literacy.

Foreword

Towards a balanced understanding of information overload – a short foreword to the book.

I am delighted to introduce this important anthology on one of the key challenges of the digital age: information overload. It is a sign of our times and also an accomplishment of the editors to shed light on this crucial topic from many different perspectives, and in so many diverse contexts.

The present anthology strongly argues the case that information overload is an omnipresent challenge that merits close examination through various research approaches. It also makes the important point that there is no panacea for the information overload problem. Rather, we need solutions that fit the respective context and specific type of information and thus enhance our information skills in diverse and flexible ways.

It is thus another accomplishment of the present volume that it does not only discuss the (at times severe) problems or symptoms associated with information overload, but also brings together authors who present (and critically discuss) solutions to the data deluge that we face today.

A last important accomplishment of this book that I would like to highlight is that that the editors have assembled authors who address the information overload phenomenon on different levels, hence not only focusing on the role of the individual knowledge worker, but also taking into account the institutional or technical parameters that increase or reduce information overload.

Having researched information overload for over twenty years now myself, I can only wish that this research field will continue to flourish and attract so many diverse researchers, as in the present volume. To the readers, I now wish stimulation from the chapters, inspiration from their findings, and at times, also irritation in order to critically reflect on one's own approach to the ever-growing information offer.

Martin J. Eppler
University of St. Gallen, Switzerland

Preface

Information overload is a phenomenon already identified a long time ago. It refers to what happens when individuals are faced with a volume of information greater than their processing capabilities allow in the period of time available, causing constraints on the ability of the individuals to solve problems. The wide availability of information that we are currently witnessing brings additional importance to the problem, making it urgent that individuals and organizations continually develop techniques and strategies to filter, select and process the most appropriate information to solve their problems. It has been addressed by several areas of knowledge like information science, behavioral sciences or information and communication technologies.

The development that has taken place in recent years in the field of communication technologies and, in particular, in the field of technologies generally referred to as social media encourages a new thinking on the problem of information overload, given that these technologies represent channels through which the volume of information transmitted is hugely larger than using more traditional communication technologies. Thus, today a new layer on the information overload problem has emerged, which is the issue of communication overload. In fact, communication networks we are using today require new attention to the subject: not only to the amount of information received, but also to the communication processes associated with it. Current trends and evolving technologies such as the internet of things, transmedia and the combined use of various devices and communication channels further complicate this issue.

This book organizes and presents a set of chapters which provides the research community and others with a wider view of the causes, approaches and trends on the subject of information and communication overload. A particular emphasis is put on the relation of this subject with the use of Information and Communication Technologies (ICT). Some of the objectives of this book are:

- Frame the concept of information overload, in theory and in experimental terms;

- Extend the concept of information overload with a wider idea that also includes communication overload, and in that way integrating the challenges posed by today's communication technologies;
- Present current and future approaches seeking to solve the problem of information and communication overload in different contexts and perspectives.

EXPECTATIONS

The creation of this independent publication aims to organize and disseminate the research trends and findings of theoretical, empirical and experimental studies worldwide. It can be valuable to everyone involved in the development of creative and new approaches to solve the problem of information and communication overload that are consequence of the new technological advances.

The editors hope that this book can be useful for practitioners as well as for researchers in fields such as information science, information management and other areas which may be related to this topic, namely, information systems, knowledge management, social media, engineering, human-computer interaction or psychology. Furthermore, it intends to be useful to managers making them more aware of this issue and realize how the effects of information and communication overload can be controlled and mitigated, and how organizations can manage the issues imposed by this subject as well.

Finally, through the dissemination of research works and findings on this topic, this publication can also be helpful to inspire and develop further research studies by researchers with interests directly or indirectly related to information and communication overload.

ORGANIZATION OF THE BOOK

This book is organized in 3 different sections and 13 chapters.

The first section, "Overview," gives the reader an introduction to the book main theme. It has three chapters. The first chapter provides an overview and a bibliometric study on information and communication overload. The other two chapters are more specific, concentrating on the email overload issue (Chapter 2) and on the relation between information overload and *PostPhotography* (Chapter 3). These three chapters include a relevant number of appropriate references which can be very useful to a novice on the theme as well as to a more experienced researcher. The first section has the following chapters:

- Chapter 1, "An Overview on Information and Communication Overload," presents a wide overview on information and communication overload, and is intended to be used as an introductory chapter for the book. It deepens in the literature to expose the main concepts and to focus not only on the information perspective of the overload phenomena but also on the communication perspective. The concepts are presented in a triad of individual, organizational, and societal perspectives of this issue. Another triad is also used, namely the causes, the symptoms and solutions for this problem, in line with previous work of other authors. The results of a bibliometric analysis based on data from SCOPUS are described showing that many of the issues published under the information overload topic are, in fact, communication overload problems and challenges. However, slight variations between consecutive years were identified and the analyses show a steady trend on the number of published works on the subject, with Computer Science being the most prominent scientific area.

- Chapter 2, "Email Overload: Framing the Concept and Solving the Problem – A Literature Review," focuses on the specific issue of email overload and frames this concept under the more general idea of information overload, identifying some of its causes and consequences. A literature review is provided giving the reader an overview of the published literature on the subject. The chapter is very organizationally-oriented and some solutions that have been proposed are described and discussed. This chapter emerges as a positive contribution and valuable reading to those who want to introduce the email overload issues.

- Chapter 3, "Photographers Without Photographs: The Internet as Primary Resource," under the main idea of creating a reflection about the present and future status of photography in the 21st century, takes the information overload issue to open a discussion on the "reformulation of *photographic fact*", in the words of the authors. Two different perspectives of the contemporary photographer are discussed: that of a photographer as an image producer and that of a photographer as someone that collects images from the internet and appropriates them, but not necessarily produces them. *PostPhotography* is discussed and presented as a new discourse in the search of a sustainable scenario for photography. Thus, in this chapter, the information overload, specifically the image overload, which has been highly leveraged by the current massive sharing of images on the Internet, is a cause of this change on photography prospective.

The second section, "Heterogeneous Factors of Overload," includes five chapters approaching diversified aspects of information and communication overload. The second section has the following chapters:

- Chapter 4, "Managing Information, Communication, and Technologies in Schools: Overload as Mismanagement and Miscommunication," starts from the idea that the contemporary landscape of ICT causes problems on using and managing information, not only in organizations or through social communication, but also at schools. The amount of information available to the schools' actors seems to increase those problems. This chapter clearly illustrates that the information mismanagement may be strongly associated to information overload. The author uses a case study to analyze three main key areas: school/teacher – pupil interaction; home-school communication; and the impact of ICT on education attainment. The major conclusions are that a process of monitoring and evaluating the use of ICT in the school must be implemented and also that a cost-benefit analysis of the investments made on devices and other aspects should be done. Finally, the author argues that a policy that gives the different actors a perspective on the use of ICT for teaching and learning could be disseminated.
- Chapter 5, "Perpetual Mobile Availability as a Reason for Communication Overload: Experiences and Coping Strategies of Smartphone Users," focuses on a specific cause of communication overload, namely on the "perpetual mobile availability". The research aims to know how users experience that availability and which strategies they develop in order to avoid communication overload. A qualitative study was implemented. A sample of 24 smartphone university student users participated in the data colleting process, through a diary study and in-depth interviews. The results are largely presented, showing that the participants experience mobile communication and deal with communication overload in divergent ways.
- Chapter 6, "The Fishtank Paradigm of Experience: Merging Time, Space, Activities, Emotions, and People," describes a project that aims to provide tools that people can use on the smartphone to manage their time and overcome information overload. Creating an environment that concentrates and combines a number of different technologies is the solution proposed. The project team includes core resources from artificial intelligence/semantics, from development and from design. Three focus groups were required to collect information on different aspects of how users manage their time. A design space concept emerged and three prototypes were produced and evaluated. The author looks at the future developments of integrating the system with other devices such as smart watches or interactive materials.

- Chapter 7, "Information and Communication Overload: Can DIGCOMP Help?," concentrates on the examination of DigiComp as a possible tool to help dealing with information and communication overload. The chapter describes the main ideas of DigiComp, which aims to be used as a European framework to understand and develop the citizens' digital competences. The authors analyze the relationship between digital competence and information and communication overload and then propose some future research directions, namely questioning the use of DigiComp as a contribution to the activities of curricula planning and certifying, or measuring the benefits of applying DigiComp.

- Chapter 8, The Impact of Information and Communication Technologies on Economic Growth and Electricity Consumption: Evidence From Selected Balkan and Eastern European Countries," assuming that digital economy has information overload as one of its issues, analyzes the impact that ICT has on economic growth and electricity consumption on Balkan and Eastern countries. The authors analyze the ways that ICT affects economic growth and also present an empirical analysis, in which they used panel data techniques. Results of this research show that electricity consumption and economic growth have positive consequences from ICT adoption. However, these results have drawn the authors' attention and awareness to the information overload, which may arise from this adoption.

The third section, "Solution Proposals," shows five chapters that, in one way or another, are concerned with solutions that could help to mitigate the issue of information and communication overload. The third section has the following chapters:

- Chapter 9, "Developing Healthy Habits in Media Consumption: A Proposal for Dealing With Information Overload," proposes a digital healthy diet to overcome the problems caused by the online consumption, which is characterized by a set of key factors, including information overload. The author argues that there are three keys to include on the proposed diet, namely producing knowledge on how to technologically handle information overload; dealing with attention and cognitive overload; and disconnect regularly from the digital network. In order to make this proposal useful to the users, a proper media education approach would be necessary. The author adds some future research directions related with emotional management and with factors that influence consumers' behavior.

- Chapter 10, "Shared and Distributed Team Cognition and Information Overload: Evidence and Approaches for Team Adaptation," draws attention to the relation between information overload and team cognition, which means that it focuses on an organizational perspective. Grounded on the literature, the chapter reviews and discusses empirical results of the relation of team mental models and transactive memory systems with information overload. Then, authors propose strategies and tools to deal with information overload situations, based on team cognition updating adaptation. The dysfunctional effects of team cognitions are among the future research directions proposed by the authors. The chapter concludes arguing that a social solution for information overload could be the synchronization and adaptation of team cognition.

- Chapter 11, "Information Management in Fab Labs: Avoiding Information and Communication Overload in Digital Manufacturing," describes a project about avoiding information and communication overload in Fab Labs, which is an international network of laboratories of digital fabrication created by the Center for Bits and Atoms at MIT. This research is part of a project to implement such a lab in a Brazilian university, and emerged due to the difficulties of managing information on these labs and thus avoiding information overload. A sample of 22 labs answered to a questionnaire and the results show that information overload is a concern on these labs. However, providing proper funding and keeping the lab running emerged as a more critical factor. The authors then propose a model to structure and save information aiming to minimize information overload.

- Chapter 12, "Information Overload in Augmented Reality: The Outdoor Sports Environments," provides solutions for using augmented reality in the outdoor sports context avoiding information overload. Considering the use of mobile devices, factors such as attention dispersion, the most appropriate data for each case and the social acceptance of using augmented reality in the outdoor sports environments are questioned. The chapter describes an empirical study that involved interaction tests with end-users. Research instruments used include observation, a questionnaire and structured interviews. The authors conclude that in order to avoid information overload, balance and simplicity are the key characteristics for solutions using augmented reality in outdoor sports contexts.

- Chapter 13, "Information Overload as a Challenge and Change for Educational Media Literacies," discusses the idea of changing the way people deal with information overload by improving digital media literacies. A historical perspective of the information overload concept is presented, and then updated with a digital layer. The authors analyze and compare two different approaches of media literacy, German and Anglo-American, and systematize both reducing them to their essentials. The chapter concludes proposing that a combined approach would be valuable, using some more idealistic ideas from the German discourse and some more pragmatic features from the Anglo-American media literacy models.

In addition to the aspects that have been considered in organizing the sections of this book, other dimensions that may be relevant to the reader may be identified. Thus, some chapters deal with educational contexts and digital literacies (Chapters 4 and 13), while others focus on new trends in technology and on the use of new media (Chapters 3, 5, 6, and 12). Some chapters deal with the individual dimension (Chapters 3, 5, 6), others deal with the organizational dimension (Chapters 4, 10, 11), and others address the societal dimension (Chapter 8).

Rui Pedro Marques
University of Aveiro, Portugal, Portugal

Joao Batista
University of Aveiro, Portugal

Acknowledgment

The editors would like to acknowledge the contribution of all participants in this project.

Firstly, because this book would be nothing without the chapters which compose it, the editors would like to express gratitude to the authors of the chapters, who contributed with their so valuable expertise and effort to this book.

Then, the editors would like to recognize the Editorial Advisory Board members for their contribution in ensuring both the scientific and academic quality and coherence of chapters and the accuracy in the double-blind review process.

Moreover, sincere recognition is also addressed to the effort and the very important contribution of the reviewers to this publication process. Some authors also served as reviewers. We highly appreciate their double task.

Finally, a special acknowledgment is given to Professor Martin Eppler for his availability and kindness in writing the foreword of this book. He is one of the highest regarded experts on the book topic and his participation in this project greatly enhanced the impact of this publication. The editors feel very honored.

Without the support of all participants, this book would not have become a reality. Thank you.

Rui Pedro Marques
University of Aveiro, Portugal, Portugal

Joao Batista
University of Aveiro, Portugal

Section 1
Overview

Chapter 1
An Overview on Information and Communication Overload

Joao Batista
University of Aveiro, Portugal

Rui Pedro Figueiredo Marques
University of Aveiro, Portugal

ABSTRACT

This chapter presents an overview on information and communication overload. The theme is contextualized and the main concepts are discussed based on the published literature. The individual, the organizational and the social perspectives are considered. To deepen this discussion, the authors developed a bibliometric analysis, which demonstrated the steady increase of interest in this topic, apparently enhanced by new developments in information technology. These technologies have presented solutions for some problems, but at the same time they have raised new issues of information overload. The bibliometric analysis also shows that many of these new issues are communication issues, contributing to justify our argument that, currently, the problems of information overload and communication overload are interrelated.

INTRODUCTION

Consider the following quote by Barnaby Rich: "one of the diseases of this age is the multiplicity of books; they doth so overcharge the world that it is not able to digest the abundance of idle matter that is every day hatched and brought forth into the

DOI: 10.4018/978-1-5225-2061-0.ch001

world" (Price, 1963). This quote was made in 1613, at a time when books would be quite rare and usually reserved for individuals of relatively privileged social classes. It highlights the difficulty to digest, or internalize, the amount of information that was produced and disseminated. The ability to digest the information you have access to is a factor related to the decision-making capacity. However, it contributes positively to the decision-making process or, conversely, it can cause stress and difficulty (Jackson & van den Hooff, 2012; Mulder, de Poot, Verwij, Janssen & Bijlsma, 2006). From the pieces of information available, books or other, which are to be chosen and digested by a person so that he or she can be properly informed in order to make a decision? What formats and properties should these pieces of information have in order to be digested efficiently and thereby rendered useful? What communication technologies should be used so that a person can receive the information in due time to make a decision?

These and other similar questions are the basic motivation to writing this chapter around the main idea of information overload. In general, information overload relates to the causes, the consequences and the solutions, or countermeasures (Eppler, 2015; Eppler & Mengis, 2004), to situations in which the excessive amount of information prevents people, organizations, and societies, from taking the most appropriate decisions.

The development of communication networks, including those based on the use of Internet has added a new layer to the problem of information overload. In fact, the amount of information that is currently exchanged online, namely through technologies such as email and social networks, force people to face another issue prior to information overload. The traffic information that is exchanged between people, on their individual, organizational or social roles, is now so high that the existence of a problem that can be called communication overload is easily recognizable (Cecchinato, Bird & Cox, 2014; Thomée, Dellve, Härenstam & Hagberg, 2010; Yin, Davison, Bian, Wu & Liang, 2014). Communication overload means that the exchange of information and the communication messages that people deal with exceed their capacity to manage them. This in what regards analyzing information and messages content, filtering out what seems more relevant or that should be given attention to so that contents can be digested.

We believe that these two issues are inextricably linked today: given that currently most of the information is sent and received digitally through online communication networks, and given the amount of communication held and information exchanged, the two problems become interdependent.

The next section of this chapter presents the concepts of information overload and communication overload and their relationship. From that short review, it results clear that a more systematic review of literature is needed. Thus, the results of a starting effort on that review are described in a new section, consisting of a bibliometric analysis of these two concepts and on how, in the literature, they have been linked. The Scopus database was the main source for the bibliometric analysis. These two sections result in a discussion and concluding remarks, and some research perspectives on this problem are then suggested.

This chapter is expected to be useful for those practitioners and researchers alike who are starting on the "overload" issue, as well as for others who, having some knowledge of the subject, are looking for a current view.

Information, Information Overload and Communication Overload

The concept of information is essential in the approach taken in this chapter. In general, from a systemic perspective, information results from data processing. For example, the inflation rate of a country in a given year results from a number of mathematical operations on a large data set. These data are collected, filtered, subjected to calculations, and then the result of this process is a value, corresponding to the inflation rate, which can then be released. If this information is digested by individuals, it can then eventually be used in political, economic and other decision-making. A journalistic piece is also regarded as information. In fact, a piece of news, such as news presented on a TV station, results from the collection of different data formats (texts, images, videos, etc.), which are then processed by journalists, or are subject to operations such as filtering, analysis, recombination, or other, to produce some new information, which can then be presented as a piece of news. This piece, if and when digested by individuals, can then be used in decision-making processes.

Information is thus something that is pursued, that is sought and that presents some informative power. It is a new result, a different perspective on any issue, or any news. When individuals receive new information, they must decide whether it is relevant to them, i.e. if it can be useful in their decision-making processes. If so, in order to use this information, it is necessary to digest it. The term information digestion has been used by some authors (Eppler, 2015; Eppler & Mengis, 2004; Price, 1963) when relating to the process that humans do, or need to do, to appropriate information and internalize it as a result of their learning. Thus, this information becomes part of their inner resources, and is then available for use. From our perspective, this use is primarily related to decision-making processes, i.e. to all kinds of situations in which individuals are faced with the need to make decisions, and thus control the course of their actions. In these situations, they may use their inner resources or seek other resources when they feel they are not sufficiently informed, or do not have the most appropriate information to support their decision.

Individuals make decisions of various kinds. Individual decisions, for example, are usually related to one's personal needs and thus essentially affect their life. For example, when an individual intends to purchase a car or a house and does not have the sufficient capital, he or she will need to know about the conditions for a credit, the fees and charges, the taxes and so on. After collecting and digesting this information the individual can then equate possible solutions and eventually make a decision.

Decisions can also be made at the organizational level. For example, in case of negative financial results in a given fiscal year, a company will have to make decisions aiming to attain more positive results in the future. Its collaborators should then, through a collective process, identify, collect and filter relevant and appropriate information for this decision making. Although the collaborators are individuals participating in this process, decisions are not individual. Given the organizational nature of this process, their tasks are combined in a common context to make decisions.

Finally, decisions can also be societal. A society is shared by a wide range of individuals, as happens in an organization. In an organization it is expected that individuals share a set of values and observe the rules governing their activities, often being paid for that. A society is a more general entity, in which individuals are subject to frameworks of values, rules, patterns of behavior but, at the same time, at least in democratic societies, they have the freedom and the right to influence its course and are not paid just because they are members of society. On the contrary, they often contribute to their society in financial terms, through various tax collection mechanisms. Societies also make decisions that affect the majority of their members. See the recent case of the referendum in the United Kingdom, called Brexit. The output of the United Kingdom decision to leave the European Union was taken collectively by all its members that decided to exercise their right to vote. For that decision, each voter collected and disseminated information shared by political parties, interest groups, and the media in general. Every citizen was allowed to choose the media by which he or she selected and filtered the information, and eventually digested it in order to make a decision on its own vote. Each citizen decided on his own vote. However, in this specific case the most relevant decision was taken by society as a whole, i.e., the decision about the direction of the majority of votes.

In today's world, all these mentioned examples face the issue of info communicational overload, i.e. face the challenges posed by information overload and, in addition, the communication overload. As mentioned in the previous section, these terms are interrelated. More than that, we argue that these two concepts are just one issue in terms of the ability of individuals, organizations and societies to make their own decisions.

Several different definitions of information overload have been presented, addressing this issue in different ways (Edmunds & Morris, 2000; Eppler & Mengis, 2004). One of the most used has been referred to as inverted u-curve (Eppler, 2015; Schroder, Driver, & Streufert, 1967), which essentially establishes a cause-effect relationship between the amount of information available and the capacity of individuals to make decisions. Thus, the more the available information, the higher the decision-making capacity. This trend is reversed when the information is excessive, hindering its possibility of being digested efficiently and thus contributing negatively to the decision making. At that point, information overload occurs. According to this model, there is a balance between the amount of information and the decision-making capacity, and there´s a peak that corresponds to the highest decision-making ability. If the amount of information continues to grow beyond that peak, the decision-making capacity gradually diminishes.

Although this definition is very clear and helps to understand the concept of information overload, it is also very subjective to apply in real situations, because many different variables, such as the personal characteristics, the context, and others, are not controllable. Also, this definition appears to be insufficient, because it just integrates two dimensions: the decision-making capacity and the amount of information. Other dimensions of the problem have been identified. For example, some authors have sought the causes, symptoms and solutions and the relationship between them, through a conceptual framework that includes 5 main causes (Eppler, 2015; Eppler & Mengis, 2004). One of the causes is that many individuals have limited capacity to filter and digest the information they receive. Their capacity also varies and they are affected by environmental factors or context (Eppler & Mengis, 2004; Haase et al., 2014; Haase, Ferreira, Fernandes, Santos, & Jome, 2015; Ruff, 2002). Technology is another factor that may cause information overload. Information and Communication Technologies (ICT) allow us to produce very large amounts of information and, more importantly, to disseminate this information through multiple communication channels, which can cause various problems such as systems usability, the efficient use of email, or in systems integration (Eppler & Mengis, 2004; Fuglseth & Sørebø, 2014; Harris, Harris, Carlson, & Carlson, 2015; Mittelstädt, Brauner, Blum, & Ziefle, 2015; Ruff, 2002).

Organizations are also causes of information overload. Organizations are dynamic systems, so their processes must be efficient and well-coordinated as well as the people and technologies that are part of these processes. Thus, if the change and the process dynamics are not properly managed, information overload can easily occur (Eppler & Mengis, 2004; Reinke & Chamorro-Premuzic, 2014; Ruff, 2002). The increasing complexity of processes may also influence information overload. The multitasking activities, the constant interruptions and delays in interdependent tasks are some organizational causes of information overload (Eppler & Mengis, 2004; Jackson & Farzaneh, 2012; Lee, Son, & Kim, 2016; Rennecker & Derks, 2013; Ruff, 2002).

The properties of the information that is disseminated and assimilated by individuals are another possible cause of information overload. Eppler addresses this particular aspect in the context of information quality, i.e. in terms of the properties that allow information to be more easily understood and, then, resulting in a higher value as far as it is used (Eppler, 2015). In search for the properties that make information easier to digest, and anticipating solutions to situations of information overload, Eppler indicates that information must be relevant; it must be sound; the process of production, dissemination and use must be optimized; and the necessary infrastructure for information management must be reliable.

Several other authors focus on the causes and factors associated with information overload. In particular, Jackson and Farzaneh identified intrinsic factors in the literature, such as the amount of information, the information processing capacity requirement, and the available time. They also identified extraneous factors such as the characteristics of information (e.g. complexity or ambiguity), information quality (usefulness, relevance, validity), the task and the process parameters (e.g. interruption, multi-tasking), and personal factors (e.g. skills, cognitive style, motivation). Sources of information were also identified as an extraneous and intrinsic factor (Jackson et al., 2012).

Symptoms of occurrence of information overload are diverse and are felt by many individuals. It is estimated that about one third of office workers and more than half of managers regularly face information overload situations (Klausegger, Sinkovics, & Zou, 2007). The symptoms may be of individual nature, such as stress, anxiety or fatigue (Bawden & Robinson, 2009). Changes in performance and efficiency in organizational processes, or changes in the ability to communicate and manage the exchange of information necessary for the operation teams, can also be symptoms of information overload (Ellwart, Happ, Gurtner, & Rack, 2015; Klausegger et al., 2007). However, as Eppler and Mengis highlighted, the main question is on how the performance of individuals is affected in the decision-making process (Eppler & Mengis, 2004).

Eppler also presents some solutions to the problem of information overload. A solution may be increasing information quality and improving the properties of the available information, as aforementioned (Eppler, 2015). However, the variety of solutions is very large and depends very much on the causes and symptoms that may be identified in each case. Technological solutions can be used to mitigate information overload and, in the case of organizations, to promote organizational efficiency. Technology may also be used to define user profiles for information access. This definition should be appropriate in order to ensure that users have correct access to information according to their duties and responsibilities, avoiding information overload and communication overload (Cecchinato, Bird, & Cox, 2014). However, if preventive approaches are adopted, problems of information and communication overload may be lighter and have a lower impact. Individuals and organizations may eventually plan and design their access to information processes and select communication channels which are most appropriate to their needs, thus preventing situations of information and communication overload.

Many of the concerns that have been revealed about information overload are, in fact, concerns related to communication processes. For example, Eppler and Mengis indicate three types of information concerning the overload situation, as "retrieval information, organization, and analysis processes", "decision processes", and "communication processes" (Eppler & Mengis, 2004). Regarding the "communication processes", they identify various situations, such as the use of groupware applications or email. From our point of view, these situations are related to communication overload to the extent that what is at issue is the management of the communication process itself and not necessarily the information digestion process of the messages that are exchanged. Thereby, the fact that we are daily flooded with messages that reach us through numerous communication channels demands that we have to give attention to the management of these messages before we can possibly observe the content of some of them. The phenomenon of communication overload currently appears to be very important, despite not new. For example, Meier proposed in 1963 a set of measures to deal with a problem of communication overload in a university library (Meier, 1963). However, with the advent of the Internet and the multiple communication technologies associated with it, this phenomenon has gained a considerable importance. For example, in a study of rate and delay in overload, Cho et al. detected increased levels of communication overload in either synchronous or asynchronous communication channels (Cho, Ramgolam, Schaefer, & Sandlin, 2011). The phenomenon of communication overload, also known as connection overload (Larose, Connolly, Lee, Li, & Hales, 2014), has been studied in relation to various technologies, such as electronic mail (Cecchinato et al., 2014; Reinke & Chamorro-Premuzic, 2014; Rennecker & Derks, 2013) or social networks (Lee et al., 2016).

All the points we raised throughout this section relate to the individual or organizational perspective of information and communication overload. Some authors include a third perspective - customer information overload - which "affects customer spending strategies" (Butcher, 1995; Jackson et al., 2012). However, the social and societal perspective also seems to be very important. The overload problem does not arise only in situations of communication between individuals or organizations but also between social or groups in societies. In this sense, Bergamaschi highlights the role that newspapers, TV networks and other media play in the multiplication of similar news, thus creating a social effect of communication overload (Bergamaschi & Leiba, 2010). Others address the issue of communication overload with over communication and miscommunication within movements of political activism (Nielsen, 2009). In these cases, the overload of information and communication in social terms are concerned, which means that these phenomena can influence and enhance the direction of societies, independently of each of its citizens or organizations they are affiliated with.

High levels of over communication and miscommunication may eventually be related to the society of uncertainty where we live today (Bauman, 2007). In fact, in Western societies, we currently live in a time that allows almost everyone to access to all kinds of information wanted, and all the communication channels are basically available. But at the same time, everything is very uncertain in people's lives, organizations and society itself. Many societies seem to have set aside their power to promote new ideas. On the contrary, they seem increasingly subdued to the power of capital. Because the media and the communication channels are now less institutional, the production of information and its dissemination seem to go in the same direction. They are increasingly private and in numbers unimaginable before. Every individual and organization may now produce and provide all the information they want. And they can do it for free or apparently so, at least if they accept to pay through advertising and by collecting their data and data related to interactions between these powerful media actors. The fact that everyone is able to establish their communication channel to access and disseminate all the information they want seems to be another layer in liquid and uncertain society proposed by Bauman.

A BIBLIOMETRIC ANALYSIS

This section aims to make an overview on the evolution of the research on information overload and communication overload from 2006 to 2015. In order to achieve this purpose we used the Scopus, one of the largest abstract and citation databases of international and scientific peer-reviewed literature, to search and gather the most relevant scientific works on these topics. We present some statistics and a brief review on the topics which are addressed in the most cited and impactful works. Three surveys were conducted: first, we searched for works on information overload, then on communication overload, and finally on both topics simultaneously, in order to understand the influence that these themes represent, individually and jointly, in the scientific communities. Data were exported to a spreadsheet from which the following graphs were generated.

The first search was made by the term "Information Overload" in the title, abstract and keyword fields, limited to the years 2006-2015 and to the existence of at least one of the keywords "Information Overload" or "Information Overloads". The source code of this search was:

```
TITLE-ABS-KEY("Information Overload")
AND (LIMIT-TO(EXACTKEYWORD,"Information Overloads")
```

```
OR LIMIT-TO(EXACTKEYWORD,"Information Overload"))
AND PUBYEAR > 2005 AND PUBYEAR < 2016
```

1410 documents matching this criterion were found. From these documents we can observe that the number of published papers increased during the ten-year period under study. Figure 1 shows the evolution of the number of published documents during that period. This number practically tripled in ten years, and it was found that 2012 was the year with more publications on this subject, with 200 documents.

According to Figure 2, most publications on this topic are conference papers. This document type accumulates nearly 70% of publications. Almost 30% corresponds to journal papers, and a residual percentage belongs to other document types, namely reviews and book chapters.

Research on information overload is more obvious in Computer Science, with almost half of publications. The other subject areas with interest regarding this topic are: Engineering, Mathematics, Social Science and Business, Management and Accounting, as represented in Figure 3.

In the subject of Computer Science, we found publications which address many themes. Those with more documents found were: Recommender Systems, Filtering, Social Networking, Information Systems and Information Retrieval. Some other topics with fewer publications were also found, such as: Information Management, Artificial Intelligence, World Wide Web, Algorithms, Human-Computer Interaction and Electronic Commerce among others.

In the area of Computer Science, we highlight the most cited works. For example, Bo and Benbasat (2007) addressed the topic of information overload on electronic commerce, including the use of recommendation agents helping consumers in

Figure 1. Number of published documents on information overload from 2006 to 2015

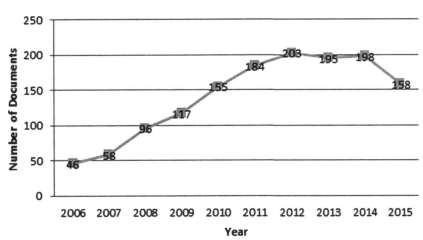

Figure 2. Distribution of publications on information overload by document type

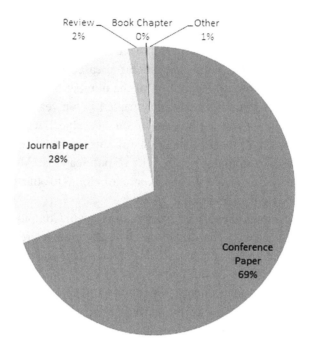

Figure 3. Distribution of publications on information overload by subject area

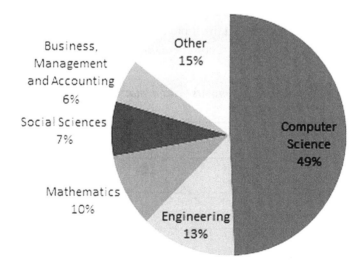

online searches through content recommendations, reducing information overload and increasing the quality of consumers' decisions. Bawden and Robinson (2009) identified and discussed some of main issues and potential problems associated with information overload. Nevertheless, the most cited publications in this period focus primarily recommender agents in electronic business and in social networking (Chen, Chen, Zheng et al., 2012; Park & Lee, 2008; Xu, Wu, Li et al., 2009).

In the Engineering subject, recommender systems are the most cited in papers. They are presented as an important factor in reducing the negative impact of information overload (Bobadilla, Ortega & Hernando, 2012; Forsati & Meybodi, 2010; Shinde & Kulkarni, 2012).

In Mathematics, the algorithms which allow the improvement of recommender systems efficiency continue to be a major concern in combating information overload as well as the efficiency of method of collecting and filtering information (Krause & Guestrin, 2011; Lü & Liu, 2011; Shambour & Lu, 2011).

In Social Sciences, we continue to find a strong emphasis on research of recommender systems and information filtering techniques (Bobadilla, Ortega & Hernando, 2012; Savolainen, 2007; Zhou, Xu, Li, Josang & Cox, 2012) and on email overload (Thomas, King, Baroni, Cook, Keitelman, Miller & Wardle, 2006).

In the Business, Management and Accounting themes, the reduction of information overload to improve consumer choices and decisions in the online environment continues to be the major concern for some researchers (Bo & Benbasat, 2007; Kuksov & Villas-Boas, 2010; Park & Lee, 2008). Furthermore, works on Technostress are also frequently cited. Technostress is also a relevant topic because the organizational use of ICT may result in negative cognitions in individuals, such as information overload and interruptions (Tarafdar, Tu & Ragu-Nathan, 2010).

Another search was made with the term "Communication Overload" in the title, abstract and keyword fields, limited to the years 2006-2015 and to the exact keyword "Communication Overload". The source code of this search was:

```
TITLE-ABS-KEY("Communication Overload")
AND LIMIT-TO(EXACTKEYWORD,"Communication Overload")
AND PUBYEAR > 2005 AND PUBYEAR < 2016
```

Regarding the obtained results, we can observe that the number of documents associated to the topic communication overload is sharply lower than the number of documents obtained in the previous search. This search resulted in 28 documents during the period under study. Because this number is small, the evaluation of the publication evolution in these years is not significant (Figure 4). Furthermore, as depicted in Figure 5, it is noted that the obtained publications are conference papers and journal papers, and the number of conference papers is slightly higher than the journal papers, making a total of 60% of documents.

As shown in Figure 6, this topic is addressed mainly in Computer Science, with almost 50% of publications. It also has some publications in the Engineering and Social Sciences.

The works which address communication overload are divided mainly into two main levels: at the organizational level, the causes and consequences of communication overload are presented and discussed, as well as its impact on workers' operational performance, largely because of interruptions due to an inadequate communication policy (Karr-Wisniewski & Lu, 2010; Stephens, 2008); the consequences of technostress are also addressed in the organizational context of communication overload (Hung, Chen & Lin, 2014); and at the telecommunications level, routing algorithms of data packets in networks are conceptualized and optimized in order to minimize the effects of communication overload (Guo, Liaw, Deng & Chao, 2010; Hung, Chen & Lin, 2014; Li & Gong, 2009; Razzak, Elmogy, Khan & Alghathbar, 2012; Wu, He & Xu, 2009).

Another search was made by the terms "Communication Overload" and "Information Overload", or "Information and Communication Overload" in the title, abstract and keyword fields, limited to the same period of time used in the previous searches. The source code of this search was:

```
TITLE-ABS-KEY(("Communication Overload" and "Information Over-
load") or "Information and Communication Overload")
AND PUBYEAR > 2005 AND PUBYEAR < 2016
```

Figure 4. Number of published documents on communication overload from 2006 to 2015

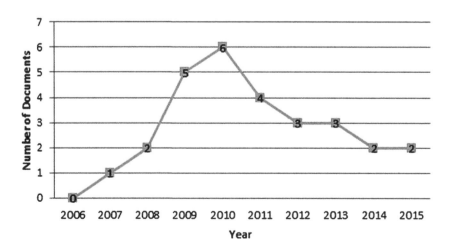

Figure 5. Distribution of publications on communication overload by document type

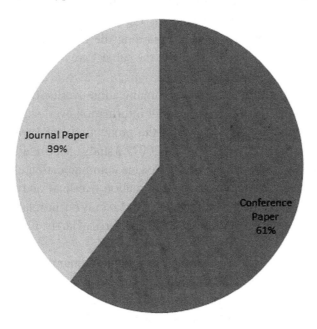

Figure 6. Distribution of publications on communication overload by subject area

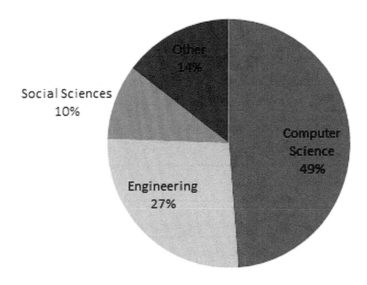

The search resulted in only 5 documents, as shown in Figure 7, of which 3 are journal papers and 2 are conference papers (Figure 8). The reduced results prevent us from making a proper assessment regarding the evolution of the number of publications in the last 10 years and about the subject areas in which this topic has been studied.

In the context of information and communication overload, some works were found, such as studies on the relationship of information overload, communication overload, and technology overload with the productivity of knowledge workers (Karr-Wisniewski & Lu, 2010; Karr & Lu, 2007); a study on the relationship between communication overload and the use of diverse communication channels and the relationship between communication, information overload and job satisfaction (Cho, Ramgolam, Schaefer & Sandlin, 2011); and a study on the relationship between technology overload and work-family conflict (Harris, Harris, Carlson & Carlson, 2015).

After this study, we noticed that the interest in communication overload is apparently still very low, given the difference of the number of publications related to the two topics. This result is surprising when compared to what the literature states with regard to the increased interest in information and communication overload, and summarized in the previous section, stating that the Digital Age is facing various challenges posed by information overload and, additionally, by communication overload. Thus, if the two concepts are interrelated, we should have observed a more balanced outcome in this bibliometric analysis.

Figure 7. Number of published documents on information and communication overload from 2006 to 2015

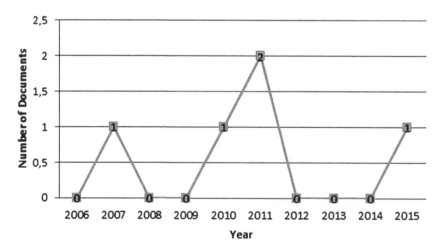

Figure 8. Distribution of publications on information and communication overload by document type

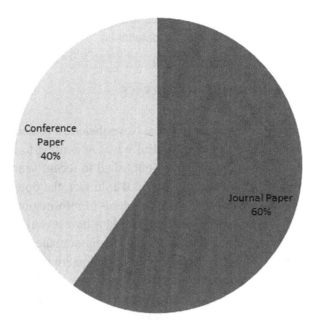

However, if we analyze the results of the first search, in which the term information overload was used as a sole search key, we find several documents whose focus is precisely what is defined as communication overload. Here are just a few examples: how excess of communication via email can induce information overload (email overload) (Kammerer, Sprenger, Hetzenecker & Amberg, 2012; Ritchie, Gilleran, Lucas, Woods & Rivero, 2013; Sobotta, 2015; Sobotta & Hummel, 2015); the contribution of the social media, including the underlying conversations and interactions, to information overload (Gomez-Rodriguez, Gummadi & Schölkopf, 2014; Imran, Castillo, Diaz & Vieweg, 2015; Kooti, Aiello, Grbovic, Lerman & Mantrach, 2015; Palekar, Atapattu, Sedera & Lokuge, 2015; Sasaki, Kawai & Kitamura, 2015; Y. Xu & Pasi, 2015), some works on social sensing as cause of information overload (Al Amin, Li, Rahman, Seetharamu, Wang, Abdelzaher, Gupta, Srivatsa, Ganti, Ahmed & Le, 2015; Qi, Aggarwal, Turaga, Sow & Anno, 2015), among other topics.

In order to have a better idea of the weight of these situations in the imbalance of the results obtained, we could identify, in the context of information overload, about 40 documents related to email overload, and over 170 publications related to social media, which have not been classified on the communication overload topic, even if they have some subjects related to this topic. The cause of this finding is unknown but may be related to the fact that communication overload is a recent issue and still emerging when compared with information overload, and the authors are not even aware that their work may be perfectly framed on this topic or they may be afraid that their work can be indexed and associated to a still growing topic and thus lose some visibility in the scientific databases.

CONCLUSION AND FINAL REMARKS

The issue of information overload is not new. Nevertheless, it remains a very current topic which has been addressed to in several ways. According to the bibliometric analysis presented, the number of papers published in recent years has showed a rising trend, despite the slight decline after 2012. In fact, the opportunities of the digital age have created solutions to some problems of information overload but at the same time they have created new challenges. Many have arisen from the development of communication technologies that enable to disseminate and exchange huge amount of information. These exchanges of information are now so intense and so present in the lives of individuals, organizations and societies, that they pose a new problem: the problem of communication overload. The bibliometric analysis shows that the problem of communication overload has often been addressed, although it is often classified as information overload. These two problems are, however, interrelated. Although the majority of the literature found place attention on the fields of individuals and organizations, we see that the issues of information and communication overload are also problems that affect and are affected by societies themselves, which is a perspective that deserves to be further researched.

REFERENCES

Bauman, Z. (2007). *Liquid Times: Living in an age of uncertainty*. Cambridge, UK: Polity Press.

Bawden, D., & Robinson, L. (2009). The dark side of information: Overload, anxiety and other paradoxes and pathologies. *Journal of Information Science*, *35*(2), 180–191. doi:10.1177/0165551508095781

Bergamaschi, S., & Leiba, B. (2010). Information overload. *IEEE Internet Computing*, *14*(6), 10–13. doi:10.1109/MIC.2010.140

Butcher, H. (1995). Information overload in management and business. In *IEE Colloquium Digest*. London: IEE. Doi: doi:10.1049/ic:19951426

Cecchinato, M. E., Bird, J., & Cox, A. L. (2014). Personalised Email Tools: A Solution to Email Overload? In *CHI'14 Workshop on Personalised Behaviour Change Technologies* (pp. 1–4). ACM.

Cho, J., Ramgolam, D. I., Schaefer, K. M., & Sandlin, A. N. (2011). The Rate and Delay in Overload: An Investigation of Communication Overload and Channel Synchronicity on Identification and Job Satisfaction. *Journal of Applied Communication Research, 39*(1), 38–54. doi:10.1080/00909882.2010.536847

Edmunds, A., & Morris, A. (2000). The Problem of Information Overload in Business Organisations: A Review of the Literature. *International Journal of Information Management, 20*(1), 17–28. doi:10.1016/S0268-4012(99)00051-1

Ellwart, T., Happ, C., Gurtner, A., & Rack, O. (2015, July). Managing information overload in virtual teams: Effects of a structured online team adaptation on cognition and performance. *European Journal of Work and Organizational Psychology, 5*(5), 812–826. doi:10.1080/1359432X.2014.1000873

Eppler, M. J. (2015). Information quality and information overload: The promises and perils of the information age. In L. Cantoni & J. A. Danowski (Eds.), *Communication and Technology* (pp. 215–232). Berlin, Boston: De Gruyter; doi:10.1515/9783110271355-013

Eppler, M. J., & Mengis, J. (2004). The Concept of Information Overload: A Review of Literature from Organization Science, Marketing, Accounting, MIS, and related Disciplines. *The Information Society, 20*(5), 325–344. doi:10.1080/01972240490507974

Fuglseth, A. M., & Sørebø, Ø. (2014). The effects of technostress within the context of employee use of ICT. *Computers in Human Behavior, 40*, 161–170. doi:10.1016/j.chb.2014.07.040

Haase, R. F., Ferreira, J. A., Fernandes, R. I., Santos, E. J. R., & Jome, L. M. (2015). Development and Validation of a Revised Measure of Individual Capacities for Tolerating Information Overload in Occupational Settings. *Journal of Career Assessment, 24*(1), 130–144. doi:10.1177/1069072714565615

Haase, R. F., Jome, L. M., Ferreira, J., Santos, E. J. R., Connacher, C. C., & Sendrowitz, K. (2014). Individual Differences in Capacity for Tolerating Information Overload Are Related to Differences in Culture and Temperament. *Journal of Cross-Cultural Psychology, 45*(5), 728–751. doi:10.1177/0022022113519852

Harris, K. J., Harris, R. B., Carlson, J. R., & Carlson, D. S. (2015). Resource loss from technology overload and its impact on work-family conflict: Can leaders help? *Computers in Human Behavior, 50*, 411–417. doi:10.1016/j.chb.2015.04.023

Jackson, T. W., & Farzaneh, P. (2012). Theory-Based Models of Factors Affecting Information Overload. *International Journal of Information Management*, *32*(6), 523–532. doi:10.1016/j.ijinfomgt.2012.04.006

Klausegger, C., Sinkovics, R. R., & Zou, H. (2007). Information overload: A cross-national investigation of influence factors and effects. *Marketing Intelligence & Planning*, *25*(7), 691–718. doi:10.1108/02634500710834179

Larose, R., Connolly, R., Lee, H., Li, K., & Hales, K. D. (2014). Connection Overload? A Cross Cultural Study of the Consequences of Social Media Connection. *Information Systems Management*, *31*(1), 59–73. doi:10.1080/10580530.2014.854097

Lee, A. R., Son, S. M., & Kim, K. K. (2016). Information and communication technology overload and social networking service fatigue: A stress perspective. *Computers in Human Behavior*, *55*, 51–61. doi:10.1016/j.chb.2015.08.011

Meier, R. L. (1963). Communications Overload - Proposals from the Study of a University Library. *Administrative Science Quarterly*, *7*(4), 521–544. doi:10.2307/2390963

Mittelstädt, V., Brauner, P., Blum, M., & Ziefle, M. (2015). On the Visual Design of ERP Systems The – Role of Information Complexity, Presentation and Human Factors. *Procedia Manufacturing*, *3*, 448–455. doi:10.1016/j.promfg.2015.07.207

Nielsen, R. K. (2009). The Labors of Internet-Assisted Activism: Overcommunication, Miscommunication, and Communicative Overload. *Journal of Information Technology & Politics*, *6*(3–4), 267–280. doi:10.1080/19331680903048840

Price, D. J. de S. (1963). Little Science, Big Science. Book, New York: Columbia University Press.

Reinke, K., & Chamorro-Premuzic, T. (2014). When email use gets out of control: Understanding the relationship between personality and email overload and their impact on burnout and work engagement. *Computers in Human Behavior*, *36*, 502–509. doi:10.1016/j.chb.2014.03.075

Rennecker, J., & Derks, D. (2013). Email overload: Fine-tuning the research lens. In D. Derks & A. B. Bakker (Eds.), *The psychology of digital media at work*. New York, U.S.A.: Routledge.

Ruff, J. (2002). Information Overload: Causes, Symptoms and Solutions. Harvard Graduate School of Education.

Schroder, H. M., Driver, M. J., & Streufert, S. (1967). *Human information processing - Individuals and groups functioning in complex social situations*. New York, U.S.A.: Holt, Rinehart, & Winston.

KEY TERMS AND DEFINITIONS

Bibliometric Analysis: A quantitative method that enables the evaluation of the development of research fields based on the analysis of scientific literature.

Communication Overload: The phenomenon that occurs when individuals, organizations, or societies are not able to deal and process all the communication processes they are involved in.

Communication Process: Exchange of messages and information between different actors.

Decision-Making Process: A process used when individuals, organizations, or societies apply information to make decisions, giving meaning to the information used.

Digital Age: The period when data, information and communication are mainly represented and processed by digital technologies.

Information Overload: The phenomenon that occurs when individuals, organizations, or societies are not able to digest all the information they are supposed to.

Overload: Excessive amount of something.

Chapter 2
Email Overload: Framing the Concept and Solving the Problem – A Literature Review

Ana Lúcia Terra
Polytechnic Institute of Porto, Portugal

ABSTRACT

In this chapter email overload is presented as a component of information overload and some of its causes and consequences are identified. Furthermore, an analysis on the skills required to deal with information overload is made. Then, a critical literature review about the concept of email overload is realized, stressing aspects such as the amount of messages, personal characteristics and skills or technological issues. Solutions for this organizational problem are presented based on relevant case studies from the literature review. Key components to consider in email overload management are also identified, including information management techniques and technological options, training, time management and information behavior (individual and organizational).

DOI: 10.4018/978-1-5225-2061-0.ch002

INTRODUCTION

Nowadays, information environment can be characterized by its super connectivity. Due not only to the multiplication of mobile devices that access information (laptops, notebooks, tablets, smartphones, and other gadgets), but also to the significant improvements involving access to wireless communication networks, with an almost complete geographical coverage in most developed countries, at an increasingly low cost. This environment, where information is available on the Internet without temporal or physical boundaries and with a minimum degree of effort and investment, presents new challenges for individuals who have to respond to constant requests and need to know how to focus their attention and processing capacity. In this sense, information overload is the flip side of the value of open communication channels.

In organizational and professional contexts, the use of information and communication technologies has resulted in the diversification of means of communication (letter, telephone, fax, SMS, email, instant messaging, etc.). Thus, organizational communication, both internal and external, has become more immediate, informal and intense (Ramsey, Hair, Renaud, 2008). Edmunds and Morris (2000), from a literature review on information overload in business organizations, claim that this abundance of information, instead of better enabling people to do their jobs, threatens to engulf and diminish his or her control over the situation. Based on this finding, it is important to understand what information overload in a professional environment is and how it materializes. Given the intensity of email use within organizations, it is certainly relevant to study it to understand information overload.

In recent decades, email became omnipresent in personal and organizational lives thus contributing to information overload. In this sense, managing emails remains a major challenge for organizations (Sumecki, Chipulo, Ojiko, 2011). By the late nineties, organizations' investments in email services were supported by communication costs savings. When compared with the use of phone, it definitely increases the information flows speed, resulting therefore in an increase in employees' productivity. But over time, this perspective has been rethought considering the experience with organizations' daily routine. In fact, because of its socio-technical features, email has become invasive due to the number of daily messages received and sent, and the time spent. Email overload became a reality. Nevertheless, both organizations and their employees recognize email as an essential source of corporate information for the daily functioning in all of its dimensions. As such, this informational asset needs to be managed, integrating a comprehensive approach to the organization's information management strategy.

In order to accomplish this, it is important to understand the concept of email overload and its relation with information overload. After a literature review about information overload and email overload, solutions to cope with the amount of email messages based on case studies are presented. Understanding the origin and consequences of information overload is the main objective of this literature review. Another goal of our approach is to highlight the contribution of information literacy skills to cope with the information overload in both personal and organizational areas. Literature review on email overload aims to identify the reasons for email overload, to present definitions of the concept and to frame its components. Another goal was to list solutions for dealing with email overload, serving as a foundation to create a model that allows categorizing the components of email overload and its relationships.

INFORMATION OVERLOAD CONCEPT

The term information overload has gained notoriety because of the mention made by Alvin Toffler, in a book published in 1970, although it was first noted in the work of Bertram Gross, *Managing of organizations: the administrative struggle*, published in 1964. According to Bawden & Robinson (2009), information overload may be considered as major communication pathology of recorded information, identified as the "paradox of choice". This paradox stems from the existence of too much information available, exacerbated by the existence of multiple formats and channels for its communication. This fact finds its roots in the invention of printing and suffered a significant boost during the nineteenth century and especially in the twentieth century, with the growth of scientific and technical literature production besides the improvement and enlargement of the States bureaucratic machinery. It is also directly related to technological developments linked to the production and storage of information records, such as the invention of printing, new means of re-production and, of course, with the Information and Communication Technologies.

Despite this finding, still in the late nineties, Tidline (1999) considered that the information overload is a myth of modern culture, understanding the myth as a "non-scientific" process which confirms the reality of an elusive phenomenon, as an overarching prescriptive belief. Thus, mythology of information overload, like all myths, has a vague origin, created in response to a change from industrial to an information-based economy. This story confirms the reality "perceived" about the information society while allowing the expression of emotions like anxiety or boredom in this society. In this sense, information overload mythology gives meaning to that reality and to an adjustment to it.

Although this approach is conceptually interesting and can help understand information overload as a social construction, we must contextualize it in the time it was formulated. At that time, in the late nineties, the flood of structured and un-structured data stored and available to be accessed, and which today is an objective reality, occurred beyond expectations reaching unimaginable numbers. There are numerous studies, both of academic (e.g., Hilbert, 2014) and commercial origin (e.g., EMC & IDC, 2014), seeking to quantify the information in the world and its growth rate. Although the data collection methodologies and calculations can be questionable, it is undeniable that the trend is for a rapid and overwhelming growth of information created, stored, distributed and accessed. Thus, according to the EMC & IDC report (2014), in 2020, the digital universe will have as many digital bits as the number of stars in the universe. Digital content is doubling in size every two years and by 2020 the data we create and copy annually will reach 44 zettabytes, or 44 trillion gigabytes. In 2013, this figure did not exceed 4.4 zettabytes. This digital universe is being created by everyone using a digital device: from more than 2 billion people living their lives and millions of enterprises doing their work online, and by millions of sensors and communicating devices sending and receiving data over the Internet. This fact implies problems at a storage level, because the world's amount of available storage is growing slower than the digital universe. In 2013, the available storage could hold just 33% of the digital universe. By 2020 it will be able to store less than 15%.

In popular culture, and in the scientific literature, this fact has been perceived and expressed by various names such as "infobesity", "information avoidance", "information anxiety", "data glut", "library anxiety", "information pollution" or "data smog" (Tidline, 1999; Bawden & Robinson, 2009). For the scientific community, the definition of information overload concept has been the subject of diverse and complementary approaches (Edmunds & Morris, 2000; Eppler & Mengis, 2004; Jackson & Farzaneh, 2012). It appears that interdisciplinary approaches are uncommon although necessary to find solutions to this problem (Eppler & Mengis, 2004). It is also noteworthy that some authors (Meadow & Yuan, 1997) argue that we can have data overload, but not information overload. This finding is based on the assumption that the information contained in a message exists regardless the receiver of that message. However, what usually happens is that there are more messages that demand our attention than those to which we can pay attention to and assimilate. As such, there may be the sense of overload but it is not information overload, but data overload.

In the view of Bawden, Holtham, & Courtney (1999: 249), "information overload occurs when information received becomes a hindrance rather than a help when the information is potentially useful." It emphasizes the quantitative component of the information received by the individual as an element that hinders the use of its qualitative components in a given context. Note that in this setting, quantitative excess will depend on the awareness and skills of the individual receiving the message. So, information overload can be understood as a subjective experience, depending on the subject and the context in which they operate, not as an absolute objective reality, as evidenced by some case studies (Allen & Shoard, 2005; Benselin & Ragsdell, 2016). In fact, based on an empirical study, Bawden, Holtham, & Courtney (1999: 251) point out that some of the respondents believe that "one is overloaded to the extent that one wishes to be overloaded". In addition to the individual component, contextual aspect is also crucial. Allen & Shoard (2005) stressed its importance in order to understand the complex ways information flows within the organization, how it enters and how it leaves. It is essential to analyse the organizational context or organizational design reported by Eppler & Mengis (2004). Since the trend is for organizations to have an open information environment, where information is heavily shared, individuals are exposed to increasingly numerous and varied information. Thus, there is the relationship between Personal Information Overload and Organizational Information Overload. As pointed out by Jackson & Farzaneh (2012) model, an organization consists of more than one individual who contributes to the addition of information, and iteratively updates and retrieves from the organization's information sources. In addition, the organization is greater than its individual parts.

Hiltz & Turoff (1985: 682) consider that information overload means "delivery of too many communications and to an increase in social density that gives individuals access to more communications than they can easily respond to". They also associate the concept with what they designate by information entropy, "whereby incoming messages are not sufficiently organized by topic or content to be easily recognized as important or as part of the history of communication on a given topic" (Hiltz & Turoff 1985: 682). In turn, this will make individuals fail to respond, respond less accurately, respond incorrectly, ignore some features, recode inputs in a more compact/effective form or quit in extreme cases. In order to avoid cumbersome situations, they emphasize the importance of structures able to distinguish interesting messages from the not interesting, which will also help to synthesize and organize information. However, in addition to structures, namely technological, to positively cope with information overload, individuals need to develop skills to handle the excess requests. In fact, the experienced users develop effective ways to address what could be overload; while beginners tend to overextend themselves trying to be fully informed on a multitude of activities. The success of technological structures to tackle information overload relies on their ability to provide options for individuals to filter out material, so that each can control content in their own way. In this sense, "overload, within the context of an organization, is essentially a behavioral phenomenon. It makes more sense to address inappropriate behavior through social norms and sanctions than to obscure the problem with software "(Hiltz & Turoff, 1985: 689).

Each approach emphasizes specific elements that can be categorized in different ways. Eppler & Mengis (2004) refer to five types of reasons that lead to information overload: personal factors, information characteristics, task and process parameters, organizational design, and information technology. The combination of these factors leads to information overload which assumes different configurations depending on the interaction intensity of each of these elements. These five causes of information overload will influence two key variables: the information processing capacity (including, for example, personal characteristics) and the information processing requirements (often determined by the nature of the tasks or processes). Jackson & Farzaneh (2012) distinguish intrinsic factors, that directly influence the information overload, and extrinsic factors, that contribute indirectly to information overload but have a direct effect on intrinsic factors. Intrinsic factors include the amount of information, regarding its availability and accessibility, and the information processing requirement, and available time. External factors include the information characteristics (complexity, ambiguity, uncertainty, and novelty), the quality of information (utility, relevance, and validity), task and process parameters (task complexity, task novelty, task interruption and multi-tasking) and personal factors (level of prior experiences, personal skills, cognitive style, person's motivation and personal situation).

Besides the causes that lead to information overload, it is also important to identify its consequences. At an organizational and professional environment, information overload is associated with the loss of workers' efficiency and decrease of productivity. Loss job satisfaction, difficulties in personal relationships, health problems and postponement of important decisions are other consequences derived from information overload. Benselin & Ragsdell (2016) argue that information overload has become a common phenomenon with a wide range of professions suffering from it. Furthermore, in a study based on 45 surveys and five semi-structured interviews, they found that there may be a link between the work experience and information overload since working as an administrator was the common link amongst those who had never suffered from it. So it seems that skills developed in administrative functions, such as dealing with large amounts of e-mails, maintaining file systems and multi-tasking, help prevent the feeling of information overload. However, these findings seem to contradict a literature review on information overload in business organizations made by Edmunds & Morris (2000). According to their analysis, the existing studies point to the fact that managers feel bombarded by information (too much, too fast, too late) but claim not getting all the information they need to perform their jobs. There is a dilemma because managers receive too much information but do not access adequate information.

As noted by Bawden & Robinson (2009), an oriented behavior to address information overload is "satisficing", also known as "bounded rationality" and conceptualized in economic theory. It is a model for choices and decision making in which the set of options available is not fully known, thus it is not possible to compare the benefits of each solution. It implies choosing information sources and selecting information within the framework that is adequate enough but that is not the best available. The use of satisficing tactics and the judgment of what is "enough information" is a common way of dealing with complex information environment. However, it is important to note that the satisficing tactics must be carefully applied, and must be based on actual skills and rational assumptions. If not so, this information behavior leads to information avoidance or a random, limited information sources' choice. Thus, one can distinguish between appropriate/good satisficing and inappropriate/bad satisficing. In any event, there is too much potentially relevant information for a perfectionist approach to be feasible. The most important point to consider is that satisficing tactics have to be put into practice in a rational way and not arbitrarily. This implies that individuals are aware of their information needs, time and material constraints and preferences in terms of information use.

These assumptions refer to the information literacy skills, as categorized in various standards. Thus, the *Australian and New Zeeland Information Literacy Framework* (Bundy, 2004) includes four competencies that refer directly to the information overload management ability. Those are: the information literate person recognises the need for information and determines the nature and extent of the information needed; the information literate person finds needed information effectively and efficiently; the information literate person manages information collected and generated; and the information literate person applies prior and new information to construct new concepts or create new understandings. Also *SCONSUL Seven Pillars of Information Literacy* (SCONSUL Working Group on Information Literacy, 2011) presents an information literacy model with particularly relevant skills for managing information overload. The first pillar is related to the ability to identify the personal need for information; the second involves assessing current knowledge and identifying gaps; the third refers to the construction of strategies for locating information and data; the fourth relates to the location and access to information that is necessary; the fifth reviews the research process and compares and evaluates information and data; and the sixth is related with the ability to organize information in a professional and ethical manner. Thus, pillars are focused on identifying, defining, planning, collecting, evaluating and managing information resources, all of which are essential ingredients to tackle information overload.

In summary, one can conclude that the person able to manage information overload is the one that is able to enjoy its benefits while avoiding its problems. These abilities are inherent to an information literate person as defined in various standards and can be synthetized as showed in Figure 1. So, it implies the ability to identify personal and organizational information needs and to identify information, designing and applying relevant search strategies. In this way, the individual becomes able to focus his/her approach to information, recognizing the personal and external factors, allowing them to map out the best way to meet his/her needs, adapting

Figure 1. Skills to manage information overload

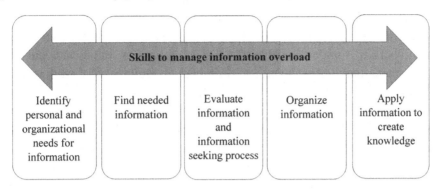

strategies and research resources of information. In this sense, it implies the use of mechanisms to cope with the excessive amount of information. Critical thinking on the information gathered and the information search process in itself also contribute to cope with information overload to the extent that it promotes an evaluation of the performed route and of the accessed resources. Thus, it will resolve problems related to the intrinsic nature of the information, namely its quality, particularly its complexity, ambiguity, novelty or credibility. Finally, skills focused on the use of information and the creation of new knowledge will highlight the skills related to the use of comparison and integration strategies between old and new information, creating knowledge and new ways of understanding. These five competencies support the individual information processing capacity, a key component to deal with information overload both at a personal and organizational level.

EMAIL OVERLOAD CONCEPT

A 2015 report and another of 2016 from the Radicati Group (2015, 2016) accounts for 2.6 billion email users, estimating that by 2020 this number will rise to 3 billion, with about a third of the world population using this form of communication. Thus, from an average of 1.7 accounts per user we will reach an average of 1.9 accounts per user. These numbers are explained because the use of an email account is required in a variety of situations (to shop online, to gain access to online portals, banking, etc.). In 2015, the number of emails sent and received per day reached a total of 205 billion, and it is expected to reach 246 billion in 2019. In 2015, the number of business emails sent and received per user totalled 122 emails per day, and it is expected that by 2019 the average reaches 126 messages sent and received by each business user. Dabish & Kraut (2006), in an academic study, using a sample of 484 respondents, collected different values, with a daily average of 41 emails received, 32 read messages and 21 sent messages. As for Burgess, Jackson, & Edwards (2005), in a study conducted in a business environment, accounted for an average of 23 emails received per day per employee. Nevertheless, according to these numbers, it is understandable that a great number of studies indicate e-mail as the primary source of personal and organizational information overload (Allen & Shoard, 2005; Bawden & Robinson, 2009).

Reasons for multiplication of incoming emails are analysed by several authors. Vacek (2014b; Vacek, 2014a) points out the fact that knowledge workers do not wish to receive information printed on paper or that many types of computer generated reports and forms were transformed in emails, such as newsletters, booking confirmations, invoices, event reminders or delivery notices. The use of email communication for internal purposes also explains the growing amount of messages. When analysing the reasons that lead to the use of email, Hanrahan, Pérez-Quiñones, & Martin (2014) report that reading messages and participating in conversations are the most common reasons while the time spent with managing and screening emails is insignificant. They identified twelve categories to explain access to e-mail inbox, and it is possible to relate them to the growing number of email messages and also with the amount of time spent handling the email inbox. Among these reasons prevails routine (many participants check their email first thing in the morning, right after lunch or when they first arrive to work) and notifications (participants cited their phone buzzing or receiving desktop notifications). The need to write and send a message is the third reason cited. Participants also report to check their email when they do not have anything specific to do. The remaining seven reasons represent a less significant number of choices and include varied reasons: anxiety (when they do not consult the mail for long periods of time they get concerned they may have received an important message), curiosity (they feel the urge to know whether they have received any messages), expecting communication (when participants were anticipating the arrival of a specific message from someone), inbox (participants initiated the session because their inbox caught their attention), previous awareness (participants cited that someone mentioned an important email in a conversation or they saw an email in the previous session), redefining (participants logged in to find out something specific), unread count (participants sometimes notice they have a few unread emails and decide to read them) and not reported (when participants selected "nothing" for motivation).

However, just like for the concept of information overload, there is no unanimous definition of the email overload concept, with approaches from several scientific fields, including Information Systems, Management, Human Resources, Psychology and Information Science, among others.

McMurty (2014) emphasizes the subjective perception of each individual by claiming that email overload is defined as the feeling of being overwhelmed by the constant flow of messages appearing in the inbox and the inability to manage the high volume of messages effectively. In the same line of thinking, Dabbish & Kraut (2006) assume the difficulty of determining whether email overload is a real phenomenon felt by the knowledge worker, or a backhanded expression of nostalgia for the communication methods of the past. Nevertheless their definition is based on the perspective of individuals. Thus, they also use the term information overload to express email users' perceptions that their own use of email has gotten out of control because they receive and send more emails that they can handle, find, or process effectively. They emphasize the personal feeling of overload, stressing the subjective component of the situation. It is also interesting to take note of the results from a study regarding email use in a Czech university (Vacek, 2014b). The author found a significant difference between estimated number of emails received by an average user (246,4) and the average number of emails really retrieved from data reports (115). This data seems to indicate that email overload has a strong component of individual subjectivity. It is not simply an objective reality in the sense that it depends on the feelings of each individual, certainly influenced by personal skills to handle information. Ingham (2003) also states that email overload is a very personal experience: one person may receive 200 messages a week and not feel overloaded, whilst another may also receive 200 messages a week and feel overwhelmed by them and hence, overloaded. To better understand the importance of individual perception, it may be appropriate to establish a relationship between the way of dealing with email and personal characteristics, as did Reinke & Chamorro-Premuzic (2014).

These personal characteristics will determine the feelings of stress associated with managing a large number of messages or the pressure felt to respond quickly to messages. The connection between email and stress was also addressed by Barley, Meyerson & Grodal (2011). For these authors, email overload is not a matter of the number of messages received, it is the joint product of the time spent handling messages, the anxieties individuals feel, the norms of responsiveness they accept and reproduce, and the daily pattern of communication activities that they could not control. In contextual terms, this experience of email overload is aggravated when organizations place employees on multiple teams and make greater use of distributed work in their efforts to globalize. In addition, those who have responsibility for dependents or other obligations outside work that restraint them from checking their email outside the workplace also experience higher email overload. In their sociomaterial approach, they conclude that "it would seem that handling more messages bolstered the respondents' sense of coping because processing email reduced the size of their inbox and allayed the anxiety of allowing emails to go unanswered. Interestingly, the more time people spent tackling their email, the more overloaded they felt, but the more messages they handled, the more they felt they could cope "(Barley, Meyerson & Grodal, 2011: 899).

Whittaker & Sidner (1996) seem to have coined the term "email overload" underlining the fact that email inboxes were far more complex than a simple container of incoming messages, since it contains emails with different status/type (to do, to read, messages of indeterminate status and ongoing correspondence). However, as referred by Dabbish & Kraut (2006), in the late eighties and early nineties, when information technologies and electronic communications systems began their way into organizational work contexts, some researchers predicted that these technologies were going to change the workplace configuration and eventually lead to overload problems.

One of the changes derived from email use is the constant interruptions in the remaining tasks that knowledge workers are dedicated to, as noted by Gupta, Sharda, & Greve (2011) in a literature review on the subject. In this regard, they stressed that whenever someone receives an email, the employee needs additional time to switch between the task in hands and read/reply to the email.

In fact, considering the time these employees spend dealing with email, Ducheneaut & Bellotti (2001) state that the email has become a habitat, in the sense that it is the place where they spend most part of their working time, receiving, doing and delegating tasks. They also add that the network effect leads to this trend becoming infectious across the organization. Indeed, they found out that many people use e-mail throughout the day. Email is the major mean of non-face-to-face communication, it is the main mean of document exchange, and many people use it as an information management tool for scheduling activities or managing contacts. Thus, email overload arises largely from the fact that it is improperly used to conduct some routine tasks. They also claim that email experience leads to the "addiction effect": the more experience people have with email, the more frequently they check it and it also leads to a higher incidence of organizational activities in e-mail (for example, organizing meetings and documenting activity) (Ducheneaut & Bellotti, 2001). Therefore, in this perspective, email overload is the result of misuse that is given to this mean of communication. Similarly, Vacek (2014a) points out six causes of email overload: internal forwarded emails with attachments sent to many recipients (for example when one receives a call for papers and forwards it to everybody no matter if others are interested or not); internal or forwarded emails sent to many recipients some of them having no direct relation with the issue; internal emails with attachments because employees use their email account as a document management system, creating redundant copies of files for each recipient; all emails sent to many recipients; internal replies when a phone call could be more efficient; and all emails with attachments. So, according to this author, the factors that cause inboxes to fill up with emails include the number of email messages, the number of attachments, using email for internal communication, sending the same message to more than three recipients, the number of unjustified replies and the number of forwards.

Applying the "theory-based model of factors influencing information overload" of Jackson and Farzaneh (2012) to the analysis of email overload, Sobotta & Hummel (2015) argue that the amount of emails received or stored is not the core of the problem but rather the limited capacity of human beings to deal with emails and email caused factors.

However, to restrict email overload to the lack of human capacity for assimilation may be too simplistic and limiting. Soucek & Moser (2010) argue that email overload comes from the interplay of three factors: large amount of incoming information, inefficient workflow and poor communication quality. The ease with which e-mail messages are created, sent and received, with very low costs, explains its widespread use, with a direct impact on their numbers. The inefficient workflow is associated with a dysfunctional use of email programs beyond their basic communication functions, using it as documents archive or to schedule performed tasks. Email messages are often deficient in their quality, presenting poor communication quality. Compared to business letters, email messages are more spontaneous and less formal, this leads to superficiality and ambiguity, that fails to give recipients enough information to act upon and fosters misunderstandings.

Another explanatory approach to email overload is to emphasize technological aspects, such as the inefficiency of email clients to provide an inbox structure that facilitates prioritization email, information structuring and workflow management (Szostek, 2011). The fact is that some automatic screening techniques (like spam filters or junk filters) preventing some emails from reaching the user, diverting them into folders based on a pre-defined rule set, also may lead to the omission of potentially relevant information (Schuff, Turetken, & D'Arcy, 2006). On doing so, they are potentially not a good solution for dealing with email overload.

WAYS TO DEAL WITH EMAIL OVERLOAD

Having in mind the complexity of email overload, in literature, it is possible to find a very wide range of proposals to solve the problem with serious consequences in terms of individual and organizational action.

According to Bawden, Holtham, & Courtney (1999) scientists using information systems and services in a pharmaceutical research organization considered that the solution to information overload was self-discipline in focussing on important things and self-education in managing personal information (eg file handling, best practices in using e-mail or what to store and how). In this case, the point was not a technical solution but rather changes in information behavior. In a study conducted in an UK police station, Allen & Shoard (2005) also found the same patterns. The authors identified strategies used by officers to deal with e-mail overload and concluded that they prioritize and filter received e-mails, choosing what is relevant for their profession or relevant for their personal interests. Due to a time management issue, they tend to define as a priority message the ones that they can process more quickly, applying a selective attention to information. They also apply strategies such as queuing, approximation, multi-parallel processing and escaping. For example, they use the approximation technique responding in a vaguely way, through short messages.

Other approaches emphasize the importance of the context and focus on traditional information management. In a study conducted in three separate companies (Ducheneaut & Bellotti, 2001), it was found that there was a relationship between the age of e-mail user and an increase of complex filing schemes, especially with the creation of an increasing number of folders to group messages. These folders tend to be organized by four criteria: sender (either the person or the distribution list), organization (for example, the client or the professional body), project (a coordinated effort or contractual undertaking) and personal interests (either professional or private). This grouping of related messages helps preserving meaningful context for historical communication and activities and is not only a strategy for further information location. They also noted that the nature of the organization influences the way people organize their email messages in folders. For instance, in the organization which is structured by projects, the arrangement of folders also follows this logic; in the hierarchical organization of departments, folders reflect this structure; while in another organization, folders are divided as they relate to personal or professional messages. Furthermore, they found that the creation of folder hierarchies is superficial, not exceeding two levels because users believe that this form of organization makes the messages location more time consuming and difficult. However, a relevant model to assess the adequacy of folder management must take into account not only the total number of folders but essentially the number of active folders. As a strategy to manage email overload, for the studied sample, authors discovered that the sort feature appears to be more popular than the search, because it can be used to faster specify search criteria (date, sender, name, subject, etc.) and that opening the search tool and typing criteria is much slower and thus, less efficient.

In their seminal work, Whittaker & Sidner (1996) identified three strategies for handling email overload by users, based on two criteria: 1) whether or not users currently use folders, 2) whether they "clean up" their inbox on a daily basis. These three strategies correspond to three informational behavior profiles of email users: no filers (no use of folders), frequent filers (folder users who try and clean up their inbox daily), and spring cleaners (folder users who only clean up their inbox periodically). Typically, no filers make no current use of folders but rely on full-text search to find information. As a result of not using folders, their inbox was huge, including a large number of conversational threads; over half of their inbox was old information which arrived more than 3 months ago. As a strategy to reduce the size of the inbox, they resort to periodic purges in which they delete large numbers of old items or copy them to a separate independent archive. Frequent filers go to great lengths to minimize the number of messages in their inbox. They keep messages into folders or delete them daily. So their inbox contains relatively few messages and essentially have new messages. They make a frequent use of folders, using them profitably so there are few empty or useless folders. Spring cleaners deal with the overload of their inbox with intermittent clean-ups, usually monthly or quarterly. They make heavy use of folders, even if sometimes in a not proper way. Their inboxes have large number of messages, with a significant amount of old messages. From these three profiles, frequent filers are those that best deal with email overload but it stems from a large investment of time to organize their inbox and can change with the progressively increase of incoming and outgoing messages.

In addition to the manual classification of e-mails folders, email services providers have developed tools for supervised and semi-supervised classifications of e-mails (Koprinska, Poon, Clark, & Chan, 2007). These tools can help spring cleaners in the systematic organization of their messages and allow time savings both to them as to frequent filers, and support the changing habits of no filers. The proposal for an automatic classification of emails system is also a solution, to the extent that such system can be designed in a way to limit the cognitive load on users even as the volume of email messages increases. The design of a system that automatically creates a folder structure based only on the content of messages (text body, date, sender and receiver) can also be a solution (Schuff, Turetken & D'Arcy, 2006).

Another categorization strategy for email managing is to distinguish the cleaners from keepers (Gwizdka, 2004). Cleaners transfer future task/event information from email programs. They have greater control of their email behavior, not allowing incoming messages to interrupt the activities they are undertaking and setting specific times to read the messages. As a rule, they do not use email to handle messages related to tasks, to-do's or events. As for keepers, they use email as habitat and keep future task/event in email programs. They let incoming emails interrupt other activities and read messages all the time. They also tend to use email to keep and handle messages related to tasks, to-do's or future events.

Another way to deal with email overload is managing the time devoted to the use of this communication mean. There is no unanimity regarding the best policy to time devoted to email management. There are very different proposals ranging from the possibility of constantly monitoring messages arriving in the inbox to setting strict timetables for this task, as well as days without access to email. In the perspective of Gupta, Sharda & Greve (2011), when the interruption frequency of the tasks that are being carried out to check the email increases, the performance on the primary task will decrease. Applying Kahneman's Single-Resource Theory, Gupta, Sharda & Greve (2011) suggest that segregating the time during which emails and other tasks are given higher priority for processing, thereby reducing the interaction between the two, can potentially reduce the number of interruptions. Having this in mind, they introduce the notion of "email-hour" slot. Thus, the total hours of daily work can be divided into two categories: one during which a high priority to the email is given, and that will be the "email-hour" slot, and another during which priority is given to primary tasks which will be the "non-email hour" slots. By tailoring the length of each email-hour slot and adjusting its number on each working day, you can reduce the number of outages without jeopardizing the achievement of the primary tasks. In this sense, they conclude that the controlled interruption policy such as processing email twice or four times a day will likely keep a better balance between email response time and task completion time than the continuous email processing policy or once-a day email processing policy. However, the fact that knowledge workers tend to frequently use email as a synchronous way of communication, feeling the need to respond immediately and, in turn, expecting quick answers, despite the asynchronous nature of email (the receiver can respond when convenient), exacerbates the tendency to uncontrolled interruptions. This type of disruption is further facilitated and encouraged by the accessibility of email from mobile devices and home computers.

However, the solution from Gupta, Sharda & Greve (2011) does not seem suitable for all contexts. The data gathered by Dabbish & Kraut (2006) suggests that checking email whenever new messages arrive, rather than checking it at restricted times, is one method for reducing email overload. The explanation suggested by the authors is that checking emails at restricted intervals means that email messages pile up in such a way that there are more messages to deal with on average when email is checked than if messages were dealt with continuously. Thus, although dealing with a high number of messages is associated with email overload, this overload is lower among those who read messages as they enter their mailbox.

In the solutions presented to deal with email overload, Sumecki, Chipulu, & Ojiako (2011) noted that literature tends not to emphasize the link between organizational and individual strategies. The individual perception of each employee about critical information contained in e-mails is related to the organizational culture but this aspect does not seem to be taken into account in most of the research that has been carried out. Based on the results of a study that collected 710 valid questionnaires, it was found that one type of email overload attenuator is the perception of the criticality of email as a business tool. When both the "inbox critical" (number of messages in the inbox considered business critical) and "email critical" (level of agreement that e-mail is a critical business tool) are larger, the smaller the feeling of email overload. According to the authors, an individual is more likely to send non-business critical emails if s/he receives more emails per day, if s/he accesses email more frequently while traveling on business, and if s/he accesses emails constantly and on notification rather than at specific times. Thus, they concluded that the more an individual accepts that e-mail is a critical business tool, the lower overload s/he experiences. So email overload can decrease in two ways: by reducing the number of non-business critical messages circulating and by a greater perception of email as a critical business tool. In this sense, the solutions needed to remedy email overload relate also to organizational culture and not to technological issues, since technology has already solved the spam problem, which was one of the biggest initial email problems.

The impact of workers training for the use of email appears to be also an interesting bet to reduce the problems associated with its use, in particular the overload. Among the problems associated with email, and promoting overload, Burgess Jackson & Edwards (2005) identified the information deficiency, often due to the poor use of the subject line, or the existence of poorly targeted emails, as many incoming emails are irrelevant or untargeted. Misuse of email, rather than other forms of communication, such as the telephone or face-to-face communication, also unnecessarily increases overload. Another problem is emails that are difficult to read because of drafting issues, requiring more time to be understood or worse, causing misunderstandings. Faced with these problems, authors have developed and implemented a training program to a sample of 20 individuals and subsequently evaluated their skills. Thus, they concluded that there has been an improvement in the quality of emails received as a result of the training completion for email senders. Training has been a success at improving employee's ability to write emails that are easy to read and that are straight to the point. The way employees use the subject line to convey information about the content and the urgency of an email was also improved. This is important for employees that receive large numbers of email and find it difficult to process their inbox.

A training intervention was also developed and conducted by Soucek and Moser (2010) in order to enhance individuals' information processing capabilities by improving media competencies to cope with large amount of email, improve personal workflow and increase email literacy. The aim of the training program was to advise trainees on how to modify or extend already existing self-management techniques to email management that fits their working routines. Overall, the trainees reported fewer problems with media usage and less work impairment. The training helps to cope with the amount of email received and reduces trainees' feelings of being overwhelmed and disrupted by incoming information. Thus, the training intervention was particularly effective with respect to coping with large amount of email. Authors assume that the causes for the alleviation of information overload are due to enhanced information processing abilities of participants. However, the training has a marginally significant effect on email strain. Furthermore, results reveal no effect concerning superficial and ambiguous communication because the trainees still perceive email communication more ambiguous when compared to alternative communication media like face-to-face communication or telephone. Additionally, in order to reinforce training effects, it is recommendable to train members of existing workgroups together, allowing the common understanding and use of email communication to be disseminated within organizational units. Paying attention to organizational-level factors, like organizational policies regarding email communication, can also be a valuable insight for successful trainings.

Another approach to deal with email overload, suggested in the literature, is to identify technological features from email clients to serve the needs of email users. In a study that investigated the latent user's needs regarding email handling practices Szostek (2011), in order to propose implications for the design of future inbox mechanisms, identified six types of needs. Three of the requirements are related to email organization (the process of assessing each new message and deciding on when and how to handle it) and include email annotation, reliable structure and no urgency to classify. Email annotation is defined as the possibility to indicate the relative importance of an email and also its relation to other emails. Reliable structure implies the provision of an inbox structure that remains simple and does not change with time. No urgency to classify emails can be defined as a need to minimize the often-occurred urgency to classify incoming emails into folders or labels, which requires an immediate assessment of their future importance. The other three requirements pertain to email retrieval aspects (a process in which an email that is already in the inbox needs to be found and reassessed), namely informative overview, flexible sorting and efficient search. Informative overview of emails can be defined as the email arrangement that reflects the temporal overview of messages and also their relevant characteristics such as priority and relationship with other messages. Flexible mail sorting can be understood as the provision of multiple customizable views on the inbox allowing the possibility to arrange emails according to their different characteristics through customizable sorting criteria and also by having the possibility to filter emails by more than one criterion. Finally, efficient search possibilities imply the ability to search and browse mails according to multiple criteria, including new ways of presenting historical data and also to be able to preserve the semantic annotation of archived emails, which would likely improve their findability at a later time. Vacek (2014b) also stressed technological solutions to improve email, including the creation of an internal repository for knowledge transfer, to bring ontology in email communication, to work with metadata for machine processing and to define automatic workflows for repeating actions.

Having in mind questions raised in the literature, it is possible to identify two main components to manage email overload [Figure 2]. These components include

Figure 2. Components to consider in email overload management

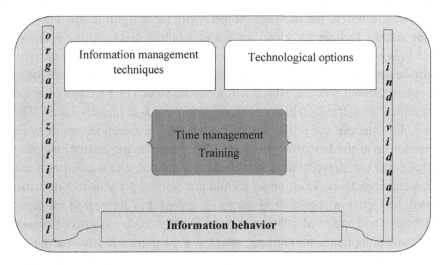

information management techniques (such as skills to create a hierarchical structure of folders or to assign tags to messages) and technological options provided by email clients (such as search options or sorting options). These solutions will only produce positive results if they are supported by training and consider especially the importance of time management. Moreover, it is important to stress that information behavior, at both individual and organizational level, is the backdrop where email overload happens and therefore always has to be considered. Detailed information on the components to consider on email overload management is presented below.

As defined by Bates (2010), information behavior is the term used to refer to the many ways in which human beings interact with information, namely the ways in which they use and seek information. To understand this relationship between people and information, it is important to consider not only the individual perspective, but also the organizational context in which that relationship takes place. Thus, information behavior is determined by personal and organizational characteristics, in particular by information culture, perceived as the socially shared patterns of behaviors, norms, and values that define the significance and use of information (Choo, Bergeron, Deltor, Heaton, 2008). Therefore, a subjective perspective of information overload is emphasized, essentially an individual/organizational feeling, determined by the skills, at personal and organizational levels, to deal with an objective reality that is the amount of information, embodied in this case in the form of emails. These skills include information management techniques applicable to all emails' lifecycle (creation/reception, analysis, organization, search/retrieval, use, evaluation and disposal/retention). The creation/reception include aspects related to writing standards, the definition of tasks which justify the use of email or alternative communication forms, the identification of senders' levels of importance or with the description of the messages subject with meaningful terms. The analysis involves reading techniques, identification of required tasks and the frame of the subject in organizational procedures, among other things. The organization is related to the implementation of standards and strategies to structure email messages in an organizational scheme, which will facilitate search and recovery, including, for example, a classification plan or assigning keywords to identify issues. The use requires, for example, the proper use of institutional distribution lists or avoid the systematic use of the functionality "reply all". Furthermore, institutions must ensure that email use supports organizational performance, and is consistent with its mission and objectives. Thus, email should not be used for sensitive information, personal, protected or confidential purposes, unless it is authorized for organizational matters and approved safety measures. The logs in the system can be used for auditing and compliance monitoring, which is very important because the system must be prepared to provide legal evidence in electronic form. Finally, evaluation and disposal/retention imply that emails are kept, protected and preserved in accordance with appropriate retention periods. Thus, the e-mail system should not be subjected to indiscriminate eliminations and message records must be managed to be accessible to authorized employees. The technological options cover all components of the IT infrastructure that will frame the use of the email system which must be aligned with the organizational structure and its procedures. Additionally, it should enable functionalities for managing information overload, through the aggregation of messages or setting the allowed size for storing messages, etc. A special emphasis should be given to time management, with training on techniques to organize working time, determining or not slot hours for consultation and reply to emails. By attending to these components, managers can define an email management policy, at organizational level to overcome the problems arising from email overload. Thus, the overall organizational performance may be improved.

CONCLUSION

For knowledge workers, email is the place where they spend the most part of their working time, receiving, doing, and delegating tasks. Additionally, in the workplace, email has become one of the most important and common mean to communicate within the organization and with clients and other stakeholders. This implies a constant flow of incoming messages and a pressure to react almost immediately, conducting to the sensation of inability to manage the high volume of information effectively. So email overload contributes to information overload understood as the delivery of too many communications. This implies an increase in social density that gives individuals access to more communications than they can easily respond to, creating information entropy, when individuals fail to respond, respond less accurately, respond incorrectly, ignore some features, recode inputs in a more compact/effective form or quit in extreme cases. So information overload occurs when information received becomes a hindrance rather than a help when the information is potentially useful. However, not all the literature is unanimous about that, arguing that the amount of emails received or stored is not the core problem, but rather the limited capacity of human beings to deal with emails, pushing them towards their capacity limit.

The research about email overload should be approached from different perspectives. It also needs to include research into personal information overload and the effects on an individual's ability to cope with solving problems and making decisions and research into the problem of organizational information overload, encompassing both paper and electronic information systems. These issues are especially relevant in the analysis of the email overload concept considering that, at a professional level, email involves aspects related to personal information management but also to information management in the organizational context.

In terms of future research, this literature review on information overload and email overload can be the basis for empirical studies relating to the factors that mitigate or accentuate the misuse of this communication tool. Another possible line of research is creating a summary of advices or guidelines in order to define guidelines of an organizational email management policy, framed in the wider context of an information management policy.

REFERENCES

Allen, D. K., & Shoard, M. (2005). Spreading the load: mobile information and communications technologies and their effect on information overload. *Information Research*, *10*(2).

Barley, S. R., Meyerson, D. E., & Grodal, S. (2011). E-mail as a source and symbol of stress. *Organization Science*, *22*(4), 887–906. doi:10.1287/orsc.1100.0573

Bates, M. J. (2010). Information behavior. In *Encyclopedia of Library and Information Sciences* (pp. 2381–2391). New York: CRC Press.

Bawden, D., Holtham, C., & Courtney, N. (1999). Perspectives on information overload. *Aslib Proceedings*, *51*(8), 249–255. doi:10.1108/EUM0000000006984

Bawden, D., & Robinson, L. (2009). The dark side of information: Overload, anxiety and other paradoxes and pathologies. *Journal of Information Science*, *35*(2), 180–191. doi:10.1177/0165551508095781

Benselin, J. C., & Ragsdell, G. (2016). Information overload: The differences that age makes. *Journal of Librarianship and Information Science*, *48*(3), 1–14. doi:10.1177/0961000614566341

Bundy, A. (Ed.). (2004). Australian and New Zealand Information Literacy Framework. Adelaide: Australian and New Zeeland Institute for Information Literacy. Retrieved from http://www.caul.edu.au/content/upload/files/info-literacy/InfoLiteracyFramework.pdf

Burgess, A., Jackson, T., & Edwards, J. (2005). Email training significantly reduces email defects. *International Journal of Information Management*, *25*(1), 71–83. doi:10.1016/j.ijinfomgt.2004.10.004

Choo, C. W., Bergeron, P., Deltor, B., & Heaton, L. (2008). Information culture and information use : An exploratory study of three organizations. *Journal of the American Society for Information Science and Technology*, *59*(5), 792–804. doi:10.1002/asi.20797

Dabbish, L. A., & Kraut, R. E. (2006). Email overload at work: an analysis of factors associated with email strain. *Proceedings of the 2006 20th anniversary conference on Computer Supported Cooperative Work ICSCW '06* (pp. 431–440). New York: ACM. doi:10.1145/1180875.1180941

Ducheneaut, N., & Bellotti, V. (2001). Email as habitat: An exploration of embedded personal information management. *Interaction*, *8*(5), 30–38. doi:10.1145/382899.383305

Edmunds, A., & Morris, A. (2000). The problem of information overload in business organisations: A review of the literature. *International Journal of Information Management*, *20*(1), 17–28. doi:10.1016/S0268-4012(99)00051-1

EMC, & IDC. (2014). The digital universe of opportunities: rich data and the increasing value of the internet of things. Retrieved from http://www.emc.com/leadership/digital-universe/2014iview/index.htm

Eppler, M. J., & Mengis, J. (2004). The concept of information overload: A review of literature. *The Information Society: An International Journal*, *20*(5), 325–344. doi:10.1080/01972240490507974

Gupta, A., Sharda, R., & Greve, R. A. (2011). Youve got email! Does it really matter to process emails now or later? *Information Systems Frontiers*, *13*(5), 637–653. doi:10.1007/s10796-010-9242-4

Gwizdka, J. (2004, April 24-29). Email task management styles: the cleaners and the keepers. *Proceedings of theConference on Human Factors in Computing Systems*, Vienna, Austria (pp. 1235–1238). doi:10.1145/985921.986032

Hanrahan, B. V., Pérez-Quiñones, M. A., & Martin, D. (2014). Attending to Email. In *Interacting with Computers*.

Hilbert, M. (2014). What is the content of the worlds technologically mediated information and communication capacity: How much text, image, audio, and video? *The Information Society: An International Journal*, *30*(2), 127–143. doi:10.1080/01972243.2013.873748

Hiltz, S. R., & Turoff, M. (1985). Structuring computer-mediated communication systems to avoid information overload. *Communications of the ACM*, *28*(7), 680–689. doi:10.1145/3894.3895

Ingham, J. (2003). E-mail overload in the UK workplace. *Aslib Proceedings*, *55*(3), 166–180. doi:10.1108/00012530310472651

Jackson, T. W., & Farzaneh, P. (2012). Theory-based model of factors affecting information overload. *International Journal of Information Management*, *32*(6), 523–532. doi:10.1016/j.ijinfomgt.2012.04.006

Koprinska, I., Poon, J., Clark, J., & Chan, J. (2007). Learning to classify e-mail. *Information Sciences*, *177*(10), 2167–2187. doi:10.1016/j.ins.2006.12.005

McMurty, K. (2014). Managing email overload in the workplace. *Performance Improvement*, *53*(7), 31–37. doi:10.1002/pfi.21424

Meadow, C. T., & Yuan, W. (1997). Measuring the impact of information: Defining the concepts. *Information Processing & Management*, *33*(6), 697–714. doi:10.1016/S0306-4573(97)00042-3

Radicati Group. (2015). Email statistics report 2015-2019. Retrieved from http://www.radicati.com/wp/wp-content/uploads/2015/02/Email-Statistics-Report-2015-2019-Executive-Summary.pdf

Radicati Group. (2016). Email market 2016-2020. Retrieved from http://www.radicati.com/wp/wp-content/uploads/2016/01/Email_Market_2016-2020_Executive Summary.pdf

Ramsay, J., Hair, M., & Renaud, K. V. (2008). Ubiquitous connectivity & work-related stress. In P. Zemliansky & K. St. Amant (Eds.), *Handbook of research on virtual workplaces and the new nature of business practices* (pp. 167–182). Hershey, PA, USA: IGI Global. doi:10.4018/978-1-59904-893-2.ch013

Reinke, K., & Chamorro-Premuzic, T. (2014). When email use gets out of control: Understanding the relationship between personality and email overload and their impact on burnout and work engagement. *Computers in Human Behavior, 36,* 502–509. doi:10.1016/j.chb.2014.03.075

Schuff, D., Turetken, O., & DArcy, J. (2006). A multi-attribute, multi-weight clustering approach to managing b e-mail overload. *Decision Support Systems, 42*(3), 1350–1365. doi:10.1016/j.dss.2005.11.003

SCONSUL Working Group on Information Literacy. (2011). The SCONUL seven pillars of information literacy: core model for higher education. Retrieved from http://www.sconul.ac.uk/sites/default/files/documents/coremodel.pdf

Sobotta, N., & Hummel, M. (2015). A capacity perspective on e-mail overload: how E-mail use contributes to information overload. Proceedings of the 48th Hawaii International Conference on System Sciences (pp. 692–701). IEEE. doi:10.1109/HICSS.2015.89

Soucek, R., & Moser, K. (2010). Coping with information overload in email communication: Evaluation of a training intervention. *Computers in Human Behavior, 26*(6), 1458–1466. doi:10.1016/j.chb.2010.04.024

Sumecki, D., Chipulu, M., & Ojiako, U. (2011). Email overload: Exploring the moderating role of the perception of email as a business critical tool. *International Journal of Information Management, 31*(5), 407–414. doi:10.1016/j.ijinfomgt.2010.12.008

Szóstek, A. M. (2011). Dealing with my emails: Latent user needs in email management. *Computers in Human Behavior, 27*(2), 723–729. doi:10.1016/j.chb.2010.09.019

Tidline, T. J. (1999). The mythology of information overload. *Library Trends, 47*(3), 485–506.

Vacek, M. (2014a). Email Overload: Causes, Consequences and the Future. *International Journal of Computer Theory and Engineering, 6*(2), 170–176. doi:10.7763/IJCTE.2014.V6.857

Vacek, M. (2014b). How to survive email. *Proceedings of the 9th IEEE International Symposium on Applied Computational Intelligence and Informatics* (pp. 49–54). IEEE.

Whittaker, S., & Sidner, C. (1996). Email overload: exploring personal information management of ernail. *Proceedings CHI '96* (pp. 276–283). doi:10.1145/238386.238530

Chapter 3
Photographers without Photographs:
The Internet as Primary Resource

Hernando Gómez Gómez
Universidad Europea de Madrid, Spain

Enrique Corrales Crespo
Universidad Europea de Madrid, Spain

ABSTRACT

The modern society establishes a complex relationship that combines the visual overload derived from technology insertion which is adapted to the today´s needs and executed through devices swiftly embraced. In this certain sense, one of the most overloaded environments currently is, in fact, the photography. The internet and digital mass media development have promoted to get a surprising image surplus, impossible to distinguish between the real occurrence and the photographic observed event. Therefore, is necessary to contemplate a sustainable scenario in photography. It must determinate a balance between images which are produced, consumed and those which can be assumed by society. The photography evolution and the new denomination PostPhotography installs a brand new discourse initially literal, linked to words and needing a unit of speech to make exist the images.

DOI: 10.4018/978-1-5225-2061-0.ch003

BACKGROUND

The main intention in *PHOTOGRAPHY OVERLOAD. Photographers without Photographs. The Internet as Primary Resource* article is to create a reflection about present and future photography in XXI century society. The information overload in the contemporary society gives an opportunity to go in depth about brand new photographic uses and, above all, post-photographic practices. The final aim is the description and analysis of several strategies that has been considered sufficiently representative in this paradigm shift.

MAIN FOCUS OF THE CHAPTER

The chapter aims to open a debate about the reformulation of photographic fact. The image overload produced by the new information and communication technologies has changed the photography prospective. In this sense, we propose a debate related to the displacement that occurs from photographer as an image producer to the photographer as collector of images obtained from the Net.

INTRODUCTION

One of the main consequences of information overload in the digital era is oversaturation of photographic images. This fact causes the nature of photography to change from one related to index to one related to the appropriation, editing and transformation of images. In this article, we intend to demonstrate how this communication overload is directly linked to new photographic/postphotograpic uses and practices.

We take as our starting point the indisputable fact that in the twenty-first century we are exposed to the greatest overload of images ever in the history of mankind, most of them of photographic origin. This fact is fundamentally changing the nature of photography, reformulating practices, interpretations, meanings, categories and relationships with the medium.

This scenario strikes us as especially exciting because it represents the definitive emancipation of the photographic medium from the visual submission referred to by Joan Costa (1991). This submission occurs when an image aims to reproduce or represent a reality outside of itself, when it tries "to present the appearance of an absent object" (Costa, 1991, page 8). If photography seeks to find its autonomy in visual submission, it will basically be redundant. Photography's current insubordination is reminiscent of painting's evolution towards pure creation since the mid-nineteenth century.

In this study, we pay special attention to contemporary photographic practices which use the internet as a primary resource. There are some visual artists we like to define with a certain degree of irony as anti-photographers, to borrow the term used by Nancy Foote (2004). The term refers to artists who use multiple strategies such as appropriation, editing, re-contextualization, intervention, redefining archives, etc. We understand the term appropriation to mean the action of taking possession of images already captured by others without contemplating the concept of authorship. The creation of photographs is dismissed and undervalued precisely because of information overload in the digital era. However, the mere fact that the artist reuses existing images causes the appeal of its discourse to have an impact on the debate about excess (understood as an overload).

Many of these practices were already present in the avant-gardes but have been updated through digital media and practices, leading to a profound reflection on the ontology of the medium. Robert Shore, in his recently published book Post-Photography: The Artist with a Camera (2014), focuses on this relationship with the photographic, including it among contemporary post-photographic practices. *See Laurence Aëgerter art work* "Healing Plants for Hurt Landscapes"

Dealing with these types of photographic practices forces us to redefine Photography and relate it to what is being called Post-Photography; identifying and delimiting the syntactical elements of the medium on the one hand, and the semantic universe of the photographic and post-photographic construct on the other.

Therefore, throughout our essay we will address different characteristics and qualities that from our point of view are redefining Photography. We will start with a formal approach to Photography/Post-Photography and subsequently propose a semantic analysis of the photographic construct. We will discuss the relationships and evolution of the index, understood as an ontological element of Photography, and its replacement by the trace in Post-Photography. We will also consider the impact of image overload on information ecology, as well as its repercussions for artistic authorship issues and the categorization of digital artworks.

TOWARDS AN ONTOLOGY OF POST-PHOTOGRAPHY

One of the main problems we encounter when talking about Photography and Post-Photography concerns the confused and confusing terminology. On what grounds do we make a categorical distinction between Photography and Post-Photography? Can we establish a real difference between these disciplines? Are they really different things?

We consider it appropriate to try to pinpoint the constituent and/or distinctive elements of Photography and Post-Photography, seeking to define these elements from a syntactic point of view. In this respect, we are aware that comparing photography

Figure1. Laurence Aëgerter, Healing Plants for Hurt Landscapes, Coast of Japan 2015. Manipulation of Google images for news photographs of a diversity of disasters in different parts of the world
Retrieved in May, 2016; http://laurenceaegerter.com/portfolio-item/healing-plants-for-hurt-landscapes-photos/

with linguistics has led many authors into murky waters with often catastrophic results, since considering the medium from semiotic perspectives has usually meant neglecting formal, visual or artistic characteristics in favour of communicative aspects, with all the advantages and disadvantages that this entails.

Barthes asserted that:

"...photographs are signs which don't take, which turn, like milk. Whatever it grants to vision and whatever its manner, a photograph is always invisible: it is not it that we see" (Barthes, 1992, p 34).

This is changing in the digital culture; post-photographic practices draw our attention to the medium, the form, rather than to the information deriving from its interpretation, as was usually the case in classical photography.

It is in this sense that we believe the advent of digital photography is allowing a similar evolution to that undergone by painting in the nineteenth century.

"Photography is clearly the most important event in the history of the plastic arts. Simultaneously a liberation and an accomplishment, it has freed Western painting, once and for all, from its obsession with realism and allowed it to recover its aesthetic autonomy" (Bazin, 1990. Page 30).

Figure 2. Kenta Cobayashi, Green Mist #Smudge, 2015. Cobayashi selects and manipulates digital images, both his own and from the internet. His main aim is purely visual and abstract, moving away from any representative interest
Retrieved in May, 2016; http://hyperallergic.com/297369/developing-the-edges-of-japanese-photography/

We believe that Post-Photography and the evolution of Photography towards digital environments entail the emancipation of the referent, thereby enabling it to become increasingly autonomous as a visual language.

Bazin spoke in 1946 about the psychological fact that the photographic image represents: "a psychological fact, to wit, in completely satisfying our appetite for illusion by a mechanical reproduction in the making of which man plays no part. The solution is not to be found in the result achieved but in the way of achieving it." (Bazin, 1990, Page 27). This naturalistic automatism is closely linked to the positivist notion of industrial progress so in keeping with the inspirations of the period in which the medium emerged. "... Between the originating object and its reproduction there intervenes only the instrumentality of a non-living agent" (Bazin, 1990. Page 28)

After the nineteenth-century pictorial approach, the early twentieth century sees photography stake its claim as the offspring of modernity and progress. Stieglitz's straight photography makes photography aware of its virtues and structural characteristics. Direct photography is concerned with details, with representative perfection, texture, optical excellence, framing, focus in/out, the quality of the result... in short, with all those elements that distinguish it from painting. This straight photography, without pictorial concessions, would soon influence European creators and all subsequent modern photographic trends, while also having a huge influence on the development of historic avant-gardes and opening up a range of creative possibilities.

But our society is very different from classical Modern Society; in our postmodern and late-capitalist context everything is diluted. We have gone from a society based on the means of production, in which wealth was supported by the gold standard, by the material, by the object, by the territory... to a diluted society. "All that is solid melts into air", as Marx said in 1848; a liquid capitalism, as referred to by Bauman (2002), where virtually nothing is palpable. This scenario also produces a soft, uncertain, speculative image, which is precisely the image provided by digital.

Post-Photography is characterized by the immateriality of the medium; it is not objective, but rather information, numerical code... Therefore, it responds much better to the idea of information flow, the absence of concrete materiality, the superfluousness of the object.

Figure 3. Mishka Henner, (Staphorst Ammunition Depot) Dutch Landscapes, 2011
Retrieved in May, 2016; https://photoworks.org.uk/mishka-henner-dutch-landscapes/

"... Digital photography is the result of an economy that favours information as merchandise, opaque capital and invisible telematic transactions. Its matter is language, codes and algorithms." (Fontcuberta, 2010, p. 13).

Post-Photography tends towards transcoding, as we will see, and this characteristic certifies the voluble nature of the medium. A matter that is demonstrated in Mishka Henner's artwork.

Fred Ritchin goes further, pointing out the dual nature of Post-Photography and comparing it with the nature of light, wavelength and quantum physics: "The universe is both Newtonian and quantum. The universe is both analogue and digital; they coexist. Light –and photography is about light– functions as wave and particle simultaneously." (2009)

In our attempt to dissect Post-Photography we take the digital image categorization established by Lev Manovich (2005). The author provides a list of features of digital images which tally with certain post-photographic practices. Manovich established the following main features: digitization, modularity, automation, variability and transcoding. A review of contemporary photography allows us to easily detect one or more characteristics that define the artist in the configuration of contemporary Post-Photography.

In the first stage of Post-Photography's evolution there is a natural transfer of the photographic device towards the digital medium. The need to operate with a known model justifies the need to digitally reproduce the analogue model. This process goes so far as to emulate certain formal defects or photographic noises while digitizing.

Digital photography discovers and proposes new applications that will modify and gradually transform photography into something else. Devices and cameras are changing and developing in response to these particularities of the digital universe that did not exist in traditional photography.

Digitization uses a numerical code that can be reinterpreted and reprogrammed, as well as transmitted and shared. In this sense, all digital images are accompanied by metadata, allowing their origin to be traced. Furthermore, the level of noise and system failures will gradually become post-photographic variations.

The raw material of the digital image is easily alterable numerical code; transcoding information is revealed as one of the great potential strengths of digital culture. Unlike analogue photography before it, digital photography does not produce an image but instead generates code. This code, even being obtained by a photosensitive matrix, can then transform the photograph into whatever we want; all we have to do is use the same code and reconfigure it.

Glitch Art uses RAW photo files and recodes them in software designed for other uses. Such practices are an interesting example of the reconfiguration of photography. This kind of strategy shows the importance of the sign in Post-Photography as opposed to the index of the Photographic image.

The modular construction of the digital image is one of the most characteristic elements of contemporary images. There are numerous examples in the field of Post-Photography that point to the modular, fractional, serial or complex organization of images. The basic construction of the digital image stems from the grouping of pixels, units which have the same characteristics and are grouped together or modulated in order to obtain new results. The grouping logic thus obtained produces larger-scale objects which in turn consist of independent parts, each of which is made up of smaller parts: a superstructure that exhibits a fractal logic as opposed traditional linear logics. As can be seen Figure 4.

Process automation is another common resource in digital and post-photographic practices. The digital environment allows automation in most processes of creation, manipulation and access. However, this automation has a downside: it tends to unify results, and so the application of industry-predesigned automated elements makes the user feel like a creator when actually he/she is the consumer, an idea already raised by Flusser (2001). On the other hand, automation processes can produce some really interesting and transgressive deconstructions of image, placing the result in a poorly defined category in which the random, the automatism and

Figure 4. Joan Fontcuberta. Googlegrams
Retrieved in May, 2016; http://www.fontcuberta.com/

Figure 5. Miguel Ángel Tornero. Random Series. 2010
Retrieved in May, 2016; http://www.bethanien.de/en/exhibitions/the-random-series/

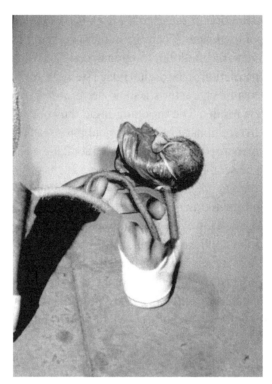

the unexpected are combined. Processes which can clearly be seen in Miguel Angel Tornero's art work.

The lack of apparent materiality and limited objectuality of digital media are further remarkable features. The common point of access to the digital image is the screen, but this is misleading. We think we know the reality through the flat image from our computers, without bearing in mind its constructive elements, such as scale, size, resolution, colour, finish, etc. Therefore, the screen both unifies and flattens our experience as viewers/customers.

We are witnessing how the screen is expanding and being used like a creative support, hence the proliferation of jobs that use multiscreen fragmentation or Thumbnails as a compositional strategy. Various media make up the final document in a hypermedia logic.

Undoubtedly, our perception of the world is directly related to our construction of reality, and our contemporary reality is fractured, rhizomatic, modular, non-localized (nonlocality). The central question is whether technology derives from our understanding of world or vice versa, or maybe both.

Figure 6. Lucas Blalock, Tire II, 2011
Retrieved in May, 2016; http://www.ramikencrucible.com/blalock-images-xyz/

"The concept is that all media change us. The media change us, we create new media, they change us -it's dialectical- but it puts us on different pathways" (Ritchin, 2009).

If André Bazin referred to the psychological fact in describing the nature of Photography, now -nearly 80 years later- we can say that Post-Photography responds to the psychological fact of the contemporary citizen and therein lies an important part of its ontology.

FROM PAW PRINT TO TRACE

Perhaps one of the most important changes linked to Post-Photography, and which we have already referred to, is the end of the index:

"conventional photography was defined by the notion of a light footprint produced by visible appearances of reality. Some systems of photorealistic digital synthesis have replaced the notion of trace with recording without trace that is lost in a spiral of mutations" (Fontcuberta, 2010, p. 13).

Barthes proposed the noema1 "It has been" as being characteristic of the medium; "The photograph is literally an emanation of the referent" (Barthes, 1992). It therefore loses its validity, and for two reasons: the absence of a referent, and attenuation of its use as an element of memory.

Nowadays, photographs are consumed instantly, and in most cases they are never recalled or remembered. We often only see them when we take them and share them, and we usually destroy them to free up our hard drives.

This absence of use and sense of memory explains the success of apps like Snapchat. This application automatically deletes the photo after 10 seconds; it ceases to exist, and it is precisely this characteristic that has made the app so popular. The picture is therefore pure message and operates in a similar manner to oral transmission, leaving no trace, no certification of what happened.

In argent2 photography the index character prevailed against the iconic

"... No matter how fuzzy, distorted, or discoloured, no matter how lacking in documentary value the image may be, it shares, by virtue of the very process of its becoming, the being of the model of which it is the reproduction: it is the model" *(Barthes, 1992, p. 28).*

Today, the issues relating to index and physical contiguity raised by Dubois (1994) and Schaeffer (1990) are becoming diluted like Post-Photography itself, and this change is undermining one of the cornerstones of the medium.

The documentary character and its connection to the record on which analogue photography was based for over a century was supported by a relationship of contiguity with the represented element, a relationship of physical proximity. Even in Pictorialism, in staged or constructed photography, the physical presence of the elements (fictionalized or otherwise) and the contiguity of light (understood as formed elements in the image) were always necessary.

Today, post-photography does not certify the relationship with contiguity; that index relationship. This feature radically changes the status of the medium: Post-Photography is all narrative and the relationship is closer to the notion of icon than that of index:

"What is important about the icon is the resemblance to the object (...) what is important in the index is that the object should actually exist and be contiguous to the emanating sign]" *(Dubois, 1994, p. 59).*

Therefore, Post-Photography is composed of code, and although this may no longer be based on the index, it does provide a particular and distinctive element in relation to Photography. This element can be defined as: information trace.

Metadata are hidden in any digital image; they are concealed informative elements, key information. Therefore, the digital photograph can be traced, followed, monitored. We can find out who took it and where, with which camera, diaphragm, etc., and this information changes the informative status of the post-photographic image.

The trace, together with the proliferation of applications and social networks (Flickr, Pinterest, Instagram, Facebook, etc.) based on the transmission of photographs, clearly indicates that one of the main features of Post-Photography is diffusion, propagation, the aspect of reminiscence being far less important than it used to be.

"Transmitting and sharing photos works well as a new system of social communication, like a ritual behaviour that is also linked to particular rules of ethics and courtesy. Among the rules, the first states that the flow of images is indicative of vital energy, which brings us back to the initial ontological argument of "I photograph, therefore I am". (Fontcuberta 2010).

Many post-photographic practices become an act of self-affirmation, a map of our construction of reality, an information trace that gradually forms a network of connections, before ultimately becoming a personal marketing artefact. Paradoxically, the only objectification that Post-Photography produces is that of the user. To paraphrase Richard Serra, "you are consumed, you are the product of television" (Serra, 1973), which we can now update to "we are consumed, we are the product of internet".

We think we produce photographs, but it is the photographs that produce us.

SEMANTIC UNIVERSE OF THE POST-PHOTOGRAPHIC CONSTRUCT

The way in which we understand and represent the world may have inherited something from the semantic principle for the creation of language, especially if we understand photography as a writing mechanism, or rather as the materialization of thoughts. We can observe very similar processes to those undergone by linguistic signs since their inception.

The constituent elements of the post-photographic process do not differ greatly from the norms established in pure language. The digital image is formed through an individualized process in every single pixel, and language does not understand speech without taking into account every word and all the morphemes, monemes... or minimum units of meaning.

Traditional photography also takes into account a discursive framework, but, unlike Post-Photography, based on the mere presence that the elements have in an image.

Given the excess of images being created at any given moment, a different framework such as that of language is useful for understanding that even in the act of speaking there is no constant terminological or expressive production that cannot be assumed by the linguistic system. A reasonable time for assimilation is required. That is, language reuses all its tools to communicate and, therefore, assumes a sustainable, recycling behaviour. If a system as important as language prioritizes the proper functioning of all its rules and norms, for the sake of expressing in order to communicate, how is it possible that such a specific discipline as photography seeks to produce simply by collecting or accumulating? To raise our self-esteem?

Post-Photography contains a distinctive feature in relation to photo collection/ collecting (see the work of Penelope Umbrico), something that did not occur to the same extent in classical photography. In the latter, the element was much more individualized and focused on a single shot, which would generally be interpreted as a whole in the pictorial mode.

However, reality shows us that the shift from individual photos to series -even though the latter has existed since the advent of photography- has gained momentum at an exponential rate as history and photographic practices have progressed. Notable examples include Gerhard Richter's Atlas and Hilla and Bernd Becher's industrial archaeology, works whose form is dependent on the composition of all their individual parts; works in the form of a grid, or a mosaic, works intended to be observed as a whole.

Current proponents of the idea of accumulation include Eric Tabuchi and his cumulative creation of alphabets formed of individual letters on the backs of trucks

Figure 7. Sunset Portraits, 2011, Penelope Umbrico
Retrieved from http://www.penelopeumbrico.net/sunsetportraits/sunsetportraits.html

Figure 8. Bernd Becher and Hilla Becher, Blast Furnaces 1969–95
Retrieved from http://www.tate.org.uk/art/artworks/becher-blast-furnaces-p81236

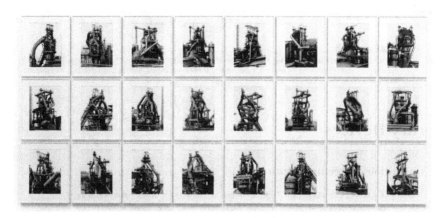

encountered by chance while driving along French roads; and Richard Simpkin, who has spent a lifetime collecting photos of himself posing with famous people; the obsession with celebrities endures, the fetishistic pursuit of VIPs continues, although all these photos contain a large dose of irony that aids recall.

In these cases, an effect is produced between the observer and the observed that borders on cognitive semantics and dilemmas that arise in relation to the psychic mechanism of this two-way interaction.

If two abovementioned concepts, irony and accumulation, are considered intrinsic to Post-Photography, an obvious reality becomes strikingly apparent: both are included in the list of stylistic devices that language uses to embellish the message. Two major institutions responsible for the categorization of figures of speech attest to this:

Therefore, the poetic component clearly forms part of the essence of the new photographic era, and so writing through images will never cease to be a communicative act that changes with the times while always safeguarding the relationship.

If construction of the post-photographic image follows the precepts of logical semantics, then it assumes that traditional relationship between the linguistic sign and reality, although this time completely different to what is commonly assumed. Both traditionally and nowadays, the norms and rules for a correct and unambiguous communicative act are of irreplaceable importance.

It is undeniable that Post-Photography represents a new way of conceiving spaces and messages, which reuses images and points to the danger of overproduction, which compiles and regroups, etc. However, there is something that it is unable to cast aside, even without knowing what it is: the word.

Figure 9. Figures of speech definition (Own elaboration, 2016)

 **POETRY** FOUNDAION

Figure of speech

An expressive, nonliteral use of language. Figures of speech include *tropes* (such as hyperbole, irony, metaphor, and simile) and *schemes* (anything involving the ordering and organizing of words—anaphora, antithesis, and chiasmus, for example). Browse all terms related to figures of speech

Literary Devices

Definition and Examples of Literary Terms

Definition of Accumulation

Accumulation is derived from a Latin word which means "*pile up*". It is a stylistic device that is defined as a list of words which embody similar abstract or physical qualities or meanings with the intention to emphasize the common qualities that words hold. It is also an act of accumulating the scattered points. Accumulation examples are found in literary pieces and in daily conversations.

The internet age forces us to name, to label… the system needs to discriminate through the icon, the signifier. No signifier, no meaning. And again, the word takes precedence over the image, meaning being the common denominator.

Sartori's homo videns3 (1998) is the evolution of homo sapiens, supplanting words with pictures. We are introduced to the new human being, its main source of education (the virtual space, cyberspace, the media, etc.) and, in particular, the relationship with the transience of images. This event diminishes proper analysis, judgment and conceptualization.

As soon as images are published, the concept of absolute truth exists, without considering whether there has been manipulation and, if so, the possible consequences. Written discourse, however, has always been questioned and debated in forums where words on paper constituted reliable proof of the author's thoughts. Gadamer (1977) states that in terms of cultural formation we have gone from being readers to mere spectators (today we would even say users), forgetting the real individual meaning of each significant minimum unit and prioritizing the visual speed and comprehension of the immediate message. The author advocates the reading experience, understood as a conversation with the text and after which the reader will never be the same again. It states that "comprehensive reading is not the repetition of something past, but participation in a felt present" (1977, p. 471). Alluding to all this, Post-Photography is eminently a current event that transcends fixed genres. It implies participation in the moment.

Returning to a principal theme of this essay, one of the most commonly used terms in this new conceptual age is appropriation. Taking images from the internet is normal practice nowadays and, in fact, hardly surprising given that the detachment and distancing of authorship encourages such acquisition by third parties. However, if we forget the desire to protect our property and instead focus on the democratisation of art, then Post-Photography would go deeper into more disinterested and unselfish territory. Fontcuberta prefers the term adoption, which implies sharing.

The literal meaning and terminological use of some concepts in photography, fully updated to this virtual age, is obvious. Semantics acquires real relevance through discursive references (appropriation, storage, transcoding, modularity, etc.)

Some authors argue that reading images is far removed from merely looking at them. Some might think that is a metaphorical way of referring to the act of looking, albeit for much more abstract and profound purposes. However, the theory put forward by Acaso (2006) seems quite consistent with post-photographic discourse; no reading without a voluntary act of looking, no reading without obtaining the relevant information, without the mental product created and understood... and as a result, the critical thinking generated therein. Therefore, this is a systematic and linguistic act. "If you learn to read, you are in control; if you only see, others are" (Acaso, 2007, page 90). In the era of information overload and digital communication, it is especially important to be able to read images in order not to lose control over information. In this way, the contemporary individual will not be easily manipulated by the suggestions found in images that come from mass media. Understanding an image's constructive codes and the references included in it offers the observer a better critical point of view.

Reading is preceded by semantic, syntactic and phonological knowledge; no such knowledge, no understanding. Would this diminish the meaning's poetical value? Traditionally, literature has established certain clearly defined standards to determine whether poems or other literary works have been realised correctly, incorrectly, brilliantly, terribly..., and according to what criteria? Through a well-chosen, beautiful and/or meaningful combination of symbols. Therefore, it can be argued that if Post-Photography continues with this logical system of operation, it will never offer banality or mere representation.

Post-Photography's semantic field also includes traditional photography and its genres: photojournalism, commercial, artistic, scientific and medical photography, etc. All these areas include the photographic image, albeit with all their major differences. It is not a matter of genre but of overall intrinsic meaning.

In one of his Discourses, Galileo announced the greatest of inventions that would give voice to the word: the set of 24 symbols (at that time) which made up the alphabet. Their combinations would culminate in speeches, statements, passions..., and in whatever human beings had in mind and needed to materialize. Port-Royal Grammar philosophers built on these premises, claiming that through the infinite combinations of 25-30 sounds the various movements of the soul would be revealed.

Today's Post-Photography assumes compilation as part of poetic discourse through the unlimited combination of all the elements present.

The importance of neuroscience in the study of language, regardless of its nature, is relevant and crucial for understanding the whole process of artistic creation. Chomsky (2002) assembled a comprehensive collection of abstract computational models (cognitive science) and conducted a material study of language and the brain's cognitive system. Basically, language is a natural object that is physically located in a very specific part of the brain and is a biological element of any species. Under this premise, any form of linguistic expression stemming from the mental construct produced in the intellect will be regarded as a real or unreal speech act. It need not be manifested through actual words, but simply by preserving the semantic structure that is established in the formal language system and with the aim of being coherent.

This new way of understanding images regards the photograph not just as a mere object but as an individual code with its own meaning. The 2.0 framework sees the zeros and ones as a universe full of informative and creative possibilities, capable of generating expressions that have never been considered or glimpsed by even the most visionary people. In this respect, an intrinsic feature of Postmodernism is equivocation or the ability to interpret the artistic code and the manipulation and reconstruction of images from different perspectives. It is time to abandon the pure stream typical of Modernity and act with more passion. Now, artists roundly reject technical perfection and its implications for the artistic life, to the extent of being able to generate pieces of art without being considered professional photographers. The concept of hybridization is now assumed to be characteristic of this new era.

Therefore, the future of photography promises to be complex and full of mysteries and uncertainties.

The new photography's construction of discourse or semiotic construct will overcome prejudices regarding an issue which may well never have existed before in the context of art: the concept of authorship. Creation is relative and now detached. However, if the act of speaking requires an infinite combination of some minimum units of meaning for it to coexist with the message, why has a closed system like art put the figure of the artist before the content of the message? This contradicts the principle of communication.

Therefore, the experience of dispossessing in order to donate could be positive. Or in other words, why not consider the exquisite corpse5 as a starting point for artistic creation?

So far in this essay we have addressed the subject of post-photography with the intention of creating a framework that defines the main features we believe are present in contemporary image trends. Now it is time to take a look at some examples of artists and their works in order to illustrate clearly the elements defined above.

In the eighties and nineties, a number of artists who could now be seen as pioneers of post-photography carried out a series of artworks that shed light on a kind of debate between photography and post-photography.

Artists such as Keith Cottingham, Aziz + Cucher, Loretta Lux, Wendy McMurdo and Nancy Burson produced works that questioned the notion of photograph as objective document. Nancy Burson's Beauty Composite (1982) and Big Brother (1983) are particularly interesting in that they consist of digital combinations of pre-existing images. In the first work she fuses portraits of Hollywood actresses, while in Big Brother she uses digitally combined photographs of great dictators. Burson's strategy ties in perfectly with our subject matter: photographers who do not take photos and artists who use the internet as their primary resource.

In 1994 Matthias Wähner created an artwork by incorporating digital elements into documentary photographs of historic milestones, thus calling into question the documentary nature of press photography.

Photojournalism is being reformulated through Post-Photography, forced to change, broaden its gaze, and understand that every photograph is an opinion and, therefore, a construct. We saw proof of this transformation in 2011 when World Press Photo, one of the most important photojournalism contests, awarded photographer Michael Wolf an honourable mention for A Series of Unfortunate Events, a work composed entirely of images taken from Google Street View.

In this and other projects in which he uses Google View as a principal source, Wolf takes Cartier Bresson's idea of "the decisive moment" and updates it in digital terms. Our society's panoptic obsession means that the image maker does not

Figure 10. Nancy Burson, Big Brother, 1983
Retrieved June, 4, 2016 from http://www.vam.ac.uk/users/node/2583

Figure 11. Mann ohne Eigenschaften, Matthias Wähner (the artists inserts himself into timeless photos)
Retrieved June, 4, 2016 from http://www.lostateminor.com/2012/08/17/matthias-wahner/

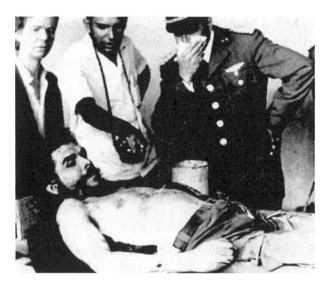

Figure 12. Series of Unfortunate Events, Michael Wolf, 2010
Retrieved in June, 4, 2016 from http://photomichaelwolf.com/#asoue/24

even have to take photos, but instead simply selects them, fishing them out of the popular ocean of images that the internet is fast becoming.

David Thomas Smith is an Irish photographer who studied Documentary Photography and is currently developing artworks with satellite images obtained in various ways. These images are recomposed and arranged in such a way as to prompt aesthetic and anthropological reflections.

Figure 13. Trinity Nuclear Test Site, New Mexico, USA - Testing of Early Atomic Bombs, David Thomas Simth
Retrieved June, 4, 2016 from http://david-thomas-smith.com/ARECIBO

Mishka Henner uses Google Maps Satellite for various purposes. In Dutch Landscapes (2011) he selects images censored by the Dutch government, whose use of visually striking camouflage lends a particularly interesting mosaic-like aspect to the final piece.

Laurence Aegerter proposes a symbolic connection between image and reality. The artist takes journalistic photographs from Google depicting natural disasters such as earthquakes, tsunamis and floods. These photographs are processed by the inhabitants of the places affected and subsequently digitized.

The omnipresent camera offering online access is the main point of interest in the work of Kurt Caviezel, who uses publicly accessible netcams to develop his artworks. In today's society we are surrounded by cameras that record everything and send those images immediately to internet. Accessing these images is much simpler and easier than we may think. Caviezel looks for dissonant elements in these recordings, as in his Self Portraits series, for example, where the moment at which the shadow cast by the streetlight security camera itself is captured within a

Figure 14. Kurt Caviezel, Animals, 2012
Retrieved June, 10, 2016 from http://www.kurtcaviezel.ch/animals/index.html

kind of involuntary self-portrait project. Especially striking, however, is his Animals series in which the author selects moments where insects suddenly appear in front of the camera lens.

On numerous occasions it is the user who makes his or her private images public in a complex and perverse exercise of online self-affirmation. In this sense, the internet is full of personal and private images... intimate pictures which can easily be accessed and reused by the rest of the community. It is here where the authorship debate becomes futile; as soon as we upload an image it belongs to everyone except us. It can immediately be manipulated, republished, redistributed … or subjected to all kinds of perversion. In this respect, visual artist Jon Haddock's Internet Sex Photos project (2007) is especially interesting. The artist begins by selecting amateur photos found on internet, images that the users themselves upload in an unprecedented exercise of exhibitionism/voyeurism. Haddock intervenes by blatantly erasing the posing subjects. The result conveys an irrepressible frustrated desire while giving meaning to all the incidental and accessory objects present.

Like John Haddock, Penelope Umbrico is another artist whose raw materials are images that have been uploaded to internet by users, and she is particularly interested in the overproduction of images in our society. In her case, the idea of collective photography, the clear absence of authorship, and the relationship between consumer and image maker are markedly present.

Figure 15. Jon Haddock, Internet Sex Photos, 2007
Retrieved June, 14, 2016 from http://www.howardhouse.net/artists/haddock/HH00648.html

Figure 16. Suns (From Sunsets) from Flickr, 2006-ongoing, Penelope Umbrico
Retrieved June, 14, 2016 from http://www.penelopeumbrico.net/Suns/Suns_Index.html

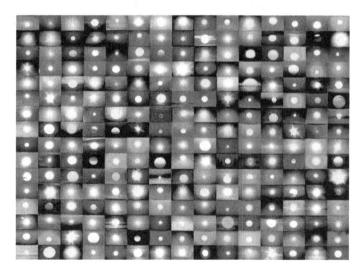

Every day sees an increase in photographic practices that do not involve taking photographs. We have chosen some examples that, in our opinion, strongly support our theories, but obviously they are neither the only possible examples nor necessarily the most remarkable. We simply believe they serve the purpose of illustrating our ideas.

The photograph becomes raw material in post-photographic practices. Photography no longer speaks of the absent object it represents, but instead has become pure matter for creative ends.

CONCLUSION

It is undeniable that the revolution that is being generated around photography and the photography network goes far beyond a mere shift from chemical to digital. The new era entails the acceptance of new values.

The old safeguarding of authorship and the artist's creative process has given way to a kind of soft, fuzzy and nonlinear co-authoring. This co-authoring sometimes reaches a certain level of debauchery and licentiousness in the use of images and photographs. Richard Prince's controversial use of Instagram selfies is a good example of irregular practices involving other people's photographs. This reconfiguration of authorship is not only accepted by the artistic community, but also welcomed and celebrated by the authors themselves. Post-Photography is clearly imbued with the spirit of appropriation. Each individual element, like a tile in a mosaic, will become an essential part of the final artwork. This way of working emphasises the idea of "modularity" that is so ubiquitous in digital culture

The evolution of Web 2.0 and the growing use and sophistication of mobile devices, combined with a free flow of information along the endless internet superhighway, have made it very easy to access and capture online images. The most important effect of this evident image overload on creative photography is the gradual replacement of the "camera shot", the act of taking photographs, with the "screenshot", the virtual capture of existing images. These readymade images have the same uses and meanings as the syntactical element in language.

The status of photography has changed considerably from its inception to the present day, just as society has also changed from nineteenth-century positivism to the crisis of discourse in our contemporary late-capitalist era.

During the twentieth century, theories of photography encompass Benjamin's aesthetic positions associated with the Frankfurt School; streams of thought based on the theories of Barthes, by the structuralist thought of Saussure and Jakobson; the cultural crystallization and technological determinism proposed by Flusser; and ultimately "the end of photography" (perhaps this is what post-photography is), as intimated by Fukuyama's idea of "the end of history".

By the end of the twentieth century, photography is in the midst of an obsessive postmodernist reconfiguration, to a large extent dominated by technical, technological and instrumental aspects, as Horkheimer anticipated after the second world war in his celebrated work, Critique of Instrumental Reason (2002). Today, photography is just a simulacra, as in Blade Runner. We build our reality using simulated constructions based on images that we assume are real.

Photography has undergone a technological and digital development whose end result is being called post-photography. The nature of post-photography is diverse, rhizomatic and messy, thereby altering conceptions of the image and its associations.

Since the turn of the century, communicative acts have taken on unforeseen new modes and forms. Internet, the emergence of social networks, photography apps and platforms, all have combined to create a vast and swirling ocean of images. Baudrillard's expression "pure circulation" has acquired a real and intense meaning in the post-photographic world.

In this context, silver salts will be transformed into binary codes, but this time the signifier and the signified will remain intact. Strings of ones and zeros will make up the image and, despite this new constructive event, photography will still have a certain written character.

Uncertainty could be the state of mind built by post-photography. Post-photography is about unease, insecurity and distrust, whereas Photography was about faith in science, positivism and trust. Is impossible for us to understand our environment without technology; we construct our meaning through technology. Pics, images and photos go viral at lightning speed and the scope of this contagion is uncertain and infinite.

The image is no longer a representation of the temporal order. Post-Photography represents itself, as J.L. Brea suggests: a tendency to disappear, a great mediating power and capacity for symmetrical reproduction and cloning. It will not really matter if the image is real or not; what really matters is the path it takes through cyberspace, the image as a whole.

The temporary nature of Post-Photography is of no consequence.

The image taken and the final image might not be the same thing or may even be susceptible to mutation. The artwork made up of other people's images excludes the individual, their genetic code, their identity. In the new Post-Photography era, each image works like a cog in a wheel, an indispensable part of a whole.

What we have now is a non-hierarchical and decentralized paradigm. There is no categorization. Artistic generosity prevails in this infinite cyberspace. However, this lack of order does not involve chaos; Adorno (2004) suggests that law and order must be understood as a great facilitator of life itself. Without order we could probably exist, but only quite marginally. Post-Photography does not aim to dismantle a pre-established visual system but rather to complement it with context.

Some theorists agree that the classic semiotic partnership of signifier-signified and consideration of the iconographic and semantic code are disappearing and being replaced by the transfiguration, modification and postproduction of images. Just as Derrida defined phonocentrism (1971) as being the hegemony of speech with respect to writing, we can declare the supremacy of the image over the word. Therefore, in this new era, discourse should be revived and developed in order to be consistent with these post-photographic practices.

Post-Photography is probably considered part of our social condition, but there also exists a point of view that has to do with its "non-definition". We may well not know very much about the attributes of image communication in this digital era, but it is a proven fact that we are redefining the image, and only through study and reflection can we understand the structural framework of Post-Photography practices. The term 'Post-Photography' simplifies the uncomfortable situation of Photography, and in fact, certain theorists such as Joan Fontcuberta are already saying this is just a temporary name awaiting modification with a view to better explaining the concept in all its complexity.

REFRENCES

Acaso, M. (2007). *Esto no son las torres gemelas: cómo aprender a leer la televisión y otras imágenes*. Madrid: Catarata.

Barthes, R. (1992). *La cámara lúcida, Nota sobre la fotografía.* Barcelona: Paidós Comunicación.

Bauman, Z. (2012). *Modernidad Líquida,* Madrid: Fondo de cultura Económica de España.

Bazin, A. (1990). *Qué es el cine, cap. Ontología de la imagen Fotográfica.* Madrid: RIALP.

Chomsky, N. (2003). *Sobre la naturaleza y el lenguaje.* Madrid: Cambridge University Press.

Costa, J. (1991). *La fotografía entre sumisión y subversión.* México: ed. Trillas.

Dubois, P. (1994). *El acto fotográfico, De la representación a la recepción.* Barcelona: Paidós Comunicación.

Flusser, V. (2001). *Hacia Una filosofía de la Fotografía.* Madrid: Editorial Síntesis.

Fontcuberta, J. (2010). *La cámara de Pandora, la fotografía después de la fotografía.* Barcelona: Gustavo Gili.

Fontcuberta, J. (2011). Por un manifiesto postfotográfico. *Lavanguardia.* Retrieved from http://www.lavanguardia.com/cultura/20110511/54152218372/por-un-manifiesto-posfotografico.html

Foote, N. (2004). *"Los Anti-fotógrafos"*. *In D. Fogle (Ed.), The last picture show: artistas que usan la fotografía. Tendencias conceptuales de 1960 a 1982. Catálogo de exposición*. Vigo: Fundación MARCO.

Gadamer, H. G. (1977). *Verdad y método I*. Salamanca: Sígueme.

Horkheimer, M. (2002). *Crítica de la razón instrumental*. Madrid: Trotta.

Lister, M. (1997). *La imagen fotográfica en la cultura digital*. Barcelona: Paidós.

Manovich, L. (2005). *El lenguaje de los nuevos medios de comunicación: la imagen en la era digital*. Barcelona: Paidós.

Ritchin, F. (2009). Awakening the Digital. *Foam Magazine*, 21, Winter.

Ritchin, F. (2009). *After Photography*. New York: Norton & Company.

Sartori, G. (1998). *El Homo videns: la sociedad teledirigida*. Madrid: Taurus.

Schaeffer, J.M. (1990). *La imagen precaria: del dispositivo fotográfico*. Barcelona: Cátedra.

Serra, R. (Director). (1973). *Televisión Delivers People* [Film].

Shore, R. (2014). *Post-Photography: The Artist with a Camer*. London: Laurence King Publishing.

KEY TERMS AND DEFINITIONS

Appropriation: It is the artistic action of taking photographs made by others and to create a new art piece.

Figures of Speech: It refers to those mechanisms that alter the normal use of language in order to obtain a stylistic effect. It helps to attract attention, surprise by its originality and possess a great power of persuasion.

Glitch Art: Use of digital defect as a creative element while the image processes.

Noema: Content of a thought.

Post-Photography: Those practices derived from medium photographic digitalization. Some practices related to the use and digital image edition of photographic origin.

Sustainable Behavior: The creation of an artistic action derived from photographs made by other authors implies a sustainable positive act. The great novelty of Post-Photography is that the large number of images can be reused.

ENDNOTES

[1]   Noema: Content of a thought

[2]   Argent: Silver salts and chemical used in the photographic process

[3]   Homo videns: See *Homo videns. Televisione e post-pensiero* by Giovanni Sartori.

[4]   The English translations that appear in *Verdad y método I* have been taken from various sources by authors.

[5]   Exquisite corpse: from the original French term *cadavre exquis*. A technique used in Surrealism, which involves a group of people assembling different images or words.

Section 2
Heterogeneous Factors of Overload

Chapter 4

Managing Information, Communication and Technologies in Schools:
Overload as Mismanagement and Miscommunication

S. T. Ahmed
UAE University, UAE

ABSTRACT

One of the most crucial areas in which information and technologies need to be managed in our information-rich society is in schools. Whilst information overload is often associated with organisations or social communication, schools represent the intersection of several stakeholders for whom information and communication must be managed effectively. Using a case study of a school in a Gulf State, this chapter analyses how mismanagement and miscommunication relating to the use of ICT is hindering the educational progress of children by examining school/teacher-pupil interaction; home-school communication, and; the application of ICT in the curriculum. It presents a professional and parental perspective on how the use and management of information technologies and effective communication are critical in maintaining acceptable levels of educational achievement. It draws on the experiences of both pupils and parents and uses a framework of participant observation to illustrate the problems of information overload as mismanagement and miscommunication.

DOI: 10.4018/978-1-5225-2061-0.ch004

INTRODUCTION

Information enjoys a special status in our contemporary society and whilst writers continue to debate the details of this 'information society', most are convinced that the availability of information, and the concomitant development of information and communication technologies (ICT), is the defining feature of our times (Webster, 2006).

The information society and ICT revolution are heralded in public discourses as unprecedented societal changes and have thus been used to promote a vast number of initiatives and reforms, including ICT in education (Nivala, 2009, p. 435).

Nivala (2009) continues that education has been the focal point of information society strategies because they have touted the use of ICT in enhancing education and because education is seen as a means for progressing into the information age. Following the ushering in of the information society, deterministic discourses have been "saturated by the view that technology is the only way to keep education up to date and relevant, thus leading to better results in teaching and learning" (Selwyn et al., 2001, cited in Nivala, 2009, p. 436).

As information becomes more widely available in all spheres of life, the proper use and management of this information in schools poses challenges to all those involved in the educational process. Apart from the obvious concerns about unsuitable material available to children online, schools are responsible for educating children about how to use and manage ICT to enhance knowledge and develop life skills. Misuse of technology in the classroom is an issue of growing concern for educational institutions, practitioners and parents alike and unless there is open and effective communication between schools, students and parents it will be difficult to understand the role of ICT in teaching and learning. Access to an increasing variety of information channels does not mean that parents are better informed of the decisions being made by schools or that they are familiar with the policies and procedures that schools are supposedly practicing. Similarly, creating a number of media through which to disseminate information does not necessarily guarantee a more knowledgeable school community if these channels are not used efficiently.

The immediate implication of information 'overload' is that there is too much information available but the concept is extended here to include not just the potential of having an overwhelming amount of information in schools but also a number of other factors such as information mismanagement; miscommunication; 'underload' and even deliberately withholding information. Overload also refers to the smokescreen created by a school to convince parents that lots of information is available because several channels for disseminating information exist, but in reality very little is actually being communicated. Whilst it is plausible that mismanagement can occur even when a limited amount of information is available, the likelihood of mismanaging information is greater when more is available, hence the strong link between overload and mismanagement. Just as there is a blurring of data from information; information from ICT; ICT from knowledge; or any of these from globalisation and the information society (Nivala, 2009), this chapter proposes that in practice there is a blurring of factors associated with information overload. Making reference to Kajtazi's (2011) concept of 'information inadequacy' which she used to analyse "dramatic situations" (human failures, natural disasters etc.), the idea is applied here to an "everyday situation", that is, school. Kajtazi (2011) identifies information 'lack' and 'overflow' as two factors that cause inadequacy and most of these have resonance with the case study used in this chapter.

Information Lack:

1. **Information is Non-Existent:** Characterized by failure to communicate information in situations when actions are unforeseen, usually due to mismanagement.
2. **Information is Insufficient:** Characterized by failure to communicate on-time information. Lack of awareness, mismanagement and difficulty in understanding represent failure to act in a timely fashion.
3. **Information is Censored**: Characterized by serious violation of information. Such information is usually hindered intentionally, secretly and illegally for the purpose of suppressing original information that is intended for the people and that may be significant for people's needs.
4. **Information is Undelivered:** Characterized by incompetent acts of humans, with a dual outcome. The act is either undertaken intentionally by prohibiting the use of information or the undelivered information is caused by lack of awareness.

Information Overflow:

5. **Information is Ambiguous:** Characterized by lack of control of information. It is usually accompanied by miscalculations and lack of accurate evidence that misleads important decision-making processes.
6. **Information is Redundant:** Characterized by duplication or even multiplication of the same information (repetition of information's message in synonyms or with the same excessive expression) due to lack of control or lack of awareness.
7. **Information is Irrelevant:** Characterized by types of information that have no validity and are shared by unknown sources. Such information holds misinterpretations.
8. **Information is Undervalued:** Characterized by mismanagement that may cause misinterpretation of information, possibly by lack of awareness. (Kajtazi, 2011, p. 6).

These characteristics are used here to frame the idea of information overload in our digital age and include more than simply quantifying the amount of data or information that can be accessed. The interconnectedness and indeed overlap of these characteristics demonstrates that the definition of overload must be multifaceted and have the ability to include emerging concepts that we have not yet experienced in our information society. Arguably the distinction between information and communication overload and mismanagement is becoming increasingly unclear because of their intertwined nature. Having identified the potential for experiencing overload in different aspects of our lives, the need to examine exactly how this manifests itself in practice is done by applying theoretical ideas to real contexts and in this instance the context is schools. The school being used as a case study in this chapter is a small international school in a Gulf country. It was established in 2007 and currently has approximately 250 students. The facts and information used to illustrate the issues in the chapter are drawn from the experiences of parents and pupils at the school and make reference to material provided by the school. As individual instances the examples cited in this study may appear of little consequence, but as collective practice at the school they have resulted in an example of how information overload, taken in its broadest sense, and the implementation of ICT have failed to enhance teaching and learning.

Background

The introduction of ICT into schools has affected infrastructure, applications, policies, teaching, communication and learning and whilst almost every educational institution has embraced them, the issue of whether and how much they impact on student achievement and progress continues to be examined. There is general agreement that ICT have the potential to enhance the learning experiences and attainment of students but this can only be considered in the context of "whole school characteristics" (Tearle, 2003). Fu (2013) lists several benefits of using ICT in her study of schools in Singapore, including the ability to:

- Access digital information efficiently and effectively.
- Support student-centred and self-directed learning.
- Produce a creative learning environment.
- Promote collaborative learning.
- Improve teaching and learning quality.

Moreover, the impact of new technologies on increasing student motivation to learn and increasing their expectations of what they can achieve has been documented (Cunningham et al., 2003). These benefits have been recognised throughout the world but Hammond (2014) argues that whilst "the contribution of ICT has not been negligible" (2014) excessive optimism should be avoided because "ICT has had only a modest impact on schools" (Hammond, 2014, p. 191) and expectations of what ICT can achieve need to be realistic. The adoption and use of ICT require an understanding of the context within which they exist if their role and impact is to be gauged with any level of accuracy.

Rather than seeking to endow ICT with special properties and powers it would be better to accept that the principal agents in the teaching and learning process are teachers and their pupils, and that if both parties commit to the use of what is undeniably a powerful tool, then improved learning is very likely to occur (Goodison, 2002, p. 211).

Furthermore, in analysing the British Educational Communities and Technology Agency (BECTA) reports, Goodison (2002) notes that of the five factors identified as being especially important in using ICT to improve standards, 'high quality teaching' is the first (the other four being school support for ICT, access to ICT, pupils' ICT skills and pupils' positive attitudes to ICT). ICT does not operate in a vacuum and research, as well as common sense understanding, point to the fact that it is an appendage to the teacher, not a replacement for them and that even the latest, cutting edge technology cannot compensate for poor teaching. There are examples of schools that have acquired relatively good resources but not put them to very good use. "It is difficult to imagine how ICT resources in themselves can contribute to improved attainment unless they are being used constructively within the teaching context" (Goodison, 2002, p. 206).

Vanderlinde, Dexter and van Braak (2012) studied the content of 31 ICT policy plans in primary schools in Flanders (Belgium) and concluded that the integration of ICT in teaching and learning can only be successful when schools implement the ICT curriculum into practice and translate the broadly formulated ICT attainment targets into concrete teaching and learning activities. They identified that leadership practices and government involvement influence this process but that a comprehensive ICT policy needs to be "grounded in a vision of education and ICT integration with implications for how the school organisation should provide supportive conditions" (Vanderlinde, et al., 2012, p. 506) for teaching practices and learning activities. Similarly, when Lim (2007) studied effective and ineffective integration of ICT into schools in Singapore, she recommended that at the school level it is essential to "set a clear vision of ICT integration strategies for the school and [that] this vision must be shared by all members of the school community" (Lim, 2007, p. 89). In addition, both teachers and students have to have ICT competency and for ICT-mediated lessons to succeed teachers must be clear what the objectives are in order to determine how ICT tools are used.

Similarly, Mishra and Koehler (2006) propose a framework in which they emphasise studying *how* technology is used in schools, rather than merely believing introducing technology into schools is enough. The Technological Pedagogical Content Knowledge model (TPCK, later known as TPACK) identifies three main knowledge components in the learning environment; technology; pedagogy and content.

TPCK is an emergent form of knowledge that goes beyond all three components. TPCK is the basis of good teaching with technology and requires an understanding of the representation of concepts using technologies; pedagogical techniques that use technologies in constructive ways to teach content; knowledge of what makes concepts difficult or easy to learn and how technology can help redress some of the problems that students face; knowledge of students' prior knowledge and theories of epistemology; and knowledge of how technologies can be used to build on existing knowledge and to develop new epistemologies or strengthen old ones (p. 1028-1029).

They argue that quality teaching requires a nuanced understanding of the complex relationships of these three key elements and thoughtfully interweaving them will result in successful technology integration in teaching and learning.

Concurrent with the introduction of ICT in schools, there is a need for parents to be informed and involved in the policies and procedures relating to their use. There is ample evidence in the literature about the benefits of effective home-school communication and a report by Henderson and Mapp (2002) finds that "there is strong and steadily growing evidence that families can improve their children's academic performance in school and have a major impact on attendance and behaviour" (p. 239). Family involvement is critical because it has a considerable impact on student achievement; it supports and positively influences student learning at home and school, improving achievement, and; it has a positive influence regardless of cultural background, education and income levels. This fact has not changed because of the advent of new media technology and it remains a key feature in determining the educational experiences and achievement of pupils. Where there is a breakdown in communication between school and home or miscommunication is taking place, this will disadvantage children.

Although our society is now saturated with information and data, scholars are conscious of the negative impact of communication technologies and the need to manage the amount and type of information we receive. In the educational context, whilst the Internet has enhanced teaching in many ways, it has also brought new challenges, such as keeping tasks from becoming unmanageable and reducing data smog (Young, 2005). Schools have to achieve a balance between overwhelming parents with information (for example, when school websites provide several links with related but copious amounts of information that become a distraction) and understanding that parents require key, timely information in order to support their children's education. It is about understanding that 'less is more' and that *quality* is more important than quantity (Harris, 2013). Thus, the ubiquity of ICT tools in our information rich society (and individual institutions) demonstrates the increasing potential for overload and subsequent mismanagement.

INTERSECTIONS OF INFORMATION AND COMMUNICATION

School/Teacher-Pupil Interactions

A key area in ensuring the effectiveness of learning is communication between schools/teachers and pupils. This relates to communication of simple instructions and organisational matters on a daily basis and extends to overarching information that should be made available to pupils such as the curriculum, learning goals, assessments and marking criteria. Before the advent and widespread adoption of ICT, this communication took place through methods including face-to-face interaction; hard copies of material, and; student notebooks or diaries. Now, however, even with several means of communication in place, pupils at school still feel unaware and uniformed of basic issues relating to their education. Overreliance on technology, which has not been managed well, to undertake the work previously done in low-tech ways has often resulted in gaps because the role of teacher as direct information provider has been replaced with technology. For example, where homework was set using a group email, it was not always clear what was expected of students and they did not receive replies to their questions in time to complete the homework by the deadline. No formal/written email 'protocol' was given to pupils so that they could understand how to keep in touch, what time frames were expected for responses and what alternatives they had if emails were not working. Similarly, tasks set through Edmodo and similar web based communication tools frequently posed problems because of connectivity; lapse in notifications coming to recipients; a constant need to refresh the programme to ensure messages were being downloaded, etc. This meant that information did not always reach the children on time and even 'disappeared' on occasions.

This illustrates how information 'underload' is taking place whereby pupils (and parents) are missing important information because of different understandings of the correct usage of ICT. It relates to Kajtazi's (2011) idea of both information lack (insufficient) and overflow (ambiguous). Furthermore, there was no school-wide or even class-wide standard set so that pupils knew, for example, that each week they would receive their homework on a set day through a set channel. An efficient and well-organised model of ICT usage should convey clearly to pupils that they can access certain information from one particular place rather than using them on an ad-hoc basis. This example of mismanagement of ICT and information demonstrates that the adoption of technologies needs to be considered carefully and the effectiveness of communication needs to be continuously assessed so that students know how, where and when to obtain information. Other schools in the region have continued to give weekly homework in printed form and parents found that this was a more effective way of knowing what was expected. The regular homework paper was reassuring to parents too because they were expecting this paper to come home on a fixed day and contain all the information needed to complete the work. However, because children at this school could receive information relating to homework in one of at least 3 electronic ways – messages, emails and Edmodo, the potential to 'miss' the correct channel is obvious and it results in information being 'undelivered' (Kajtazi, 2011). The pragmatic approach would be to select one channel through which particular information was given, enabling better management and productivity.

Google docs was another programme that was sometimes used and this caused problems for the iPad (the mobile device used by the school) for two main reasons: the first was that Word is not available on iPads with which Google docs is compatible, and the second was that Internet access is needed to use the programme. On several occasions students had to wait until the next day to receive the information in an alternative format if the teacher did not reply to their email the same evening. If children were required to add something to the document and recirculate, this would again cause inconvenience because they were unable to make a contribution or see the contribution of others. Technology requires a supportive infrastructure which if not available renders the tools of little or no value (Cunningham et al., 2003) and it is the responsibility of schools to ensure this infrastructure exists before it initiates ICT programmes.

Children were not involved in monitoring, evaluation or feedback (formal) about their use of ICT. The school did offer some opportunities for them to voice their opinions or dissatisfaction with particular aspects of ICT but parents were aware that they felt bored having to continuously complete homework using the same application (app) and the effects on their health (eye-strain, potential of RSI in fingers/ hands, etc.) was not considered. Individual children and parents were always able to give their opinions on any aspect of ICT usage but the school did not initiate a channel whereby pupils could review and continually update the school on their experiences. The Student Council was a potential mechanism through which this could have taken place but it was not utilised to include this. The school had the opportunity to set up a monitoring and evaluation system to examine the advantages and disadvantages of ICT usage that could have been used as a model of good practice across the country had it recognised the value of doing so. This could then have served as a model to other schools.

Home-School Communication

A similar problem existed for communication between parents and the school. The traditional letter to parents has been mostly replaced by a number of communication channels but 'important' information was still sent by letter to make sure parents actually received and read it, suggesting that this was the most effective method of communicating information. Having a number of new channels certainly did not mean communication became more effective. In fact, the opposite was often the case because parents were expected to look in several different places to get information and may easily have missed important material because they had not used the correct channel and were not aware new information had been made available. Informal networks amongst parents compensated for this deficiency as information was circulated between them and this was a responsibility taken on by parents because they were aware of the problems the school had with communicating information.

Whilst in some cases information was missed because it was not publicised properly, in other cases information was presented in such a way that its essence was lost. Communication about the curriculum provides an example of this information overload to the extent that parents were left unable to answer simple questions such as 'what is my child doing in maths?'. Providing a webpage to disseminate curriculum information is something many schools have done and most parents expect this as part of the 21st century school system. However, the delay in composing and uploading data created a void in the basic information that parents require regarding the curriculum. The preoccupation with ICT, soft copies and online versions of essential material excused the school from providing a simple printed (or printable) version of key information (to which pupils and parents are entitled). A whole academic year passed and the curriculum website was still 'under construction'. Numerous requests were made by parents for even a brief but up-to-date curriculum so that they could understand what their children were supposed to be studying during the year but this was never provided and the school continued to delay the website, citing 'technical problems' as an excuse. This illustrates how information was certainly insufficient, if not non-existent, and it may even have been censored because the school had not in fact produced up-to-date, relevant information. This example also relates to all four aspects of information overflow (Kajtazi, 2011).

The decision to introduce tablets in a 1-to-1 programme (for Grade 3 and upwards) was a decisive move for the school towards becoming an IT-rich institution.

However, no discussion or consultation took place prior to this initiative and even after it had been rolled out parents were never involved or consulted about why apps were chosen; which apps they felt were useful or appropriate; which they did not want their children to have access to; how the use of these apps was to be monitored and evaluated; whether the school regularly (if at all) checked children's browsing history, and; how much time children were spending using tablets compared to traditional forms of learning. Furthermore, no analysis was undertaken of how use of tablets and applications translated to achieving of learning outcomes and goals for different subjects. There was no progression in the use of applications as students moved to higher grades. The same applications were used for several grades and the same exercises were being carried out on them. This is another example of how the school did not fulfil its commitment of 'involving parents in learning' (as stated in several places, including its website and annual report) and in fact excluded them completely from the decisionmaking process. Even the children were not consulted about how they felt about any of these issues, which does not reflect best practices adopted by other educational institutions that have surveyed the student body to understand their opinions on the introduction and use of ICT (specifically iPads).

The conventional Parent Teacher Association (PTA) was dismantled at the school, eliminating the commonly recognised means through which parents' concerns are raised. Instead, an 'open door' policy was encouraged, whereby parents could communicate their queries to the school via email (or even in face-to-face meetings). This strategy proved consistently ineffective. Many parents attended many meetings about the lack of information about the curriculum; unclear assessment structures; poor quality of Arabic as a second language; individual student progress; the need for more challenging work; internet security, etc., but very little – if any – action was actually taken by the school. Notes were often taken during these meetings to document what was discussed but follow-up was usually feeble and eventually most parents relented accepting that the school was eager to set up meetings but had little intention of taking parents' concerns seriously if they did not fit into the school's agenda. Student websites were another vehicle through which parents were to be informed of and involved in their children's schoolwork, but they became ineffective after receiving little effort on the part of teachers, and therefore children. In addition, the nature of the internet, servers and other hardware and software issues often meant information was not provided and when it was provided, depth and quality were not adequate.

Not surprisingly, communication was one area identified by many parents as being problematic and this was something the school acknowledged and promised to work on in order to improve. Parents complained that information was given at short notice; it wasn't clear where the information would be made available; not enough details were given on the events calendar; it wasn't always apparent which version of information was the latest/most up-to-date, etc. A number of initiatives were taken by the school to involve and communicate with parents, such as Coffee Mornings and Information Sessions, but these did not provide the essential information parents had been requesting, such as a comprehensive curriculum; detailed feedback and marked student scripts; explanations of comments made on school reports, or; an understanding of how assessments linked to subsequent work. When parents requested information about assessments, there was a lack of willingness to provide this and only upon being asked several times were assessments copied and given to parents, but without any context or explanation. Parents often struggled to understand the core activities within the school and one mother at a Coffee Morning said she was sure the school was doing something, but she 'didn't know what it was that the school actually did'.

ICT Framework

Pupil Learning: The Impact of ICT on Educational Attainment

Do ICT tools enhance pupils' learning experience and academic achievement? This is a key question that continues to be debated but which was never asked or examined using evidence by the school. Decades after the introduction of computer technologies into schools, quantifying the effect of ICT on attainment is still a challenge. Robertson (2002) argued that at the turn of the century, after twenty years of ICT in Scottish and English primary schools, it remains "a marginal force in the education of 5-12 year-olds" (p. 404). Does use of ICT develop skills amongst students? This question may be answered more easily and without necessarily having to present tangible evidence because as children become familiar with using technologies and new media tools, they automatically increase their repertoire of skills.

The apparent problem at the school is that most teachers are trying to transfer their responsibilities to technology and there is no doubt this will disadvantage the students (Wright, 2013). Previously pupils were expected to complete maths and literacy tasks that then had real teacher input (marking and feedback and therefore continuous assessment) but applications and online tools such as *Raz-Kids* (English) and *IXL* (maths) are now breaking this communicative process. Data on pupil progress was never made available to parents as an initiative from the school itself though it is available as part of the applications (to teachers and parents). In addition, the limited feedback that pupils received about their work on these applications throughout the year did not lead to any demonstrable progress or development. Teachers have even told pupils simply to do '20 minutes of IXL' for daily homework with no input about level, no connection to progress and no consideration of the child's learning journey. Teachers never gave pupils the time for individualised, detailed feedback on the use of these tools by accessing the data available about completed exercises, correct and incorrect answers and areas of weakness. Those parents who made the effort to access the information for themselves were not supported by the school in their desire to understand what the data meant and were not given explanations as to why pupils were not being set work at the right level according to the achievements shown by the data. IXL has a section on 'Analytics' which gives a detailed breakdown of the exercises and topics completed by the child, how long they took to complete each task, the results, areas to work on, etc. all of which help the student, teacher and parents understand the level and progress of the child. Again, lack of information at the onset and no communication during the years these apps were used meant parents were unable to connect their usage to the overall curriculum and the intended learning outcomes for each subject. Information was undervalued (Kajtazi, 2011) as the school failed to make an effort to relay it to parents for whom it would have helped considerably in gaining an understanding of their children's work. Judging by the abstract nature of the curriculum and the work/homework set for children it is perfectly plausible to state that teachers themselves did not access or use this data or analytics to inform their decisions about teaching (both individual and class level). The *Harnessing Technology* report by BECTA (2010) found that teachers used ICT for assessment activities to varying degrees but unless the results of these assessments were then used to inform future teaching and learning, there was little point in employing applications or online assessment tools.

Lim (2007) writes about teacher competency being a critical factor in the effective integration of ICT into schools. However, when teachers themselves are not able to use new applications it is difficult to see how students will benefit from any learning activities or achieve the outcomes of the task. *Comic Life* was at least one such application that children were asked to use to complete homework, but because the teacher admitted she had not used it before, they were left on their own to try and understand how to navigate it and complete their work. Lack of planning and synchronisation between what teachers knew and what was expected of children was clear in several instances. The school selected a number of other apps for children to use but these were of poor quality compared to what would have been available on more professional devices, namely computers. Weaker alternatives to Word and Excel are available as iPad applications but their compatibility, interfaces and usability render them problematic, especially for students who have not been exposed to such programmes.

Research using technology (Internet) is an example of how an abundance of information can be gathered at the outset (overload) but often not yield data of good, academic quality. Harris (2013) explains how presenting fewer resources can fight information overload for teachers but this principle can be applied to pupils of all ages so that their searches are streamlined to give them access to meaningful and appropriate data. It also helps them develop time management skills and 'weed out' sources to make better choices. An instinctive reliance on technology is perhaps to be expected from digital natives but they need to understand that it may not be the most academic route to take. There are a number of more academic search engines available as alternatives to Google but pupils were not taught about these.

Mobile Devices and iPad Programmes

Zalaznick (2013) notes that 'the rise of 1-to-1 programs has pushed a surge of mobile devices into schools' (p. 82) and that this is creating a whole new logistical challenge for administrators and authorities. In the case of private schools, the authorities and bodies overseeing these challenges need to work very closely with the schools to monitor and manage these programmes, otherwise there is a danger that schools can operate without being accountable. He warns that 'the most common mistake is buying first and asking questions later' (p. 85). Unfortunately, in the fervour to be seen as tech-savvy, some schools have done just that. Replacing reading from books with reading applications on devices such as tablets has meant a loss of the skills and know-how that children gain from conventional techniques. On the one hand there are fears that children will not even be able to handle a pen or pencil (Kershaw, 2013) and, at the other end of the spectrum, their exposure to using computers and keyboards (more akin to professional/work environments) is limited due to the preference of tablets and mobile devices.

The debate about whether iPads are the best choice for schools has been taking place for some years now since many were enthusiastically adopted after their launch in 2010. For instance, the USA embarked on several ambitious iPad initiatives, including 1-to-1 programmes, in what has been described by some as a 'buying craze' in which millions of dollars were spent on the devices (Mageau, 2012). iPads were expected to contribute towards increasing student engagement, especially because of the 'novelty' factor, bringing creativity into teaching and learning and introducing new skills to students. However, as Mageau (2012) notes, what schools should be concentrating on are "initiatives in teaching and learning that are supported by professional development, new curricula, authentic assessment and yes, technology" (p. 2), rather than iPad initiatives.

There was dissatisfaction amongst parents with the iPad programme at the school but this was not communicated to the school through any formal channel and it may have been that the school was genuinely unaware of the concerns of parents with regards to this matter. The fact that the school had no PTA was probably a factor in impeding this concern from being raised at the level of the whole school community. Children were using their iPads at home to play games; were spending more time on them than parents would wish, and; some sibling jealousy was also occurring between younger siblings who had not yet reached the grade in which the devices were given to individual pupils. Academically, parents were not convinced that using an iPad was the most effective way for children to learn and children were limited in the number and range of applications being utilised. Suggestions were made by parents to introduce a computer lab, housing a small number of PCs, considering the size of the school, so that pupils could develop essential IT skills alongside the use of tablets. Children struggled to use a proper keyboard (preferable for longer assignments and extended periods of use) because they had only been given access to tablets at school. Even laptops were not made available though both students and parents had requested them. Schools around the world are reconsidering their sole reliance on iPads because they do not have proper keyboards and are not powerful enough tools for creating all types of work. The iPad offers many applications and has educational value, but using it to write a one thousand-word paper, for instance, is not necessarily utilising it in the most efficient way (Waters, 2010).

As the initial iPad euphoria has subsided, there is greater recognition that these devices form part of the technology landscape of educational institutions. Some schools are trading these devices for laptops because they have experienced short-comings for older students and there is a perception amongst both teachers and students that they were more for fun and playing games whilst laptops were more for schoolwork (McNeil, 2016). Other schools are adopting a mixed-device approach so that students have access to both iPads as well as more robust desktop or laptop machines because each serves a different purpose (Waters, 2010). Another factor affecting the popularity of the iPad is increased competition from similar devices on the market, including the Chromebook and Netbook. Maddux (1986, in Falloon, 2014) describes this phenomenon as the 'pendulum syndrome' where

educational innovations usually surrounded by hype or bold and ambitious claims are hastily adopted by schools, to be followed by disillusionment and eventual abandonment, when they inevitably fail to meet the overinflated expectations (p. 319).

Whichever device a school decides to adopt, it needs to relay information about choices to parents so they can understand the school's objectives and understand the role technology will be playing in education. The more information that is given to parents, the more confident they will feel about what the school's policies are and how their children should benefit from the introduction of these programmes. "As schools continue to integrate this new technology into their curriculum, a strong mobile device management (MDM) solution is compulsory to support these requirements" (Gentile, 2012, p. 12) and again this must be made available to the whole school community, including students and parents. These MDMs include issues relating to security, management and content delivery, and should be understood before the devices are purchased and given to pupils.

Online Safety

Of greater concern than the absence of a clear policy framework and general training in using ICT was the fact that from the time pupils were given access to their own devices (to use at school and home), they received no training, advice or awareness on how to 'stay safe' online. Not all parents felt it was appropriate for younger pupils to have access to their own devices and, by extension, to the Internet, but as it was school policy that they should do so, little choice was available to 'opt-out'. Neither was any choice given to opt-out of applications that were deemed potentially unsafe by parents, for example YouTube. At no point before or during the time pupils had access to iPads were they taught about safety as a specialised subject. A global citizenship programme was talked about but this did not translate into practice and in the 4 years that children have embarked on the 1-to-1 programme, they have never been given training in using ICT safely; had a reporting mechanism for inappropriate usage explained to them; had details about what constitutes online 'dangers'; taught about the concept of cyber-bullying, etc. Some of these areas are mentioned in a usage agreement but this is inadequate to equip the children to use their devices with awareness and confidence about reporting problems. Ribble (2011) writes about the fact that global citizenship is more than just a set of dos and don'ts in the guise of Acceptable Use Policies (AUPs) and needs to encompass broader concepts of how to respect technology; understand what is appropriate and why; and learn how to use technology effectively. For schools such as the one in this case study that have not yet embarked on any effective global citizenship programme or instruction, Ribble's book offers lesson plans on 'Foundational Lessons' at the end of which he presents 'technology use scenarios' for students to make choices, and a variety of questions and exercises that stimulate debate about the practice of digital citizenship. Furthermore, Ribble echoes what a number of parents at the school had been advocating for some time, that is, that parents too need to be involved in digital citizenship 'lessons'. "Parents are the primary educators of their own children, [so] they too need to be involved in the process of understanding digital citizenship" (Ribble, 2011, p. 138).

Only when an incident occurred in which pupils accessed pornographic images did the school retrospectively, and rather clumsily, prepare an A4 sheet of paper that was an attempt to reassure parents that an Internet safety policy had been in place since the beginning of the iPad programme. Prior to this no communication had taken place between the school and parents or between the school and pupils about how ICT were going to be used and monitored and how the children's safety and welfare were going to be maintained and guaranteed (notwithstanding aspects of IT that are beyond total control). Whilst the usage agreement listed possible problems with access to online material, it made no mention of how the school intended to protect pupils and no details were given of the companies, software or hardware that were being employed for safety. In theory the children only accessed such applications and programmes under teacher supervision, but being able to guarantee that misuse would not take place is almost impossible. The only way to eliminate access to unsuitable videos on YouTube, for example, would be to remove the programme from the device or restrict its access through the browser. The school did not communicate with parents to obtain their opinions on whether programmes and applications such as YouTube or even using Internet search engines were in fact of any significant educational benefit, and whether they would yield a tangible improvement in the academic performance of pupils. The censoring of information (Kajtazi, 2011) at all stages of this incident resulted in mistrust between parents and the school and reflected poorly on its ethical practices.

SOLUTIONS AND RECOMMENDATIONS

The purpose of this chapter is not to criticise the use of ICT in schools, as it would be difficult to dismiss the potential for enhancing teaching and learning using these tools. However, if these tools are not managed and integrated into the wider framework of learning, they become a distraction rather than an enhancement to learning. Traditional learning should be complemented by the use of ICT and they must be integrated into the curriculum to result in effective learning and skills development. Whilst it is not easy to accurately measure the impact of ICT, it is clear that when they are used in an unstructured way, they will not achieve their full potential in supporting children's learning.

The educational process, including the use of ICT, must be continuously appraised in order to ensure it is fulfilling its desired outcomes. In all cases where the school was undertaking any of these ICT related activities, no monitoring or evaluation of the effectiveness of learning was undertaken. If at all it was, this crucial information was never relayed to parents. As a result, parents were obliged to approach the school for information rather than the school fulfil its responsibility of informing parents about developments taking place in their children's learning and achievement within the ICT framework. One of the Standards of the CIS (The Council of International Schools, by which the school is currently aiming to be accredited) was to keep parents informed about important issues relating to their children's progress and development and to 'involve parents in learning' (a motto of the school). If the school genuinely wants to involve parents and values their contributions, then it needs to improve its communication with them and encourage more open dialogue with all those concerned with the educational endeavour.

Monitoring and evaluation must be given priority by all schools if they are to evaluate the role of ICT in the curriculum and satisfy themselves, pupils and parents that ICT are benefiting children, academically and otherwise. Some form of cost-benefit analysis that considers the investment made into purchasing devices and setting up the programme along with the time spent on them and weighing this up against how pupils have improved in their core skills is essential in convincing the stakeholders that technology is being used successfully. The same applications continued to be used for several years indicating that no evaluation had taken place. Children were dissatisfied with the use of some applications because they were not user-friendly or were inept at allowing them to complete their work, but they were not given sufficient opportunity to give feedback. New apps were added but little information was given about why these were chosen, what purpose they intended to serve and what skills students would obtain from them. Information sessions on other aspects of school life were arranged but the school never organised anything relating to its approach to ICT or disseminated a 'policy' (a policy did not in fact exist or at least was not made available to parents) which is fundamental if there is to be effective implementation of the objectives of using ICT tools for teaching and learning.

FUTURE RESEARCH DIRECTIONS

Relatively soon after ICT were introduced into schools around the world, research sought to understand their impact on teaching and learning. Now that they have become part of the everyday life of schools, it does not mean their impact should be taken for granted. It is still imperative that those involved in the education sector continue to examine the role being played by ICT for individual pupils and schools as a whole. Information mismanagement, overload, underload and miscommunication are concepts that are becoming increasingly important in our lives, both professional and private. In an educational setting there must be still greater emphasis on identifying the problems, real and potential, which relate to our relationship with information – how it is managed, accessed, interpreted and utilised. Schools must take the lead in managing how this information is communicated to parents to ensure they remain informed participants in the education of their children. Furthermore, the children themselves must be seen as competent agents in their own educational journey and need to be involved, if not in the decision-making, then at least in ongoing appraisals.

CONCLUSION

The school has consistently failed to communicate with parents about how ICT is being used and what outcomes and impact its introduction has had on the teaching and learning experiences at the school. There seems to have been a belief that bringing new technologies into the classroom would automatically satisfy parents because it is seen as being 'progressive' and no effort has been made to engage with the main stakeholders – students and parents – on how the presence of mobile devices in particular has added any value to the educational experience. The same fears that are being realised about social media breaking down the face-to-face communication process and real 'human' interaction can be seen taking place in the educational context, especially at schools. Technology is rendering the teacher 'absent' in a number of situations where he/she would previously have been the main catalyst for engaging and motivating students. If students undertake online or device based exercises, these must be followed by teacher input to enable children to understand their strengths and weaknesses. ICT tools and usage are a means to achieve certain outcomes and not an end in themselves. It is unacceptable to roll-out hardware and software on such a grand scale and not have in place a rigorous mechanism, independently administered, to check how educational technologies are being used and if they are having any influence on how and what is being taught and learnt.

This chapter is not a review of the applications or devices being used by the school but an analysis of *how* these are being used and how their use is being communicated to parents. It is an attempt to evaluate their use and recommend that this needs to be reconsidered to increase their potential to enrich pedagogies and academic experiences. It also identifies that the inability or unwillingness on the part of schools to communicate with parents has an adverse effect on the educational experiences and attainment of children. Using the school as a case study, this chapter has argued that availability of information does not equate to acquisition of knowledge and the relationship between the two is further complicated when the burden is placed on the shoulders of ICT alone. Having an array of ICT tools and a variety of channels through which information can be disseminated does not result in well informed stakeholders because it is the management of this information that is key to effective communication – ensuring neither overload, underload or inadequacy.

The concept of information and communication overload is unpacked by applying it to the experienced reality of an institution which, whilst priding itself on being at the forefront of digital innovation and using the latest technologies, has shown that the use of ICT tools in an abstract manner does not result in achieving desired educational goals and is further hindered when communication is weak. Having described various relationships and situations in which information overload is occurring, the contention in this chapter is that overload encompasses several interconnected phenomena and that these can be better understood when they are examined in the context of a tangible situation such as the one presented here.

REFERENCES

British Educational Communications and Technology Agency (BECTA). (2010). *Harnessing Technology Schools Survey 2010.*

Cunningham, M., Harris, S., Kerr, K., & McEune, R. (2003). *New technologies supporting teaching and learning.* Slough: National Foundation for Educational Research.

Falloon, G. (2014). What's going on behind the screens? Researching young students learning pathways using iPads. *Journal of Computer Assisted Learning, 30*(4), 318–336. doi:10.1111/jcal.12044

Fu, J. S. (2013). ICT in Education: A Critical Literature Review and Its Implications. *International Journal of Education and Development using Information and Communication Technology, 9*(1), 112-125.

Gentile, M. (2012). The importance of managing iPads in the classroom. *The Education Digest. Essential Readings Condensed for Quick Review, 78*(3), 11–13.

Hammond, M. (2014). Introducing ICT in schools in England: Rationale and consequences. *British Journal of Educational Technology, 45*(2), 191–201. doi:10.1111/bjet.12033

Harris, C. (2013). Less is more. *School Library Journal, 59*(6), 7–8. PMID:23312511

Henderson, A., & Mapp, K. (2002). *A new wave of evidence: The impact of school, family, and community connections on student achievement.* Austin: Southwest Educational Development Laboratory.

Kajtazi, M. (2011, September 27-28). Information Inadequacy: The Lack of Needed Information in Human, Social and Industrial Affairs. in DM., Hercheui, D., Whitehouse, W. McIver, Jr., & J. Phahlamohlaka, (Eds.) Proceedings of the 10th IFIP TC 9 International Conference on Human Choice and Computers, 2012, Amsterdam, The Netherlands. Retrieved from https://pdfs.semanticscholar.org/3c02/e75efec30ab-c5051e0fa9bb7905a3e9b6ad8.pdf

Kershaw, A. (2013, December 2). Tablets mean children 'struggle to use a pencil'. *The Scotsman.* Retrieved from http://www.scotsman.com/news/education/tablets-mean-children-struggle-to-use-a-pencil-1-3216500#ixzz4DickYPcS

Lim, C. P. (2007). Effective integration of ICT in Singapore schools: Pedagogical and policy implications. *Educational Technology Research and Development*, *55*(1), 83–116. doi:10.1007/s11423-006-9025-2

Mageau, T. (2012). Stop buying iPads, please. *Technological Horizons in Education Journal*. Retrieved from http://online.qmags.com/TJL0912/default.aspx?pg=2&mode=1#pg2&mode1

McNeil, E. (2016, June). Maine teachers trade iPads for laptops. *Education Week*, *8*, 4.

Mishra, P., & Koehler, M. J. (2006). Technological Pedagogical Content Knowledge: A framework for teacher knowledge. *Teachers College Record*, *108*(6), 1017–1054. doi:10.1111/j.1467-9620.2006.00684.x

Nivala, M. (2009). Simple answers for complex problems: Education and ICT in Finnish information society strategies. *Media, Culture & Society*, *31*(3), 433–448. doi:10.1177/0163443709102715

Ribble, M. (2001). *Digital Citizenship in Schools* (2nd ed.). Arlington, Virginia: International Society for Technology in Education.

Robertson, J. (2002). The ambiguous embrace: Twenty years of IT (ICT) in UK primary schools. *British Journal of Educational Technology*, *33*(4), 403–409. doi:10.1111/1467-8535.00277

Tearle, P. (2005). ICT Implementation: What makes the difference? *British Journal of Educational Technology*, *34*(5), 567–583. doi:10.1046/j.0007-1013.2003.00351.x

Vanderlinde, R., Dexter, S., & van Braak, J. (2012). School-based ICT policy plans in primary education: Elements, typologies and underlying processes. *British Journal of Educational Technology*, *43*(3), 505–519. doi:10.1111/j.1467-8535.2011.01191.x

Waters, J. K. (2010). Enter the iPad (or Not?). *Technological Horizons in Education Journal*. June 2010.

Webster, F. (2006). *Theories of the Information Society* (3rd ed.). Abingdon: Routledge.

Wright, P. (2013, June 20). Why new technologies could never replace great teaching. *The Guardian*. Retrieved from https://www.theguardian.com/teacher-network/teacher-blog/2013/jun/20/technology-not-replace-teaching-learning

Young, J. R. (2005). Knowing When to Log Off. *The Chronicle of Higher Education*, *51*(33), 1–5.

Zalaznick, M. (2013). Managing the move to mobile. *District Administration*, (December), 82–85.

KEY TERMS AND DEFINITIONS

Applications: Also known as 'apps', are programmes or software with a specific purpose normally used on mobile devices. The apps used by the school were those available for Apple devices (mainly the iPad).

Comic Life: "The app with everything you need to make a stunning comic from your own images." https://plasq.com

CIS: The Council of International Schools. "The Council of International Schools (CIS) is a membership community committed to high quality international education". http://www.cois.org The school is currently seeking accreditation from CIS.

Edmodo: "The safest and easiest way for educators to connect and collaborate with students, parents, and each other". https://www.edmodo.com Available on all devices but normally used by higher grades.

IXL: "IXL is the Web's most comprehensive math and language arts practice site". https://nz.ixl.com The school normally uses it for math.

Overload: The concept of having too much information made available so that it becomes difficult to focus on the specific aspect required by the user/reader. Overload should not be limited only to the amounts of information available but also how these ever-increasing amounts are managed and how effectively they are communicated.

Raz-Kids: "The award-winning website where K-5 students go to read — anytime, anywhere!" https://www.raz-kids.com

Underload: The term here refers to the loss or blurring of important information because it is not clear through which channel this information is being made available.

Chapter 5
Perpetual Mobile Availability as a Reason for Communication Overload:
Experiences and Coping Strategies of Smartphone Users

Bernadette Kneidinger-Müller
University of Bamberg, Germany

ABSTRACT

Mobile communication media such as smartphones have dramatically increased the social availability of users. The perpetual contact is experienced quite ambivalently, not only as a big advantage of technological development but also as a new reason for increasing communication overload. This chapter details how people evaluate mobile availability in their everyday lives and how they cope with experiences of overload and stress. Using the transactional theory of stress and coping (Lazarus & Cohen, 1977), data from a diary study and qualitative interviews with German smartphone users are analyzed. The findings emphasize the high level of subjectivity that influences how everyday experiences of smartphone usage and mobile availability are evaluated.

DOI: 10.4018/978-1-5225-2061-0.ch005

INTRODUCTION

The term *communication overload* was first introduced in the context of an amplification of communication channels at the workplace. Nowadays communication overload has increasingly entered the private sphere (Harper, 2010). A main reason can be seen in the mobilization of Internet-connected communication devices, first and foremost the smartphone. Whereas the "perpetual contact" (Gergen, 2002) in the mobile phone era was limited to a one- or two-channel (calls or/and SMS) communicative experience, smartphones have introduced a new multidimensionality of mobile interaction channels by making all types of computer-mediated communication available without time or space constraints (Turkle, 2008). But this communicative deliberation also causes a new complexity of communication practices that can result in "technostress" (Weil & Rosen, 1997) and communication overload. Communication overload is defined as a state when communication demands from information and communication technology channels exceed users' communication capacities (Cho et al., 2011). Communication overload can interrupt users' daily tasks (Cho et al., 2011) and increase stress levels as well as the risk for certain diseases (Lee et al., 2016).

As a theoretical background, the "transactional theory of stress and coping" (Lazarus & Cohen, 1977) is used to analyze stress experiences and related coping strategies as a transactional process. Based on a research review, this paper discusses four characteristics of smartphone usage that could be potential precursors of communication overload and stress emotions:

1. "Perpetual contact",
2. Technologically induced availability expectations,
3. Parallelization of communication channels, and
4. "Doubling of space".

Using data from an empirical project, we will analyze the theoretically discussed stress experiences and stress inducers during smartphone usage.

BACKGROUND

Mobile Communication as Stress Inducer

In many public discussions and even scientific studies, digital media such as mobile computers and mobile phones are frequently mentioned as stress inducers in the everyday lives of many people (Barley, Meyerson, & Grodal, 2011; Lee et al., 2014).

Especially smartphones with their potential usage as mobile "minicomputers" can lead to technostress (Lee, Jin, & Choi, 2012; Lee et al., 2014; Palfrey & Gasser, 2013). Technostress is defined by Weil and Rosen (1997, p. 5) as stress that is a direct or indirect result of the use of technology. It often is discussed as an emotional consequence of communication overload (Chen, 2015, p. 734). Moreover, most studies about digitally induced communication overload and stress focus on the use of digital information and communication media in the work context (e.g., Barley et al., 2011; Grandhi & Jones, 2010; Jackson, O'Conaill, & Frohlich, 2012; Lee et al., 2014; Wajcman et al., 2008). Hardly any research has been done on stress-inducing mobile communication behavior in the private context. With this paper, the author intends to contribute to closing this research gap.

Chen focused his work on "mobile technostress" and highlighted the new need for permanent multitasking as especially stress inducing (2015, p. 735). Even outside the work context, many situations exist where individuals have to handle more than one task simultaneously because of the perpetual contact created by mobile communication media (Sellberg & Susi, 2014). Mobile phone users have to decide which incoming call, message, e-mail, or voice mail should be answered first. Additionally, all forms of mediated communication can reach the individual during face-to-face interactions so that interactions with co-located people and with only virtually present people have to be coordinated instantaneously. This can lead to feelings of tension and irritation (Chen, 2015, p. 735).

The results of this type of research indicate a simple solution for "mobile technostress": reduce the use of mobile communication media. However, a large amount of evidence shows that it is not that easy. For a group of users, being outside the everyday communication stream (see also Vincent, 2005) may lead to feelings of stress or other negative emotions. For example, Walz (2012) found that nearly two-fifths of respondents felt some kind of anxiety when they did not have their smartphones with them. In addition, the ability to remain in perpetual contact with others via the Internet may provide a feeling of belonging and social support (see also Oh, Ozkaya, & LaRose, 2014; Valkenburg, & Peter, 2007). Therefore, perpetual availability may not only induce stress because of an overload of messages but also because of a new form of dependence on this permanent communication stream. The opposite of a communication overload can be seen in a negatively experienced form of communication abstinence and a lack of interaction.

Transactional Model of Stress and Coping Transferred to Mobile Communication

Independent of the inducers of stress, the emotional reaction has to be taken seriously, as already highlighted by Lazarus and Cohen in their paper about environmental stress (1977). They distinguish three types of stress, namely life events, chronic stress, and daily hassles. Stressful life events are, for example, the death of a person close to one or contracting an acute disease, and a stressful job or problems in the family can cause chronic stress. Daily hassles are minor occurrences such as missing a train, but they can result in chronic stress if they occur frequently. Stress induced by communicative overload can be categorized, according Lazarus and Cohen's categorization of stress types, as daily hassles (Lazarus & Cohen, 1977, p. 192) but can also result in chronic stress if the overload lasts persists (Hefner, & Vorderer, 2016, p. 238). Following Lazarus and Cohen's "transactional model of stress and coping," stress has to be treated as a transactional phenomenon that depends on the individual meaning a person places on the stress-inducing stimulus. Based on this model, stress always occurs in a person–environment transaction. The individual significance of the external stressor is mediated by the person's appraisal of the stressor and by social and cultural resources that can be used to handle the situation (Lazarus & Cohen, 1977).

These early assumptions of Lazarus and Cohen are supported by recent studies about digital stress. They identified four steps of appraising potential stressors and coping with them that can be transferred even to digital forms of stress: In the first step of Lazarus and Cohen's (1977) model, "primary appraisal," the individual evaluates the significance of the situation and the stressors themselves. In the second step, "secondary appraisal," the controllability of the stressor and the individual coping resources are evaluated. In the third step, "coping efforts," actual strategies are implied to handle the situation and reduce the feeling of stress. The coping strategies can include "problem management" strategies that aim to change a stressful situation and "emotional regulation" that should change how the individual thinks or feels about the stressful situation. The "outcomes" (e.g., psychological well-being, a functional status) occur after the coping strategies have been implemented (Glanz et al., 2002, p. 213).

Communication Overload and Coping Strategies

Smartphone users have to develop a mobile availability management strategy to avoid experiencing communication overload. Transferring the transactional theory of stress and coping to experiences and coping strategies in the context of mobile communication habits and experiences of communication overload, the four steps could be described as follows: A person receives a call and a text message simultaneously during a face-to-face interaction with a close friend. The individual has to evaluate the communicative and social needs of three potential interaction partners (on the phone, via text message, and face-to-face) who want to communicate with the person. The stress level experienced in this situation depends on how problematic and challenging the individual perceives the situation (primary appraisal). During the secondary appraisal stage, the person thinks about what he or she could do to organize the three competing communications—the higher the perception of control over the situation, the lower the experienced stress level. Coping efforts appear when the individual decides on a potential coping strategy and acts accordingly, and by choosing a problem management strategy, the person tries to change the situation, for example, by turning off the smartphone so that no further incoming calls or messages can cause disturbance. By choosing emotional regulation, the individual redefines the situation and the connected feelings, for example, by defining the face-to-face interaction as more important than interactions with absent people via smartphone. Consequently, the decision regarding which conversation should be continued becomes easier, and the stress-inducing situation is neutralized. Independent of the coping strategy, at the end, the individual should have organized all communications so that he or she does not perceive them as cognitive overload ("outcomes"). The appraisal of and coping with communication demands are treated as main factors that influence the perception and experience of digital stress (Hefner & Vorderer, 2016, p. 241). Therefore, communication overload and stress cannot be measured by counting the number of incoming messages or social contacts a person has, but the individual's short- and long-term resources have to be considered. Additionally, the personality of a user and the specific context of use seem to influence how individuals appraise and cope with communication demands (Hefner & Vorderer, 2016, p. 241).

MAIN FOCUS OF THE CHAPTER

The Research Questions

The smartphone as a form of a mobile minicomputer with Internet connection not only offers the user various interpersonal communication methods but also a new amount of perpetually accessible information via online media, social media, and all other forms of online content. Thus, the use of the smartphone may provoke multiple forms of information and communication overload depending on the specific usage. This paper addresses mobile communication as a form of person-to-person interaction. Information from other online sources such as online media or social media form another part of the information and communication flood that reaches users via their smartphones is discussed in detail in this chapter. Hence, we are not examining general digital stress, defined as "stress resulting from a strong and perhaps almost permanent use of information and communication technology (ICT) that is triggered by permanent access to an inconceivable amount and diversity of (social) content" (Hefner, & Vorderer, 2016: 237). Instead, we are discussing the significance of mobile communication technology for person-to-person interactions and its potential to increase or decrease feelings of communication overload and stress in everyday life. A review of current studies revealed that coping strategies in the context of communication overload are still under-researched (Lee et al., 2016). The author aims to fill this gap by answering the following research questions:

RQ1: How do users experience mobile availability via smartphone?
RQ2: Which coping strategies do users develop to avoid communication overload caused by mobile communication?

Before answering these research questions using data from a diary study and qualitative interviews with smartphone users, four characteristics of smartphone usage should be discussed that can be potential causes of mobile technostress.

"Perpetual Contact" as Stressor

Smartphones, as personal communication devices, have become an everyday companion for many users. Consequently, individuals have to handle an "increased amount and promptness of digital communication with connected others" (Hefner, & Vorderer, 2016: 238). Being available is experienced as something necessary, helpful, and calming (Kang & Jung, 2014; Ling & Yttri, 2002). Moreover, the human need to maintain social relationships and interact with other individuals described in Baumeister and Leary's (1995) concept of the "need to belong" explains why smartphones are experienced as important relationship tools. Hefner and Vorderer (2016, p. 242) identified a "permanent communication vigilance" for incoming messages and a need to habitually check the smartphone for any news (Oulasvirta et al., 2012). Therefore, situations where the smartphone is not available or does not work may be experienced as threatening and stressful. Concepts such as "fear of missing out" (Przybylski et al., 2013) describe the negative emotional experiences of individuals that are out of the communication stream for some time and have to handle the feeling that they are not aware of the ongoing activities and interactions of others (Cheever et al., 2014). Thus, many users never switch off their smartphones, which puts them in a "connected presence" (Licoppe, 2004) with others 24 hours a day. The question arises if this should be interpreted as an indicator for a dependence on the smartphone as a technological device or a dependence on perpetual social connection.

Permanent connectedness also can be discussed from another perspective: The communication flood demands resources in terms of the users' time, attention, and cognitive capacity (Hefner & Vorderer, 2016: 239). Moreover, permanent communication vigilance means a permanent alertness that requires mental effort (Warm, Parasuraman, & Matthews, 2008). Hence, many users experience this perpetual contact (Katz & Aakhus, 2002) as stressful and disturbing (Bailey & Konstan, 2006; Misra & Stokols, 2012; Rettie, 2009). In contrast to communication overload in organizational environments, communication overload in the private sphere cannot be interrupted by leaving the office, which is why Tarafdar et al. (2007) talk about a techno-invasion. The smartphone is with one at all times; thus, so is the continuous stream of mobile-transmitted communication. It has to be asked how smartphone users experience this perpetual contact in their everyday lives, under which circumstances people experience it as a stress-inducing or stress-reducing factor, and how people cope with the technologically offered opportunity of around-the-clock availability.

Technologically Induced Availability Expectations

Because of the simplification of mutual mobile reachability, smartphones cause a new complexity in availability management. Being available is no longer a question of technical reachability but a question of social availability. Studies show that the amplified technological reachability via smartphones increases expectations of social availability and quick responses (Campbell, Ling, & Bayer, 2014; Grintner et al., 2006, p. 441; Grintner & Eldridge, 2001; Ling, 2004). The expected duration between reading a message and responding to it varies between different communication channels (Avrahami et al., 2008, p. 285; Licoppe, 2004, p. 137; Rettie, 2009, p. 434). The quicker and easier a message can be exchanged, the more instant the reaction should be. Today, many users feel obligated to respond immediately even to text messages (Bailey & Konstan, 2006; Church & de Oliveira, 2013, p. 356; Hall & Baym, 2012, p. 316; Quan-Haase & Collins, 2008). This is particularly the case if it is assumed that the person is technically reachable via a specific channel at the moment the message is sent (Rettie, 2009, p. 434).

The introduction of read notifications in chats and mobile messaging applications can further intensify the experienced obligation to respond immediately (Church & de Oliveira, 2013; Mai et al., 2015; O'Hara et al., 2014). This can be seen as an example of how even low-level technological developments can influence social communication experiences. Generally, device manufacturers intend to develop technical solutions that help users to handle the increasing amount of communication, for example by introducing automated interactions. These technical solutions can increase individuals' opportunities to control their availability (Baron, 2008; Schroeder, 2010, p. 80). For example, using caller ID, people can decide whether they want to respond to every incoming call and message at particular moments. In text-based communication channels, individual status updates can be used to inform others of one's own availability or to obscure one's actual availability status (Hancock et al., 2009; Quan-Haase & Collins, 2008, p. 534). How such technological solutions support coping strategies or further increase experiences of communication overload and stress should be an important research topic for further study.

Besides the social expectations and specific characteristics of the interaction situation, individual personality factors can influence availability expectations and their consequences for communication overload. Hefner and Vorderer (2016) assumed that "highly agreeable and/or conscientious individuals suffer more severely from perceived obligations to respond, and consequently have a higher perception of obligation in the first place than individuals scoring lower on these traits" (p. 242). Additionally, a high susceptibility to peer pressure (Dielman, Campanelli, Shope, & Butchart, 1987) combined with an "always-on" peer-group mentality is seen as a potential predictor for perceived stress. Another personality trait that could relate to stress appraisal is the locus of control: the more in control of their lives people feel, the fewer stressors they identify (Abouserie, 1994).

Being socially available includes the decision to answer a call or a message. Consequently, being socially unavailable can be interpreted as the conscious decision to refuse to respond to another person (at least at a certain moment). The social unavailability of a contacted person seems to become a situation that is difficult to accept, can evoke negative feelings (see also Church & de Oliveira, 2013, p. 356; Mai et al., 2015), or is experienced as a threat to the quality of the relationship (Licoppe, 2004, p. 145). Users develop various strategies to cope with social availability expectations. White lies (Camden et al. 1984), or so-called "butler lies" (Hancock et al., 2009; Birnholtz et al., 2010), are used to manage unwanted contact or conversation break offs without violating social expectations and norms. "Butler lies" describe a process of denying that one is available. Previously, another person (the butler) usually would fulfil this function by telling the contacting person that the individual is not present. Today, this task increasingly is fulfilled by technological solutions. Moreover, social unavailability frequently is masked with excuses about fictitious activities or technical problems (see also Grintner et al., 2006, p. 441; Hancock et al., 2009, p. 517; Birnholtz et al., 2013). Further coping strategies could be predefined times of usage and non-usage of the smartphone as well as the development of and compliance with codes of behavior for smartphone use in different social contexts (see also Plant, 2002, p. 37f).

In summary, availability alone does not predict stress; only the subjective appraisal of social availability expectations results in stress (Misra & Stokols, 2012; Thomèe et al. 2011). Therefore, the individual and social availability expectations have to be analyzed in more detail to determine under what conditions incoming calls or messages have to be answered immediately.

Parallelization of Communication Channels

Smartphones cause the disappearance of a linear communication structure that was typical for landline telephony. Whereas phone calls can be received and answered only one after the other, smartphones with their multidimensional communication channels lead to an increased parallelization of incoming calls and verbal, textual, and visual messages a user receives simultaneously via multiple channels. This multimodal connectedness (Chan, 2014) increases the challenge of maintaining an overview of messages received and sent. Besides changes in mobile person-to-person communication, the mobile usage of social media especially amplifies the communication flood that can be characterized as a specific form of network communication. Social networking sites (SNSs) not only increase the amount of communication but also are connected with a new demand for permanent active self-presentation and self-monitoring (Hefner & Vorderer, 2016, p. 243). According to La Rose et al. (2014), permanent mobile availability on SNSs may lead to a "connect overload."

Multimodal connectedness via smartphones has forced people to multitask (Chen, 2015, p. 735), and they can experience this in different ways. On the one hand, social interactions are simplified because smartphone users can choose from a wide range of communication channels and switch between them according their needs (Isaacs et al., 2012; O'Hara et al., 2014). On the other hand, the multiplicity of communication channels makes social interactions more complex because smartphone users have to decide which communication channel is most appropriate for each individual interaction. This can result in an overload of options and choices, which again may result in stress (Hefner & Vorderer, 2016, p. 245; Rim et al., 2011; Schwartz et al., 2002). Therefore, many smartphone users develop strategies to handle the permanent stream of communications via various channels. For example, Lee et al. (2012) showed that individuals who report higher technostress levels were more likely to make calls than to choose text-based communication forms such as e-mails or text messages. They interpreted it as an indicator that such individuals avoid using the smartphone as a minicomputer due to technostress (Lee et al., 2012).

"Doubling of Space"

The "multimodal connectedness" via smartphones not only causes a parallelization of communication channels but also a parallelization of communicative spheres. Whereas in traditional face-to-face interactions only physically present people could participate in a conversation, because of mobile phones even physically absent people have become part of a face-to-face conversation. The smartphone compensates for physical absence and gives the mobile interaction partners a new form of "absence presence" (Gergen, 2002). This can be interpreted as a simplification of interaction because the technology allows the participation of absent people in a conversation and makes them part of the face-to-face interaction. At the same time, it causes an increased complexity of the interaction situation because it goes along with a competition between mediated (online) communication and face-to-face interactions. Scannell (1996) discusses these changes of interaction contexts under the term "doubling of space." The new complexity of the interaction situation appears with the parallelization of a "colocated" and a "remote" communication community that competes for the attention of the smartphone user (de Souza, 2006, p. 262). That also means a multiplication of communication flows that have to be handled and can result in communication overflow.

The Empirical Project

This paper chooses a qualitative approach to analyze mobile-induced communication overload and stress in more detail. As Chen (2015, p. 740) criticizes, the majority of current studies investigated mobile technostress based on questionnaires. Therefore, a two-step qualitative research project with 24 German smartphone users should offer more in-depth insights in usage experiences and coping strategies. The smartphone usage habits were analyzed with a combination of a self-administrative diary study and in-depth interviews. All participants were recruited by students from a sociological research seminar at a German university. The participants were selected based on their age (between 20 and 30), sex, and smartphone ownership. In the first step, in the diary study, 14 women and 10 men between 21 and 30 years old, mainly students (22 persons, 2 working full-time), documented on three determined days (Friday, May 29, 2015; Sunday, May 31, 2015; Tuesday, June 2, 2015) every SMS and every message that was received or sent on their favorite mobile messaging application (WhatsApp: 18 persons, Threema: 4 persons, Line: 2 persons) using an electronic diary grid. For each message, various aspects were coded, such as the day, time, and location where the message was received or sent, initials of the interaction partner, relationship with the interaction partner, content of the message, form of the message, motivation to write the message, group message vs. single message, and whether a face-to-face interaction partner was present at the moment when the message was sent or received. In total, the 24 study participants recorded 3,224 messages for three days. After the diary study, all participants were interviewed about their smartphone usage behavior, their motivations, and especially their experiences with mobile availability in different situations and contexts. All interviews were audio-recorded, transcribed, and analyzed using a qualitative content analysis (based on Mayring (2008), supported with the software package atlas.ti). Based on the exploratory focus of the study, all codes and categories are applied inductively to the interview material. All interviews were reread and recoded in several coding runs so that a coherent coding schema was applied to all texts.

THE FINDINGS

Perpetual Availability

The fact that mobile phones allow users to stay in "perpetual contact" with physically absent people independent of time and space was frequently mentioned during the interviews. The interviews revealed an ambivalent evaluation of increasing mutual availability. Positive as well as negative experiences were reported, sometimes both at the same time. When asked about the advantages and disadvantages of smartphones, eight persons instantaneously named permanent availability as a positive aspect, whereas six persons named it a negative aspect. Some of them experienced the permanent mobile availability as an advantage and disadvantage at the same time, as expressed by a man:

It [the smartphone] is with you every time. You are always available ... Texting has many advantages. It's a great opportunity to communicate, but at the same time it's kind of exhausting and you have to consider whether this capacity is lacking anywhere else. And it can cause stress ... (Man, 27 years old)

Nevertheless and independent of the individual evaluation of perpetual availability, the majority of the participants (14 persons) are available on their smartphone 24 hours a day or at least "always on" during the daytime (3 persons). The individual availability management does not predict the appraisal of the perpetual contact. There are participants who are always available but do not feel any stress or communication overload. Whereas other participants report strong feelings of pressure, stress, and communication overload because of their perpetual availability. Referring to the model of Lazarus and Cohen (1977), these answers illustrate how different the evaluation of a potential stress-inducing situation can be during the "primary appraisal" stage. At the "secondary appraisal stage," the individuals think about possible solutions to reduce negative feelings that could result from perpetual availability. A coping strategy of many participants is a restriction of technological availability in special situations or at special places to avoid stressful situations.

After a very hard workday, when I am already 16 to 17 hours on my feet and I know that I don't have to get up early the next morning, I switch off the phone. (Man, 23 years old)

But switching off the phone does not work for anyone as a coping strategy against communication overload. Some participants who regularly switch off their phones nevertheless report feelings of stress or pressure. Others even report increased negative feelings in cases where they cannot be available on their phone. Being out of the "communication loop" is experienced as more stressful than the permanent stream of communications (c.f. Hefner & Vorderer, 2016, p. 242).

Increased Expectations of Social Availability

Smartphones increase expectations of social availability. As a consequence, the social unavailability of others can be experienced as a problematic social situation (Church & de Oliveira, 2013, p. 356; Licoppe, 2004, p. 145; Mai et al. 2016). Quite strong availability expectations were expressed in various interviews. Four interview participants explicitly report dissatisfaction when a person does not respond to a message or a call even though the interviewee knew that the contacted person was able to answer and carried his or her smartphone with himself or herself all day.

If I know that the person always carries around the smartphone with himself, then I really expect his availability. (Man, 27 years old)

Two interview participants go a step further and even interpret the duration until they receive a response to their text messages as an indicator of their place in the friendship hierarchy, as one man describes it:

That is totally depending on the person. If I know that someone only uses his mobile during his lunch break, then I could not insist on an immediate response. That's totally okay. But when another person has nothing to do the whole weekend and nevertheless she doesn't answer, it's really not cool. In this case, I know where I'm placed on the friendship hierarchy of this person. (Man, 30 years old)

The analysis of such experiences of dissatisfaction in the case of missing or delayed answers of contacted persons is especially important because they are reflected in individual availability management. Based on their own expectations and experiences about the availability of others, smartphone users make presumptions about the availability expectations of their interaction partners. Thirteen of the 24 interview participants experience some stress answering incoming calls or messages immediately. The experienced pressure depends on the contents of the messages (10 people) or on the person who sent the message (one person).

Of course, important messages have to be answered quickly. But I don't feel any obligation to answer unimportant messages immediately. It's my time and I can organize it by myself. (Man, 26 years old)

Some users report a need for quick responses to avoid negative reactions and feelings by others.

Certain persons get a quick response because I noticed that they are waiting for my reaction, and if you don't answer quickly, they let feel you how they are thinking about it. (Woman, 24 years old)

In close relationships, mutual mobile availability is expected to be much stronger than that in weak ties, as one man reports his expectations:

From my partner or my close friends, I actually expect an immediate response depending on the urgency of a message ... The closer a relationship—with family or close friends—the higher is my expectation to get an immediate response to certain topics. (Man, 30 years old)

This quote highlights the significance of relationship strength for the evaluation of availability. For strong relationships, the perpetual availability can be experienced a positive way to stay in contact even over distance, but for weak relationships, an immediate response and intensive communication are not expected. Mai et al.'s study about the Facebook chat (2015, p. 299) shows similar influences of the relationship strength on the response expectations.

In general, it can be said that availability expectations for one's own person are much higher than the expectations for the availability of others (similar to findings of Mai et al., 2015, p. 300). Twelve people explicitly report that they do not expect others to be continuously available. Only five people express the expectation that their interaction partners should be always available. The expectation of others' availability depends strongly on the situation and the contents of the exchanged messages or calls. Availability is strongly expected in urgent cases or personal emergency (9 persons) and if the interaction was arranged in advance (12 persons).

Status Display and Read Notifications as Stress Inducers

Either I respond immediately or I try not to open the message directly, so that it appear as "not read," in the case that I want to answer it later. (Man, 27 years old)

This citation impressively shows how technological settings may intensify the availability pressure. Consequences of technological changes become especially obvious with the introduction of "read notifications" in the mobile messaging application WhatsApp in 2014. An automated status appears when a user has opened a message. Together with the receipt confirmation and the time of the last online status, it offers the interaction partner a detailed feedback about the online activities of a user. These automated notifications appear unless the user deactivates them actively. The "read notifications" can be described as an "awareness cue" (Oulasvirta et al., 2007) that are used to compensate the lack of social cues that can be transmitted in computer-mediated interactions compared to face-to-face interactions. However, preliminary empirical findings indicate negative effects of such notifications too. The displayed information may increase response pressure. (Birnholtz et al., 2013; Church & de Oliveira, 2013, p. 356; O'Hara et al., 2014, p. 1139).

The automated notifications were discussed with the interviewees. Most of them do not have deactivated notifications (18 persons); only 6 persons (3 men, 3 women) deactivated it actively. One person reports that she deactivates the notifications temporarily to reduce the expectation of answers when she is on holiday and she is not permanently connected to the Internet. Four persons explain that they do not change the settings because they want to see the online status of their contacts and to get read notifications from them. A deactivation of one's own status would enable the user to see the status of others.

I didn't deactivate my online status because that's the only way to see if others are online. For me, it doesn't matter if anyone can see that I'm online; that has never bothered me. The others have to live with the fact that they see my online status and that nevertheless I don't answer a message, that's it. But I want to see the status of others, it's a kind of certainty. (Woman, 22 years old)

In general, 12 interview participants experience increased stress because of the read notifications in mobile messaging applications, 7 do not agree with it, 1 person expresses a very ambivalent opinion, and 4 participants do not have any view about the topic.

These read notifications of some messengers really increase the pressure when you have already read a message but haven't answered yet. Thus, I tend to read a message later or answer immediately. (Man, 27 years old)

But not only negative experiences with read notifications are reported. Two participants experience the read notification as stress reducing because they do not need to answer a message just to write that they had received and read the message.

The two checks in WhatsApp reduce the stress to respond immediately to messages because now you can see automatically if I have already read a message or not. (Woman, 24 years old)

Four interviewees describe the notifications as helpful additional information about the daily life of others, and three see it as a feedback about the recent well-being of their interaction partners. The time of the last online status of a person is used to draw conclusions about whether someone had arrived at the destination or whether someone is already awake.

Sometimes when you write someone a message, it only matters if you know that he has read the message. I don't know an answer anymore ... That's quite nice because you get the feeling that the person is okay because she has been online. Nothing had happened to her while she was driving in her car, for example. (Woman, 24 years old)

It can be suggested that the automated notifications can even be experienced as technologically supported ways to reduce communication overload and feelings of stress because they reduce the response pressure (cf. O'Hara et al., 2014, 1139f)

The displayed online status is also used for the selection of the communication channel. If the online status shows that a person has not been active for some time, the interviewees report that they use this information to switch to another communication channel to reach the person.

It's a somewhat urgent situation, and then you see that the person isn't online and no blue checks appear in WhatsApp. Then I decide to call the person, that's how I do it. (Woman, 22 years old)

This can be interpreted as another coping strategy to avoid an overload of messages by choosing the most appropriate communication channel. A conscious selection of communication channels reduces the probability of the unavailability of others which would go along with waiting for responses for a long time. Additionally, a conscious channel selection can help reduce the number of communications on parallel channels by focusing on the one that seems to offer the highest probability to reach a person. However, a negative consequence would be that the decision to choose the more "invasive" channel (phone call) could increase stress for the contacted person. This underlines the close interdependence of the multidimensionality of availability and the multidimensionality of communication channels, which leads to the next paragraph.

Multidimensionality of Communication Channels

The high variety of available communication channels is experienced as a positive innovation but also sometimes as a problematic situation. Especially the practice of "channel blending" (Isaacs et al., 2012; O'Hara et al., 2014) is described in many interviews. Most frequently mentioned is the combination of telephone calls and text messages. For example, a text message is sent to coordinate a subsequent phone call, or a text message is sent after a call to add information to an already discussed topic.

Most of the time you start writing text messages, and then you decide to call the person. Everything can be merged depending on the amount of information that should be exchanged. For a lot of information, a call is better; for less information, the messenger is better. (Man, 27 years old)

A multidimensionality of communication also occurs when more than just one conversation is held on various communication channels simultaneously. Such a parallelization of conversations with different people on different communication channels has already been experienced from all interview participants.

When I'm unsure about the availability of a person in the specific moment, I send a text message first because text messages can be ignored much easier than a call and they are not so obtrusive as a call in the case that the mobile setting is put on "loud." And after the message, I wait if the person responds. (Man, 25 years old)

With such forms of channel combinations, the interviewees try to avoid problems that appear because of calling a person in an inappropriate situation. Text messages are seen as less invasive and disturbing because they create an asynchronous form of communication that allows a response with time delay (cf. Avrahami et al., 2008, p. 285; Licoppe, 2004, p. 137). The examples illustrate the different characteristics of telephone calls and text messages and how they are used to reduce feelings of communication overload and stress on both sides—the sender and the receiver of a message or a call. Speech-based communication is associated as a more invasive form of communication, but it increases the possibility to get a quick and direct reaction from the contacted person, which can reduce negative experiences for the sender because he or she does not have to wait for an answer. Text-based communication is seen as more unobtrusive and therefore reduces the receiver's potential for stress. Most participants experience the possibility to combine different communication channels as positive and helpful. However, some users describe the switch between various communication channels as confusing or unnerving.

It's sometimes really annoying when you are at the university and write messages on Facebook and after that you switch to WhatsApp or another mobile messenger when you are on the go. And after that you switch to some other channel ... That's really unnerving. (Man, 23 years old)

The technologically offered "multimodal connectedness" (Chan, 2014; Schroeder, 2010) increases the amount of communication and the challenge of keeping the overview over messages which may result in communication overload and stress. But at the same time, the option to select the most appropriate communication channel for the specific communication need can help reduce communication overload by minimizing the number of communications that have to be exchange. Additionally, stress could be avoided by choosing a less invasive communication channel that reduces the pressure of answering a phone call immediately in inappropriate situations. This again indicates the influence of a high level of subjectivity if one and the same usage practice is experienced as stress inducing or, on the contrary, as a coping strategy against communication overload.

The Doubling of Space

The already mentioned parallelization of communicative spheres that occurs when mobile communication intrudes face-to-face interactions and the other way around has to be treated as another special situation where communication overload could be experienced. The analysis of the diary documentations suggests a quite frequent practice of parallel communication via smartphone during face-to-face interactions. Nearly a quarter of all recorded messages (23%) were sent or received in the presence of a face-to-face interaction partner. In the sample, women exhibit this behavior more frequently (25% of all messages) than men (20%). Based on the diary data, six participants can be characterized as highly frequent parallel communicators because more than half of their recorded messages are sent or received in the presence of others. During the interviews, many participants express their preference for textual communication on their smartphone in the presence of others because a telephone call is experienced as much more disturbing in ongoing face-to-face interaction.

I mainly use text messages. Sometime even telephone calls happen, but in such cases I always leave the room. When I'm answering a call, it only happens with a good reason, and I interrupt the interaction with my conversation partner for a moment totally. (Woman, 25 years old)

Leaving the room to answer an incoming telephone call during a face-to-face interaction can be seen as one coping strategy to reduce the complexity of the social interaction and the communication stimuli that have to be handled simultaneously. A quite similar strategy of coping with overstimulation because of communicative interactions was already mentioned in the early paper of Lazarus and Cohen (1977, p. 194f), where they discussed the strategy of disengagement of individuals as a way to protect themselves against excessive stimulation.

Half of the interview participants (12 persons) have already experienced some criticism about their parallel communication habits. Most of them completely understand these critics because they experience the negative consequences of parallel communication themselves. Thirteen interviewees describe calls or messages that are sent or received during a face-to-face interaction as a distraction from the conversation and an expression of missing attention from the interaction partner.

I really experience such habits as very impolite because the attention should be with the physically present conversation partner and not additionally on other channels. (Man, 27 years old)
Nine persons talk about a disturbance in the communication flow.
You are distracted, don't get everything. The conversation cannot flow. (Woman, 23 years old)

Even a self-exclusion of the parallel communication from the copresent interaction partner(s) (nine persons) and a lack of interest in the present interaction partner (six persons) is experienced.

It's really disturbing because you get the feeling that the person isn't present anymore but is stuck in the virtual reality. And you get the feeling that this is more important for this person than the conversation with you. (Woman, 24 years old)

But why are people acting as parallel communicators when they evaluate such habits as so negative? A closer look at the motivations of the messages that are sent or received with copresent face-to-face interaction partners reveals that parallel communication happens not only as a way to coordinate urgent matters (30%) but also as a kind of habit or a way to escape boring face-to-face conversations (33%).

If I'm bored in a conversation, I start typing on my mobile. (Man, 23 years old)

To sum up, the usage of smartphones for parallel communication can be seen as a special phenomenon that results from the technologically enabled permanent availability of individuals. The communication situation does not only become more complex because of an increased amount of communication, but even a new complexity of communication spaces has to be handled as well. Smartphone users have to consider both spaces—the physical and the virtual space—as potential communication spheres. Both spheres imply potential communication overload and stress. And because of the doubling of space, potential stressors can jointly affect the individual if the user is not able to address the flood of communications and develop coping strategies for each sphere.

LIMITATIONS AND FUTURE RESEARCH DIRECTIONS

The empirical findings of this paper are based on a qualitative study with a strong exploratory orientation. Therefore, the generalizability of the findings is limited. Majority of the participants were students and belong to a quite restricted age cohort. Their usage habits and experiences cannot be transferred without restrictions to social groups with other sociodemographic, educational, or economic characteristics. For example, it could be questioned whether older or younger people report different experiences of "mobile technostress" or whether the special life stage of being a student influences mobile communication behavior, as some studies indicate (Coclar & Sahin, 2011; Tu, Wang, & Shu, 2005). Nevertheless, the quite divergent experiences and usage habits of the participants highlight the variety of individual mobile communication experiences and how people cope with communication overload in very different ways.

CONCLUSION

The researcher examined why mobile availability has to be analyzed from two perspectives—as a reason for communication overload and stress experiences as well as a coping strategy that lessens social fears and stress. The empirical findings underline the assumption that interpersonal smartphone communication and even an increased number of messages exchanged do not necessarily predict communication overload and stress. The effects of the communication flood can be measured only by considering the individual appraisal of a communication task, individual resources and personality traits, and social expectations and contextual factors. The ambivalent experiences and evaluations of communication situations indicate that there is a narrow divide between mobile communication as a reason for communication overload, which could lead to stress, and mobile communication as an indispensable tool for satisfying the social needs of belonging, connection, and social support, which could reduce stress.

Such ambivalent effects could be observed for all four of the characteristics of smartphone usage discussed. The multidimensionality of communication communities that manifest when physically absent people become virtually present in face-to-face interactions is seen as an opportunity to maintain contact with people who are living apart. However, negative experiences are reported when the copresence of absent people in face-to-face interactions leads to a competitive situation for the attention of the smartphone user or in situations where face-to-face interactions are repeatedly disrupted by incoming calls or text messages.

The multidimensionality of communication channels allows the conscious and purposeful selection of the most appropriate communication channel for the specific situation, the communicative intention, or the interaction partner. Additionally, it allows users to communicate simultaneously with many people. Nevertheless, this new option to choose from an unmanageable variety of communication channels can also increase feelings of stress and confusion, because it necessitates putting more thought into the selection of a communication channel (overload of choices and options). Additionally, it can be quite difficult to maintain an overview of the simultaneously occurring interactions take place via multiple communication channels (multitasking). All the reported experiences can be seen as indicators for communication overload.

Due to the simplification and complexity of interpersonal communication experienced in the mobile communication society, smartphone users develop new strategies to handle perpetual contact. Because of automated information on availability, new ways to strategize availability management could be observed. For example, participants report special techniques for reading messages without using messaging applications to avoid sending read notifications that would increase the pressure to answer immediately. Other coping strategies include special behavioral routines developed to handle problematic situations of parallel communication during face-to-face interaction such as leaving the room or switching off the mobile device in specific situations.

Finally, and contrary to many public discussions, mobile communication via smartphones can be a reason for communication overload and experiences of stress, but this does not have to be the case. Using the transactional theory of stress and coping as theoretical framework for the analysis of smartphone usage experiences, the researcher has shown how individual appraisal of the specific interaction situation and the available resources for coping with these situations influence the evaluation of and the strategies for managing potential problems of communication overload caused by interpersonal communication via smartphone. Therefore, the four characteristics of smartphones mentioned as potential inducers of communication overload and stress feelings may not be evaluated as risk factors in general. The awareness of smartphones as stress inducing and stress relieving devices should be kept in mind in future studies about the individual and social effects of digital devices in everyday life. Moreover, these findings should be considered in the development of future technical solutions for interpersonal communication via mobile devices.

Knowledge about the positive effects of perpetual contact is already successfully used for the establishment of social networking sites. These platforms explicitly address the human needs of staying in continuous contact with others, of connection with others, and of belonging to a social group. The perception of perpetual contact as a stress inducing condition received significantly less attention from a technological perspective. Developers of mobile devices and software for digital interactions would be well advised to develop more technological solutions that support the users in handling individual and social availability expectations. Technological solutions could serve as an amplification of the individual resources available to cope with potentially stressful communication situations and reduce the probability of stressful experiences. Furthermore, when the communication flood is discussed as a cognitive and social challenge in the mass media, technological devices or solutions that help with managing the amplified communication context would offer new economic opportunities for device and software developers. Keeping such psychological, social, and even economic aspects in mind, further studies should analyze the framing conditions for the benefits and risks of smartphone communication in greater detail. This should help to identify social and technological solutions to overcome the problem of communication overload due to mobile communication and increase the potential of smartphone interactions as a coping strategy for various forms of daily hassles.

REFERENCES

Abouserie, R. (1994). Sources and levels of stress in relation to locus of control and self-esteem in university students. *Educational Psychology*, *14*(3), 323–330. doi:10.1080/0144341940140306

Avrahami, D., Fussel, S. R., & Hudson, S. E. (2008, November 8-12). IM Waiting: Timing and Responsiveness in Semi-Synchronous Communication. *Proceeding of the CSCW'08*, San Diego, California, USA (pp. 285-294).

Bailey, B. P., & Konstan, J. A. (2006). On the need for attention-aware systems: Measuring effects of interruption on task performance, error rate, and affective state. *Computers in Human Behavior*, *22*(4), 685–708. doi:10.1016/j.chb.2005.12.009

Barley, S. R., Meyerson, D. E., & Grodal, S. (2011). E-mail as a source and symbol of stress. *Organization Science*, *22*(4), 887–906. doi:10.1287/orsc.1100.0573

Baron, N. S. (2008). *Always On: Language in an Online and Mobile World*. New York: Oxford University Press. doi:10.1093/acprof:oso/9780195313055.001.0001

Baumeister, R. F., & Leary, M. R. (1995). The need to belong: Desire of interpersonal attachments as a fundamental human motivation. *Psychological Bulletin, 3*(3), 497–529. doi:10.1037/0033-2909.117.3.497 PMID:7777651

Birnholtz, J., Guillory, J., Hancock, J. T., & Bazarova, N. (2010, Feb. 6-10). "on my way": Deceptive Texting and Interpersonal Awareness Narratives. *Proceedings of the2010 ACM conference on Computer supported cooperative work*, Savannah, Georgia, USA, 1-4. doi:10.1145/1718918.1718920

Birnholtz, J., Reynolds, L., Smith, M., & Hancock, J. (2013). Everyone Has To Do It: A joint action approach to managing social inattention. *Computers in Human Behavior, 29*(6), 2230–2238. doi:10.1016/j.chb.2013.05.004

Camden, C., Motley, M. T., & Wilson, A. (1984). White Lies in Interpersonal Communication: A Taxonomy and Preliminary Investigation of Social Motivations. *Western Journal of Speech Communication, 48*(4), 309–325. doi:10.1080/10570318409374167

Chan, M. (2014, August). Multimodal Connectedness and Quality of Life: Examining the Influences of Technology Adoption and Interpersonal Communication on Well-Being Across the Life Span. *Journal of Computer-Mediated Communication. Online First, 12*. doi:10.1111/jcc4.12089

Cheever, N. A., Rosen, L. D., Carrier, L. M., & Chavez, A. (2014). Out of sight is not out of mind: The impact of restricting wireless mobile device use on anxiety levels among low, moderate and high users. *Computers in Human Behavior, 37*, 290–297. doi:10.1016/j.chb.2014.05.002

Chen, L. (2015). Mobile Technostress. In Y. Zheng, (Ed.), Encyclopedia of Mobile Phone Behavior (pp. 732-744). Hershey, PA, USA: IGI Global.

Church, K., & de Oliveira, R. (2013, August 27-30). *What's up with WhatsApp?Comparing Mobile Instant Messaging* Behaviors with Traditional SMS. Proceeding of the *Mobile HCI '13*, Munich, Germany (pp. 352-361). doi:10.1145/2493190.2493225

Coclar, A. N., & Sahin, Y. L. (2011). Technostress levels of social network site users based on ICTs in Turkey. *European Journal of Soil Science, 23*(2), 171–182.

de Souza e Silva, A. (2006). From Cyber to Hybrid: Mobile Technologies as Interfaces of Hybrid Spaces. *Space and Culture, 9*(3), 261–278. doi:10.1177/1206331206289022

Dielman, T. E., Campanelli, P. C., Shope, J. T., & Butchart, A. T. (1987). Susceptibility to peer pressure, self-esteem, and health locus of control as correlates of adolescent substance abuse. *Health Education Quarterly*, *14*(2), 207–221. doi:10.1177/109019818701400207 PMID:3597110

Gergen, K. J. (2002). The Challenge of Absent Presence. In J. Katz & M. Aakhus (Eds.), *Perpetual Contact: Mobile Communication, Private Talk, Public Performance* (pp. 227–241). Cambridge: Cambridge University Press. doi:10.1017/CBO9780511489471.018

Glanz, K., Rimer, B., & Viswanath, K. (2002). *Health Behavior and Health Education*. San Francisco, USA: Wiley.

Grandhi, S., & Jones, Q. (2010). Technology-mediated interruption management. *International Journal of Human-Computer Studies*, *68*(5), 288–306. doi:10.1016/j.ijhcs.2009.12.005

Grintner, R. E., & Eldridge, M. (2001, September 16–20). y do tngrs luv 2 txt msg? *Proceedings of the 7thEuropean Conference on Computer-Supported Cooperative Work (ECSCW)*, Bonn, Germany (pp. 219–238).

Grintner, R. E., Palen, L., & Eldridge, M. (2006). Chatting with Teenagers: Considering the Place of Chat Technologies in Teen Life. *ACM Transactions on Computer-Human Interaction*, *13*(4), 423–447. doi:10.1145/1188816.1188817

Hall, J. A., & Baym, N. K. (2012). Calling and texting (too much): Mobile maintenance expectations,(over)dependence, entrapment, and friendship satisfaction. *New Media & Society*, *14*(2), 316–331. doi:10.1177/1461444811415047

Hancock, J., Birnholtz, J., Bazarova, N., Guillory, J., Perlin, J., & Amos, B. (2009, April 4-9). Butler Lies: Awareness, Deception, and Design. Proceedings of the *CHI '09*, Boston, MA, USA (pp. 517-526).

Hefner, D., & Vorderer, P. (2016). Digital Stress. Permanent Connectedness and Multitasking. In L. Reinecke & M. B. Oliver (Eds.), *The Routledge Handbook of Media Use and Well-Being: International Perspective on Theory and Research on Positive Media Effects* (pp. 237–249). New York: Routledge.

Isaacs, E., Szymanski, P., Yamauchi, Y., Glasnapp, J., & Iwamoto, K. (2012, February 11-15). Integrating Local and Remote Worlds Through Channel Blending. *Proceeding of the CSCW'12*, Seattle, Washington, USA. doi:10.1145/2145204.2145299

Kang, S., & Jung, J. (2014). Mobile communication for human needs: A comparison of smartphone use between the US and Korea. *Computers in Human Behavior*, *35*, 376–387. doi:10.1016/j.chb.2014.03.024

Katz, J. E., & Aakhus, M. (2002). *Perpetual Contact. Mobile Communication, Private Talk, Public Performance*. Cambridge: Cambridge University Press. doi:10.1017/CBO9780511489471

Lazarus, R. S., & Cohen, J. B. (1977). Environmental Stress. In I. Altman & J. F. Wohlwill (Eds.), *Human Behavior and Environment* (Vol. 2, pp. 90–127). New York: Plenum. doi:10.1007/978-1-4684-0808-9_3

Lee, S., Jin, S., & Choi, B. (2012): The influences of technostress and antismart on continuous use of smartphones. *Paper presented at World Congress on Engineering and Computer Science*, San Francisco, CA, USA.

Lee, Y., Chang, C., Lin, Y., & Cheng, Z. (2014). The dark side of the smartphone usage: Psychological traits, compulsive behavior and technostress. *Computers in Human Behavior*, *31*, 373–383. doi:10.1016/j.chb.2013.10.047

Licoppe, C. (2004). "Connected Presence": The emergence of a new repertoire for managing social relationships in a changing communication technoscape. *Environment and Planning. D, Society & Space*, *22*(1), 135–156. doi:10.1068/d323t

Ling, R. (2004). *The Mobile Connection*. Germany: Elsevier.

Ling, R., & Yttri, B. (2002). Hyper-coordination via mobile phones in Norway. In J. Katz & M. Aakhus (Eds.), *Perpetual Contact: Mobile Communication, Private Talk, Public Performance* (pp. 139–169). Cambridge: Cambridge University Press. doi:10.1017/CBO9780511489471.013

Mai, L. M., Freudenthaler, R., Schneider, F. M., & Vorderer, P. (2015). I know youve seen it! Individual and social factors for users chatting behavior on Facebook. *Computers in Human Behavior*, *49*, 296–302. doi:10.1016/j.chb.2015.01.074

Mayring, P. (2008). *Die Praxis der qualitativen Inhaltsanalyse (2nd ed.)*. Beltz.

Misra, S., & Stokols, D. (2012). Psychological and health outcomes of perceived information overload. *Environment and Behavior*, *44*(6), 737–759. doi:10.1177/0013916511404408

O'Conaill, B., & Frohlich, D. (2012). *Timespace in the workplace: Dealing with interruptions. Proceedings of Human Factors in Computing Systems* (pp. 262–263). Denver, CO: ACM Press.

O'Hara, K., Massimi, M., Harper, R., Rubens, S., & Morris, J. (2014, February 15-19). Everyday Dwelling with WhatsApp. *Proceedings of the Mobile Apps for Enhancing Connectedness CSCW '14*, Baltimore, MD, USA (pp. 1131-1143). doi:10.1145/2531602.2531679

Oh, H. J., Ozkaya, E., & LaRose, R. (2014). How does online social networking enhance life satisfaction? The relationships among online supportive interaction, affect, perceived social support, sense of community, and life satisfaction. *Computers in Human Behavior*, *30*, 69–78. doi:10.1016/j.chb.2013.07.053

Oulasvirta, A., Rattenbury, T., Ma, L., & Raita, E. (2012). Habits make smartphone use more pervasive. *Personal and Ubiquitous Computing*, *16*(1), 105–114.

Palfrey, J., & Gasser, U. (2013). *Born digital: Understanding the first generation of digital natives*. New York: Basic Books.

Plant, S. (2002). *On the mobile. The effects of mobile telephones on social and individual life*. Motorola.

Pryzbylski, A. K., Muraryama, K., DeHaan, C. R., & Gladwell, V. (2013). Motivational, emotional, and behavioral correlates of fear of missing out. *Computers in Human Behavior*, *29*(4), 1841–1848. doi:10.1016/j.chb.2013.02.014

Quan-Haase, A., & Collins, J. L. (2008). Im there, but I might not want to talk to you. *Information Communication and Society*, *11*(4), 526–543. doi:10.1080/13691180801999043

Rettie, R. (2009). Mobile Phone Communication: Extending Goffman to Mediated Interaction. *Sociology*, *43*(3), 421–438. doi:10.1177/0038038509103197

Rim, H., Turner, B. M., Betz, N. E., & Nygren, T. E. (2011). Studies of the dimensionality, correlates, and meaning of measures of the maximizing tendency. *Judgment and Decision Making*, *6*, 656–579.

Scannell, P. (1996). *Radio, television and modern life: A phenomenological approach*. Oxford, UK: Blackwell.

Schroeder, R. (2010). Mobile phones and the inexorable advance of multimodal connectedness. *New Media & Society*, *12*(1), 75–90. doi:10.1177/1461444809355114

Schwartz, B., Ward, A., Monterosso, J., Lyubomirsky, S., White, K., & Lehman, D. R. (2002). Maximizing versus satisficing: Happiness is a matter of choice. *Personality and Social Psychology*, *83*(5), 1178–1197. doi:10.1037/0022-3514.83.5.1178 PMID:12416921

Sellberg, C., & Susi, T. (2014). Technostress in the office: A distributed cognition perspective on human-technology interactions. *Cognition Technology and Work*, *16*(2), 187–201. doi:10.1007/s10111-013-0256-9

Tarafdar, M., Tu, Q., Ragu-Nathan, T. S., & Ragu-Nathan, B. S. (2007). The Impact of Technostress on Role Stress and Productivity. *Journal of Management Information Systems*, *24*(1), 301–328. doi:10.2753/MIS0742-1222240109

Thomée, S., Härenstam, A., & Hagberg, M. (2011). Mobile phone use and stress, sleep disturbances, and symptoms of depression among young adults-a prospective cohort study. *BMC Public Health*, *11*(1), 66. doi:10.1186/1471-2458-11-66 PMID:21281471

Tu, Q., Wang, K., & Shu, Q. (2005). Computer-related technostress in China. *Communications of the ACM*, *48*(4), 77–81. doi:10.1145/1053291.1053323

Turkle, S. (2008). Always-on/always-on-you: The tethered self. In J.E. Katz (Ed.), *Handbook of Mobile Communication Studies* (pp. 121–138). Cambridge, MA: MIT. doi:10.7551/mitpress/9780262113120.003.0010

Valkenburg, P. M., & Peter, J. (2011). Online communication among adolescents: An integrated model on its attraction, opportunities, and risks. *The Journal of Adolescent Health*, *48*(2), 121–127. doi:10.1016/j.jadohealth.2010.08.020 PMID:21257109

Vincent, J. (2005). Emotional Attachment to Mobile Phones: An Extraordinary Relationship. In L. Hamill & A. Lasen (Eds.), *Mobile World. Past, Present and Future* (pp. 95–104). London: Springer. doi:10.1007/1-84628-204-7_6

Wajcman, J., Bittman, M., & Brown, J. E. (2008). Families without borders: Mobile phone connectedness and work-home divisions. *Sociology*, *42*(4), 635–652. doi:10.1177/0038038508091620

Walz, K. (2012): Stress Related Issues Due to Too Much Technology: Effects on Working Professionals. *MBA Student Scholarship*. Retrieved from http://scholarsarchive.jwu.edu/mba_student/12

Warm, J. S., Parasuraman, R., & Matthews, G. (2008). Vigilance requires hard mental work and is stressful. *Human Factors*, *50*(3), 433–441. doi:10.1518/001872008X312152 PMID:18689050

Weil, M. M., & Rosen, L. D. (1997). *Technostress: Coping with Technology @Work, @Home, @Play*. New York: Wiley.

KEY TERMS

Communication Overload: A feeling of too much communication reaching a person. The Individual feels incapable to handle the incoming messages or calls.

Coping Strategies: Strategies that are used to handle a situation that is experienced as problematic, negative, or stressful.

Mobile Availability: The status of a person being reachable via mobile communication.

Mobile Communication: All forms of communication that are conducted using a mobile communication medium for textual, visual, or verbal interactions.

Parallel Communication: A verbal or text-based conversation with an absent person via mobile phone during the interaction with a face-to-face communication partner.

Perpetual Contact: The situation that a person is available to others all the time, mainly via mobile communication media.

Transactional Theory of Stress and Coping: An important theory of Lazarus and Cohen (1977) that discusses the process of stress experiences and coping as a transactional process that is strongly influenced by the individual perception of the situation and individual coping resources.

Chapter 6

The Fishtank Paradigm of Experience:
Merging Time, Space, Activities, Emotions, and People

Silvia Torsi
University of Trento, Italy

ABSTRACT

Time management as an important source of wellbeing is here described along with the opportunities to link this activity to physical space, contacts and mobile personal cloud. The user-centered design of a novel agenda is the theme of this chapter. Some user studies were carried on, concept design and rough evaluations followed. The fishtank paradigm of interaction is here presented. It overcomes the linear perception of time and provides a gradient of devices for attention starting from peripheral awareness to proper notification according to the urgency of the tasks to execute. The final aim of the project is to support prospective as like as autobiographical memory in order to live the present time at its' fullest.

INTRODUCTION

Time management is becoming an essential field in which major research efforts are being made (e.g. Google Now, Apple Siri). It is clear that the opportunities derived from mobile ICT, Web 2.0, GPS infrastructures, and mobile cloud technologies are increasing the possibilities to deliver novel lifestyle enhancements by optimizing the work, life, activities, interactions with communities, and personal lives of individuals. These material conditions provide the opportunity to set up new ways to perceive

DOI: 10.4018/978-1-5225-2061-0.ch006

time and manage daily life. The Witmee project described here (Torsi & Giunchiglia, 2015) maximizes the social and psychological potential of these possibilities (Figure 1). This paper introduces a new opportunity: to improve time management by combining a number of existing technologies into a single environment that can provide meaningful visualizations and a customizable level of peripheral awareness. Evidently, there are many existing tools for these tasks, but they are not integrated into a single device nor related to an individual's actions. The added value in centralizing tools is that the system can shadow the user and provide tangible support for daily life, without forcing users to to step across different applications in order to manage tasks. Current technologies are revealing unprecedented ways to support all the different facets, duties, social roles, interests, and multiple identities of individuals. In the same way, new forms of awareness are equally available: being conscious about peers and family location, group activities and all that will allow people to get synchronized (Tolmie, Pycock, Diggins, MacLean, & Karsenty, 2002). Accordingly, this richness of roles, relationships and possible activities can be effectively supported by a system that helps people to better coordinate activities of daily living (Torsi & Giunchiglia, 2015). The project originated from a desire to create a different kind of agenda to fulfil the needs of individuals when managing different aspects of their daily life.

Figure 1. A diagram of the overall aims of the project

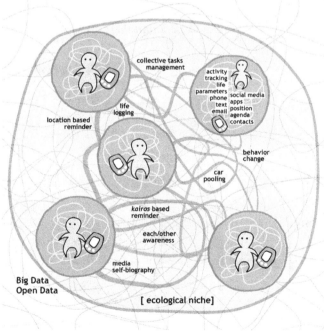

THE PROJECT TEAM

The research group consists in: an Artificial Intelligence/Semantics core that is to create meaningful entities that will sort, rank and manage the contents the system has already collected. Afterwards, a development core integrates the computational resources and relates them to the metaphor that the system offers, and a design core responsible for the delivery of visualizations and notifications (Figure 2). The AI and the design cores work in parallel to determine the overall vision of what is desired: a virtual life companion helping users to manage daily living in the interplays across working activities, personal life and relationships. The development core, then, integrates the platforms, the infrastructures, and the applications involved in the system to produce a working prototype. This contribution focuses on the design core made by an HCI researcher and three computer scientists.

The AI/Semantics Core

The work started with the effort of the AI scientists to combine data in innovative ways, in order to create combinations that, converted into suggestions, awareness, and logistic support, would really improve the user's quality of life. Their task was to find ways to finalize, reduce, sort, organize, combine, and present Big Data all the while having in mind the quality of daily life of an individual as the central objective.

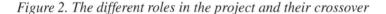

Figure 2. The different roles in the project and their crossover

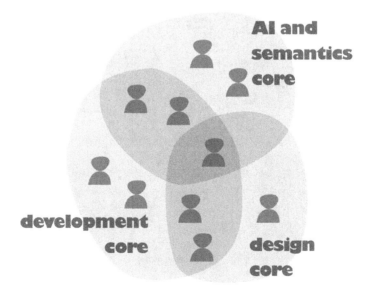

Figure 3. The main areas of interest for the AI/semantics core

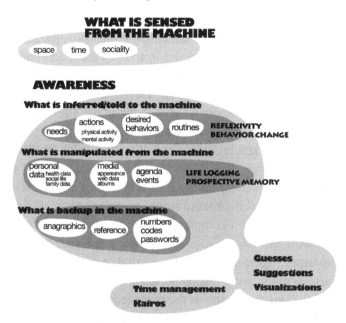

The AI core created weighted taxonomies in order to combine them in original ways, as the system needed to recognize the user and the context. Dynamic data had to be the outcome of the different variables. Time, space, people, activity, life parameters and environment were the variables through which the system had to compute what was known about the user, in order to provide effective suggestions. The system would continuously attempt to understand what the user is doing and learn from the user's behavior and explicit feedback. Similarly, the system has to provide dynamic management and presentation of contacts, which automatically reacts to data such as location, activity, plans, availability or proximity. Life parameters were also important in order to support healthy choices. Media was used to provide the fundamental data for the system to aggregate, combine, store, manage, and present information, in order for the user to build personal autobiographical memories and share them (Giunchiglia & Hume, 2013; Kim & Giunchiglia, 2012, 2013; Chenu Abente, Zaihrayeu & Giunchiglia, 2013; Zeni, Zaihrayeu & Giunchiglia, 2014).

The Design Core

The design core focused on user's needs, the development of the concept, user's modelling, and a scenario-based design (Torsi, 2015). Big Data can be a resource for a better living, but at present faces the risk of becoming information overload (Bawden & Robinson, 2009; Heyligen, 2004). The implementation core of this project was the following: gathering information from the user's parameters, friends', family's and colleagues' smartphones, and from open data, and combine them in order to convey to the user location-based reminders for optimizing the users' use of time and improve their quality of life. The Design core interests are centered on wellbeing, peace of mind and happiness of the individual. These are modeled from a cognitive perspective as a result of enjoying the present time to its fullest that can be found into the theorizations of *flow* (Csikszentmihalyi, 2013). The personal life of the user is then perceived as a continuous flow of life. For example, the life backup can be useful for lifelogging in order to fine-tune the future with the past and provide achievable steps in order to reach an objective.

The design core provided a complementary contribution in the design of the services offered with the help of user studies (focus groups in particular) and a theoretical framework (while analyzing the cultural origins of cognitive categories like: time, space, activity, emotions, especially when considered together). The intention was for the system to support the management of the past and the organization of the future (optimizing time, advanced planning, suggestions, etc.) in order to relieve the user from living in those dimensions, and to allow them to be fully present in the actual moment. Another important theoretical element was to direct

Figure 4. The design dimensions of the project

efforts into providing the user with the means to live single experiences, in which time, space, people, activities, and feelings are felt as a unique whole. The idea behind it was to subvert modern-Fordist time perception (Duncheon & Tierney, 2013; Hassard 2002) in favour of more human dimensions, like conviviality, experience, expanding present time, space/time, circularity (Harvey, 1989; Hodges, 2008) and so on. Another observation in regard to the actual framing of time as linear was that most people were overloaded by both daily duties (Brandimonte et al. 1996) and memories of the past (Rubin et al., 1986). From a distributed cognition perspective (Kirsh, 2013; Sutton, 2007) the project presented the necessity to provide support for both of them, in order to unburden the user from them and allow him to live the present time at its fullest (Csikszentmihalyi, 1990). The design core, therefore, developed a novel way to connect these functionalities with people and take into consideration their limited attention. The idea was to have an interface embodying tools ranging from peripheral awareness to direct notification (Alexanderson, 2004) for supporting the algorithms of the computer scientists.

RELATED WORK

The aim of the project was to provide a new purpose of smartphone-based services for maximizing the potential of the available infrastructures. Therefore, the design core (whose work is the theme of this chapter) crossed the main current paradigms related to this field, in order to deliver them in novel combinations and with understandable interaction styles. The following state of the art time management tools survey is more a design core search for insights rather than being an exhaustive review.

Google Now and Apple Siri

Literature describes Google Now and Apple Siri (Manjunath, 2014; Koubek, Procházka, & Šťastný, 2013), personal assistant tools that have similar features to our project intent. Google Now is an artificial intelligence personal assistance application that conveys information by combining user and context-situated information (weather, time, places, and paths). Google Now uses cards in order to display suggestions to the user; Apple Siri, instead, is a voice-controlled natural language interface. Its technology is based on tagging and combining locations, events, contacts etc., into information meaningful for the user. Thus, the objectives of the research were: (1) to integrate the existing features of Google Now and Siri with the services designed while working with the focus groups (2) to prototype and evaluate novel ways to convey the information, especially with an innovative paradigm of interaction and a set of tools ranging from awareness to notification.

Task Management Systems

Those are the tools to create, manage and be use as a support for prospective memory (Brandimonte, Einstein, McDaniel, 1986). Task management involves complex feelings, in which anxiety combines with being busy, perceived as a positive social value, along with feelings of inefficiency and low self-esteem (Lesher & Senger, 2011). In this sense, a new way to manage the tasks can be to allow personalization, offer heterogeneity, facilitate slowing down processes as an alternative to busyness, and encompass situated context factors. Among the vast landscape of multiplatform applications for these practices, Evernote seems to be one of the most successful (this claim also arose during the focus groups), especially in relation to its mobile cloud-based architecture, the richness of input devices, the choice of the formats for visualizing notes, and several possibilities to share and export them (Graham, 2011). In this direction, the use of tablets represents further enrichment by bringing specific and new, effective practices and actions, e.g. for annotating, storing and retrieving data (Buttfield-Addison, Lueg, Ellis, & Manning, 2012).

Mobile Cloud Computing

The main added value of cloud computing is the delivery of computational resources, data and services through the Internet, the most diffused network in the world. It is a pervasive technology in which infrastructures converge to provide shared services. Mobile cloud computing combines mobile computing, the Internet and cloud computing. It adds the use of cloud resources for processing and storage on a multi-platform range of tools (Qureshi, Ahmad, & Rafique 2011). From these technologies, new design potentials emerged (Amin, Bakar, & Al-Hashimi, 2013). The most important for our purposes is the possibility to combine contextual data, coming from physical environment, GPS or Big Data. In addition Personal Cloud delivers other orders of data that can be aggregated with the latter with the aim of increasing the quality of life of the owner. Data, the information stored in the user's tools (e.g. contacts, agenda, notes, profiles etc.), life parameters, personal information coming from the user's smartphone sensors, peers and family data, and resources coming from the environment. This set of architectures in our envisioned system lends itself to ongoing change and is capable of taking new shapes by recombination and re-computation, according modifications of the context.

Location Based Services

It is not possible to consider space as disconnected from self-consciousness, identity, practices, artifacts, emotions, cognition, relationships, and communities (Dourish,

2006). Cybercartography (Taylor, 2005) allows for this connection to occur by providing new material conditions. Sharing data for synchronizing people with each other is a major source for growing Social Capital, new practices, sensibilities, identities, (McCullough, 2006; 2007) social habits, and are sources of well being (Bilandzich & Foth, 2012). Some authors (Hochman & Manovich, 2013; Schwartz & Halegoua, 2014) raise the hypothesis that GPS based technologies provide novel forms of spatial intelligence and awareness, especially related to media geo-tagging. Data level of the single individual provides the unitary, modular, scalable set of measures from building a collective intelligence coming from individuals' data (Heyligen, 2004), and creating additional opportunities, such as the concept of *smart cities* (e.g.Caragliu, Del Bo, & Nijkamp, 2011). In this project, the primary aim was to create the building blocks, starting from the single individual and enabling him to access and produce added value throughout infrastructure-enabled practices. Some early examples of services now consolidated have been ridesharing (Furuhata, Dessouky, Ordóñez, Brunet, Wang, & Koenig, 2013), contacts' proximity detection (Hung, Hu, & Lee, 2013), location-based networks for tourism and applications based on the check in practice (Li, Sohn, Huang, & Griswold, 2008). It is possible also to model the cognitive and social expansion Web 2.0 that a digital localization has brought (Wilson, 2012; Schwartz & Halegoua, 2014; for a state of the art concept see Gartner, 2012).

Self-Tracking for Behavior Change

There are some relevant theoretical approaches about the possible supporting role of behavior change in ICT (e.g. Torsi, Wright, Mountain, Nasr, Mawson, & Rosser, 2010; Li, Dey & Forlizzi, 2011). An example of mapping devices across human physiological data is in Waltz (2012). Rooksby, Rost, Morrison, & Chalmers (2014) present interview studies that provide taxonomies about the main topics related to tracking practices: walking, physical exercise, food and drink, weight and size, sleep. They also list the main possible strategies related to tracking: directive, documentary, and diagnostic tracking. Some individuals measure themselves while seeking for positive feedback, while for others this is just a self-referential practice. It is also possible to list specific individual reasons for self-tracking (Conroy, Yang, & Maher, 2014). Regardless the reasons, there are other voices addressing the human contradictions, resistance, cognitive obstacles and potential dysfunctional behaviors that the *quantified self* brings with it (Waltz, 2012; Calvo & Peters, 2013; Kehr, Hassenzahl, Laschke, & Diefenbach, 2012).

Media Management Applications for Autobiographical Memory

Rather than just being analytical, memory is a constructive process through which the individual reinforces his own self, his models, and his schemata (Barclay p.95 in Rubin, 1986). The design implications follow: technologies might support: recollecting (re-living life experiences), reminiscing (having the same feelings), retrieving (finding them), reflecting (reviewing past experience, analyzing it from the present self's perspective), and remembering intentions (recalling delayed intentions, Sellen & Whittaker; 2010). Some authors (Petrelli & Whittaker; 2010; Whittaker, Kalnikaite, Petrelli, Sellen, Villar, Bergman, Clough, & Brockmeier 2012) show different practices specifically related to memories. Physical mementos are preferred for their physicality, or for the feelings of ownership, and assurance they provide while storing them safely in boxes, albums or drawers, for years on end. Younger generations, instead, (especially teenagers) are highly proficient to digital media and online sharing. These youngsters could not afford to save all this volume of media they produce in a physical format, thus, they use tags (Tsur & Rappoport; 2012), editing, sharing, posting, multi-platforms facilities and easy exportation of media across different applications (Abolfazli, Sanaei, Gani, Xia, & Yang, 2014). Consequently, the applications provide powerful means for easy media management (Kietzmann, 2012). Smartphones' digital picture taking and video shooting capabilities increase volume and introduce chances, immediacy and spontaneity (Whittaker et al., 2012). All of these elements contribute to extremely transparent and easy ways to engage in a process of reflective practice triggered by media (Bowen & Petrelli, 2011). The users can appreciate self-disclosure (e.g. by means of selfie practice: see Warfield, 2014) and being commented upon, liked, or republished, while maintaining and fostering relationships (Utz, 2015). Thus, those media hubs are based on a participatory culture, where people can be at the same time consumers, producers and distributors of media, such as videos on YouTube (Shifman, 2012). Flickr (Lerman & Jones, 2006) and pictures on Instagram (Hochman & Schwartz, 2012) were born as photo sharing Web 2.0 platforms, while maintaining the main ways to structure contracts and manage communication, like social browsing, commenting, editing, social tagging, etc. One interesting aspect of Instagram is the geo-temporal tagging, which identifies the pictures basing on time and the space in which they have been taken (Hochman & Schwartz, 2012). Contextually, users participate to new forms of shared narratives and evolution of cultures (Eco, 1990; Giaccardi, 2003). Mementos are not relegated into private boxes or family albums anymore (Petrelli & Whittaker; 2010) but tend to converge to grow individual identity and foster collective awareness (Kietzmann, 2012; Heyligen, 2004).

Novel Interaction Styles

With the propagation of touch screens as interaction tools for smartphones and tablets, the issue of novel approaches and insights toward affordance has become even more compelling, because new functionalities and practices require the creation of updated and effective conceptual models. In this frame, making efforts to mimic physical affordances appear to be the best way to proceed (Matei, Faiola, Wheatley, & Altom, 2012). Accordingly, the aesthetics of interaction (Overbeeke, Djajadiningrat, Hummels, Wensveen, & Prens, 2005) describe rich affordances providing positive experiences while meeting the perceptual-motor, cognitive and emotional skills of the user, and focusing on experience, enjoyment, expressiveness, identity and appropriation. Some authors provide means for conveying physicality into conceptual models and interaction styles (Löwgren, 2007; Elmqvist, Moere, Jetter, Cernea, Reiterer, & Jankun-Kelly, 2011; Jacob, Girouard, Hirshfield, Horn, Shaer, Solovey, & Zigelbaum, 2008). Inventories of multi-touch gestures for interactive surfaces are also listed in several studies (Hinrichs & Carpendale; 2011; Ruiz & Lank, 2011). In the Witmee project, the design core wanted to interpret the development of the system shadowing the user and supporting them in daily life activities by creating a set of ad hoc interaction styles. Metaphors had to address the (imagined) physicality of the tools, for example using perceptual modes to provide affordances, e.g. the *peephole* metaphor of interaction (Yee & Ka-Ping, 2006) that allows the user to manage large sizes of visual data even with the small screen of a Smartphone. This interaction style represents an interesting solution to overcome the smartphones' screen dimensions shortage. The *peephole* metaphor is based on the perceptual capacity of imagining a continuous and wider workspace than the screen used; one that the user cannot entirely see, but that affords navigation by moving the screen across a larger space. The combination of the *peephole* interaction style and the touch-based interaction can allow interesting metaphors, such as zooming back and forth on the (virtual) interaction space.

Soundscapes

A soundscape is a component of the natural acoustic environment, consisting of natural sounds, including animal calls and, for instance, the sound of thunder or of any other natural element. Soundscapes have an evolutionary value in that they provide background knowledge about the absence of risk for the animals (Krause, 2008). They are pleasant and calm. For example, the soundscape of a family can be reassuring, indicating ongoing routine without the intrusion of daily problems (Oleksik, 2008). Brazil & Fernstrom (2007) indicate some possible approaches in order to use this valuable tool in ICT. In the last 30 years, research has been conducted both in music theory and ICT on soundscapes. Mapping data with a peripheral value by means of soundscapes is a natural extension. The periphery of attention is the main perceptual device for this (Bakker et al., 2010). All perceptual systems, attention included, have an array of awareness levels, starting from its center (notifications, like changes in the environment) and sliding to the periphery (where nothing happens; this is the background awareness of tranquillity). Changing of individual or external conditions make these stimuli move back and forth throughout this gradient. Peripheral awareness and soundscapes are tightly related and provide a fundamental, ecological, evolutionary, conservative, calm and pleasant state of mind to human beings. It would be interesting to modulate soundscapes while providing transitions to be mapped from the interplay between peripheral awareness and notification. If peripheral awareness is a component of soundscape, earcons and auditory icons could be used to respond to notification. They have been compared by Garzonis, Jones, Jay, & O'Neill (2009), and sorted according to their specificities and potential functions.

Tactile Interfaces

Brazil & Fernstrom (2007) describe and analyze tactile cues as interaction tools. Frank A. Geldard (1957) made a theoretical presentation on touch, and described tactile interaction as of a crucial importance in the array of human perceptions. Geldard insists on the topic of information overload (oversaturation) for senses like ophthalmoception and audioception, by affirming that it is possible to make use of tactile interaction to address this issue. This author also points out the evolutionary value, the potential to provide background knowledge (i.e. peripheral awareness), and the richness, complexity, and reliability of tactile interfaces, with which it is possible to provide combinations of communicative patterns. In the past five years there has been some breakthrough research that combines peripheral awareness paradigms with tactile cues (e.g. Hemmert, 2008; Pielot & Oliveira, 2013; Brewster & Constantin; 2010) and even with auditory cues (Hoggan et al., 2009).

Considerations

The previously described areas were a source of inspiration for user interface design that also helped the team to focus on specific objectives and to share ideas, visions, and develop theoretical frameworks about the system. It became clear that this innovation would be an adjusted combination of ideas coming from all of the different fields listed above. This work also created a set of future directions, which will be described in due time.

THE USER STUDIES

An important stage of the project was the setting up of a cycle of three focus groups (specific for user experience design as described by Kuniavsky, 2003), each having different purposes: to ask people about how they perceive time, to make use of support for managing daily life, and to ask them about their routines, their most recurrent activities, and what facilitates or slows down these activities. Members of the design core ran the focus groups, presenting a set of "how to use" case scenarios that represented the new system in action in daily use contexts and asking the participants to speak freely about the credibility, the soundness, the level of identification and the appropriateness of each scenario. The opportunity was also taken to document individual's narrative pattern in order to evaluate the acceptance of the design concepts incorporated (Rosson & Carrol, 2008). Additionally, the design core performed a card-based design workshop (Halskov & Dalsgård; 2006).

The First Focus Group: Location Based Reminders

The first focus group explored prospective memory and evaluated the location-based reminder functionalities of the envisioned system. Each focus group trial lasted for ninety minutes and was based on a collective interview during which the participants were invited to comment upon the use case scenarios: the core concept behind Witmee. Two people ran the focus group: one who was asking questions and one who was facilitating the discussion. The participants were five graduate, Master and Ph.D. students of Computer Science, Cognitive Science and Social Sciences. The session was recorded, transcribed, and then the results were clustered according to affinities, similarities, listings and oppositions in order to establish certain patterns in their findings of what emerged. The participants agreed to make digital annotations for work and agenda activities, and use paper and sticky notes for their private lives. The multi-platform interoperability and the synchronization of electronic notes appeared to suit better work delayed intentions, while for the immediacy of home duties, shopping, and leisure time the handiness of paper and pencil worked better. People tend to stick reminders all over the house, in crucial places such as: the refrigerator, the entrance door, etc. Unfortunately, these notes can lose their impact over time or are misplaced. Besides, there are always the same things (e.g. wallet, keys, sunglasses etc.) to look for when exiting the house that are far more important. One other major source of memory load is food procuring and replacing, especially perishable food items like: bread, milk, et cetera. As for the delayed intentions, the participants seem to manage complex daily living activities by taking into consideration all the elements. In fact, our ideas about location-based reminders were in general well accepted in this focus group. Pieces of information like to know if the bus is late (or the weather forecast) before going out of home, self-organizing weekly electronic agenda, reciprocal awareness and synchronization of time and space with close friends and family members, automatic management of itineraries, self-regulating organization of phone calls, were also well received. The idea of a system that would record and present all relevant information within a context, in order for the user to better manage their daily life, duties and relationships was considered a good solution. Some issues (concerning privacy) were raised, though: a number of participants wished a very high level of personalization and easy ways to modify the settings according to the ongoing situation. Nevertheless, interesting observations were made about the possibility to convert everything into reminders and notifications, and also the opportunity to convert the old reminders into biographical information. In fact, reminders seem to have some capacity to evoke past emotions.

The Second Focus Group: *Kairos* Based Reminders

After the findings obtained from the first focus group, other information was needed for the project. The design core wanted to investigate the potential users' opinions about the construct of the "opportune moment" (*kairos*), as an alternative to schedules. The second focus group also lasted for ninety minutes and was run by an interviewer and a facilitator. It, too, was audio recorded, transcribed and analysed. Six participants were available, one from the area of community design, and the other five from computer sciences. *Kairos* (Fogg, 2003) is a theoretical construct from persuasive technology with reference to mobile ICT that provides ways to convey behaviors by focusing upon the opportune context. The interviewees in the focus group apparently reacted in a contradictory way to the scenarios, while raising issues on invasiveness more than on privacy. Accordingly, the form factor (the way information is conveyed, the rhetoric of the services) has a fundamental role for the acceptance of these aspects. Thus, it is more a matter of how suggestions are presented that makes them acceptable or considered irritating. This led the design core to think about intertwining persuading technologies and a newly developed novel *etiquette* to render applications *polite* and thus, to facilitate the daily life of people without disregarding discretion and a feeling of appropriateness. In particular, offering diverse possibilities and preferences instead of having an imperative tone, would be one possible way to respect the free will of the users and their need to feel in control. There are contingencies like: strikes, accidents on the pathway, postponed meetings and so on, that are good to know as soon as they occur, preferably before leaving home or soon after, or coincidences such as: a friend that is having a cup of coffee a few metres from where you are while you are returning from work, one's favorite shop having a sale, being close to one's partner's favorite gift shop a few hours before their birthday or an anniversary. Facebook birthdays, notifications, likes, comments are often used to maintain relationships at a distance that can be difficult to keep otherwise. The stress fell more on these aspects: context sensitive agenda functionalities, coordinating with friends, intimacy, relationships both close and remote compared to the ones presented in the first focus group. They were broadly accepted along with the restrictions described.

The Third Focus Group: Awareness

With this focus group, the qualitative research core wanted to elicit the attitude of the participants toward topics like: behavior change, self-efficacy, self-monitoring, or measuring and visualizing one's own physical activity, or working hours (or distractions e.g. social networks, news, personal emails, etc.), as well as balancing work and private life, cultivating interests and, in general, managing personal high level goals. The overall team wanted to incorporate these practices into the system (by implementing life logging and Big Data functionalities), but were aware of the ambiguous attitude people have toward self-tracking technologies (Kehr, Hassenzahl, Laschke, & Diefenbach, 2012; Waltz, 2012; Calvo and Peters, 2013) potentially bringing counterproductive reactions, and, as a consequence, disaffection toward the proposed systems. The focus group lasted ninety minutes and was audio taped, transcribed and analysed. There was one interviewer, one facilitator and five partici-pants from different areas and of different ages. The participants were asked what they monitor mostly about themselves: diabetes, dieting, sleeping hours. As far as workwise, they listed: computer time, posture, and breaks; some of them mentioned inefficiencies experienced from needing to coordinate themselves with co-workers. As expected, the scenarios were accepted, but with many comments; these results marked again the frailty of this ICT area and the ongoing need to find effective paradigms of use that would be widely accepted. Discretion, politeness, presenting possibilities instead of imposing, providing motivations, offering alternatives were some important elements of persuasion that the participants highlighted in order to appreciate those type of services. A lot of weight was also put on personalization: the system should take into account the user's personal and individual awareness of time and distance. For example, fifty minutes can be perceived very differently from person to person and vary according to the situation; in the same way, half a mile will be thought or felt in a diverse manner between two individuals.

The Design Workshop: The Right Moment

Along with the focus groups, the design core felt the need to ask our research group to deepen the concept of *kairos*, in order to use it in the best way possible. Four computer scientists were invited (e.g. Halskov & Dalsgård, 2006) in order to exploit what happenstance, coincidences, and accidents would mean in their personal life and to convert those insights into design concepts. An interviewer and a facilitator ran the workshop that was again audiotaped, transcribed and analysed. The results suggested that the systems hints should not interfere with the cycles of activities and that they should fit among tasks without causing distraction. Issues of personalization were brought: the opportune moment was felt as a personal matter. In this sense, the ability of the system to learn from its user was crucial. Different kinds of opportune moments were found. For example, when a tourist is visiting a city, he can receive notifications about restaurants for three reasons:

1. Notification of all the restaurants around him,
2. Notification of a good restaurant close to him, or
3. Notification of a good restaurant when the system knows the user is hungry.

As emerged from the focus group about awareness, people feel and perceive time, space and activities in individual and diverse ways. Therefore, they observed that personal perception of time intervals, or physical distances can be an issue when coordinating with others. Consequently, any system must account for such individual differences, and ought to learn from any negative feedback. In general, the finalization of a suggestion should be ranked somehow in order for the system to learn from it. It should know by itself that there are times and places when people do not want to be disturbed, even without switching on that function on the smartphone. There are at least three important specifications: for how long the user does not want to be interrupted, the importance of the issue or of the person that is calling, and the urgency of the topic.

Considerations

With these user studies the design core found interesting developments of the original ideas among the various participants. Notifications were well accepted, even though the participants considered switching them off at times. The highest possible levels of personalization were requested, as well as the option to switch off parts of a service, a whole service, or all even all of them. Unexpectedly, the issue of privacy did not affect a lot the evaluation of our scenarios, whilst participants shared explicit resistance to the idea of self-tracking feedback. We realized that the participants rely a lot upon the ability of the system to learn from the user, and they have expectations regarding this ongoing symbiosis between the system and the user. Our tools to increase awareness of others, coordination, presence, intimacy, and relationships were welcomed. After analyzing the overall focus groups and the design workshop, the team delved into understanding the expectations and the needs of the participants of the services that were being considered for development.

THE EMERGED DESIGN SPACE

After selecting a set of services from the user studies, the design core had to provide ideas for building a conceptual model and a set of visualization tools for delivering the services offered by the system.

The focus groups raised several issues regarding the tone, the appropriateness and the politeness of the way the system made suggestions to the user. The HCI researcher tried to interpret the need of the focus group participants to have control over a system that would otherwise risk being obtrusive, irritating or inopportune.

The initial idea was to make the system looking like a human cartoon, but according to Lachman (1997), anthropomorphic interfaces involve attention mechanisms, social rules, attributions of meaning and investments that could interfere with the interaction. The personification of a system can give the user an initial perception of inferiority, that result in bestowing negative feelings toward the intelligence of the system, distracting attention from the needs of interaction, be involuntarily grotesque, and cause aggression and anxiety. Lachman (1997) introduced the possibility of making use of animism to develop interaction paradigms. In animism all things in the world have a spiritual agency (i.e. soul, spirit, intelligence, perception, sensitivity, communication skills, etc.). Animistic interfaces allow the user to interact with the system with scalable levels of attention, allowing them to shift the focus from the background to the foreground with greater elasticity than that of humanlike avatars. Lifelike behaviors, small events, light variations, sound signals or vibration cues can be used effectively in the paradigm of animism (Lachman, 1997). The intelligence poured into things is also consistent with situated cognition (Kirsh, 2013), and with the construct of *nonhuman agencies* (Jacob et al., 2008). Examples in HCI are lifelike tactile vibration (Brewster & Costantin, 2010) and auditory displays (Roginska, 2013).

Hence, in order to answer one of the main tenets of the focus group participants, unobtrusiveness was identified with peripheral awareness, and politeness with an organism living in symbiosis with the user.

Therefore, we decided to use soundscapes and natural sounds, lifelike vibration cues, objects and animations in order to present the metaphor of living and taking its inspiration from life itself (and appropriateness) from user's data, parameters and behaviors. Accordingly, Lackmann (1997) stresses upon the fact that, when humans walk down the street and see buses and taxis, or hear sirens and dogs barking, usually this is not to be considered an overload of information. The environment around us produces a whole set of visual, kinaesthetic, or tactile information, providing background knowledge of the environment.

The aim was to design and evaluate an interface that provides notifications in an array of non-obtrusive cues. In particular, there could be sets of interaction styles starting from peripheral awareness and ending in a direct notification. The scientific ground of this vision is to consider these gradients ranging from inattention to full attention as an evolutionary, conservative, function of human cognition. For example the periphery of the visual cone is involved into controlling the context (of either the environment or the background) thus preventing accidents (Gibson, 1966). If something happens in the periphery of the visual cone, we immediately react bringing that element into the centre of our attention.

From the HCI perspective, the conceptual model of symbiosis means to create an interaction paradigm ranging from peripheral awareness to notification while ensuring to the minimum that the interaction is neither unnecessarily nor obtrusive or irritating. The information that the system provides to the user can be categorized between two extremes:

1. Notifications; providing the foreground knowledge, with a request for an immediate action (e.g. to modify a user's path toward the office in order to pay a bill due in 24 hours), and
2. Peripheral awareness, providing background knowledge (calm technologies).

The peripheral awareness lies at the boundary between inattention and attention. It is information with non-urgent request of action: the user's daughter just left her volleyball training and is going home. The Witmee dialogue with the user can provide awareness about relatives, friends and close colleagues, and reminders of various kinds:

1. Things to do with a close deadline,
2. Odds to make things the user ought to do for which there are space-time conditions, or
3. Things the user should and can do easily with a minor deviation from their path (location-based reminders).

An example of a *kairos*-based reminder is the system telling the user after work that friends are gathered just a few blocks away. Another case is informing the user after work that they are running out of bread, or milk, or that the day after is an important data such as the stepmother's birthday and that the user is in the vicinity of her favorite shop. Background knowledge is equally important. There is a need to store complex spatial-temporal-activity-social patterns occurring within a user's family in order to enhance the coordination and optimization of resources. Another exemplar chance for the system to improve the quality of life of its user is to provide reciprocal awareness among two or more people having arranged an appointment. The behaviors and movements of each of them will allow the computation, notification, and benefit of moving the time of the appointment if those involved are running late.

The design core intended to create a set of different media: soundscapes (Krause, 2008), auditory displays (Roginska, 2013), life like animistic and symbiotic organisms (Lackmann, 1997; Raghunath, Narayanaswami, & Pinhanez, C, 2003), peripheral or notification vibration cues (Pielot, M., & Oliveira, R. D., 2013, Hemmert, 2008; Brewster & Brown, 2004; McLean, 2008). The idea was to make use of them in order for the user to always receive perceptual cues about their parameters, duties, or family life. The range started from: "everything is ok" and moved toward: "your partner will be at home in forty minutes", and arrived at: "your colleague is waiting for you in room 24D in the next five minutes". Those parameters would change and move according to the other's behavior, whilst minimizing dead times and optimizing *kairos*. Those tools were aimed to provide support for prospective memory (or *delayed intentions*, Brandimonte et al., 1996). The main goal was to free the individual from living in the future and allow them to enjoy the present time at its fullest. It can also provide and organize the media backup for an automatic construction and contextualization of autobiographical memory (Chalfen, 1989; Andrews, Paniagua, & Torsi, 2011; Rubin, 1986). In this way, it is possible to create a system that aggregates information in order to build a consistent life story of the individual (Bruner, 1987; 1991).

EARLY PROTOTYPING AND EVALUATION

After selecting and ranking a range of services from the scenario evaluation, the design core moved towards the initial steps of interface design. Three explorative rough prototypes were produced and informally evaluated. This phase sought to provide general directions for a more focused prototyping phase. Initially, there was a lot of sketching, especially during the first iteration, which was made with paper prototypes (Snyder, 2003), broadly summarizing some of the most central scenarios of interaction. The second set of prototypes was made with video animations and the third by means of diagrams and visual descriptions. Evaluations had a group-based focus, consisting in questionnaires and free discussions. Three cycles of prototyping and evaluation guided ideas of what potential users would like to have, and the team proceeded using the elements that the participants liked the most from each of the prototypes.

The First Prototype

The first prototype was aimed at condensing an experience into a single whole, represented by spheres of different sizes, colors, and textures. The dimension time can be considered as a cultural construction based on artifacts (like the clock). The attempt was directed from overcoming linear perception of time and space as an abstract and computational dimension, the sharp division between work, family, relationships and leisure, and the mechanization of one's daily life. The aim was to provide an artifact for novel ways to perceive time and the related self (Csikszent-mihalyi, 1990; Damasio, 2012) and to allow people to live more intensely during the present time by providing supporting tools for prospective (Brandimonte et al., 1996) and autobiographical (Rubin, 1986) memory. The design core sought ways to represent living in the present time with its concretion of temporal, spatial, activity emotions, and relate the dimensions as a unitary whole (Dewey, 2005; Wright & McCarthy, 2004). Time, space, people, activities, tools and emotion had to converge in a single whole experience. Therefore the HCI researcher made sketches on *bubbles* (McDuff, Karlson, Kapoor, Roseway, & Czerwinski, 2012), containing the representations of the described dimensions (Figure 4). Sets of complex experiences were visualized in an alternative way with respect to linear time so that to convey the idea of single unities in which the elements of the experience converged. The objective of the first paper prototype was to attempt to provide a novel visualization that allow space, time, people, activity, mood and experience to converge in a single visual unit (Figures 5, 6 and 7).

The early paper prototype described was, then, evaluated. The results were encouraging, but nevertheless there was a need to provide new sources of richness for the interaction styles developed. In particular there was a desire to strengthen the idea of providing a symbiotic form of life, taking its parameters and level of suitability from the overall data. Not wishing to start from scratch, there was a desire to add more elements of sense in order to fully deploy the expressive and support potential of the system. This crystallized the idea of providing the user with isomorphic visualizations of their agenda, so they can choose the preferred solution according to personal taste or the ongoing needs of the day, week, or month.

The Second Prototype

The second prototype followed another interaction paradigm. The main concept was not new for HCI literature: to visualize data by means of an aquarium (Gordon-Beckford, 2015). Several attempts were made using paper prototypes, and a video animation was ultimately selected to present and evaluate the new vision (Figures 8, 9 and 10). This took inspiration from some experiences in ICT employing the

Figure 5. This drawing shows a portion of the first paper prototype. It describes how the user can obtain the magnification of an activity in terms of a sequence of different actions he needs to carry on. The larger is the sphere, the more time the activity takes

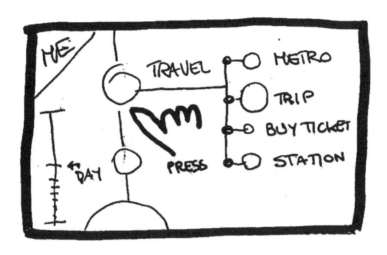

Figure 6. This is a detail of a table representing the first paper prototype. It shows a unity of experience and the related information radiating from it by means of smaller, interconnected sub-unities. The use of fingers is a design technique, as the team sought to develop ways to manually exploit, analyze, and obtain information by means of specific touchscreen manipulating options

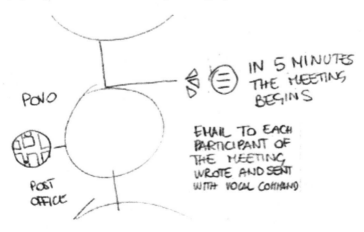

Figure 7. This table shows the weekly overview of activities designed for the first paper prototype. Here it is possible to observe the effort required to take a step forward from the linear visualization of time

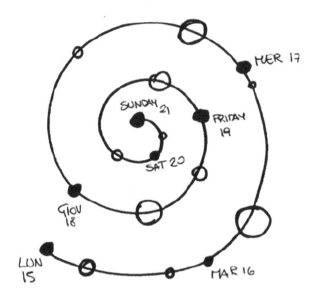

metaphor of the aquarium. The first game is *The Happy Aquarium* on Facebook, in which the user has to nourish and care for the fish in their aquarium (Di Loreto & Gouaich, 2010). Another example is the famous *Tamagotchi* portable electronic game of the past decade (Desmet & Hassenzahl, 2012). An important contribution was made with the collective game *Fish'n Steps*, (Lin, Mamykina, Lindtner, De-lajoux, & Strub, 2006) in which large screens in the canteen of a workplace show the overall weekly walking activity of the employers in each room. The rich world of aquarium gave us the possibility to address different and numerous data. In the aquarium metaphor, the fish represented complex entities of experiences (like the bubbles in the first prototype). In the same way, we used underwater plants to show specific exercises such as: steps, stairs, lifting weights and every activity measurable by motion sensors like accelerometer, pedometer and gyroscope. Thus, plants stand for personal objectives (Consolvo, KIasnja, McDonald, Avrahami, Froehlich, LeGrand, Libby, Mosher & Landay, 2008). The clarity of water represents mood and the color is for excitement. All the visualizations in the aquarium can be performed in two ways: by notification and by peripheral awareness. They represent the result of algorithms situated between relevance and urgency.

Relevance is given by from the context. The aquarium is a complex visualization summarizing the awareness of where the user is, which event they participate to, the people with which they surrounded themselves, the objective they aim to achieve and the activity they are involved in. Fish floating into the water represent *unity of experience* and are differentiated by race, color, size, and behavior. Almost all the communicative issues of the system can be represented and interpreted by the fish metaphor; they symbolize: place, time, activities, and the individuals involved. They silently swim on the aquarium screensaver and have a number of associated audible features like: bubbles, water flowing, and the fish knocking at the screen for notification.

This visualization had to be an animation taking its life from the user's data and parameters, and it had to run like a screensaver on the smartphone screen. The aquarium metaphor is intended to be a screensaver and the interface appears as a silent and slow-moving visualization consisting in fish, plants, water, colors, shapes, and animations, in order to monitor, give feedback, notify, provide awareness, and reassure. The aquarium is activated by the data and the parameters it receives from the user, their contacts, and their surrounding environment. The aquarium is made of several visual elements, which can be seen at a glance as peripheral awareness or even during down moments. Entities can leave the background and come to the foreground of attention and "become" a notification if there are emergencies, or if there are spatial-temporal coincidences for important or pleasurable activities (Figures 11, 12, 13). This second prototyping phase was supported by a video animation that was presented to groups of potential users to be evaluated. Following the description of the system and the projection of the video, there was a free discussion

Figure 8. The concept of the aquarium includes: the clarity of the water (mood and excitement), the plants (objectives and behavior change) and the fish (complex evolving entities)

Figure 9. One of the main objectives of the system is to provide connectivity between members of a family, friends and close colleagues, in order to optimize reciprocal coordination

Figure 10. In order to maximize the expressivity and the visualization potential of the complex and multifaceted aspects of the user's identity, lifestyle, interests, etc., the fish can change its shape, size, and color

and an individual questionnaire to fill in. The results were encouraging (Torsi & Giunchiglia, 2015). People liked the idea of assigning tasks and events to flowing fish and expressed them with this visualization. The decision was taken to create further visualizations with the same behavior but with different items: jewels instead of fish. This was done for graphic design and personal preference purposes (Consolvo et al., 2008).

Figure 11. This is a diagram explaining the constituting elements of an entity that is visualized as a fish. Effort was made in order to maximize the unitary aspects of the experience, by providing symbiotic fish that are taking their healthy appearance from user's parameters

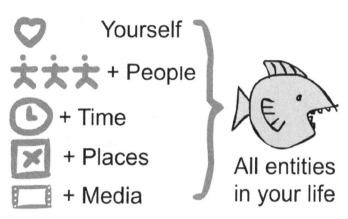

Figure 12. Two examples of situations in which plants can be used: counting steps and reading ebooks. Increasing exercise and behavior change can be supported by the system giving feedback to the user to help them to improve their lifestyle

The Third Prototype

The new concept was going to take the best from the two previous prototypes while maintaining what had already been achieved. The design core wanted to preserve the convergence of time, space, people, activity, environment and emotion in a single

Figure 13. Notifications can be used to maximize kairos, e.g. suggesting the user modified itineraries to buy groceries, cat food or to meet friends that are in the vicinity

visual unity, and made a trial with simpler, less lively objects that were still reactive and dynamic, and whose behaviors could be altered according to new parameters. Different marbles, each with its color, shape and behavior, were sketched floating in the space of the device, ranging from peripheral awareness behavior to notification. The representation of goals in terms of plants and the transparency of the background for mood or excitement were preserved. The marbles were tools representing the user's "entities". The *peephole* method of visualization (Yee, 2003) was maintained as well. This paradigm of interaction makes use of the human capability to imagine a larger space, partially unavailable to the human eye, where things can move freely. This space can be accessed and explored by accessing the smallest window of the device, i.e. its monitor, by moving the screen around this larger, virtual space. This is an effective metaphor because it leverages the human capacity of imagining things that do not always fit into the visual cone (Gibson, 1966). It is possible to go ahead with this visualization by finding cues for ranking the behavior and visibility of our entities (marbles), that is by shifting non-attention, peripheral awareness to attention. With the use of the peephole modality it is possible to naturally map ranges across these three states of human excitement. Marbles would be small and slowly float within the interface area, then gradually become larger and louder when they, in turn, are converted to notifications. This interplay was to be supported by applying past and current research on hearing and tactile displays. Hence, the perceived space

Figure 14. In this example, the visualization of the gradient between peripheral aware-
ness and notification is visualized in terms of transparency or of density of colour

of the screen was larger than the device, and ideally the screen could be used to explore this larger space of interaction, rather than a peephole. The behavior of the marbles in the peripheral awareness mode would be to bounce across this enlarged, virtual space, until they gradually and ultimately shift into the notification modalities. A perceptual path towards attention was needed for when the system asked for immediate behavioral response. A visual analysis on the possible appearance of the marbles was made, in order to maximize the choices for them to be connected to entities (Figure 14).

Future Research Directions

The following step could be the creation of usage case scenarios based on storyboards for the next evaluation stage. At present, the team intends to conduct systematic research on the multi-modal range of communication cues available, ranging from in-attention, peripheral awareness, polite suggestions, and all the way to notifications. This will include not only video animation but also sounds and vibrations. There is a desire to pursue iterations of design and evaluation of a systems ecology that supports contextual information, coordination, Big Data, Life Logging, and a user's parameter data into a multi-platform ecology of artifacts. The team envisage the future system to be integrated into smart watches, tangible user interfaces (Valdes, Eastman, Grote, Thatte, Shaer, Mazalek, Brygg & Konkel, 2014), jewelry (Wallace, 2007), textiles (Karahanoğlu & Çiğdem, 2011; Kan et al., 2015), or interactive materials (e.g. moldable) (Ishii, Lakatos, Bonanni, & Labrune, 2012), with the scope of broadening the array of communication potential of the system and obtain more channels of peripheral awareness and natural interactions.

CONCLUSION

The project focuses on smartphones unexpressed potential to capitalize upon computation, mobility and connection to provide novel opportunities for research in HCI. The project aims at cross-referencing data sensed from the Smartphone with geographical data, agenda, contacts and the data held by a user's relatives, friends and close colleagues in order to provide suggestions aimed at improving the user's quality of life. At the moment, there is a large number of applications across numerous platforms, but it is still possible to imagine the existing need for systematic research into a deeper, new potential usages of smartphone applications: those related to sensors, GPS based technology, user input, agenda, contacts, home automation, medical devices, or integrated services, to name just a few. The design core of the project started this task with a few focus groups during their daily life, intentionally broad, in order to capture the widest notions of participants' recurring frustrations and ideas for improving their routines. Regarding the concept of new services, Distributed Cognition was the starting paradigm. This model, by means of Situated Reasoning, provides a view over human cognition as common for different possible artifacts, tools, objects and elements of the environment. Therefore, people can receive help from manipulating external representations in order to make decisions and be supported while doing that. In fact, people are able to access information into a geographical context. This ongoing interaction offers the possibility to create new chances for improving the human interaction in connection with the environment. On the one hand, connectivity and computation in motion and on the other hand, the integration of digital information represent further steps towards enforcing situated reasoning. The following task was to shape a conceptual model encompassing all these functionalities in order to deliver them to the user. Smartphones cross-sensing capability (awareness of the activities of the user's close friends and colleagues, the user's favorite places, and their activities and duties, in combination with email, texts, and Web 2.0), enriches further the potential for adopting tactile and auditory peripheral awareness or notification systems and novel ways for users to communicate with their devices (e.g. gesture-based). A life-like environment that emulates the user's data and parameters was chosen and this one also showed information about relatives, friends and close colleagues. While looking for interaction styles, the use of earcons and tactons is considered the most relevant option. In this direction, the design core considered a continuum or interplay between various gradients that are ranging from peripheral awareness to direct notification. The blurry area between attention and non-attention represents a set of information that must be kept in mind, as it may become urgent or important. While the individual moves through the environment, complex sets of events take place, and notification in motion represent a novel challenge to be incorporated into the ecological cycles occurring when one is moving around physical space. Also, the resilient and context sensitive communication opportunities that are available on smartphones increase and push forward new levels and dimensions of the human sharing of content, relating to one another, and spreading information (Torsi, 2013). These are additional opportunities that enrich the environment and can have a role in the metabolism of consciousness while cyclically coupling with the environment (Torsi, 2015).

ACKNOWLEDGMENT

This work wouldn't be possible without the supporting tutoring of Prof. Fausto Giunchiglia (University of Trento). The research leading to these results has received partial funding from the European Community's Seventh Framework Program (FP7/2007-2013) under grant agreement n. 600854 Smart Society: hybrid and diversity-aware collective adaptive systems: where people meet machines to build smarter societies http://www.smart-society-project.eu/.

REFERENCES

Abolfazli, S., Sanaei, Z., Gani, A., Xia, F., & Yang, L. T. (2014). Rich mobile applications: Genesis, taxonomy, and open issues. *Journal of Network and Computer Applications*, *40*, 345–362. doi:10.1016/j.jnca.2013.09.009

Alexanderson, P. (2004). Peripheral awareness and smooth notification: the use of natural sounds in process control work. In *Proceedings of the third Nordic conference on Human-computer interaction* (pp. 281-284). New York: ACM. doi:10.1145/1028014.1028057

Amin, M. A., Bakar, K. B. A., & Al-Hashimi, H. (2013). A review of mobile cloud computing architecture and challenges to enterprise users. In *GCC Conference and Exhibition (GCC), 2013 7th IEEE* (pp. 240-244). Piscataway, NJ: IEEE. doi:10.1109/IEEEGCC.2013.6705783

Andrews, P., Paniagua, J., & Torsi, S. (2013). Katies Swiss Trip: A Study of Personal Event Models for Photo Sharing. *International Journal on Semantic Web and Information Systems*, *9*(3), 42–56. doi:10.4018/ijswis.2013070103

Bakker, S., van den Hoven, E., & Eggen, B. (2010). Design for the Periphery. *EuroHaptics*, *2010*, 71.

Bawden, D., & Robinson, L. (2009). The dark side of information: Overload, anxiety and other paradoxes and pathologies. *Journal of Information Science*, *35*(2), 180–191. doi:10.1177/0165551508095781

Bilandzic, M., & Foth, M. (2012). A review of locative media, mobile and embodied spatial interaction. *International Journal of Human-Computer Studies*, *70*(1), 66–71. doi:10.1016/j.ijhcs.2011.08.004

Bowen, S., & Petrelli, D. (2011). Remembering today tomorrow: Exploring the human-centred design of digital mementos. *International Journal of Human-Computer Studies*, *69*(5), 324–337. doi:10.1016/j.ijhcs.2010.12.005

Brandimonte, M., Einstein, G. O., & McDaniel, M. A. (1996). Prospective Memory. Theory and Applications. Mahwah, NJ: Lawrence Erlbaum Associates.

Brazil, E., & Fernstrom, M. (2007). *Investigating ambient auditory information systems.* Academic Press.

Brewster, S., & Brown, L. M. (2004b). Tactons: structured tactile messages for non-visual information display. In *Proceedings of the fifth conference on Australasian user interface* (vol. 28, pp. 15-23). Australian Computer Society, Inc.

Brewster, S., & Constantin, A. (2010). Tactile feedback for ambient awareness in mobile interactions. In *Proceedings of the 24th BCS Interaction Specialist Group Conference* (pp. 412-417). British Computer Society.

Brewster, S. A., & Brown, L. M. (2004a). Non-visual information display using tactons. In CHI'04 extended abstracts on Human factors in computing systems (787-788). New York: ACM. doi:10.1145/985921.985936

Bruner, J. (1987). Life as narrative. *Social Research*, 11–32.

Bruner, J. (1991). The narrative construction of reality. *Critical Inquiry*, *18*(1), 1–21. doi:10.1086/448619

Buttfield-Addison, P., Lueg, C., Ellis, L., & Manning, J. (2012). Everything goes into or out of the iPad: the iPad, information scraps and personal information management. In *Proceedings of the 24th Australian Computer-Human Interaction Conference* (pp. 61-67). New York: ACM. doi:10.1145/2414536.2414546

Calvo, R. A., & Peters, D. (2013). The irony and re-interpretation of our quantified self. In *Proceedings of the 25th Australian Computer-Human Interaction Conference: Augmentation, Application, Innovation, Collaboration* (pp. 367-370). New York: ACM. doi:10.1145/2541016.2541070

Caragliu, A., Del Bo, C., & Nijkamp, P. (2011). Smart cities in Europe. *Journal of Urban Technology, 18*(2), 65–82. doi:10.1080/10630732.2011.601117

Chalfen, R. (1987). *Snapshot versions of life*. Madison, WI: University of Wisconsin Press.

Chenu-Abente, R., Zaihrayeu, I., & Giunchiglia, F. (2013). A Semantic-Enabled Engine for Mobile Social Networks. In ESWC (Satellite Events) (pp. 298-299). doi:10.1007/978-3-642-41242-4_50

Conroy, D. E., Yang, C. H., & Maher, J. P. (2014). Behavior change techniques in top-ranked mobile apps for physical activity. *American Journal of Preventive Medicine, 46*(6), 649–652. doi:10.1016/j.amepre.2014.01.010 PMID:24842742

Consolvo, S., Klasnja, P., McDonald, D. W., Avrahami, D., Froehlich, J., LeGrand, L., & Landay, J. A. et al. (2008). Flowers or a robot army? encouraging awareness & activity with personal, mobile displays. In *Proceedings of the 10th international conference on Ubiquitous computing* (pp. 54-63). New York: ACM.

Csikszentmihalyi, M. (2013). *Flow: The psychology of happiness*. New York: Random House.

Damasio, A. (2012). *Self comes to mind: Constructing the conscious brain*. New York: Vintage.

Desmet, P., & Hassenzahl, M. (2012). Towards happiness: Possibility-driven design. In *Human-computer interaction: The agency perspective* (pp. 3–27). Berlin: Springer. doi:10.1007/978-3-642-25691-2_1

Dewey, J. (2005). *Art as experience*. London: Penguin.

Di Loreto, I., & Gouaich, A. (2011). Facebook Games: The Point Where Tribes And Casual Games Meet. *GET'10: International Conference Game and Entertainment Technologies*.

Dourish, P. (2006, November). Re-space-ing place: place and space ten years on. In *Proceedings of the 2006 20th anniversary conference on Computer supported cooperative work* (pp. 299-308). New York: ACM. doi:10.1145/1180875.1180921

Duncheon, J. C., & Tierney, W. G. (2013). Changing conceptions of time implications for educational research and practice. *Review of Educational Research*.

Eco, U. (1990). *Drift and Unlimited Semiosis* (Vol. 1). Indiana University.

Elmqvist, N., Moere, A. V., Jetter, H. C., Cernea, D., Reiterer, H., & Jankun-Kelly, T. J. (2011). Fluid interaction for information visualization. *Information Visualization*.

Fogg, B. J. (2003). *Persuasive Technology: Using Computers to Change What We Think and Do*. San Francisco, CA: Morgan Kauffman.

Furuhata, M., Dessouky, M., Ordóñez, F., Brunet, M. E., Wang, X., & Koenig, S. (2013). Ridesharing: The state-of-the-art and future directions. *Transportation Research Part B: Methodological, 57*, 28–46. doi:10.1016/j.trb.2013.08.012

Gartner, G., & Ortag, F. (2012). *Advances in location-based services*. New York: Springer. doi:10.1007/978-3-642-24198-7

Garzonis, S., Jones, S., Jay, T., & O'Neill, E. (2009, April). Auditory icon and earcon mobile service notifications: intuitiveness, learnability, memorability and preference. In *Proceedings of the SIGCHI Conference on Human Factors in Computing Systems* (pp. 1513-1522). New York: ACM. doi:10.1145/1518701.1518932

Geldard, F. A. (1957). Adventures in tactile literacy. *The American Psychologist, 12*(3), 115–124. doi:10.1037/h0040416

Giaccardi, E. (2003). *Principles of metadesign: Processes and levels of co-creation in the new design space* (Dissertation). University of Plymouth.

Gibson, J. J. (1966). *The senses considered as perceptual systems*. Boston: Houghton Mifflin Company.

Giunchiglia, F., & Hume, A. (2013). A distributed entity directory. In *Extended Semantic Web Conference* (pp. 291-292). Berlin: Springer.

Gordon-Beckford, A. (2015). *Clinical Benefits of Aquarium Design*. Retrieved from http://www.sbid.org/2013/09/clinical-benefits-of-aquarium-design/

Graham, K. (2011). TechMatters: Happily "Evernote" After: Storing and Sharing Research in the Cloud. *LOEX Quarterly, 38*(1), 4.

Halskov, K., & Dalsgård, P. (2006). Inspiration card workshops. In *Proceedings of the 6th conference on Designing Interactive systems* (pp. 2-11). New York: ACM. doi:10.1145/1142405.1142409

Harvey, D. (1989). *The condition of postmodernity*. Oxford, UK: Blackwell.

Hassard, J. (2002). Essai: Organizational time; modern, symbolic and postmodern reflections. *Organization Studies, 23*(6), 885–894. doi:10.1177/0170840602236010

Hemmert, F. (2008). Ambient Life: Permanent Tactile Life-like Actuation as a Status Display in Mobile Phones. Proc. of the 21st annual NEW YORK: ACM symposium on User Interface Software and Technology (UIST).

Hinrichs, U., & Carpendale, S. (2011). Gestures in the wild: studying multi-touch gesture sequences on interactive tabletop exhibits. In *Proceedings of the SIGCHI Conference on Human Factors in Computing Systems* (pp. 3023-3032). New York: ACM. doi:10.1145/1978942.1979391

Hochman, N., & Manovich, L. (2013). Zooming into an Instagram City: Reading the local through social media. *First Monday, 18*(7). doi:10.5210/fm.v18i7.4711

Hochman, N., & Schwartz, R. (2012, June). Visualizing instagram: Tracing cultural visual rhythms.*Proceedings of the Workshop on Social Media Visualization (Soc-MedVis) in conjunction with the Sixth International AAAI Conference on Weblogs and Social Media (ICWSM–12)*, 6-9.

Hodges, M. (2008). Rethinking times arrow Bergson, Deleuze and the anthropology of time. *Anthropological Theory, 8*(4), 399–429. doi:10.1177/1463499608096646

Hoggan, E., Raisamo, R., & Brewster, S. A. (2009, November). Mapping information to audio and tactile icons. In *Proceedings of the 2009 international conference on Multimodal interfaces* (pp. 327-334). New York: ACM. doi:10.1145/1647314.1647382

Hung, Y. H., Hu, P. C., & Lee, W. T. (2013, August). Improving the design and adoption of travel websites: An user experience study on travel information recommender systems.*5th IASDR International Conference.*

Ishii, H., Lakatos, D., Bonanni, L., & Labrune, J. B. (2012). Radical atoms: Beyond tangible bits, toward transformable materials. *Interactions, 19*(1), 38-51.

Jacob, R. J., Girouard, A., Hirshfield, L. M., Horn, M. S., Shaer, O., Solovey, E. T., & Zigelbaum, J. (2008). Reality-based interaction: a framework for post-WIMP interfaces. In *Proceedings of the SIGCHI conference on Human factors in computing systems* (pp. 201-210). New York: ACM. doi:10.1145/1357054.1357089

Kan, V., Fujii, K., Amores, J., Zhu Jin, C. L., Maes, P., & Ishii, H. (2015). Social textiles: Social affordances and icebreaking interactions through wearable social messaging. In *Proceedings of the Ninth International Conference on Tangible, Embedded, and Embodied Interaction* (pp. 619-624). New York: ACM. doi:10.1145/2677199.2688816

Karahanoğlu, A., & Erbuğ, Ç. (2011). Perceived qualities of smart wearables: determinants of user acceptance. In *Proceedings of the 2011 Conference on Designing Pleasurable Products and Interfaces* (p. 26). New York: ACM. doi:10.1145/2347504.2347533

Kehr, F., Hassenzahl, M., Laschke, M., & Diefenbach, S. (2012). A transformational product to improve self-control strength: the chocolate machine. In *Proceedings of the SIGCHI Conference on Human Factors in Computing Systems* (pp. 689-694). New York: ACM. doi:10.1145/2207676.2207774

Kim, P. H., & Giunchiglia, F. (2012). Life logging practice for human behavior modeling. In *2012 IEEE International Conference on Systems, Man, and Cybernetics (SMC)* (pp. 2873-2878). IEEE. doi:10.1109/ICSMC.2012.6378185

Kim, P. H., & Giunchiglia, F. (2013). The open platform for personal lifelogging: The elifelog architecture. In *CHI'13 Extended Abstracts on Human Factors in Computing Systems* (pp. 1677–1682). New York: ACM. doi:10.1145/2468356.2468656

Kirsh, D. (2013). Embodied cognition and the magical future of interaction design.[TOCHI]. *ACM Transactions on Computer-Human Interaction*, *20*(1), 3. doi:10.1145/2442106.2442109

Koubek, T., Procházka, D., & Šťastný, J. (2013). Augmented reality services. *Acta Universitatis Agriculturae et Silviculturae Mendelianae Brunensis*, *61*(7), 2337–2342. doi:10.11118/actaun201361072337

Krause, B. (2008). Anatomy of the soundscape: Evolving perspectives. *Journal of the Audio Engineering Society*, *56*(1/2), 73–80.

Kuniavsky, M. (2003). *Observing the user experience: a practitioner's guide to user research*. Burlington, MA: Morgan kaufmann.

Lachman, R. W. (1997). *Animist interface: Experiments in mapping character animation to computer interface* (Doctoral dissertation). Massachusetts Institute of Technology.

Lerman, K., & Jones, L. (2006). *Social browsing on flickr.* arXiv preprint cs/0612047

Li, I., Dey, A. K., & Forlizzi, J. (2011). Understanding my data, myself: supporting self-reflection with ubicomp technologies. In *Proceedings of the 13th international conference on Ubiquitous computing* (pp. 405-414). New York: ACM. doi:10.1145/2030112.2030166

Li, K. A., Sohn, T. Y., Huang, S., & Griswold, W. G. (2008). Peopletones: a system for the detection and notification of buddy proximity on mobile phones. In *Proceedings of the 6th international conference on Mobile systems, applications, and services* (pp. 160-173). New York: ACM. doi:10.1145/1378600.1378619

Li, N., & Chen, G. (2010). Sharing location in online social networks. *IEEE Network*, *24*(5), 20–25. doi:10.1109/MNET.2010.5578914

Lin, J. J., Mamykina, L., Lindtner, S., Delajoux, G., & Strub, H. B. (2006). Fish'n'Steps: Encouraging physical activity with an interactive computer game. In *International Conference on Ubiquitous Computing* (pp. 261-278). Berlin: Springer Berlin Heidelberg. doi:10.1007/11853565_16

Löwgren, J. (2007). Inspirational patterns for embodied interaction. *Knowledge, Technology & Policy*, *20*(3), 165–177. doi:10.1007/s12130-007-9029-1

Manjunath, K. U. K. (2014). *Location Based Context-Aware Systems* (Doctoral dissertation). University of Birmingham.

Matei, S. A., Faiola, A., Wheatley, D. J., & Altom, T. (2012). The role of physical affordances in multifunctional mobile device design. *Models for Capitalizing on Web Engineering Advancements: Trends and Discoveries: Trends and Discoveries*, 306.

McCullough, M. (2006). On the Urbanism of Locative Media [Media and the City]. *Places, 18*(2).

McCullough, M. (2007). New media urbanism: Grounding ambient information technology. *Environment and Planning. B, Planning & Design*, *34*(3), 383–395. doi:10.1068/b32038

McDuff, D., Karlson, A., Kapoor, A., Roseway, A., & Czerwinski, M. (2012). AffectAura: an intelligent system for emotional memory. In *Proceedings of the SIGCHI Conference on Human Factors in Computing Systems* (pp. 849-858). New York: ACM. doi:10.1145/2207676.2208525

Oleksik, G., Frohlich, D., Brown, L. M., & Sellen, A. (2008). Sonic interventions: understanding and extending the domestic soundscape. In *Proceedings of the SIGCHI conference on Human Factors in computing systems* (pp. 1419-1428). New York: ACM. doi:10.1145/1357054.1357277

Overbeeke, K., Djajadiningrat, T., Hummels, C., Wensveen, S., & Prens, J. (2003). Let's make things engaging. In *Funology* (pp. 7–17). Dordrecht: Springer Netherlands. doi:10.1007/1-4020-2967-5_2

Petrelli, D., Bowen, S., & Whittaker, S. (2014). Photo mementos: Designing digital media to represent ourselves at home. *International Journal of Human-Computer Studies*, *72*(3), 320–336. doi:10.1016/j.ijhcs.2013.09.009

Petrelli, D., & Whittaker, S. (2010). Family memories in the home: Contrasting physical and digital mementos. *Personal and Ubiquitous Computing*, *14*(2), 153–169. doi:10.1007/s00779-009-0279-7

Pielot, M., & Oliveira, R. D. (2013). Peripheral vibro-tactile displays. In *Proceedings of the 15th international conference on Human-computer interaction with mobile devices and services* (pp. 1-10). New York: ACM.

Qureshi, S. S., Ahmad, T., & Rafique, K. (2011). Mobile cloud computing as future for mobile applications-Implementation methods and challenging issues. In *2011 IEEE International Conference on Cloud Computing and Intelligence Systems* (pp. 467-471). Piscataway, NJ: IEEE. doi:10.1109/CCIS.2011.6045111

Raghunath, M., Narayanaswami, C., & Pinhanez, C. (2003). Fostering a symbiotic handheld environment. *Computer, 36*(9), 56–65. doi:10.1109/MC.2003.1231195

Roginska, A. (2013). Auditory icons, earcons, and displays: Information and expression through sound. *The Psychology of Music in Multimedia*, 339.

Rooksby, J., Rost, M., Morrison, A., & Chalmers, M. C. (2014). Personal tracking as lived informatics. In *Proceedings of the 32nd Annual ACM Conference on Human Factors in Computing Systems* (pp. 1163-1172). New York: ACM.

Rosson, M. B., & Carrol, J. M. (2008). Scenario-based Design. In A. Sears & J. A. Jacko (Eds.), *The Human-Computer Interaction Handbook. Fundamentals, Evolving Technologies and Emerging Applications*. Lawrence Erlbaum Associates.

Rubin, D. C. (1986). *Autobiographical memory*. New York: Cambridge University Press. doi:10.1017/CBO9780511558313

Ruiz, J., Li, Y., & Lank, E. (2011). User-defined motion gestures for mobile interaction. In *Proceedings of the SIGCHI Conference on Human Factors in Computing Systems* (pp. 197-206). New York: ACM.

Schwartz, R., & Halegoua, G. R. (2014). The spatial self: Location-based identity performance on social media. *New Media & Society*.

Sellen, A. J., & Whittaker, S. (2010). Beyond total capture: A constructive critique of lifelogging. *Communications of the ACM, 53*(5), 70–77. doi:10.1145/1735223.1735243

Shifman, L. (2012). An anatomy of a YouTube meme. *New Media & Society, 14*(2), 187–203. doi:10.1177/1461444811412160

Snyder, C. (2003). *Paper prototyping: The fast and easy way to design and refine user interfaces*. Burlington, MA: Morgan Kaufmann.

Sutton, J. (2008). Material agency, skills and history: Distributed cognition and the archaeology of memory. In *Material agency* (pp. 37–55). New York: Springer US. doi:10.1007/978-0-387-74711-8_3

Tankoyeu, I., Stöttinger, J., Paniagua, J., & Giunchiglia, F. (2012). Personal photo indexing. In *Proceedings of the 20th ACM international conference on Multimedia* (pp. 1341-1342). New York: ACM. doi:10.1145/2393347.2396474

Taylor, D. R. F., & Lauriault, T. (Eds.). (2006). *Cybercartography: Theory and practice* (Vol. 5). Amsterdam: Elsevier.

Tolmie, P., Pycock, J., Diggins, T., MacLean, A., & Karsenty, A. (2002). Unremarkable computing. In *Proceedings of the SIGCHI conference on Human factors in computing systems* (pp. 399-406). New York: ACM.

Torsi, S. (2013). Notification in Motion. Theoretical Frameworks and Design Guidelines. *JMMT: Journal of Man. Machine and Technology*, 2(1), 1–11.

Torsi, S. (2015). Design for Consciousness in the Wild: Notes on Cognition and Space. *Analyzing Art, Culture, and Design in the Digital Age*, 279.

Torsi, S., & Giunchiglia, F. (2015). *Early prototyping for prospective memory, behavior change and self-biography*. ARTECH 2015. 7th International Conference on Digital Arts – Creating Digital e-Motions, Óbidos, Portugal.

Torsi, S., Wright, P., Mountain, G., Nasr, N., Mawson, S., & Rosser, B. (2010). The self-management of chronic illnesses: Theories and technologies. In *2010 4th International Conference on Pervasive Computing Technologies for Healthcare* (pp. 1-4). Piscataway, NJ: IEEE.

Tsur, O., & Rappoport, A. (2012). What's in a hashtag? Content based prediction of the spread of ideas in microblogging communities. In *Proceedings of the fifth ACM international conference on Web search and data mining* (pp. 643-652). New York: ACM.

Utz, S. (2015). The function of self-disclosure on social network sites: Not only intimate, but also positive and entertaining self-disclosures increase the feeling of connection. *Computers in Human Behavior*, 45, 1–10. doi:10.1016/j.chb.2014.11.076

Valdes, C., Eastman, D., Grote, C., Thatte, S., Shaer, O., Mazalek, A., & Konkel, M. K. et al. (2014). Exploring the design space of gestural interaction with active tokens through user-defined gestures. In *Proceedings of the SIGCHI Conference on Human Factors in Computing Systems* (pp. 4107-4116). New York: ACM. doi:10.1145/2556288.2557373

Wallace, J. (2007). *Emotionally charged: A practice-centred enquiry of digital jewellery and personal emotional significance* (Doctoral dissertation). Sheffield Hallam University.

Waltz, E. (2012). How I quantified myself. *IEEE Spectrum, 49*(9), 42–47. doi:10.1109/MSPEC.2012.6281132

Warfield, K. (2014). *Making selfies/making self: Digital subjectivities in the selfie.* Academic Press.

Whittaker, S., Kalnikaite, V., Petrelli, D., Sellen, A., Villar, N., Bergman, O., Clough, P., Brockmeier, J. (2012). Socio-technical lifelogging: Deriving design principles for a future proof digital past. *Human-Computer Interaction, 27*(1-2), 37-62.

Wilson, M. W. (2012). Location-based services, conspicuous mobility, and the location-aware future. *Geoforum, 43*(6), 1266–1275. doi:10.1016/j.geoforum.2012.03.014

Wright, P., & McCarthy, J. (2004). *Technology as experience.* Cambridge, MA: The MIT Press.

Yee, K. P. (2003). Peephole displays: pen interaction on spatially aware handheld computers. In *Proceedings of the SIGCHI conference on Human factors in computing systems* (pp. 1-8). New York: ACM. doi:10.1145/642611.642613

Zeni, M., Zaihrayeu, I., & Giunchiglia, F. (2014). Multi-device activity logging. In *Proceedings of the 2014 ACM International Joint Conference on Pervasive and Ubiquitous Computing: Adjunct Publication* (pp. 299-302). New York: ACM.

Chapter 7
Information and Communication Overload:
Can DigComp Help?

Margarida Lucas
University of Aveiro, Portugal

António Moreira
University of Aveiro, Portugal

ABSTRACT

Information and communication overload have gained a new dimension in today's digital world. The exposure to the volume of information being distributed has probably never been so high due to the rapid increase of communication channels at our disposal. Facing great volumes of information (and communication channels) may cause constraints in our personal and professional lives and therefore it requires the ability to deal with and solve the problems related with them. This chapter presents the DigComp, a tool that proposes a set of knowledge, skills and attitudes that are part of digital competence, one of the eight key competences for lifelong learning and essential for participation in our increasingly digitalised society. It takes the stance that the DigComp may work as a foundation for "calculating" the boundaries of that so-called overload. The intention is to find in this tool the right ally to gauge the acquisition of competences that will make any user more critically aware and proactive towards the ways s/he deals with communication and information in her/his daily routines.

DOI: 10.4018/978-1-5225-2061-0.ch007

INTRODUCTION

As information and communication are both vast and channeled through a variety of means and supports, they can induce overload. And this – information and communication overload – is a concept which has been around since the very beginnings of the discussion of publicity and marketing principles that lead practitioners in these areas to elect them as an object of study. However, due to the technological advances operated in the past few decades, studies on the subject have extended to other areas.

Our general purpose in this chapter is to introduce the reader to DigComp (Ferrari, 2013; Vuorikari, Punie, Carretero & Van den Brande, 2016), a common framework of reference that proposes 21 competences structured in five competence areas, the first two – "Information and data literacy" and "Communication and collaboration" being of particular interest for the present work. The framework, which is currently being fine-tuned, allows us to be able to describe each competence and attribute it a certain degree of skill in its performance, therefore establishing a relationship between the observed individual performance and the level at which the common framework of reference places its display. This comparison or gauging mechanism will eventually allow us to infer the areas of digital competence where overload may be prevented and/or detected, while at the same time offering a measure of individual performance. Although the measurement approach is not yet a reality, it is very possible that it will mimic what has been happening with other European Common Reference Frameworks of Competences (ECRFC) in other fields, especially the one that started this whole movement – the European Common Reference Framework of Competences for Languages (CEFR[1]) –, which involved renowned linguists, pedagogues, sociologists and sociolinguists, psycholinguists, language teaching methodologists, language policy makers and politicians in Europe. Relationships between digital competence dimensions and information and communication overload will be briefly exemplified and matched for clarification purposes, following the same principles and overall presentation display used in those other ECRFC.

Let us start with a few simple but enlightening examples to set the ground for the discussion that follows. In the early seventies of the last century, students taking courses in marketing and publicity were warned of the dangers of over-information, although over-communication was not an issue as such at the time. As it happens, whenever the issue of publicizing outdoors or even on the radio or television and print media, adequate "hits" to an adequate "public" under an adequate "format" to the "means of communication" was a rule of thumb to take into account and avoid overload, even if we were talking about the mere decoration of a shop window. What was essential was to be "clean", "lean", "catchy" and "memorable".

The explosion in means and forms of communication and the accrued load of unfiltered, "uncensored" information led to a double, intertwined overload: that of information and that of communication. Not long ago, say around 40 years ago or so, we would still regularly exchange letters, the odd postcard while on holiday, or make a phone call from a landline at home or from a phone booth. Getting a reply in the first cases took its time (and even this decreased with the advent of fast transportation, like the car, the steam-boat and the airplane), although this meant days, if not weeks or even months. The phone call had a very specific purpose, and was almost surgically used.

Communication overload is usually the result of human error, and can be described as a set of wrong assumptions about ourselves, the ones we communicate with, the purposes of communication, and the contexts in which such communicative events must take place. A well prepared, thought out plan that includes feasible objectives for a feasible agenda, within a set time span, gathering the right people with the required functions and roles is a very good starting point for, for instance, a meeting becoming productive. Also, too many persons involved in a very well-defined problem to be solved may become a burden, a source of entropy and an invitation to disaster, as far as resolving the problem is concerned. Adding people may also add complexity, which in turn may reduce understanding, lean and clearly set solutions and decisions and, in the long term, productivity. Just like in focus groups, size matters: the larger the number of participants, the larger the number of ideas tend to turn up. And that is why most experts in the field of research suggest a minimum of 5 and a maximum of 10 participants for a focus group to be productive (Krueger & Casey, 2009), for instance for the information and communication they provide/establish to be of value to the researcher.

The use of email is another example of communication and information that requires consideration and careful thought, as the problem gets even more acute as we look at mailing lists. Do we really need them? Do we have to hit the "reply to all" button every time something "vaguely" interesting happens? Will there be someone in the organization with the functional responsibility to do exactly that sort of filtering? If we hit the button without thinking, we are just adding another layer of overload (both communicative and informative) to the process.

The same happens with meetings, whether face-to-face or online, when they take place with a regularity that is uncalled for. If you have a pre-set timetable of meetings to discuss (usually) the same topics, you risk becoming "boring" and demobilize precisely the ones you want on your side. Meetings should serve a precise purpose and only be called when and if necessary; not because you need to control everybody's timetable (including your own), making therefore sure that you have a day when you can dispose of people at your own will (whether or not recommendable).

Letting go of control-centered attitudes is also a bonus: giving your collaborators the power to take control and responsibility for their own actions is another way to reduce communication and information overload – the keywords for this handing out of responsibility and, therefore, top-down overload is accountability, initiative and risk-taking in the resolution of problems. All these should not only be encouraged but also rewarded. You do not have to be everywhere, every time. If something is really important, it will get to you. Here, the English saying "No news is good news" applies perfectly – no overload of information, therefore no overload of communication. And that is why one should never use communication, information or collaboration tools just because that is the trend. Most of the times, the return you get from this behavior is too disruptive and expensive.

Although most of the above applies to enterprises and business relations (adapted from Tobak, 2010), they are, we would dare say, universal. And they need to be addressed by everybody who deals with digital technologies, from the very specialized expert in the field of ICT to the common citizen. A tool that may help all of us in the management of these issues of communication and information overload in the near future, and that has involved the authors in the last few months, is DigComp (Ferrari, 2013; Vuorikari et al., 2016). And this is the framework we would like to bring to the readers' attention as it can be a foundation for "calculating" the boundaries of that same overload, not in the sense of controlling it, but as a means to place a person at a certain level of development/performance as to their digital competences. The intention is to find in this framework the right ally to gauge our acquisition of competences that will make us more critically aware and proactive towards the ways we deal with communication and information in our daily routines.

Therefore, the objectives of this chapter are to address how DigComp can be used to predict current and future approaches that seek to solve the problem of information and communication overload, particularly those that are related to digital technologies, the areas of information and data literacy and communication and collaboration. It is not the intention of the authors to put forth a set of guidelines or recipes to be used blindly, but to give the reader the opportunity to keep up with the development of an ECRFC that is being developed in Europe, with the concurrence of various entities in several countries, including Portugal.

DIGCOMP: THE DIGITAL COMPETENCE FRAMEWORK FOR CITIZENS

Aims, Methodology and Structure

DigComp is a European framework proposal for the understanding and development of digital competence for all citizens. Digital competence has become part of the educational, social, economic, and political agenda since the European Commission declared it one of the eight key competences for lifelong learning and essential for participation in our increasingly digitized society (European Parliament and the Council, 2006). It is also understood as a transversal key competence enabling the acquisition of other key competences, namely "communication in the mother tongue", "communication in foreign languages", "mathematical competence and basic competences in science and technology", "learning to learn", "social and civic competences", "sense of initiative" and "entrepreneurship and cultural awareness and expression".

Being digitally competent today is an essential requirement for life (Bawden, 2008), or even a survival skill (Eshet-Alkalai, 2004) that can benefit citizens, communities and the economy and society in general regarding social, economic, political, health and cultural areas (Van Deursen, 2010). It is no longer considered just a matter of using ICT or digital technologies, but an issue that involves "a set of knowledge, skills, attitudes, abilities, strategies, and awareness that are required when using ICT and digital media to perform tasks; solve problems; communicate; manage information; collaborate; create and share content; and build knowledge effectively, efficiently, appropriately, critically, creatively, autonomously, flexibly, ethically, reflectively for work, leisure, participation, learning, socializing, consuming and empowerment" (Ferrari, 2012, pp. 3-4).

Digital competence depends mainly on two aspects: first, it depends on each person's needs, interests, and context, and has therefore to be adapted to those; second, it depends on technological availability and users' adoption practices. Therefore, digital competence also implies the ability and willingness to attend to new technological developments and practices and so its definition may change over time.

The DigComp is the result of a project launched by The Institute for Prospective Technological Studies (IPTS), one of the European Commission's Joint Research Centers (JRC), under an Administrative Agreement with the Directorate General (DG) for Education and Culture with a view to contribute to the better understanding and development of digital competence in Europe. Its development included a thorough literature review of the concept and related terms (Ala-Mutka, 2011), a collection and analysis of case studies of several digital competence frameworks (Ferrari, 2012), an online consultation with stakeholders and experts (Janssen & Stoyanov, 2012), and workshops involving interviews, the presentation of proposals, their refinement and validation.

Its overall objectives were

1. To identify the key components of digital competence in terms of the knowledge, skills and attitudes needed to be digitally competent;
2. To develop descriptors that could feed a conceptual framework and/or guidelines to be validated at European level, taking into account relevant frameworks available; and

3.   To propose a roadmap for the possible use and revision of a digital competence framework and descriptors of digital competences for citizens/all levels of learners.

Its main aims were to create a common understanding and a scientific basis to define which components should be part of every citizen's digital competence and reach consensus among the many existing initiatives across European member states. DigComp is based on the most comprehensive and rigorous review of existing frameworks and represents one of the most recent and extensive frameworks which attempts to outline what digital competence is and which specific aspects it includes.

The outputs of this project consisted of a self-assessment grid that can be used by citizens as a tool to describe and improve their own level of digital competence (included in the online version of the Europass CV), and a framework that can be used for the development and assessment of curricula, training and certification, or school programs. The framework proposed wants to be descriptive rather than prescriptive, meaning that it should be used as a reference, for instance when tailoring interventions (e.g. instructional planning, work-based learning or curriculum development) to fit the specific needs of target groups.

The structure of the DigComp was taken and elaborated from the eCompetence framework for ICT professionals (eCF[2]) and from the CEFR[3], which proposes three proficiency levels. The DigComp also proposes three proficiency levels: A (basic user), corresponding to a state of "being aware and having an understanding of"; B (independent user), which involves "being able to use"; and C (proficient user), which presupposes "being actively involved in as a practice" (Ferrari, 2013).

Since its publication, DigComp has been used for multiple purposes, particularly in the context of employment, education and training, and lifelong learning. However, the rapid change brought about by digitization to various aspects of society fueled the need for an updated version. The first of a two-phase update process was published in June 2016 (Vuorikari et al., 2016) and was modelled under a multi-stakeholder governance in which the DG for Employment, Social Affairs and Inclusion and JRC-IPTS led the management and quality assurance. Other DG were involved in the update to ensure complementarity between existing and emerging actions (e.g. e-Skills for growth and jobs, Digital Single Market, European Skills/Competences, qualifications and Occupations [ESCO], etc.).

The recent update includes changes in vocabulary used, changes in the names of competence areas, competences and competence descriptors that now include relevant updates regarding European Union (EU) legislation (e.g. EU data protection reform[4]) and a more visible and explicit alignment with other works such as the Global Media and Information Literacy Assessment Framework (UNESCO, 2013).

The second update will be published until the end of 2016 and will include, for instance, the introduction of more fine-grained proficiency levels with examples of knowledge, skills and attitudes for each of the 21 competences. The framework presented in the next section already includes the aforementioned updates proposed by Vuorikari et al. (2016).

The Framework

The DigComp identifies the key components of digital competence in terms of the knowledge, skills and attitudes required to be digitally competent. It also presents comprehensive conceptual descriptors that can help any citizen set a boundary to, or cope with, information and communication overload by providing an understanding of what s/he is supposed to do or expected to achieve in relation to information and communication in the digital world. The framework is structured around five dimensions that reflect a different aspect of the descriptors and a different stage of granularity.

Dimension 1: Competence areas;
Dimension 2: Competences that are pertinent to each area and descriptors;
Dimension 3: Proficiency levels that are foreseen for each competence;
Dimension 4: Examples of the knowledge, skills and attitudes applicable to each competence (examples are not differentiated in proficiency levels);
Dimension 5[5] : Examples on the applicability of the competence to learning and employment purposes.

The areas of digital competence identified (Dimension 1) correspond to the ones of "Information and data literacy", "Communication and collaboration", "Digital content creation", "Safety" and "Problem-solving". For each of the competence areas, a series of related competences were identified, totaling 21 (Dimension 2). Both dimensions are presented in Table 1. Competences in each area vary in number, from a minimum of three to a maximum of six. For instance, the areas of "Information and data literacy" and "Communication and collaboration" identify three and six competences respectively. The DigComp numbers the competence areas from 1 to 5 and all competences within each area are also numbered sequentially, e.g. 2.6: the first sequence identifies the competence area and the second the competence. It is worth noting that this progression does not reflect any growing achievement or any type of hierarchy.

The first competence in each area includes more technical aspects: in these specific competences, the knowledge, skills and attitudes have operational processes as a dominant component. However, technical and operational skills are also

Table 1. Competence areas (dimension 1) and competences (dimension 2)

Competence Areas	Competences
1.Information and data literacy	1.1 Browsing, searching and filtering data, information and digital content
	1.2 Evaluating data, information and digital content
	1.3 Managing data, information and digital content
2.Communication and collaboration	2.1 Interacting through digital technologies
	2.2 Sharing through digital technologies
	2.3 Engaging in citizenship through digital technologies
	2.4 Collaborating through digital technologies
	2.5 Netiquette
	2.6 Managing digital identity
3. Digital content creation	3.1 Developing digital content
	3.2 Integrating and re-elaborating digital content
	3.3 Copyright and licenses
	3.4Programming
4. Safety	4.1 Protecting devices
	4.2 Protecting personal data and privacy
	4.3 Protecting health and well-being
	4.4 Protecting the environment
5. Problem solving	5.1 Solving technical problems
	5.2 Identifying needs and technological responses
	5.3 Creatively using digital technologies
	5.4 Identifying digital competence gaps

embedded in each competence. For instance, the first competence listed in the area of "Information and data literacy" is "Browsing, searching and filtering data, information and digital content". These can be understood as more technical competences (such as knowing how to use search engines, following information presented in hyper-linked and non-linear form or browsing the Internet for information and content), whereas "Evaluating data, information and digital content", the third competence listed within this area, is more transversal and includes higher levels of understanding and critical thinking, such as judging the validity of content found on the internet or the media, evaluating and interpreting it.

Competences can be cross-referenced against competences from different competence areas and even against the key competences for lifelong learning (e.g. competences from the "Communication and collaboration" competence area, such as "Interacting through digital technologies" or "Engaging in citizenship through digital technologies", can be cross-referenced against the ability to express and interpret concepts, thoughts, feelings, facts and opinions in both oral and written form, regarding the key competence of "Communication in the mother tongue"). Cross-referencing within the DigComp can be established, for instance, between the competence "Protecting devices", which pertain to the competence area "Safety", and the competence "Storing and retrieving information" regarding the competence area of "Information and data literacy".

Many of the competences listed by the framework are overlapped and interlocked and, therefore, relevant for dealing with information and communication overload. In this chapter, however, and as previously stated, focus is placed upon the first two competence areas. The areas of "Information and data literacy" and "Communication and collaboration" are defined as rather linear, meaning that they deal with competences that are relevant to any type of activity that is carried out through digital means. They are summarized in terms of what could be subsumed as soft skills, and therefore, "Information and data literacy" implies the ability to identify, locate, retrieve, store, organize and analyze digital information, judging its relevance and purpose, whereas collaboration has to do with the ability to communicate in digital environments, share resources through online tools, link with others and collaborate through digital tools, interact with and participate in communities and networks, sustained by cross-cultural awareness. Competences pertinent to each area are described as follows (Vuorikari et al., 2016):

1.1 Browsing, Searching and Filtering Data, Information and Digital Content: To articulate information needs, to search for data, information and content in digital environments, to access them and to navigate between them. To create and update personal search strategies.

1.2 Evaluating Data, Information and Digital Content: To analyze, compare and critically evaluate the credibility and reliability of sources of data, information and digital content. To analyze, interpret and critically evaluate the data, information and digital content.

1.3 Managing Data, Information and Digital Content: To organize, store and retrieve data, information and content in digital environments. To organize and process them in a structured environment.

2.1 Interacting Through Digital Technologies: To interact through a variety of digital technologies and to understand appropriate digital communication means for a given context.

2.2 Sharing through Digital Technologies: To share data, information and digital content with others through appropriate digital technologies. To act as an intermediary, to know about referencing and attribution practices.

2.3 Engaging in Citizenship through Digital Technologies: To participate in society through the use of public and private digital services. To seek opportunities for self-empowerment and for participatory citizenship through appropriate digital technologies.

2.4 Collaborating through Digital Technologies: To use digital tools and technologies for collaborative processes, and for co-construction and co-creation of resources and knowledge.

2.5 Netiquette: To be aware of behavioral norms and know-how while using digital technologies and interacting in digital environments. To adapt communication strategies to the specific audience and to be aware of cultural and generational diversity in digital environments.

2.6 Managing Digital Identity: To create and manage one or multiple digital identities, to be able to protect one's own reputation, to deal with the data that one produces through several digital tools, environments and services.

Current uses of DigComp

Since it was first published, there have been numerous implementations at European, national and regional levels of the DigComp. These refer mainly to three categories of use:

1. Policy formulation and support,
2. Instructional planning for education, training and employment, and
3. Assessment and certification.

Regarding the first category, and just to provide an example, the DigComp has been used to develop the Digital Economy and Society Index (DESI), which bases its "Digital skills" indicators on the competence areas of "Information and data literacy", "Communication and collaboration", "Digital content creation" and "Problem solving".

As to the second category, DigComp has mostly been taken up to develop education and training initiatives for education, skills and employment purposes. For instance, it has been used to develop new training syllabi for digital competence in adult education by the Department of Education in Flanders; to develop professional development programs for teachers in various European countries (Croatia, Norway, Portugal, Spain) or guide third-sector education and training programs, such as those ran by Telecentre Europe (TE), a European non-profit organization that represents publicly-funded telecenters/telecenter networks, ICT learning centers, adult education centers and libraries across Europe.

The third category already translates into a series of initiatives. The aforementioned TE developed the online test Skillage to assess young people's understanding of ICT in an employment setting; the Ikanos project offers a free-of-charge diagnostic tool for assessing one's own digital competence in the Basque Country. Its government has also created a public service that certifies the digital competence of citizens and civil servants by using DigComp to enable companies and administrations to objectively assess the ICT skills of people in their organizations, as well as those looking to incorporate ICT in their midst.

As far as research is concerned, it is already possible to find a few studies that have used DigComp as an input for technology based activities, data collection or as an assessment tool (Evangelinos & Holley, 2014ab; Evangelinos & Holley, 2015; Velicu & Mitarca, 2016; Siiman et al., 2016). Evangelinos and Holley (2014b) found that the framework may be used to quantitatively evaluate the general level of digital competence of individuals and groups, and produce 'maps' of digital competence. Nevertheless, they point at the lack of precision that may arise when using such measurements, especially when participants are asked to self-evaluate themselves. They call for additional data to be triangulated with those collected with DigComp. They also found (2015) that the framework facilitates the design of online technology based learning activities aiming at developing digital competences in the health education curriculum. Velicu and Mitarca (2016) report some problems in adapting the framework for evaluating young children's digital competence, such as the absence of some genuine children's digital activities (gaming). Siiman et al. (2016) developed a self-report questionnaire based on DigComp to survey how often students from grades 6 and 9 used a smart device to perform a digitally competent activity. They refer the need to triangulate data gathered from tests and observations to increase the validity of the self-report questionnaires.

RELATIONSHIP BETWEEN DIGITAL COMPETENCE AND INFORMATION AND COMMUNICATION OVERLOAD

Information Overload

Information overload occurs when people are exposed to more information than they can accommodate in their capacity for information processing (Eppler & Mengis, 2004). Regarding the competence "Browsing, searching and filtering data, information and digital content", a user with a basic level of proficiency (A) is expected to know how to do some online searches through search engines, but may lack the necessary skills to avoid dealing with information and content that is irrelevant to their interests or unimportant. When such happens, chances of experiencing overload are high (Ayyagari, Grover & Purvis, 2011). Ways of dealing with irrelevant information or content received include adjusting searches according to one's specific needs, using filters and agents, refining information searches by selecting adequate vocabulary that limits the number of hits, or being able to adapt search strategies to a specific search engine, application or device. Descriptors proposed by the DigComp suggest that an independent user (B) is able to articulate information needs and select appropriate information, whereas a proficient user (C) can use a wide range of search strategies when browsing, searching and filtering data, information and digital content. For instance, s/he understands how feeds mechanisms work and uses them to be updated with information and content s/he is interested in.

Chances of experiencing information overload may also be minimized if a user is competent in "Evaluating data, information and digital content". In today's world of rapidly proliferating information, individuals must be ready to evaluate what they find and receive. Having this competence means one analyses, compares and critically evaluates the credibility and reliability of sources of data, information and digital content. The evaluation of information is often performed by applying the CRAAP[6] test, which suggests 5 criteria to evaluate information: currency (the timeliness of the information), relevance (the importance of the information for one's needs), authority (the source of the information), accuracy (the reliability, truthfulness and correctness of the content) and purpose (the reason that supports the existence of the information). Being able to assess the usefulness, timeliness, accuracy and integrity of the information or to compare, contrast, and integrate information from different sources corresponds to the highest level of proficiency proposed by the DigComp, i.e. level C. Lower levels of proficiency pose it, for instance, that a basic user knows that not all online information is reliable, but may not know how to verify the reliability of content found, which can be done by means of comparing different sources. Comparing information sources and looking for their origins as a way to judge their value is something an independent user would do, but s/he may not be ready to assess its validity, accuracy and credibility, which is something a proficient user would do. Such user would probably look at where the information came from, look at evidence supporting it, look for spelling and grammar errors or look for the author's credentials or organizational affiliations.

Also in today's world, there is an expectation that every user is competent in "Managing data, information and digital content", meaning that s/he is competent in organizing, storing and retrieving data, information and content in digital environments and in processing them in a structured environment. This is known to have a positive impact on task development, decision making, individual work performance or even reducing stress (Strother, Ulijn & Fazal, 2012). An essential attitude every user should have is acknowledging the importance of having an understandable and pragmatic storage system/scheme. A user who knows how to structure and classify information and content according to a classification scheme or method will be able to later retrieve and access it more easily. A simple example is, for instance, categorizing emails into appropriate folders based on a critical view of the emails' contents. Examples of proficiency for a basic user include knowing how to save files and content (e.g. texts, pictures, music, videos, and web pages) and knowing how to go back to the content saved. An independent user is the one who can save, store or tag files, content and information and has his/her own storing strategy, for instance, s/he classifies the information in a methodical way using files and folders to locate them easily and makes backups of information or files stored. A proficient user can apply different methods and tools to organize files, content, and information. S/he can deploy a set of strategies for retrieving the content s/he or others have organized and stored, for example, using cloud information storage services.

Communication Overload

The surge of information overload is related with the rapid increase of communication technologies. Channels available – email, instant messaging apps, news feeds, social networking sites and others growing daily – enable information to be produced and disseminated instantaneously at a fast pace and to a large quantity of people. These technologies enable individuals to communicate from anywhere at any time, but also to be reachable anywhere at any time. The increasing diffusion of communication technologies and the always connected communication environment we live in can also lead to communication overload (Rainie, Smith & Duggan, 2013; Cho, Ramgolam, Schaefer & Sandlin, 2011). This phenomenon or experience can be described as a state of feeling overwhelmed by communication technologies (Lee, Lee & Suh, 2016; Ayyagari, Grover & Purvis, 2011). Common recommendations to diminish the effects of communication overload often include checking emails at set intervals throughout the day or turning off social media notifications (Dabbish & Kraut, 2006; Chen & Lee, 2013). Even though these are valid and important suggestions, today's proficient users need to go beyond.

Taking the first competence identified by the DigComp for the area of "Communication and collaboration" as an example, which is "Interacting through digital technologies", any user may be led to believe s/he is competent in doing so. Communicating with others using basic features, such as voice messaging, SMS or send and receive emails, using a mobile phone, Voice over IP, e-mail or chat may be fairly basic for the majority of people. However, using more advanced features, such as sharing files while using Voice over IP or deciding whom to follow on micro-blogging social sites may not be so basic. In fact, these correspond to profiles of independent and proficient users respectively. Knowing the benefits and limits of different means of communication, distinguishing the most appropriate ones to any given context or purpose or being aware of the risks linked with digital communication with unknown people/services are examples of the knowledge, skills and attitudes proposed by the framework, yet another form of communication overload that is of an insidious and ever more complex nature.

"Sharing through digital technologies", which has the added facet of copyright and its legal nuances, may also contribute for communication overload if one is unaware of what and with whom one is sharing information. For instance, the simple act of providing one's email address when subscribing certain online services, commenting posts or registering for certain types of accounts may result in receiving unsolicited information or in becoming targeted with spam. Taking a proactive attitude in the sharing of resources, content and knowledge is an approach a competent user usually has, but this also implies such user has an informed opinion about sharing practices, benefits, risks and limitations. A basic user shares files and documents using simple tools, such as an email attachment, but may not know how to share them without disclosing the email addresses of the people whom s/he is sharing them with by using, for instance, the Blind carbon copy (Bcc) function. In not doing so, such user may be contributing, even if unwarily, for the communication (and information) overload of other people.

Being competent in sharing and "Collaborating through digital technologies", meaning one knows how to prevent communication overload for oneself and the others, also implies that one is competent in behaving online and knowing the norms and know-how of while using digital environments ("Netiquette"). S/he understands the dynamics of collaborative work and of giving and receiving feedback and understands the different roles needed in diverse forms of online collaboration. So, for instance, when creating a project spreadsheet to share with others so that they can comment, make changes or suggestions, one can set notifications to find out when other people have modified the project spreadsheet, and learn what they have modified. One can also choose how often one would like to be notified. This includes being notified "right away", which means receiving an email every time one of the users with whom one has shared the project spreadsheet with modifies something or receiving a daily digest email, which is a summary of the changes made by collaborators throughout the day. Chances of communication overload may reduce when adopting the last option.

"Managing digital identity" involves the ability to create, adapt and manage one or multiple digital identities as well as to deal with the data that one produces through several accounts and applications. It also involves the ability to protect oneself and others from online threats and keeping track of his/her own digital footprint. Identity exposure threats include, for example, the collection of identity information by service providers that can use it for marketing purposes. Again, just as mentioned previously, this may result in being targeted with unwanted communication.

FUTURE RESEARCH AND LIMITATIONS

Future and emerging trends, from our point of view, are vast and cannot be comprehensively listed here. We can, nevertheless, make an educated guess that attention span will be one area of DigComp that will probably be studied, given that several studies have revealed that people do not use technologies continuously. They use them, put them aside, pick them up again for the continuation of what they were doing or some other task, and so on and so forth. Moreover, the surge of new technologies is so intense and the context of their use so diverse that the question on whether DigComp will account for these aspects when the framework is applied to different age publics arises.

Also, if we focus on digitally cognitive malleability, there is also proof that people who are brought up in different cultures, even when facing technology, represent different things of what they see and experiment. For instance, the menus displayed on an interface differ from culture to culture, especially if we contrast eastern Europeans with Americans, Chinese, Arabs, etc. Writing using a keyboard in different cultures/languages may have an influence on how DigComp "measures" digital competences: another aspect to be considered.

Some open questions we pose ourselves while working on this ECRFC on digital competence are always lingering at the very back of our minds:

- What are the key success factors for attaining higher levels of performance in DigComp?
- Should DigComp be part of compulsory curricula planning, professional certification and administration? Where, when and how?
- What types of assessment are appropriate for the monitoring and evaluation of digital competences with DigComp in the background?
- How can measurements made with DigComp benefit from performance-based tests using authentic tasks?

We also recognize that there are limitations to the proposed framework, as it focuses on individual competences rather than the general approach we adopted, since there are major differences between age groups or different target groups. The present proposal can only be taken as the beginning of the discussion of conceptions and interpretations of what digital competences and social practices using digital media are about. Over time, and when more data is available, both in breadth of scope and publics and depth of approaches to its study and application, we will necessarily reach more elaborated and consolidated knowledge about the ECRFC's strengths and drawbacks, possibly implicating the adoption of other competences definitions, evaluation criteria, and classification measurements.

CONCLUSION

The digital age has brought about many positive aspects: being able to access vast amounts of information and communication channels anywhere, anytime, anyplace is only but a repeated example. Information and communication overload in its own right, and coldly looked at and analyzed, may not be that bad after all. If we can control the overload to limits that are cognitively manageable, overload has the effect of the long lingering memory that suddenly sheds light on a problem, reviving the means to solving a problem, enlightening a less vivid picture that ascribes sense to something that had long been forgotten.

One could argue that the overload is not in the information and communication; it is rather in the users of information and communication, confined by their individual traits and capacities, their professional contexts or their socio-cultural environments.

DigComp details a conceptual understanding of digital competence. It is based on a review of several digital competence frameworks and outlines 21 competences in five competence areas. It is understood as a tool that can be used by all citizens, but the level of abstraction of the competences that are foreseen in the framework allows users, institutions/organizations, intermediaries or initiative developers to refine and specify sub-competences in the terms they consider most appropriate for the target groups or context they are dealing with. Therefore, the framework and the comprehensive descriptions of each competence it provides make it applicable to many areas and suitable for the development of indicators and tests to measure digital competence. In fact, testing of DigComp and results reporting have been a call of its authors (Ferrari, 2013; Vuorikari, et al., 2016) so that the framework gains in term of validity and reliability.

The chapter examines a potentially very useful tool to help manage flows of information and communication. It is a framework that can be applied to a wide variety of settings and can be incorporated into the educational system at different stages to create digitally competent citizens. It is also something that organizations and companies will find useful in developing the skills, attitudes and knowledge of their work forces.

REFERENCES

Ala-Mutka, K. (2011). *Mapping digital competence: Towards a conceptual understanding*. Sevilha: JRC-IPTS.

Ayyagari, R., Grover, V., & Purvis, R. (2011). Technostress: Technological antecedents and implications. *Management Information Systems Quarterly*, *35*(4), 831–858.

Bawden, D. (2008). Origins and concepts of digital literacy. In C. Lankshear & M. Knobel (Eds.), *Digital Literacies: Concepts, Policies & Practices* (pp. 17–32). New York, NY: Peter Lang Publishing, Inc.

Chen, W., & Lee, K. (2013). Sharing, liking, commenting, and distressed? The pathway between Facebook interaction and psychological distress. *Cyberpsychology, Behavior, and Social Networking, 16*(10), 728–734. doi:10.1089/cyber.2012.0272 PMID:23745614

Cho, J., Ramgolam, D. I., Schaefer, K. M., & Sandlin, A. N. (2011). The rate and delay in overload: An investigation of communication overload and channel synchronicity on identification and job satisfaction. *Journal of Applied Communication Research, 39*(1), 38–54. doi:10.1080/00909882.2010.536847

Dabbish, L. A., & Kraut, R. E. (2006). Email overload at work: An analysis of factors associated with email strain.*Proceedings of the 2006 20th anniversary conference on Computer supported cooperative work* (pp. 431–440). Alberta: ACM. doi:10.1145/1180875.1180941

Eppler, M. J., & Mengis, J. (2004). The concept of information overload: A review of literature from organization science, accounting, marketing, MIS, and related disciplines. *The Information Society, 20*(5), 325–344. doi:10.1080/01972240490507974

Eshet-Alkalai, Y. (2004). Digital Literacy. A Conceptual Framework for Survival Skills in the Digital Era. *Journal of Educational Multimedia and Hypermedia, 13*(1), 93–106.

European Parliament and the Council. (2006). Recommendation of the European Parliament and of the Council of 18 December 2006 on key competences for lifelong learning. *Official Journal of the European Union, L, 394*(310).

Evangelinos, G., & Holley, D. (2014a). Developing a Digital Competence Self-Assessment Toolkit for Nursing Students. In A.M. Teixeira, A. Szűcs & I. Mázár (Eds.), *E-learning at Work and the Workplace. From Education to Employment and Meaningful Work with ICT E-learning at Work and the Workplace*, (pp.206–212). European Distance and E-Learning Network (EDEN), Annual Conference, Zagreb.

Evangelinos, G., & Holley, D. (2014b). A Qualitative Exploration of the EU Digital Competence (DIGCOMP) Framework: A Case Study within Healthcare Education. In G. Vincenti, A. Bucciero & C. Vaz de Carvalho (Eds.), *E-Learning, E-Education, and Online-Training (ELEOT)First International Conference, Lecture Notes of the Institute for Computer Sciences, Social Informatics and Telecommunications Engineering*, (pp.85–92). Cham: Springer International Publishing. doi:10.1007/978-3-319-13293-8_11

Evangelinos, G., & Holley, D. (2015). Embedding digital competences in the curriculum: a case study on student-experience of an online technology-enhanced, activity-based learning design. *Proceedings of the European Distance and E-Learning Network 2015 Annual Conference*. Retrieved 6 October 2016 from http://arro.anglia.ac.uk/577015/

Ferrari, A. (2012). *Digital Competence in practice: An analysis of frameworks*. Seville: JRC-IPTS.

Ferrari, A. (2013). *DIGCOMP: A framework for developing and understanding digital competence in Europe*. Seville: JRC-IPTS.

Janssen, J., & Stoyanov, S. (2012). *Online consultation on experts' views on digital competence*. Seville: JRC-IPTS.

Krueger, R. A., & Casey, M. A. (2009). *Focus Groups: A practical guide for applied research* (4th ed.). Los Angeles, CA: Sage.

Lee, S. B., Lee, S. C., & Suh, Y. S. (2016). *Technostress from mobile communication and its impact on quality of life and productivity*. Total Quality Management & Business Excellence; doi:10.1080/14783363.2016.1187998

Rainie, L., Smith, A., & Duggan, M. (2013). *Coming and going on Facebook*. Pew Research Center's Internet and American Life Project.

Siiman, L. A., Mäeots, M., Pedaste, M., Simons, R.-J., & Leijen, Ä. Rannikmäe, M., …, & Timm, M. (2016). An Instrument for Measuring Students' Perceived Digital Competence According to the DIGCOMP Framework. In P. Zaphiris & Ioannou, A. (Eds.), *Third International Conference, LCT 2016, Held as Part of HCI International 2016*, (pp. 233-244). Springer International Publishing. doi:10.1007/978-3-319-39483-1_22

Strother, J. B., Ulijn, J. M., & Fazal, Z. (Eds.). (2012). *Information overload: An international challenge for professional engineers and technical communicators*. Wiley-IEEE Press. doi:10.1002/9781118360491

Tobak, S. (2010). Ten ways to stop communication overload. *CBS Moneywatch*. Retrieved June 16, 2016, from http://www.cbsnews.com/news/10-ways-to-stop-communication- overload/

UNESCO. (2013). *Global Media and Information Literacy Assessment Framework: Country Readiness and Competencies*. UNESCO.

van Deursen, A. J. A. M. (2010). *Internet Skills. Vital assets in an information society* (Unpublished doctoral dissertation). University of Twente, Netherlands.

Velicu, A., & Mitarca, M. (2016). *Young children (0-8) and digital technology: A qualitative exploratory study*. National Report Romania.

Vuorikari, R., Punie, Y., Carretero, S., & Van den Brande, L. (2016). *DigComp 2.0: The Digital Competence Framework for Citizens: Update Phase 1: The Conceptual Reference Model*. Sevilha: JRC-IPTS.

KEY TERMS AND DEFINITIONS

Data: A sequence of one or more symbols given meaning by specific act(s) of interpretation.

DigComp: The European Digital Competence Framework for Citizens, also known as DigComp, offers a tool to improve citizens' digital competence.

Digital Communication: Communication using digital technology. It can be synchronous communication (real time communication, e.g. using skype or video chat) or asynchronous communication (not concurrent communication, e.g. email, forum to send a message, sms).

Digital Competence: The set of knowledge, attitudes and skills needed to take an active part in digital environments and to reap the benefits of technologies for everyday life.

Digital Environment: A context, or a "place", that is enabled by technology and digital devices, often transmitted over the internet, or other digital means, e.g. mobile phone network.

Digital Technology: Any product that allows people and organizations to communicate and share information digitally.

The Common European Framework of Reference for Languages: A tool used to describe achievements of learners of foreign languages across Europe and, increasingly, in other countries.

ENDNOTES

[1]   See http://www.coe.int/t/dg4/linguistic/Cadre1_en.asp
[2]   See http://www.ecompetences.eu/
[3]   See endnote 1
[4]   http://europa.eu/rapid/press-release_IP-15-6321_en.htm
[5]   Vuorikari et al. (2016) do not include this dimension in their publication.
[6]   See http://libguides.library.ncat.edu/content.php?pid=53820&sid=394505

Chapter 8

The Impact of Information and Communication Technologies on Economic Growth and Electricity Consumption:
Evidence from Selected Balkan and Eastern European Countries

Burcu Berke
Omer Halisdemir University, Turkey

Gülsüm Akarsu
Ondokuz Mayıs University, Turkey

Gökhan Obay
Omer Halisdemir University, Turkey

ABSTRACT

Information overload is an important issue in the digital economy. Although, information can be easily accessed and disseminated by widespread use of information and communication technologies (ICT) since 1990s; among countries, there are still significant disparities in information access and utilization as well as ICT access and usage. ICT affect economy, industries and companies holistically and have

DOI: 10.4018/978-1-5225-2061-0.ch008

important functions like increasing economic growth and promoting development. The basic purpose of this study is to analyze the impact of ICT on economic growth and electricity consumption for a group of Balkan and Eastern European countries by using other economic variables that affect electricity consumption and growth, such as income and electricity consumption for control purposes. This study employed a panel data method on a group of Balkan and Eastern European countries to verify the effect of other economic variables, primarily electricity consumption and found that ICT had positive impacts on economic growth.

INTRODUCTION[1]

Studying the rapid accumulation and dissemination of information and communication technologies (ICT) in the world and its effect on the economic growth of developed and developing countries has gained significance in recent years (Breitenbach, Aderibigbe, & Muzungu, 2005; Abdel-Kader, 2006).

These technologies have created a digital space with the following properties, such as connectivity and emergence of networked environments, inter-operability and organisational boundarylessness, and higher speed and quality of communication and information flow (Filos and Banahan, 2001, p. 2-3).

Today, the structure of global economy has changed considerably with these technologies. The reason behind such a change is the rapid expansion of technologies like personal computers, the internet and mobile phones and the comprehensive impact of these devices have on the economy. Thus, the whole world is on a trajectory towards information-based economy that is always accessible and constantly usable (Seo and Lee, 2006) and information is the core input and result of this new digital economy (Filos and Banahan, 2001; Stewart, 1998). On the other hand, not all the countries, social groups and individuals have access to information, equally. The issues of information inequality and poverty have gained great attention since 1960's (Yu, 2006). There are many definitions related to information inequality and poverty. In his definition, Sweetland (1993) considered three forms of information deprivation as information poverty such as lack of information access, information overload and self-imposed information deprivation (Yu, 2006, p. 231). Among these forms, information overload is the situation in which there is too much information to process and therefore, there is difficulty to access the necessary information and according to Filos and Banahan (2001), one problem in the digital economy is the information overload rather than access to the information based on the following argument proposed by Simon Herbert "wealth of information creates a poverty of attention" (Shapiro and Varian, 1999). This argument can be valid for countries which have higher access to and utilization of information and ICT; however, among the countries, there are significant differences in information access and utilization as well as ICT access and usage which enables them to reach the information easily as beginning by 1990s, ICT's have become one of important tools for information dissemination and access and there is a strong relation between information inequality and digital divide (Yu, 2006). Yu (2006) classified different interpretations of information inequality in the literature based on four angles: ethics, political economy, social constructivism and cognitive science. This study focused on the political economy interpretation in which "the information inequality is both determined by and contributes to the political and economic inequality" (Yu, 2006, p. 232) and by considering the significant relation between information inequality and digital divide, i.e. inequality in ICT usage and access, analyzed the effect of ICT on economic growth and electricity consumption.

It is found that studies on the relation between ICT investments and economic growth first appeared in the 1960's and generally focused on the USA. The first study on the subject belongs to Jipp (1963) who examined the relation between communication technologies and growth. In the study, Jipp approached the relation between the number of telephone lines per capita and GDP per capita as a growth rate indicator. Jipp expressed the existence of a positive relation between telephone use intensity and growth (Alleman et al. 1994). Subsequent to this, a significant number of studies were conducted in developed and developing countries, which mostly suggested that information and communication technologies generally had a positive role on economic growth. Early studies (Jipp, 1963; Hardy, 1980; Saunders et al. 1983) were unable to demonstrate long-term relations between these two variables. However, the relation between ICT development and economic growth started to appear in time series and panel data analyses after the 1990s, with Cronin et al. (1991, 1993).

Since the 1990's "information and communication technologies (ICT)" have started to affect the economic and social structures of countries in all parts of the world. Having said that, the mention of such technologies in "energy literature" corresponds to the 2000's (Takase and Murota, 2004, p. 1291). Although there are several studies in literature on the relation between energy consumption and economic growth and between ICT investments and economic growth, the number of studies that collectively investigate the relations between them are quite limited. While literature reports that ICT investments generally have a positive effect on economic growth and productivity ("productivity paradox"), the relation between ICT investments and energy consumption has drawn less attention, despite its economic and environmental impacts. So much so that investing in ICT increases the energy efficiency which in return reduces production costs (Cho, Lee and Kim,

2007, p.4730). Following the oil crises of the 1970's, studies were carried out to determine the outlook of energy consumption in the economy as the use of information technologies increased. Certain hypotheses were developed which argued that information technologies reduced energy consumption and increased economic growth. However, prior to the proliferation of internet and mobile phone usage these hypotheses disregarded the effect information technology use had on electricity consumption (Sadorsky, 2012, p. 130).

The information and communication industry entered a phase of rapid growth with the spread of internet and mobile cellular phones. As traditional mobile phones got replaced by smart phones, it became possible to share data, images and videos. While these created positive network effects it also resulted in increased electricity demand (Sadorsky, 2012, p.131). In literature the impact of ICT on electricity consumption is unknown. On one hand, ICT reorganize production processes and reduce costs by contributing to energy savings, however, on the other hand, it can lead to additional energy demand due to the energy consumed by ICT capital stock. In contrast to energy intensity, in recent years, electrical power consumption intensity has increased or has not decreased as much as energy intensity in many countries. That is why it is interesting to investigate the effect of ICT capital diffusion and production on electricity intensity (Bernstein and Madlener, 2008).

This study employs the panel data method to analyze how three different ICT indicators affect electricity consumption and economic growth in 20 selected Balkan and Eastern European countries during the 1996-2012 period. In other words, the basic purpose of this study is to analyze the impact of information and communication technologies (ICT) on economic growth for a group of Balkan and Eastern European countries by using other economic variables that affect growth, such as electricity consumption for control purposes. For this purpose, the following section first surveys theoretical and empirical literature on the subject, then presents results obtained from the analyses and tests carried out in scope of two different models (one on the effects of ICT on electricity consumption, and the other on the effects of ICT on economic growth) developed specifically for this country group. The study concludes with results and recommendations.

BACKGROUND

ICT affects the economic growth in a number of ways. According to Quah (2002), ICT improves "labor skills and consumer sophistication; and increases level of broad-based education" and therefore contributes to the economic growth through increasing labor productivity (Vu, 2011, p. 357). On the other hand, as ICT usage leads to easy access to information, investments can increase suggested by Levine (1997) which further boosts the economic growth (Vu, 2011). The first study about information and communication technologies belongs to Jipp (1963) who investigated the relation between communication technologies and growth. The study discusses the relation between the number of telephone subscriptions per capita (intensity of telephone use) and GDP per capita, used as an indicator of growth rate, and demonstrates a positive relation between the two parameters (Alleman et al., 1994). After this study, several other studies were carried out in both developed and developing countries. Authors like Hardy (1980), Chen and Kuo (1985), Cronin et al. (1991, 1993), Alleman et al. (1994), Dholakia and Harlam (1994) led the way during the 1980's and 1990's.

Empirical studies generally suggest that information and communication technologies have a "positive" effect on economic growth. For example, in their study investigating the effect of telephone usage on economic growth, Hardy (1980), Chen and Kuo (1985), Alleman et al. (1994), Madden and Savage (2000), Breitenbach et al. (2005) conducted country-specific analyses and ultimately supported the existence of a positive relation between telephone subscriptions per capita and economic growth. Meanwhile, Brock and Sutherland (2000) took a different approach and investigated the effect of telephone subscriptions per capita has on growth in industrial production but did not find such a relation.

Another group of studies discuss the effect of telecommunication investments on economic growth. Some that stand out include Dholakia and Harlam (1994), Schreyer (2000), Röller and Waverman (2001), Datta and Agarwal (2004), Lee, Gholami and Tang (2005), Lee, Levendis and Gutierrez (2012), Lam and Shiu (2010), and particularly Cronin et al. (1991, 1993). In a study carried out in the USA, Cronin et al. (1991) investigated the effect of telecommunication investments on GNP and found a positive relation between each other. Another study by Cronin et al. (1993) examined the effect of telecommunication infrastructure investments on productivity and argued that such investments had a positive effect on productivity. Similarly, after carrying out country or group specific studies, Dholakia and Harlam (1994), Schreyer (2000), Röller and Waverman (2001), Datta and Agarwal (2004), Lee et al. (2012) supported Cronin et al.'s (1991, 1993) hypothesis and agreed that telecommunication investments and telecommunication infrastructure investments had a positive effect on growth. On the other hand, Lee et al. (2005) found that telecommunication investments had a positive effect on economic growth in developed and developing countries but had no effect in underdeveloped countries. More comprehensively, Lam and Shiu (2010) investigated the relation between real GDP growth and telecommunications systems (number of landline and cellular subscribers per 100 people) as well as the relation between total factor productivity and telecommunication productivity and verified their relation had significant causality.

A separate group of studies focus on the effect of information and communications technologies on growth, productivity and total factor productivity. Different than the aforementioned studies, Jorgensen and Stiroh (2000), and McGuckin and Stiroh (2000) examined the relation between the number of computers and growth and found a positive relation between the two. Dewan and Kraemer (2000), Pohloja (2000), Roeger (2001), Colecchia and Schreyer (2002), Jalava and Pohloja (2002), Satti and Nour (2002), Oulton (2002), O'Mahony and Vecchi (2005), Timmer and Van Ark (2005), Jorgensen and Vu (2007), Hosman, Fife, & Armey (2008), Vu (2011) investigated the impact of information technologies investments on growth and/or productivity and reported a positive relation. More specific studies by Baliamoune-Lutz (2003), Jorgensen (2001), Abdel-Kader (2006), Zahra, Azim, & Mahmood (2008) take a different approach and make distinctions between the indicators of information and communication technologies. Baiamoune-Lutz (2003) used mobile phone, personal computer, internet providers and users as "indicators for information and communication technologies" for 47 developing countries and reported that these technologies had a positive role on income per capita. Jorgensen (2001) used software and human capital instead of the indicators identified for G7 countries and reported increased productivity. In his study covering Latin America, the Middle East, North Africa, East and South Asia countries, Abdel-Kader (2006) used the number of personal computer, internet users, phone subscribers and mobile phone users per 100 people as indicators and reported that these factors had a positive effect on growth. In his study Zahra et al. (2008) used mobile phone and internet subscriptions per 1000 people as indicators for low, middle and high income countries and reported that these factors had a positive relation with growth in GDP per capita.

Literature on information and communication technologies has developed over the years and there are now examples of studies associated with energy economy literature. In their study investigating the relation between electricity consumption and economic development, Ferguson, Wilkinson and Hill (2000) reported that wealthy countries had a stronger correlation between electricity consumption and creating wealth compared to poor countries. This finding suggests that it is electricity use rather than energy that plays an important role in the development of modern society. Studies evaluating the relation between ICT and electricity consumption appear later. Early on, Romm (2002) suggested that internet investments reduced electricity and energy intensity. This was followed by studies analyzing the effects of ICT on electricity and energy consumption in different country groups. In some studies, the magnitude of the effect was justified with the relative size of the income and substitution effects. For example, while in the income effect ICT increases electricity and energy consumption, in the substitution effect ICT reduces consumption of both (Bernstein and Madlener, 2008). Among these, the works of Schaefer, Weber and Voss (2003), Takase and Murota (2004), Collard, Feve and Portier (2005), Cho, Lee and Kim (2007), Bernstein and Madlener (2008), Ropke, Christensen, & Jensen (2010), and Sadorsky (2012) are noteworthy. For example, Schaefer et al. (2003) investigated the impact of mobile phone services on energy demand in Germany and found that these services increased demand. Taking a slightly different approach, Takase and Murota (2004) investigated the impact of information technology (IT) investments on energy consumption and CO2 emissions in the USA and Japan and reported different results for the mentioned countries. They reported that while IT investment led to energy savings in Japan, it increased consumption in the USA. Therefore, while the substitution effect is dominant in Japan, the income effect is in play in the USA. By using a factor demand model for the service sector in France, Collard et al. (2005) reported that electricity intensity increased with computers and software while it dropped with the diffusion of communication devices. To put it briefly, in contrast to computers and software, communication devices increased electricity efficiency and therefore contributed to a fall in electricity intensity. Similarly, Bernstein and Madlener (2008) reported that communication technologies helped save electricity in production and decreased electricity intensity in 5 different industries by using disaggregated ICT data. On the other hand, in their study investigating the impact of ICT investment, electricity tariffs and petrol prices on industrial electricity consumption in South Korea, Cho et al. (2007) reported that ICT investments contributed to a cut in energy consumption, especially in most manufacturing sectors, but increased electricity consumption in the service sector. Similarly, a study by Ropke et al. (2010) investigated the effect of ICT on household energy consumption and reported that ICT practices increased electricity consumption and that internet and social media sites created a positive network effect. Finally, Sadorsky (2012) pointed out to the positive relation between ICT and electricity consumption and urged on that three different ICT indicators (internet users, mobile cellular subscriptions, personal computers) had a positive effect on electricity consumption.

Another segment of literature consists of studies analyzing the relations between ICT and economic growth. Among these, Oliner and Sichel (2000) argued that computer hardware, software and network infrastructure stocks contributed to growth in the USA and that information technology was a basic determinant in economic growth. Another example comes from Jalava and Pohjola (2008) who analyzed ICT and electricity as the indicators of economic growth in Finland and argued that ICT had a more important role in economic growth compared to electricity. On the other hand, Yousefi (2011) investigated the effects of ICT and non-ICT capitals on economic growth in developed and developing countries. Results suggest that while investments in ICT and non-ICT capital played a fundamental role in the growth of high and upper-middle class income group countries, such investments failed to be successful in contributing to the growth of low-middle income group countries. Similarly, in their study investigating the relation between ICT and non-ICT capital and economic output in Australia, Shahiduzzaman and Atam (2014) reported a positive relation and causality relation between the two. Lee et al. (2012) reported that in Sub Saharan Africa mobile cellular phones played a more significant role in economic growth compared to land-line telephones and emphasized the importance of telecommunication infrastructure investments in growth. Finally, unlike other studies, Pradhan, Bele and Pandey (2013) included macro-variables in their study on 34 OECD countries and confirmed the presence of a causality relation between internet, economic growth, public spending and inflation.

EMPIRICAL ANALYSIS FOR THE EFFECT OF ICT ADOPTION ON ELECTRICITY CONSUMPTION AND ECONOMIC GROWTH

First, this section presents the information on data used in the analysis. Then, the authors discuss methodological issues and empirical results. In the analysis, panel data techniques are employed because given the data available for short time periods for the countries under investigation, one can gain efficiency improvement in the estimates while allowing for heterogeneity in the data.

Information on Data Employed

This study uses annual balanced panel data on 20 Balkan and Eastern European countries[2] covering the period from 1996 to 2012. This group of countries is chosen because it includes both developed and developing countries in addition to the economies in transition. This enables one to analyze the effect of ICT usage for the countries with different levels of development. Two different models are employed based on economic theory and previous literature. For electricity consumption model, the data set includes electric power consumption measured in kWh per capita ($pcec$), GDP per capita measured in constant 2005 US\$ ($pcgdp$), consumer price index with base year $2010 = 100$[3] (cpi) as a proxy for electricity price, fixed telephone subscriptions per 100 people (tel), internet users per 100 people ($int\,ernet$), and mobile cellular subscriptions per 100 people ($mobile$). All the data is transformed using natural logarithm.

Table 1. Summary Statistics

	Data for Electricity Consumption Model						Data for Economic Growth Model				
	Mean	**S.D.**	**C.V.**	**Min**	**Max**		**Mean**	**S.D.**	**C.V.**	**Min**	**Max**
lnpcec	8.07	0.50	0.06	6.52	8.87	*g*	3.97	5.03	1.27	-14.56	14.45
lnpcgdp	8.57	0.97	0.11	6.35	10.18	$lnpcgdp_{-1}$	8.54	0.98	0.12	6.35	10.18
lntel	3.20	0.48	0.15	0.65	4.05	*inf*	9.79	15.45	1.58	-1.28	154.76
lninternet	2.23	1.94	0.87	-5.37	4.36	*ICT*	0.38	0.25	0.66	0.01	0.91
lnmobile	3.17	2.05	0.65	-4.66	5.23	*population*	-0.10	0.83	8.33	-2.52	2.64
lncpi	4.49	0.50	0.11	1.21	5.36	*openness*	0.94	0.33	0.35	0.38	1.80
						capital	0.24	0.05	0.22	0.13	0.41
						lnpcec	8.07	0.50	0.06	6.52	8.87

lnpcec , *lnpcgdp* , *lntel* , *lninternet* , *lnmobile* and *lncpi* show natural logarithms of *pcec* , *pcgdp* , *tel* , *internet* , *mobile* and *cpi* . $lnpcgdp_{-1}$ is lagged GDP per capita (constant 2005 US$) in natural logarithm. C.V. is the ratio of standard deviation to the mean.

On the other hand, for economic growth model, the data set consists of real per capita GDP growth[4] (*g*), inflation (consumer prices, annual %) (*inf*), ICT index (*ICT*),[5] population growth (annual %) (*population*), openness index (*openness*),[6] capital stock (*capital*),[7] and electric power consumption (kWh per capita) in logarithm (ln *pcec*). The data is obtained from *World Bank, World Development Indicators*.

Table 1 shows the summary statistics, i.e., overall mean, standard deviation (S.D.), coefficient of variation (C.V.), minimum (Min) and maximum (Max) values for each variable. GDP of these countries under investigation grow 3.96% on average, over the period between 1996 and 2012. ICT index shows that fixed telephone subscriptions, internet usage, and mobile cellular subscriptions are low on average in these countries over the period; however, the maximum value for this index was realized in Estonia in the year of 2012 indicating the highest usage of ICT in this country among others. C.V. indicates the presence of large variability over both time and countries for especially internet usage, mobile cellular subscriptions, economic growth, inflation, and population growth. However, from Table 1, one cannot observe the differences among the countries.

In order to examine the differences among countries over the period, time averages of each variable for each country are calculated and presented in Tables 2 and 3. The countries are classified according to their level of development based on the classification of United Nations. For the period under investigation, on average, developed countries record the highest levels of electricity consumption, per capita GDP, fixed telephone subscriptions, internet usage, mobile cellular subscriptions, CPI, ICT usage, capital stock and foreign trade. On the other hand, the highest average inflation rate and population growth are observed in developing country, Turkey over the period between 1996 and 2012. Economic growth is the highest on average for the economies in transition. Country level comparison shows that, as seen from Table 2, average electricity consumption is the highest in Slovenia and the lowest in Albania over the period from 1996 to 2012. On the other hand, the highest and lowest economic growth is experienced by Georgia and Greece, respectively (see Table 3).

The examination of ICT index (see Table 3) shows that the highest ICT usage is recorded by Estonia and lowest by Armenia, on average. Estonia also has the highest internet usage and mobile cellular subscriptions while Slovenia records the highest level of fixed telephone subscriptions.

Pairwise correlations between the variables are given in Tables 4 and 5 for electricity consumption and economic growth models, respectively. Correlations show that there is not any problem of multicollinearity between the variables for economic growth model. However, for electricity consumption model, there is strong relation between *lnmobile* and *lninternet* which is an indication of multicollinearity problem. Therefore, in the estimations, this issue needs to be addressed. Moreover, pairwise correlations cannot show the direction of relation. But, the focus of this study is only on the effect of ICT usage on electricity consumption and economic growth.[8]

Methodology and Empirical Results

In this study, panel data techniques are employed in order to investigate the effect of ICT on electricity consumption and economic growth for the selected Balkan and Eastern European countries. Two models are estimated given by equations (1)

Table 2. Average values of variables employed in Electricity Consumption Model, 1996-2012

Country	lnpcec	lnpcgdp	lntel	lninternet	lnmobile	lncpi
Developed Countries	8.302	9.250	3.437	2.967	3.763	4.524
Cyprus	8.239	10.053	3.708	3.069	3.787	4.574
Czech Republic	8.710	9.439	3.372	3.102	3.980	4.580
Estonia	8.594	9.088	3.572	3.552	4.100	4.588
Greece	8.501	9.922	3.960	2.744	4.085	4.567
Hungary	8.191	9.213	3.482	2.940	3.916	4.515
Latvia	7.867	8.760	3.360	2.944	3.589	4.611
Lithuania	8.045	8.843	3.284	2.690	3.827	4.655
Poland	8.146	8.969	3.203	2.935	3.500	4.542
Romania	7.747	8.393	2.930	2.174	3.071	4.122
Slovak Republic	8.533	9.331	3.181	3.081	3.634	4.488
Slovenia	8.752	9.742	3.749	3.405	3.908	4.507
Economies in Transition	7.808	7.610	2.873	1.217	2.311	4.518
Albania	7.249	7.826	1.888	0.605	2.317	4.551
Armenia	7.294	7.210	2.944	1.056	1.577	4.606
Georgia	7.350	7.206	2.704	0.850	2.475	4.573
Kazakhstan	8.265	8.099	2.841	0.771	2.165	4.563
Macedonia	8.089	8.026	3.115	2.255	2.817	4.610
Moldova	7.519	6.642	3.081	1.269	1.985	4.413
Russia	8.642	8.490	3.241	1.935	2.780	4.299
Ukraine	8.059	7.378	3.169	0.996	2.372	4.530
Developing Countries						
Turkey	7.567	8.822	3.252	2.121	3.471	3.993

Table 3. Average values of variables employed in Economic Growth Model, 1996-2012

Country	g	lnpcgdp$_{-1}$	inf	ICT	population	openness	capital	lnpcec
Developed Countries	*3.461*	*9.217*	*7.208*	*0.459*	*-0.147*	*1.046*	*0.246*	*8.302*
Cyprus	1.108	10.042	2.725	0.434	1.634	1.192	0.217	8.239
Czech Republic	2.386	9.416	3.811	0.498	0.104	1.102	0.291	8.710
Estonia	5.194	9.040	5.891	0.555	-0.486	1.394	0.292	8.594
Greece	0.921	9.914	3.664	0.517	0.248	0.512	0.219	8.501
Hungary	2.357	9.190	8.339	0.463	-0.237	1.329	0.233	8.191
Latvia	5.773	8.705	5.711	0.428	-1.177	0.949	0.257	7.867
Lithuania	5.884	8.787	4.592	0.490	-1.144	1.097	0.217	8.045
Poland	4.332	8.927	5.884	0.408	-0.082	0.691	0.207	8.146
Romania	3.405	8.361	28.081	0.304	-0.724	0.708	0.247	7.747
Slovak Republic	4.165	9.291	5.448	0.437	0.050	1.383	0.277	8.533
Slovenia	2.545	9.717	5.145	0.517	0.196	1.144	0.253	8.752
Economies in Transition	*4.814*	*7.564*	*10.327*	*0.265*	*-0.219*	*0.844*	*0.234*	*7.808*
Albania	5.688	7.771	6.057	0.216	-0.556	0.675	0.316	7.249
Armenia	7.594	7.139	5.632	0.211	-0.465	0.705	0.254	7.294
Georgia	6.592	7.143	8.417	0.203	-0.310	0.750	0.237	7.350
Kazakhstan	6.005	8.042	10.865	0.267	0.352	0.852	0.229	8.265
Macedonia	2.412	8.003	2.419	0.320	0.339	0.899	0.210	8.089
Moldova	2.927	6.615	13.042	0.234	-0.188	1.294	0.223	7.519
Russia	4.097	8.451	19.764	0.373	-0.209	0.555	0.192	8.642
Ukraine	3.194	7.349	16.421	0.295	-0.718	1.020	0.209	8.059
Developing Countries								
Turkey	2.777	8.796	33.816	0.322	1.388	0.490	0.204	7.567

Table 4. Pairwise Correlations for Electricity Consumption Model

	lnpcec	lnpcgdp	lntel	lninternet	lnmobile	lncpi
lnpcec	1					
lnpcgdp	0.7202	1				
lntel	0.6345	0.6395	1			
lninternet	0.5018	0.5892	0.5263	1		
lnmobile	0.4172	0.5321	0.4591	0.9321	1	
lncpi	0.2105	0.1658	0.1711	0.6407	0.662	1

Table 5. Pairwise Correlations for Economic Growth Model

	g	lnpcgdp$_{-1}$	inf	ICT	population	openness	capital	lnpcec
g	1							
lnpcgdp$_{-1}$	-0.236	1						
inf	-0.1353	-0.194	1					
ICT	-0.209	0.5809	-0.3565	1				
population	-0.2122	0.3629	0.0427	0.1084	1			
openness	0.0136	0.2027	-0.2554	0.3684	-0.0458	1		
capital	0.2391	0.1078	-0.1901	0.1139	-0.0823	0.1445	1	
lnpcec	-0.1773	0.7214	-0.2279	0.544	0.1783	0.3536	0.0517	1

and (2) below including individual and time-period fixed effects into the models, therefore, allowing for country and time heterogeneity;

$$\mathbf{lnpcec}_{i,t} = \alpha_{1i} + \delta_{1t} + \beta_{11}\mathbf{lnpcgdp}_{i,t} + \beta_{12}\mathbf{lntel}_{i,t} + \beta_{13}\mathbf{lninternet}_{i,t} + \beta_{14}\mathbf{lnmobile}_{i,t}$$
$$+ \beta_{15}\mathbf{lncpi}_{i,t} + \varepsilon_{1i,t}$$

(1)

$$\mathbf{g}_{i,t} = \alpha_{2i} + \delta_{2t} + \beta_{21}\mathbf{lnpcgdp}_{i,t-1} + \beta_{22}\mathbf{inflation}_{i,t} + \beta_{23}\mathbf{ICT}_{i,t} + \beta_{24}\mathbf{population}_{i,t}$$
$$+ \beta_{25}\mathbf{openness}_{i,t} + \beta_{26}\mathbf{capital}_{i,t} + \beta_{27}\mathbf{lnpcec}_{i,t} + \varepsilon_{2i,t}$$

(2)

where, $i=1,...,20$ and $t=1996,...,2012$ show subscripts for cross-sectional units and time periods and $\varepsilon_{ji,t} \sim iidN(0,\sigma^2)$ for all i, t and $j=1, 2$. α_{ji} and δ_{jt} are country-specific and time period fixed effects (FE) where $j = 1, 2$. For equation 1, the coefficients on each variable show the elasticity estimates. First, pooled model is estimated by OLS assuming homogenous coefficients including the intercept term such that $\alpha_{1i} = \alpha_1$ and $\delta_{1t} = \delta_1$ for electricity consumption model given by equation (1) and $\alpha_{2i} = \alpha_2$ and $\delta_{2t} = \delta_2$ for economic growth model given by equation (2). If heterogeneity is ignored although it exists, then OLS estimator of pooled model will be inconsistent and biased. Therefore, intercept is allowed to differ across countries by introducing individual fixed effects to the model, therefore the equations (1) and (2) are restricted by imposing following restrictions; $\delta_{1t} = \delta_1$ for equation (1) and $\delta_{2t} = \delta_2$ for equation (2). Lastly, in addition to country-specific FE's, time period FE's are also included into the models as in the equation (1) and (2). The presence of fixed effects is tested by using F tests. Also other diagnostic tests are performed in order to check if there is misspecification in the model, such as autocorrelation and heteroscedasticity tests. If there is problem of autocorrelation and heteroscedasticity, then Feasible Generalized Least Squares (FGLS) and Feasible Generalized Least Square Dummy Variable (FGLSDV) estimation methods are applied. The details and formula for the tests can be found in Baltagi (2008). On the electricity consumption (*lnpcec*), one expects positive impacts of income (*lnpcgdp*), fixed telephone subscriptions per 100 people (*lntel*), internet users per 100 people (*lninternet*), and mobile cellular subscriptions per 100 people (*lnmobile*), whereas, negative effect of electricity price (*lncpi*) is expected.

Economic growth (*g*) is expected to be positively affected by ICT index (*ICT*), population growth (*population*), openness index (*openness*), capital stock (*capital*), and electric consumption (ln *pcec*), but negatively affected by inflation (*inf*). In equation (2), the negative and statistically significant coefficient on $lnpcgdp_{-1}$ indicates the evidence of conditional income convergence among the countries.

The estimation results are presented in Tables 6 and 7 for both models. As there is evidence of individual and time period fixed effects and also autocorrelation and heteroscedasticity problems, conclusions of the study are based on the estimation results given by the FGLSDV estimation of models with individual and time period fixed effects assuming common AR(1) coefficient which is shown in the fifth column of Tables 6 and 7. In Table 6, the estimation results of electricity consumption model show that *lnpcgdp*, *lntel* and *lnmobile* significantly and positively affect *lnpcec*. Because, higher economic activity and ICT usage are expected to be associated with increase in electricity demand. Income and price elasticities of electricity consumption are found to be 0.344 and -0.003, respectively, indicating that electricity consumption is inelastic with respect to income and price and also 1% increases in income (price) increases (decreases) per capita electricity consumption by 0.344% (0.003%). Therefore, electricity can be regarded as a necessity for group of these countries. Also, pricing policies alone is not an effective tool to influence the electricity demand and thus to guarantee the supply and demand balance. Findings further show that 1% increases in fixed telephone subscriptions per 100 people, internet users per 100 people, and mobile cellular subscriptions per 100 people are associated with 0.053%, -0.008%, and -0.015% increases in the electricity consumption, respectively. Three different measures of ICT are employed in this study as in Sadorsky (2012). Overall, one can conclude that ICT usage significantly and positively affect electricity consumption under certain assumptions.

On the other hand, the estimation results for the growth model are given in Table 7 indicating that all the variables have statistically significant effects with signs in line with the expectations except *lnpcec*. Although the effect of electricity consumption is found to be positive on growth, this effect is not statistically significant. In addition, increase in inflation has a negative effect on growth as high inflation hampers capital investments. In this case also, the findings indicate the positive effect of ICT adoption on economic growth.

SOLUTIONS AND RECOMMENDATIONS

From the previous section, the results show significant and boosting effects of ICT adoption on both electricity consumption and economic growth. Based on this result, one can conclude that while making policies related to ICT usage and development, both growth and environmental effects should be considered altogether. In addition, one cannot ignore the impact of ICT usage on electricity consumption

Table 6. Pooled and Fixed Effects Estimations of Electricity Consumption Model

lnpcec	(1)	(2)	(3)	(4)	(5)
lnpcgdp	0.274*** (0.028)	0.450*** (0.039)	0.299*** (0.047)	0.344*** (0.046)	0.346*** (0.044)
lntel	0.290*** (0.050)	0.032 (0.071)	0.107 (0.082)	0.053** (0.026)	0.051** (0.025)
lninternet	0.063 (0.052)	0.023 (0.016)	-0.006 (0.019)	-0.008 (0.008)	-
lnmobile	-0.074 (0.043)	-0.028* (0.015)	-0.030 (0.019)	-0.015** (0.007)	-0.018*** (0.006)
lncpi	0.118*** (0.034)	0.039*** (0.011)	0.014 (0.011)	-0.003 (0.015)	-0.001 (0.014)
Constant	4.352*** (0.365)	3.966*** (.471)	5.042*** (0.427)	4.422*** (0.381)	4.419*** (0.366)
R^2	0.5870	0.6328	0.9683	-	-
LM_ρ	154.84***	155.76***	150.27***	-	-
LR_H	306.05***	347.05***	383.82***	-	-
Individual FE test		181.93***		-	-
Time-period FE test[1]			1.67094*	-	-
Joint FE test[2]			2009.95***	-	-

Notes: Driscoll and Kraay (1998) standard errors are provided in parentheses for the correction of possible cross-sectional dependence, heteroscedasticity and autocorrelation. LM_ρ statistics is employed to test for first order autocorrelation in the residuals; $LM_\rho \sim \chi_1^2$ under the assumption of no autocorrelation. LR_H is the heteroscedasticity test and have asymptotic χ^2 null distribution with 20 d.f. *, **, *** show the statistical significance of test statistic at 10%, 5% and 1%. In order to save space, the estimation results are not presented for the coefficients on individual and time-period fixed effects.
1. Pooled OLS.
2. Individual FE.
3. Individual and Time period FE.
4. FGLSDV estimation with individual and time period FE. In FGLSDV estimation, common AR(1) coefficient (0.7095) is estimated for all panels.
5. FGLSDV estimation with individual and time period FE. In FGLSDV estimation, common AR(1) coefficient (0.7093) is estimated for all panels. In order to consider the problem of multicollinearity, lninternet variable is excluded from the model; however, similar results are obtained.
[1] Test in the presence of Individual FE.
[2] Joint Test for Individual and Time-period FE.

Table 7. Pooled and Fixed Effects Estimations of Economic Growth Model

g	(1)	(2)	(3)	(4)
$lnpcgdp_{-1}$	-0.631 (0.423)	-18.850** (6.624)	-12.161** (4.584)	-16.379*** (2.463)
inf	-0.060*** (0.018)	-0.083*** (0.021)	-0.066*** (0.015)	-0.062*** (0.013)
ICT	-4.575*** (1.372)	7.045** (2.738)	2.658 (3.803)	7.323*** (2.669)
population	-0.683** (0.333)	0.837 (0.555)	0.652 (0.493)	0.868** (0.368)
openness	0.640 (0.869)	12.046*** (4.000)	6.752*** (2.118)	7.286*** (1.351)
capital	21.577*** (4.857)	57.460*** (11.492)	35.110*** (7.318)	46.429*** (5.715)
$lnpcec$	-0.153 (0.780)	1.581 (2.957)	-1.527 (2.127)	1.302 (2.419)
constant	7.056 (4.902)	125.315*** (33.679)	103.563** (39.459)	102.877*** (23.018)
R^2	0.1823	0.3494	0.5777	-
LM_ρ	27.431***	39.682***	27.745***	-
LR_H	66.03***	89.96***	97.34***	-
Individual FE test		7.3789***		-
Time-period FE test[1]			10.069***	-
Joint FE test[2]			20.782***	-

Notes: Driscoll and Kraay (1998) standard errors are provided in parentheses for the correction of possible cross-sectional dependence, heteroscedasticity and autocorrelation. LM_ρ is the LM statistics to test for first order autocorrelation in the residuals; $LM_\rho \sim \chi_1^2$ under the assumption of no autocorrelation. LR_H is the heteroscedasticity test and have asymptotic χ^2 null distribution with 20 d.f. Pesaran's CD test is cross-sectional dependence tests and has asymptotic N(0, 1) distribution for large T and N $\longrightarrow \infty$. *, **, *** shows the statistical significance of test statistic at 10%, 5% and 1%. In order to save space, the estimation results are not presented for the coefficients on individual and time-period fixed effects.
1. Pooled OLS.
2. Individual FE.
3. Individual and Time period FE.
4. FGLSDV estimation with individual and time period FE. In FGLSDV estimation, common AR(1) coefficient (0.3439) is estimated for all panels.
[1] Test in the presence of Individual FE.
[2] Joint Test for Individual and Time-period FE.

and growth. The studies that did not include the ICT measures may lead to wrong policy suggestions for example related to energy conservation, energy efficiency and mitigation of greenhouse gas emissions and also wrong projections of electricity demand which is important for the planning in the sector, therefore energy security as noticed by Sadorsky (2012). Because results show ICT adoption has an important and boosting effect on electricity consumption which can further cause increase in greenhouse gas emissions. On the other hand, ICT usage increases economic growth. As a conclusion, while designing policies to increase ICT adoption, one need to consider both economic growth effects and electricity consumption growth effects, thus environmental impacts together. In order to reduce the impact of ICT usage increase, energy efficiency of ICT products, networks and data centers should be upgraded. The R&D activities should be supported for the energy efficiency improvements of ICT products.

FUTURE RESEARCH DIRECTIONS

As mentioned earlier, this study only analyzes the effect of ICT on economic growth and electricity consumption, not the effect of economic growth and electricity consumption on ICT. But this direction of relation can also be studied in the future studies. Moreover, the analysis can be applied to other set of countries or individual countries based on the data availability. In addition, as a future study, the effect of ICT usage on information overload can be analyzed by using survey data or performing experiments.

CONCLUSION

There is a strong relation between information inequality and digital divide. Although information overload is a challenging issue for the countries with higher ICT access and usage, other countries still suffer from limited access to information and ICT. Therefore, depending on data availability, this study employed the panel data method to analyze "the effect of ICT on electricity consumption and economic growth" for 20 selected Balkan and Eastern European countries under two different models over the period from 1996 to 2012. After verifying the effects of other variables, the results show that each of the ICT indicators positively affect both electricity consumption and economic growth. Based on this result, one can conclude that while making policies related to ICT usage and development, both growth and environmental effects should be considered altogether. ICT is important in reviving economic growth and promoting development (Yousefi, 2011). In terms of emerging market countries, energy protection policies are important however, policies that disregard the effect of ICT and only consider the relations of electricity demand and income are inclined to forecast energy demand lower than it really is. Similarly, energy demand forecasts that disregard the effect of ICT can also damage energy policy targets aimed at reducing greenhouse gases. Under these conditions, developing countries' policies aimed at closing the "digital divide" should focus on spreading ICT (Sadorsky, 2012).

REFERENCES

Abdel-Kader, K. (2006). The Impact of information and communication technology on economic growth in MENA countries. *EUI Working Papers, 2006/31*, 1-29.

Alleman, J., Hunt, C., Michaels, D., Mueller, D., Rappaport, P., & Taylor, L. (1994). *Telecommunications and economic development: empirical evidence from Southern Africa.* Paper presented at 10th Biennial International Telecommunications Society Meeting. Sydney.

Baliamoune-Lutz, M. (2003). An analysis of the determinants and effects of ICT diffusion in developing countries. *Information Technology for Development, 10*(3), 151–169. doi:10.1002/itdj.1590100303

Baltagi, B. H. (2008). *Econometric analysis of panel data* (4th ed.). West Sussex, UK: John Wiley.

Bernstein, R., & Madlener, R. (2008). The impact of disaggregated ICT capital on electricity intensity of production: econometric analysis of major European industries. *FCN Working Paper, 4/2008*, 1-31.

Breitenbach, M., Aderibigbe, O., & Muzungu, D. (2005). *The Impact of information and communication technology (ICT) on economic growth in South Africa: Analysis of evidence.* Retrieved from http://www.essa.org.za/download/2005Conference/Breitenbach.pdf

Brock, G., & Sutherland, E. (2000). Telecommunications and economic growth in the former USSR. *East European Quarterly, 34*(3), 319–335.

Chen, H. T., & Kuo, E. C. Y. (1985). Telecommunications and economic development in Singapore. *Telecommunications Policy, 9*(3), 240–244. doi:10.1016/0308-5961(85)90055-2

Cho, Y., Lee, J., & Kim, T. Y. (2007). The Impact of ICT investment and energy price on industrial electricity demand: Dynamic growth model approach. *Energy Policy*, *35*(9), 4730–4738. doi:10.1016/j.enpol.2007.03.030

Colecchia, A., & Schreyer, P. (2002). ICT investment and economic growth in the 1990s: Is the United States a unique case? A comparative study of nine OECD countries. *Review of Economic Dynamics*, *5*(2), 408–442. doi:10.1006/redy.2002.0170

Collard, F., Feve, P., & Portier, P. (2005). Electricity consumption and ICT in the French service sector. *Energy Economics*, *27*(3), 541–550. doi:10.1016/j.eneco.2004.12.002

Cronin, F., Parker, E., Colleran, E., & Gold, M. (1991). Telecommunications infrastructure and economic growth: An analysis of causality. *Telecommunications Policy*, *15*(6), 529–535. doi:10.1016/0308-5961(91)90007-X

Cronin, F., Parker, E., Colleran, E., & Gold, M. (1993). Telecommunications infrastructure investment and economic development. *Telecommunications Policy*, *17*(6), 415–430. doi:10.1016/0308-5961(93)90013-S

Datta, A., & Agarwal, S. (2004). Telecommunications and economic growth: A panel data approach. *Applied Economics*, *36*(15), 1649–1654. doi:10.1080/0003684042000218552

Dewan, S., & Kraemer, K. L. (2000). Information technology and productivity: Evidence from country-level data. *Management Science*, *46*(4), 548–562. doi:10.1287/mnsc.46.4.548.12057

Dholakia, R., & Harlam, B. (1994). Telecommunications and economic development: Econometric analyses of the US experience. *Telecommunications Policy*, *18*(6), 470–477. doi:10.1016/0308-5961(94)90015-9

Driscoll, J. C., & Kraay, A. C. (1998). Consistent covariance matrix estimation with spatially dependent panel data. *The Review of Economics and Statistics*, *80*(4), 549–560. doi:10.1162/003465398557825

Ferguson, R., Wilkinson, W., & Hill, R. (2000). Electricity use and economic development. *Energy Policy*, *28*(13), 923–934. doi:10.1016/S0301-4215(00)00081-1

Filos, E., & Banahan, E. P. (2001). Will the organisation disappear? The challenges of the new economy and future perspectives. In L. M. Camarinha-Matos, H. Afsharmanesh, & R. J. Rabelo (Eds.), *E-business and virtual enterprises: managing business-to-business cooperation* (pp. 3–20). Dordrecht: Kluwer Academic Publishers. doi:10.1007/978-0-387-35399-9_1

Hardy, A. (1980). The role of the telephone in economic development. *Telecommunications Policy, 4*(4), 278–286. doi:10.1016/0308-5961(80)90044-0

Hosman, E., Fife, E., & Armey, L. (2008). The case for a multi-methodological, cross-disciplinary approach to the analysis of ICT investment and projects in the developing world. *Information Technology for Development, 14*(4), 308–327. doi:10.1002/itdj.20109

Jalava, J., & Pohloja, M. (2002). Economic growth in the new economy: Evidence from advanced economics. *Information Economics and Policy, 14*(2), 189–210. doi:10.1016/S0167-6245(01)00066-X

Jalava, J., & Pohloja, M. (2008). The roles of electricity and ICT in economic growth: Case Finland. *Explorations in Economic History, 45*(3), 270–287. doi:10.1016/j.eeh.2007.11.001

Jipp. A (1963, July). Wealth of Nations and Telephone Density. *Telecommunications Journal,* 199-201.

Jorgenson, D., & Stiroh, K. J. (2000). U.S. economic growth in the new millennium. *Brookings Papers on Economic Activity, 1*, 125–211. doi:10.1353/eca.2000.0008

Jorgenson, D. W. (2001). Information technology and the U.S. economy. *The American Economic Review, 91*(1), 1–32. doi:10.1257/aer.91.1.1

Jorgenson, D. W., & Vu, K. (2007). Information technology and the world growth resurgence. *German Economic Review, 8*(2), 125–145. doi:10.1111/j.1468-0475.2007.00401.x

Lam, P. L., & Shiu, A. (2010). Economic growth, telecommunications development and productivity growth of the telecommunications sector: Evidence around the world. *Telecommunications Policy, 34*(4), 185–199. doi:10.1016/j.telpol.2009.12.001

Lee, S., Gholami, R., & Tang, T. Y. (2005). Time series analysis in the assessment of ICT impact at the aggregate level-lessons and implications for the new economy. *Information & Management, 42*(7), 1009–1022. doi:10.1016/j.im.2004.11.005

Lee, S. H., Levendis, J., & Gutierrez, L. (2012). Telecommunications and economic growth: An empirical analysis of sub-Saharan Africa. *Applied Economics, 44*(4), 461–469. doi:10.1080/00036846.2010.508730

Madden, G., & Savage, S. (2000). Telecommunications and economic growth. *International Journal of Social Economics, 27*(7/8/9/10), 893–906. doi:10.1108/03068290010336397

McGuckin, R. H., & Stiroh, K. J. (2001). Do computers make output harder to measure? *The Journal of Technology Transfer, 26*(4), 295–321. doi:10.1023/A:1011170416813

Oliner, S. D., & Sichel, D. E. (2000). The resurgence of growth in the late 1990s: Is information technology the story? *The Journal of Economic Perspectives, 14*(4), 3–22. doi:10.1257/jep.14.4.3

OMahony, M., & Vecchi, M. W. (2005). Quantifying the impact of ICT capital on output growth: A heterogeneous dynamic panel approach. *Economica, 72*(288), 615–633. doi:10.1111/j.1468-0335.2005.0435.x

Oulton, N. (2002). ICT and productivity growth in the United Kingdom. *Oxford Review of Economic Policy, 18*(3), 363–379. doi:10.1093/oxrep/18.3.363

Pohjola, M. (2000). *Information technology, productivity, and economic growth.* UNU World Institute for Development Economics Research Working Papers, No 173.

Pradhan, R. P., Bele, S., & Pandey, S. (2013). Internet-growth nexus: Evidence from cross-country panel data. *Applied Economics Letters, 20*(16), 1511–1515. doi:10.1080/13504851.2013.829170

Quah, D. (2002). Technology dissemination and economic growth: Some lessons for the new economy. In C. E. Bai & C. W. Yuen (Eds.), *Technology and the new economy* (pp. 95–156). Cambridge, MA: MIT Press.

Roeger, W. (2001). The Contribution of information and communication technologies to growth in Europe and the US: a macroeconomic analysis. *Economic Papers, European Commission Directorate-General for Economic and Financial Affairs,* 147.

Röller, L., & Waverman, L. (2001). Telecommunications infrastructure and economic development: A simultaneous approach. *The American Economic Review, 91*(4), 909–923. doi:10.1257/aer.91.4.909

Romm, J. (2002). The internet and the new energy economy. *Resources, Conservation and Recycling, 36*(3), 197–210. doi:10.1016/S0921-3449(02)00084-8

Ropke, I., Christensen, T. H., & Jensen, J. O. (2010). Information and communication technologies-a new round of household electrification. *Energy Policy, 38*(4), 1767–1773. doi:10.1016/j.enpol.2009.11.052

Sadorsky, P. (2012). Information communication technology and electricity consumption in emerging economies. *Energy Policy, 48,* 130–136. doi:10.1016/j.enpol.2012.04.064

Satti, S. O., & Nour, M. (2002). ICT opportunities and challenges for development in the Arab world. *WIDER Discussion Paper, 2002/83*, 1-15.

Saunders, R., Warford, J., & Wellenius, R. (1983). *Telecommunications and economic development*. Baltimore, MD: John Hopkins University Press.

Schaefer, C., Weber, C., & Voss, A. (2003). Energy usage of mobile telephone services in Germany. *Energy*, *28*(5), 411–420. doi:10.1016/S0360-5442(02)00154-8

Schreyer, P. (2000). *The contribution of information and communication technology to output growth: a study of the G7 countries*. OECD, DSTI Working Paper, Paris.

Seo, H., & Lee, Y. (2006). Contribution of information and communication technology to total factor productivity and externalities effects. *Information Technology for Development*, *12*(2), 159–173. doi:10.1002/itdj.20021

Shahiduzzaman, M., & Atam, K. (2014). The long-run impact of information and communication technology on economic output: The case of Australia. *Telecommunications Policy*, *38*(7), 623–633. doi:10.1016/j.telpol.2014.02.003

Shapiro, C., & Varian, H. R. (1999). *Information rules. A strategic guide to the network economy*. Boston: Harvard Business School Press.

Stewart, T. A. (1998). *Intellectual capital. The wealth of organisations*. London: Nicholas Brealey.

Sweetland, J. H. (1993). Information Poverty – Let Me Count the Ways. *Database*, *16*(4), 8–10.

Takase, K., & Murota, Y. (2004). The impact of IT investment on energy: Japan and US comparison in 2010. *Energy Policy*, *32*(11), 1291–1301. doi:10.1016/S0301-4215(03)00097-1

Timmer, M. P., & Van Ark, B. (2005). Does information and communication technology drive EU-US productivity growth differentials? *Oxford Economic Papers*, *57*(4), 693–716. doi:10.1093/oep/gpi032

United Nations. (2014). *World economic situation and prospects 2014*. New York: United Nations Publication.

Vu, K. M. (2011). ICT as a source of economic growth in the information age: Empirical evidence from the 1996–2005 period. *Telecommunications Policy*, *35*(4), 357–372. doi:10.1016/j.telpol.2011.02.008

Yousefi, A. (2011). The Impact of information and communication technology on economic growth: Evidence from developed and developing countries. *Economics of Innovation and New Technology*, *20*(6), 581–596. doi:10.1080/10438599.2010.544470

Yu, L. (2006). Understanding information inequality: Making sense of the literature of the information and digital divides. *Journal of Librarianship and Information Science*, *38*(4), 229–252. doi:10.1177/0961000606070600

Zahra, K., Azim, P., & Mahmood, A. (2008). Telecommunication infrastructure development and economic growth: A panel data approach. *Pakistan Development Review*, *47*(4), 711–726.

KEY TERMS AND DEFINITIONS

Balkan Countries: Countries in the Balkan peninsula which is in the Southeast part of Europe.

Digital Gap or Divide: It is the difference between countries in terms of technology use due to delays in the diffusion of information and communication technologies.

Eastern Europe Countries: Countries in the East part of Europe.

Economic Growth: Increase in total output produced in an economy.

Elasticity: Unit free measure showing the percentage change in one variable as a result of 1% change in another variable.

Energy Efficiency: Using less energy in order to provide same services in an optimal level.

ICT Adoption: Usage of Information and Communication Technologies which includes products such as fixed telephones, mobile cellular, internet and computers, receiving, storing, and transmitting information, electronically.

Panel Data: Data type including both time series and cross sectional dimensions in the data.

ENDNOTES

[1]   This study is partly based on Gökhan Obay's graduate thesis belonging to Omer Halisdemir University, Institute of Social Sciences.

[2]   Based on the data availability, the following countries are included which are classified as developed countries, developing countries and economies in transition: developed countries (Cyprus, Czech Republic, Estonia, Greece,

Hungary, Latvia, Lithuania, Poland, Romania, Slovakia, Slovenia), economies in transition (Albania, Armenia, Georgia, Kazakhstan, Macedonia, Moldova, Russia and Ukraine), and developing countries (Turkey).

[3]   The index is recalculated by using the base year as 2005.

[4]   Real per capita economic growth is calculated by using the following expression in which Y is the GDP per capita (constant 2005 US$); growth=

$$\left(\frac{Y_t - Y_{t-1}}{Y_{t-1}} \right) \times 100.$$

[5]   ICT index is obtained by employing the following formulae: ICT=

$$\left(\frac{tel + internet + mobile}{3} \right) \times 0.01$$ where, tel, internet, and mobile are fixed

telephone subscriptions (per 100 people), internet users (per 100 people), and mobile cellular subscriptions (per 100 people), respectively.

[6]   Openness index is calculated as a ratio of sum of Exports of goods and services (current US$) and Imports of goods and services (current US$) to GDP (current US$).

[7]   Capital stock is the ratio of Gross fixed capital formation (current US$) to GDP (current US$).

[8]   The effect of economic growth and electricity consumption on ICT usage is out of scope of this study but can be studied in the future studies.

Section 3
Solution Proposals

Chapter 9

Developing Healthy Habits in Media Consumption:
A Proposal for Dealing with Information Overload

Javier Serrano-Puche
University of Navarra, Spain

ABSTRACT

In the contemporary media ecosystem, online consumption is framed and character-ized by a number of general elements. These key factors are: a) the overabundance of information available to users (information overload); b) the speed of online interaction; c) the emergence of attention as currency; d) the multiplicity of differ-ent screens; and e) the socialization of consumption. This chapter, grounded on a comprehensive literature review, first provides a description of these elements. A digital diet is then proposed based on the development of three areas: knowing how to use the technological tools and applications to deal with information overload; learning how to manage attention and cognitive overload; and, finally, establishing regular periods of digital disconnection. The conclusion is that practicing these healthy habits leads to more useful and effective media consumption.

DOI: 10.4018/978-1-5225-2061-0.ch009

INTRODUCTION

The integration of digital technology in our daily lives is unquestionable, to the point where it is increasingly difficult to stop using it regularly because it has become such an inevitable part of our existence. As Deuze (2012) said, "we do not live *with*, but *in*, media" (p. XIII). It is a time of individuals interconnected via networks (the new social operating system) (Rainie & Wellman, 2012), who use the Internet as their platform for contact and information exchange and which they can access anytime and anywhere, thanks to mobile communication.

The omnipresence of digital devices is not, however, a simple quantitative matter, as:

their widespread presence, their level of personalization and the potential for permanent connection that they provide contribute to the reconfiguration of many aspects of daily life and to contemporary processes of subjectivation and socialization (Lasén, 2014, p. 7).

Thus, according to Lipovetsky and Serroy (2009), "the network of screens has transformed our way of living, our relationship with information, with space-time, with consumption" (p. 271).

Digital technology has favored increasing flexibility in relationships between individuals and groups, giving rise to the development of what some authors have called "networked individualism" (Wellman et al, 2003) or "networked self" (Papacharissi, 2011). In parallel with traditional relationships of belonging, transitory network relationships of a more limited scope have proliferated and are characterized by being less rigid and more dynamic, because the online environment allows users to be in company while conserving their individuality (Turkle, 2011) and provides a "sanitized" form of relationship typical of a liquid world in which identities are fluid (Bauman, 2004).

The birth of each new medium has always given rise to the start of a debate between enthusiasts and skeptics, and the Internet is no exception (Baym, 2010). However, it is needed to rise above this polarization and take a critical and nuanced approach to really understanding the impact of digital technologies and the opportunities, challenges and risks they bring in order to make good use of them. According to Area and Ribeiro (2012), there are six major realms or dimensions of learning on the Internet, as it is at once:

a universal library, a global market, a giant jigsaw puzzle of hypertextually interconnected pieces, a public meeting place where people communicate and form social communities, a territory in which multimedia and audiovisual communication take precedence, and a diversity of virtual, interactive environments (p. 14).

Compared to the reading and writing of classical literacy, this online culture now requires the development of different instrumental, cognitive and intellectual, sociocultural, axiological and emotional competences and skills. This requires an awareness of two possible dangers: limiting media education to the development of online skills and limiting online competence to its most technological and instrumental dimension by focusing on technical knowledge and procedures for using and managing devices and applications, while ignoring attitudes and values (Gutiérrez & Tyner, 2012). Ultimately, online literacy must prioritize ethical and critical learning on-screen over technological skills.

More specifically, as other authors have pointed out in this book, it is essential in this "age of hyperconnectivity" (Reig & Vilchez, 2013) to find an efficient way of managing the information overload we face on a daily basis. Otherwise, people run the risk of failing to digest all the information they consume and may ultimately be unable to convert this information into knowledge.

Based on this hypothesis, this chapter presents a theoretical and exploratory research grounded on an extensive literature review and examining theoretical and empirical studies in order to develop a meta-analysis of research on digital consumption in the contemporary media ecosystem. The materials taken into consideration include monographs, collective works published by scholarly publishers, indexed journals papers and conference proceedings mainly in the time span from 2010 to 2015.

More specifically, this paper has the following objectives, which correspond to the two main parts of this chapter: to identify and analyze the sociocultural and technological traits that affect the type of media consumption; and to recommend a "digital diet" which implies critical and beneficial use of information technologies by adopting healthy media habits.

BACKGROUND

Media consumption includes the uses and habits associated with the different media, which, in light of the process of media convergence, are currently largely subsumed by the Internet (where content associated with television, the press, magazines and journals, and radio can all be accessed, together with purely online content). This collection of information and entertainment acquired by users is conditioned by factors relating to each person's status and situation (age, sex, nationality, occupation, personal preferences, needs and expectations, etc.) and is reflected in specific forms of consumption linked to the type of medium and content, frequency, times, patterns of behavior when consuming, etc.

However, in the contemporary media ecosystem, online consumption is framed and characterized by a number of general elements. These key factors are:

1. The overabundance of information available to users (information overload);
2. The speed of online interaction;
3. The emergence of attention as currency;
4. The multiplicity of different screens; and
5. The socialization of consumption.

The first three are exogenous factors that belong to the sociological and cultural order of our times, whereas the last two refer to intrinsic characteristics of online media consumption. Each one of these will be briefly explained in the following pages.

INFORMATION OVERLOAD

Today, information is not the scarce resource it has been at previous times in history. Its importance is such that it has become commonplace to call the current era the Information Society, although the term has no single, unequivocal definition and has generated some controversy (Trejo Delarbre, 2006, p. 31-73). Other terms such as the Knowledge Society and the Networked Society have been used more recently. As Castells (1996) states, it has emerged

a specific form of social organization in which information generation, processing and transmission become the fundamental sources of productivity and power, because of new technological conditions emerging in this historical period (p. 21).

This extraordinary abundance of information is a great advantage, because more content is often instantly and freely available to the citizens. However, it also poses new challenges and may even lead to certain cognitive or psychological problems. In his 1970 book *Future Shock*, Alvin Toffler was the first to warn of information overload as a specific disorder resulting from this new social context in which individuals are equipped with neither the tools nor skills to properly absorb such a surfeit of information. Since then, more and more authors have explored this issue, either through the use of different metaphors, such as "data smog" (Shenk, 1997), "torrent of images and sounds" (Gitlin, 2003), "flood of information" (Gleick, 2011), "information pollution" (Bray, 2008) and "infoglut" (Andrejevic, 2013), or by focusing on "the dark side of information" (Bawden and Robinson, 2009), i.e., the disorders that people can develop as a result of this phenomenon, including "Technostress" (Brod, 1984), boredom (Klapp, 1986), anxiety (Wurman, 1989), "information fatigue syndrome" (Reuters, 1996), "cognitive overload" (Kirsch, 2000) and "Information Obesity" (Whitworth, 2009).

Although information overload predates the popularization of the Internet, this new digital ecosystem has made the challenges and problems associated with the wealth of information more prominent and complex. Furthermore, thanks to the popularization of mobile devices such as tablets and smartphones, access to information, which occurs primarily on the Internet, is constant and ubiquitous.

And the proliferation of screens and the accompanying rise in media consumption are displacing and diminishing the important role traditionally played by the printed book in knowledge generation and acquisition. In the digital age, knowledge is no longer seen as a finite series of accurate and reliable content organized in repositories, but as a network of unlimited discussions and arguments (Weinberger, 2012). Information itself has become a continuous flow that primarily affects journalists and other media-based professions, whose work used to be based on regular time periods, but has now evolved into a kind of non-stop journalism (Martín Algarra, Torregrosa and Serrano-Puche, 2013). However, knowledge is not synonymous with unlimited access to information or a greater flow of information, but with the "interpretation, critical understanding and even recreation of this information within a certain spatial, temporal and cultural context" and "the speed of networks and new technology platforms is not always consistent with true knowledge generation. On the contrary, it tends to lead to a form of consciousness that is fragmentary, short-term, unthinking and ahistorical" (Barranquero-Carretero, 2013, p. 429).

The Speed of Communication

One of the most important transformations associated with the consolidation of online technologies involves how people experience space and time. However, as with information overload, this is a phenomenon that dates back to the final decades of the 20th century and therefore predates the popularization of the online world as a space for social relations. In his 1989 work, *The Condition of Postmodernity*, David Harvey pointed to "time-space compression" as being a phenomenon of our times, "characterized by speed-up in the pace of life, while so overcoming spatial barriers that the world sometimes seems to collapse inwards upon us" (Harvey, 1989, p. 240).

In this process, digital technologies have historically helped shape (and have been the greatest exponent of) the "culture of speed" in the modern era, in which, as Virilio (2012) notes, "our societies have become arrhythmic. Or they only know one rhythm: constant acceleration" (p. 27).

Within this constant acceleration, however, it should be noted that the speed of the face-to-face world is different than that of the online world. Traditional social life is slower and more localized, whereas online social life is faster and without location. They are, therefore, two different space-time regimes and each is accompanied by its emotional regime, but "the coexistence of both emotional regimes causes interference between the emotional logic inherent to each one" (González, 2013, pp. 13-14). The traditional emotional regime is a regime of emotional qualities, whereas the technological regime is principally a regime of emotional intensity, in which the quantity of emotion is what matters (quantifiable by the number of likes, retweets, views, etc.).

The tremendous speed with which time is experienced (Wajcman, 2015) has brought changes in production and consumption processes, the organization of work, lifestyles and the way the brain processes information (Carr, 2010). One of the consequences of this, as Byung-Chul Han (2012) has noted, is that our reality is

poor in interruptions, in entities and intervals in which hyperactivity leaves no space for attention of the ability to listen, qualities that are essential to promoting critical thinking, creativity and social bonds (pp. 55-56).

Time has lost its narrative nature to be broken down into a mere succession of atomized presents (Han, 2015). This inflation of the "now," what Rushkoff (2013) calls "presentism," in turn influences media consumption, often characterized by the "neophilia" that leads to overrating what happens at every instant and to the desire for the new, prioritizing trivial news over valuable older information. Thus, "the excess information flow has, in some cases, led to a kind of media bulimia, compulsive real-time consumption that exhausts itself and does not resolve the need for cognitive sedimentation" (Díaz Nosty, 2013, p. 137). In some segments of the population there is a dependence on the moment, on anecdotes, on eccentric comments, by means of a succession of variable stimuli that magnify the ephemeral, like a magnetic attraction of the attention, in detriment to larger matters.

Attention as a Scarce Resource

A third element that can explain the nature of media consumption today is the fact that people's attention is the ultimate scarce resource in developed societies. There is an "attention economy" (Goldhaber, 1997; Davenport & Beck, 2001), in which content producers (and, in general, anyone who wants to communicate something) compete to grab people's attention in an attempt to occupy their available time. Hence, potential users are targeted by an extraordinarily wide range of new media and supports everywhere and all the time. The bombardment of messages and cognitive stimuli to which people are subject is especially obvious in the online environment.

Since technology allows sending more information in less time and more agents are sending messages to potential recipients, the personal "bandwidth" of information is increasing all the time. Meanwhile, the amount of time that people are able to spend on each piece of information they receive is getting shorter. The problem is essentially that "the two variables are inversely proportional to each other: the higher the 'personal bandwidth,' the shorter the 'personal attention span'" (Cornella, 2008, p. 21).

In this context of information overload and shorter attention spans, most of the content consumed by users reaches us via emotional appeals. "Memes" are gaining increasing importance in the media diet; these are the viral images, videos and ideas that circulate via the Internet, driven by the emotions of the users, both horizontally (via blogs, YouTube, Facebook, Twitter) and vertically, when traditional media venues (television, radio, newspapers) also report them with the emotional resonance they take on. Understanding and trying to predict the process of disseminating this type of content has been the subject of academic analysis (Spitzberg, 2014; Ash, 2015). It is a phenomenon that has been studied particularly in the field of advertising, where the authors agree that a necessary component for a video to be shared in the online environment is that it stirs emotions, particularly surprise and joy (Eckler & Bolls, 2011; Dafonte, 2014).

Multiscreen Consumption

The proliferation of technological devices, both fixed (desktop computers and smart TVs) and mobile (smartphones, tablets, laptop computers, wearables, etc.) has diversified consumption among multiple screens, each of which has characteristics that influence our online media habits, as evidenced in aspects such as times and frequency of use, and the level of interaction with other users and other types of content accessed via these devices.

One of the consequences of this wealth of digital devices is that some users increasingly consult several terminals simultaneously when carrying out an activity. One of the most common ways is the use of cellphones or tablets while watching television; hence the name "second screening" (Doughty, Rowland & Lawson, 2012), which has been applied to this phenomenon where mobile devices fulfill a secondary support role to the domestic "big screen." According to the report, "The Digital Consumer" (Nielsen, 2014), in the United States, 84% of smartphone and tablet owners admit to using their devices while watching TV, as they simultaneously require at least two devices to meet their social interaction, information, entertainment and work productivity needs.

This tells us that the uses of multiscreen consumption are increasingly complex and diverse. For example, Smith and Boyles (2012) note that mobile devices are not always used in connection with what is being viewed on television, but is due to the fact that that the television content does not capture the attention of the users (e.g., during an ad break) and, without completely abandoning the TV, they turn to the phone or the tablet for distraction. Thus, the "second screen" often becomes the first screen (Días & Teixeira-Botelho, 2014) because it is the one on which the person's attention is actually focused in order to interact with others, search for information, check for email and review social networks, etc.

The Socialization of Consumption

From the point of view of media consumption, mobility has been a disruptive factor insofar as it has taken the use of media out of the domestic setting and made it highly individual, now that all users have their own digital devices. Paradoxically, however, consumption has become more socialized at the same time, given the preeminence of interconnection via interpersonal networks and contacts in the online environment.

This process of socializing media consumption is evident in several ways. Information overload has led many people to increasingly rely on their social media contacts as a filter to help them make sense of the overwhelming amount of information (Rainie & Wellman, 2012, p. 18). However, this response, which is a logical in terms of human social behavior, can have a detrimental side effect. If people's reaction to escape from the information avalanche of thousands of conflicting voices is to focus their attention on a handful of media outlets sympathetic to their viewpoint and surround themselves with people of a similar ideology on social media, there is a "risk that the Internet will transform us from a cohesive society into islands enclosed within bubbles of beliefs, rather than within open spaces for exchanging ideas" (Doval, 2012). This is the "filter bubble" mentioned by Pariser (2011), i.e., the efforts made by platforms such as Facebook and Google to tailor content to users (almost always without them noticing), thus depriving them of a more holistic and inclusive view of reality and current affairs.

The growing socialization of media consumption can also be seen in the motivation behind and frequent use of multiscreen practices mentioned above. It is common for the use of cellphones and tablets while watching a television program to be driven by the urge to comment on and/or read the comments of other users on the program content (Giglietto & Selva, 2014), either on the social networks (especially Twitter) or via applications such as WhatsApp.

HEALTHY HABITS IN DIGITAL CONSUMER BEHAVIOR: A PROPOSAL

There is no doubt that the availability of information in real time and the all-encompassing presence of technology in our daily lives are realities that are not expected to diminish or disappear, but will only become more prevalent. However, it is possible for people to rethink their relationship with technology and become more aware and critical of the way they use it and the amount of time they spend on it. However, the problem is not only the existence of too much information. It stems from a broader issue relating to the culture of speed so dominant today.

As mentioned above, there is a socio-technological landscape that can easily cause media consumption to turn into so-called "information obesity" when consumers fail to convert information into knowledge (Whitworth, 2009). Just as physical obesity is not simply a result of overeating, information obesity is not simply a question of information overload, but also one of problems of mental fitness in information consumption (the lack of skill or judgement), the poor quality of the information being received, and the habit of consuming information before correctly judging its value, a habit common among those who connect to digital technologies for long periods. As will be shown below, a change of attitude towards media consumption is required to alleviate these information "disorders." To continue with the food metaphor, it is necessary to go on a digital diet. As with a nutritional diet, a digital diet plan will have some general features common to all diets and others that need to be tailored to users' digital habits and professional and personal situation.

The digital diet proposed here is not limited to a series of specific measures to manage the torrent of information, but also presents a theoretical dimension: the desire to regain the upper hand over technology by learning how to harness its enormous potential for human enrichment in fields of knowledge and communication and trying to counteract the consequences of the culture of speed (which is so evident in the digital environment), e.g., instant gratification, multitasking, superficiality and neuronal overstimulation.

Specifically, there are three keys to achieving a healthier use of information technologies and they should be implemented together:

1.   Using technology itself to resolve the information overload created by technology.
2.   Being more aware of how people receive and assimilate information, and constantly concentrating on what is truly essential in its context. At the same time, going back to merely observing information and events, without having to consciously process them.
3.   When necessary, resorting to digital disconnection, i.e., occasional or regular abstinence from digital technologies.

These lines of action are further developed in the next section.

SOLUTIONS AND RECOMMENDATIONS

Technology for Filtering and Storing Information

As stated above, information overload is one of the distinctive elements of the current media ecosystem. More specifically, all users are subject to different information flows to one extent or another (Díaz Arias, 2015). In addition to the information supplied by the mass media, there is personalized information (which each person voluntarily chooses based on his or her tastes and interests) and social information (now that information consumption has become socialized), as well as strategically targeted information such as advertising.

Thus, as other authors have noted (Miller, 2004; Savolainen, 2007; Brown, 2012; Tolido, 2012), as a first step to dealing with information overload, it is essential to establish a good system for screening information, since the problem is not information overload itself, but a failure to filter information properly (Shirky, 2010). Therefore, on a more technical and operational level, the first step is to have tools, applications and software to filter, aggregate and curate the information received constantly throughout the day. It is a good idea to refine the list of information sources consulted regularly and reduce it to a manageable number, based on the principle that you don't need to know everything, just what's important. This task also requires people to make an initial effort to think about how to apply it to their different information entry points:

- With email (by creating labels, multiple inboxes or filters based on the sender address).
- On social networks (by creating lists of users on Twitter, groups on Facebook, circles on Google+, etc., or by aggregating the content of all these channels in personalized magazines such as Flipboard or Paper.li).
- On frequently visited websites and blogs (by using an RSS feed manager such as Feedly, Netvibeso Leaf).
- On mobile devices (by adjusting the push notification settings so that they are not a constant distraction).

In order to survive the abundance of information in the digital environment, it also helps to use tools like Instapaper, Pocket and Readability, which let you save and sort texts so you can read them at your convenience (thus freeing you from the "tyranny" of real-time information). Social bookmarking applications like Diigo, Evernote and Delicious are also very helpful in this area. Other types of software can help improve your ability to concentrate, such as word processors for writing without distractions (e.g., Ommwriter and WriteRoom) and applications that enhance productivity by impeding multitasking and Internet access (e.g., Freedom and

StayFocusd). As Pérez Latre (2012) points out, "We have built amazing information highways, but have forgotten to teach how to drive. With more news and data, we will need more filtering and better selection. There is a stronger need to establish a hierarchy of information, gatekeeping and search for solid evidence" (p. 266).

Managing Attention and Cognitive Load

The second aspect of media consumption you need to develop is the habit of narrowing the focus of your attention, which, in the online environment, is constantly bombarded with multiple cognitive stimuli. As Cory Doctorow (2009) points out, whenever you log onto a computer, you are immersed in an "ecosystem of interruption technologies." It has been shown how information overload affects productivity (Hurst, 2007) and memory (Klingberg, 2009; Niada, 2010) and that the capacity for multitasking is largely a myth (Crenshaw, 2008). Therefore, cultivating concentration, focusing on the essence of information and navigating the torrent of information using what Lucchetti (2010) refers to as the "principle of relevance" are crucial skills to ensure that you do not succumb to the deluge of information and are able to achieve a fulfilled life. Practicing mindfulness by paying full attention to the present moment helps reduce stress and increase personal effectiveness (Gallagher, 2009; Goleman, 2013).

Developing your attention also involves understanding the extent of your own media consumption. As proposed by Johnson (2012), a good diet is one in which the individual consumes actual information, not just opinions, in small amounts and preferably firsthand (by going directly to the source or using intermediaries who really give the information context and analysis without distorting it). Similarly, before contributing to the dissemination of memes (i.e., "contagious" images, videos and ideas that circulate virally on the Internet), you should "stop and think, understand them, find out who started them and why, think about why they have affected you and choose whether you want to spread them or boycott them" (Rodriguez, 2013, p. 196).

Just as you need to learn how to focus your attention, you also need to learn how to develop a way to manage your cognitive load, i.e., to be capable, when necessary, of "observing" dense information flows without the need to process them in their entirety (for example, your Twitter feed and email inbox). The new skills that should be acquired by digital users include statistical thinking, data analysis and visualization, the skill to search for and filter accurate, high-quality information, the ability to synthesize, and flexible thinking, because "connecting ideas, making sense of information and knowing how to contextualize the huge amount of information we receive will be much more important than accumulating information" (Reig, 2013, p. 43).

Digital Disconnection

Another healthy measure against the tyranny of immediacy and real-time information that distinguishes the media ecosystem is being committed to long-lasting
sustainability associated with culture "as opposed to the market's increasingly rapid
obsolescence; everything is produced so as to last less and less" (Martín Barbero,
2008, p. 13). From the perspective of time, which must, in turn, be reflected in
media consumption patterns, this means finding a balance, namely: "Be fast when
it makes sense to be fast, and be slow when slowness is called for. Seek to live at
what musicians call the tempo gusto –the right speed" (Honoré, 2004, p. 15).

In the same vein, the practice of regularly disconnecting from technology is a
good remedy against "digital maximalism," i.e., the widespread belief that "connecting via screens is good and the more you connect, the better" (Powers, 2010, p. 4).
Disconnection is at the heart of a slow vision of communication (Freeman, 2009;
Serrano-Puche, 2014). This school of thought, which is applied in diverse fields such
as food, work, education, leisure, travel and city life, is presented as an antidote to
the cult of speed that dominates society today and the consequences it brings (lack
of patience, hyperstimulation, superficiality, etc.). In response, the Slow Movement
promotes a more leisurely lifestyle that avoids any increase in speed that does not
improve the quality of our different daily activities. It does not advocate slowness
for slowness's sake, but the need to find the pace best suited to the characteristics
of human actions and needs, while being aware of the best way to spend time and
what truly merits attention.

Disconnecting regularly helps users regain their attention span, since surfing
the Internet requires a particularly intensive form of mental multitasking. Regular
disconnection also ensures that online time is more enriching, since being tethered to
an incessant flow of information paradoxically decreases productivity and efficiency.

As Sieberg (2011) writes, introducing digital disconnection as a regular habit
calls for a progressive four-step plan. The first step involves rethinking the time
you spend on the Internet every day and how this time could be spent on family
and social relationships, physical activity and sleep. The second step is the actual
detox phase: ever-increasing periods of abstinence from the use of technology (perhaps starting with a few hours, then a day or the whole weekend, while resuming
other tasks). Depending on how users consume media, this step may be more or
less difficult and may require willpower and self-discipline (Schoenebeck, 2014a).
The third step is to reconnect digitally, but this time with a series of good routines,
including a firm plan for regular disconnection periods, and to reassign technology
to its rightful place in your daily schedule. The fourth step is to learn how to live
with technology and develop a renewed approach to communication and digital life,

so that your relationship with technology and your face-to-face contact with people are both natural and harmonious.

In documented studies and experiments on digital disconnection (Moeller, Powers & Roberts, 2012; Lee & Katz, 2014; Baumer et al., 2014; Schoenebeck, 2014b), all the people who managed to disconnect indicated that they experienced a sense of liberation and peace, improved communication with family members and close friends, and more time to do the things they had neglected. These benefits are consistent with the overall objective of the digital diet presented here, i.e., to find a pace of life that is appropriate for human beings, given the dynamic attractions of the information age. The potential of digital technologies is therefore harnessed in the best possible way without losing the necessary balance between online and face-to-face interaction. In fact, communication and information in both contexts are enriched and humanized.

FUTURE RESEARCH DIRECTIONS

Digital consumption, characterized by the factors described in the first pages of this chapter, always presents a strong emotional component, given that the use of technology arouses emotions in users and serves as a channel for the expression of affection. Moreover, the myriad of digital gadgets influences the way in which this affection is modulated and displayed. In that sense, a pertinent future research direction is that devoted to examining the connotations that online consumption has on human beings' emotional dimension. The development of a critical and conscious media consumption, which is associated with emotional management, still require research that will shed light on it.

Furthermore, the emergence of wearable devices—which is a step closer towards the bodily adaptation and integration of technology into the user—, advances in the design of social robots (facilitating a more 'natural' interaction with humans) and the growing expansion of the 'Internet of things,' which are making the presence of technology in daily life more ubiquitous and immersive, are some of several future lines of research that emerge as subjects of interest in this field, since they influence digital consumer behaviour.

CONCLUSION

The overabundance of information and the hypervelocity of communications are the hallmarks of today's digital ecosystem. In addition, the consolidation and generalized use of digital technologies and mobile devices with Internet access have fueled the belief that constant connection is not only technically feasible but even desirable. As a result, people are now constantly assaulted with an overwhelming amount of poor-quality information from multiple screens, but are often unable to digest this flow of information. Simply regarding it as a matter of information overload does not help define the problem or identify solutions. Instead, it is useful to consider overload as a failure to filter information and to provide the necessary resources to make it truly effective.

Therefore, people should become more aware of the extent of their media consumption and establish some guidelines to ensure that such use is truly beneficial and does not result in information obesity. As mentioned above, the proposal to adopt healthy habits of media consumption is a good practice that should be undertaken at various levels. First, a key area of this digital diet involves the proper management of the technical tools (applications, software, computer programs, etc.) users need to assist them in the task of filtering, aggregating and curating the information they receive throughout the day. It also requires users to exercise more caution and awareness concerning the type and quantity of information consumed and to learn how to exercise some control over mental attention and cognitive load management. Finally, it is necessary to regularly disconnect from digital technologies because this has been shown to be a good habit for harmonizing and mutually enriching the online and offline modes of everyday socialization.

From the perspective of media education, developing a digital diet based on these lines of action has positive consequences. Therefore, it should not be seen as a form of deprivation of a series of elements, but as a smart way to consume relevant information more effectively and develop healthy habits.

ACKNOWLEDGMENT

This paper stems from the research project "News Preferences and Use within the New Media Scenario in Spain: Audiences, Companies, Contents and Multiplatform Reputation Management". Project funded by the Ministry of Economy and Competitiveness (Spain) and the European Regional Development Fund (ERDF). Reference number: CSO2015-64662-C4-1-R MINECO/ERDF, EU.

REFERENCES

Andrejevic, M. (2013). *Infoglut: How Too Much Information Is Changing the Way We Think and Know*. London: Routledge.

Area, M., & Ribeiro, M. T. (2012). From Solid to Liquid: New Literacies to the Cultural Changes of Web 2.0. *Comunicar*, *38*(38), 13–20. doi:10.3916/C38-2012-02-01

Ash, J. (2015). Sensation, Network, and the GIF: Toward an Allotropic Account of Affect. In K. Hillis, S. Paasonen, & M. Petit (Eds.), *Networked Affect* (pp. 119–113). Cambridge, MA: The MIT Press.

Barranquero-Carretero, A. (2013). *Slow media*. Comunicación, cambio social y sostenibilidad en la era del torrente mediático. *Palabra Clave*, *16*(2), 419–448. doi:10.5294/pacla.2013.16.2.6

Bauman, Z. (2004). *Identity. Conversations with Benedetto Vecchi*. Cambridge, UK: Polity Press.

Baumer, E. P. S., Adams, P., Khovanskaya, V. D., Liao, T. C., Smith, M. E., Sosik, V. S., & Williams, K. (2013). Limiting, leaving, and (re)lapsing: An exploration of Facebook non-use practices and experiences.*Proceedings of the SIGCHI Conference on Human Factors in Computing Systems* (pp. 3257-3266). New York: ACM. doi:10.1145/2470654.2466446

Bawden, D., & Robinson, L. (2009). The dark side of information: Overload, anxiety and other paradoxes and pathologies. *Journal of Information Science*, *35*(2), 180–191. doi:10.1177/0165551508095781

Baym, N. K. (2010). *Personal connections in the digital age*. Cambridge, UK: Polity Press.

Bray, D. A. (2008, June). *Information Pollution, Knowledge Overload, Limited Attention Spans, and Our Responsibilities as IS Professionals*. Paper presented at the Global Information Technology Management Association (GITMA) World Conference, Atlanta, GA.

Brod, C. (1984). *Technostress: The Human Cost of the Computer Revolution*. Reading: Addison Wesley.

Brown, S. (2012). Coping with information obesity: A diet for information professionals.*Business Information Review*, *29*(3), 168–173. doi:10.1177/0266382112454355

Carr, N. (2010). *The Shallows: What the Internet Is Doing to Our Brains*. New York: W. W. Norton & Company.

Castells, M. (1996). The Information Age: Economy. In *The Rise of the Network Society*. Malden, MA: Blackwell.

Cornella, A. (2008). Principio de la intoxicación. In J. J. Fernández García (Ed.), *Más allá de Google* (pp. 19–22). Barcelona: Infonomía.

Crenshaw, D. (2008). *The Myth of Multitasking: How "Doing It All" Gets Nothing Done*. San Francisco: Jossey-Bass.

Dafonte, A. (2014). The Key Elements of Viral Advertising. From Motivation to Emotion in the Most Shared Videos. *Comunicar, 43*, 199–207. doi:10.3916/C43-2014-20

Davenport, T. H., & Beck, J. C. (2001). *The Attention Economy: Understanding the New Currency of Business*. Cambridge, MA: Harvard Business School Press.

Deuze, M. (2012). *Media Life*. Cambridge, UK: Polity Press.

Días, P., & Teixeira-Botelho, I. (2014). Is the Second Screen becoming the First? An exploratory study of emerging multi-screening practices.*Proceedings of the International Conference on Computer Graphics, Visualization, Computer Vision and Image Processing*. Lisbon: IADIS.

Díaz Arias, R. (2015). Curaduría periodística, una forma de reconstruir el espacio público. *Estudios sobre el Mensaje Periodístico, 21*, 61-80.

Díaz-Nosty, B. (2013). *La prensa en el nuevo ecosistema informativo. ¡Que paren las rotativas!* Barcelona: Ariel-Fundación Telefónica.

Doctorow, C. (2009). Writing in the Age of Distraction. *Locus Magazine, 62*(1), 29-35.

Doughty, M., Rowland, D., & Lawson, S. (2012). Who is on your sofa? TV audience communities and second screening social networks. In *Proceedings of the 10th European conference on Interactive TV and video—EuroiTV* (pp. 79–86). New York: Association for Computing Machinery. doi:10.1145/2325616.2325635

Doval, M. (2012). Por una dieta informativa más variada y sana. *Aceprensa*. Retrieved from http://www.aceprensa.com/articles/por-una-dieta-informativa-mas-variada-y-sana/

Eckler, P., & Bolls, P. (2011). Spreading the Virus: Emotional Tone of Viral Advertising and its Effect on Forwarding Intention and Attitudes. *Journal of Interactive Advertising, 11*(2), 1–11. doi:10.1080/15252019.2011.10722180

Eppler, M. J., & Mengis, J. (2004). The concept of information overload: A review of literature from organization science, accounting, marketing, MIS, and related disciplines. *The Information Society: An International Journal, 20*(5), 325–344. doi:10.1080/01972240490507974

Freeman, J. (2009). Manifesto for a Slow Communication Movement. In *The Tyranny of E-mail: The Four-Thousand-Year Journey to Your Inbox* (pp. 190–203). New York: Simon & Schuster.

Gallagher, W. (2009). *Rapt. Attention and the Focused Life*. New York: The Penguin Press.

Giglietto, F., & Selva, D. (2014). Second Screen and Participation: A Content Analysis on a Full Season Dataset of Tweets. *Journal of Communication, 64*(2), 260–277. doi:10.1111/jcom.12085

Gitlin, T. (2003). *Media Unlimited: How the Torrent of Images and Sounds Overwhelms Our Lives*. New York: Henry Holt and Company.

Gleick, J. (2011). *The Information: A History, A Theory, A Flood*. London: Harper Collins.

Goldhaber, M. (1997). The Attention Economy and the Net. *First Monday, 2*(4). Retrieved from: http://firstmonday.org/article/view/519/440

Goleman, D. (2013). *Focus: The Hidden Driver of Excellence*. New York: Harper Collins.

González, A. M. (2013). Introducción: emociones y análisis social. In L. Flamarique & M. D'Oliveira-Martins (Eds.), Emociones y estilos de vida: radiografía de nuestro tiempo (pp. 9-24). Madrid: Biblioteca Nueva.

Gutiérrez, A., & Tyner, K. (2012). Media Education, Media Literacy and Digital Competence. *Comunicar, 38*, 31–39. doi:10.3916/C38-2012-02-03

Han, B.-C. (2015). *El aroma del tiempo: un ensayo filosófico sobre el arte de demorarse*. Barcelona: Herder.

Harvey, D. (1989). *The Condition of Postmodernity. An Enquiry into the Origins of Cultural Change*. Blackwell.

Honoré, C. (2004). *In praise of slowness*. New York: Harper Collins.

Hurst, M. (2007). *Bit Literacy: Productivity in the Age of Information and E-mail Overload*. New York: Good Experience.

Johnson, C. A. (2012). *The Information Diet: A Case for Conscious Consumption*. Cambridge, MA: O'Reilly Media.

Kirsch, D. (2000). A few thoughts on cognitive overload. *Intellectica, 30*, 19–51.

Klapp, O. E. (1986). *Overload and boredom: Essays on the quality of life in the information society*. New York: Greenwood Press.

Klingberg, T. (2009). *The Overflowing Brain: Information Overload and the Limits of Working Memory*. Oxford, UK: Oxford University Press.

Lasén, A. (2014). Introducción. Las mediaciones digitales de la educación sentimental de los y las jóvenes. In I. Megía Quirós & E. Rodríguez San Julián (Eds.), Jóvenes y Comunicación: La impronta de lo virtual (pp. 7-16). Madrid: Fundación de Ayuda contra la Drogadicción.

Lee, S. K., & Katz, J. E. (2014). Disconnect: A case study of short-term voluntary mobile phone non-use. *First Monday*, *19*(12). doi:10.5210/fm.v19i12.4935

Lipovetsky, G., & Serroy, J. (2009). *La pantalla global. Cultura mediática y cine en la era hipermoderna*. Barcelona: Anagrama.

Lucchetti, S. (2010). *The Principle of Relevance. The Essential Strategy to Navigate Through the Information Age*. Hong Kong: RT Publishing.

Martín Algarra, M., Torregrosa, M., & Serrano-Puche, J. (2013). Un periodismo sin períodos: actualidad y tiempo en la era digital. In A. García (Ed.), Periodística y web 2.0: hacia la construcción de un nuevo modelo (pp. 73-83). Madrid: CEU Ediciones.

Martín Barbero, J. (2008). *Políticas de la comunicación y la cultura: Claves de la investigación. Documentos del CIDOB. Serie Dinámicas interculturales, 11*. Barcelona: Fundación CIDOB.

Miller, K. (2004). *Surviving Information Overload*. Zondervan.

Moeller, S., Powers, E., & Roberts, J. (2012). The World Unplugged and 24 Hours without Media: Media Literacy to Develop Self-Awareness Regarding Media. *Comunicar*, *39*, 45–52. doi:10.3916/C39-2012-02-04

Niada, M. (2010). *Il tempo breve. Nell'era della frenesia: la fine della memoria e la morte dell'attenzione*. Milano: Garzanti.

Nielsen. (2014). *The digital consumer*. Retrieved May 14th, 2014 from http://www.nielsen.com/us/en/insights/reports/2014/the-us-digital-consumer-report.html

Papacharissi, Z. (Ed.). (2011). A Networked Self: Identity, Community, and Culture on Social Network Sites. New York: Routledge.

Parisier, E. (2011). *The Filter Bubble: What The Internet Is Hiding From You*. New York: The Penguin Press.

Pérez Latre, F. (2012). The Paradoxes of Social Media: A Review of Theoretical Issues. In M. McCombs & M. Martín Algarra (Eds.), *Communication and social life* (pp. 257–274). Pamplona: Eunsa.

Powers, W. (2010). *Hamlet's Blackberry. A practical philosophy for building a good life in the digital age*. New York: Harper Collins.

Rainie, L., & Wellman, B. (2012). *Networked. The New Social Operating System*. Cambridge, MA: The MIT Press.

Reig, D., & Vílchez, L. (2013). *Los jóvenes en la era de la hiperconectividad: tendencias, claves y miradas*. Madrid: Fundación Telefónica.

Reuters Business Information. (1996). *Dying for information: an investigation into the effects of information overload in the UK and worldwide*. London: Reuters.

Rodríguez, D. (2013). Memecracia. Los virales que nos gobiernan. Barcelona. *Gestion*, 2000.

Rushkoff, D. (2013). *Present Shock. When Everything Happens Now*. New York: The Penguin Group.

Savolainen, R. (2007). Filtering and withdrawing: Strategies for coping with information overload in everyday contexts. *Journal of Information Science*, *33*(5), 611–621. doi:10.1177/0165551506077418

Schoenebeck, S. (2014a). Developing Healthy Habits with Social Media: Theorizing the Cycle of Overuse and Taking Breaks. Workshop Refusing, Limiting, Departing: Why We Should Study Technology Non-Use, Toronto, Canada.

Schoenebeck, S. Y. (2014b). Giving up Twitter for Lent: How and Why We Take Breaks from Social Media. *Proceedings of the SIGCHI Conference on Human Factors in Computing Systems* (pp. 773-782). New York: ACM. doi:10.1145/2556288.2556983

Serrano, P. (2013). *La comunicación jibarizada. Cómo la tecnología ha cambiado nuestras mentes*. Barcelona: Ediciones Península.

Serrano-Puche, J. (2014). Hacia una comunicación *slow*: El hábito de la desconexión digital periódica como elemento de alfabetización mediática. *Trípodos*, *34*, 201–214.

Shenk, D. (1997). *Data Smog: surviving the information glut*. New York: Harper Collins.

Shirky, C. (2010). It's not Information Overload. It's Filter Failure. *Mas Context*, (7), 76-85.

Sieberg, D. (2011). *Digital Diet: The 4-Step Plan to Break Your Addiction and Regain Balance in Your Life*. New York: Three River Press.

Spitzberg, B. H. (2014). Toward a Model of Meme Diffusion (M3D). *Communication Theory, 24*(3), 311–339. doi:10.1111/comt.12042

Tolido, R. (2012). Cómo apaciguar la Tormenta de Información. El impacto de la abundancia de información y las posibilidades que ofrece la tecnología de la información al tratar esta cuestión. In J. Victoria Mas, A. Gómez Tinoco, & J. B. Arjona Martín (Eds.), Comunicación 'Slow' (y la Publicidad como excusa) (pp. 277-314). Madrid: Fragua.

Tomlinson, J. (2007). *The culture of speed: the coming of immediacy*. Los Angeles, CA: SAGE.

Trejo Delarbre, R. (2006). *Viviendo en el Aleph. La Sociedad de la Información y sus laberintos*. Barcelona: Gedisa.

Turkle, S. (2011). *Alone together. Why We Expect More from Technology and Less from Each Other*. New York: Basic Books.

Virilio, P. (2012). The Administration of Fear. Los Angeles, CA: Semiotext(e).

Wajcman, J. (2015). *Pressed for Time. The Acceleration of Life in Digital Capitalism*. Chicago: The University of Chicago Press.

Weinberger, D. (2012). *Too Big to Know: Rethinking Knowledge Now That the Facts Aren't the Facts, Experts Are Everywhere, and the Smartest Person in the Room Is the Room*. New York: Basic Books.

Wellman, B., Quan-Haase, A., Boase, J., Chen, W., Hampton, K., Díaz de Isla, I., & Miyata, K. (2003). The social affordances of the Internet for networked individualism. *Journal of Computer-Mediated Communication, 8*(3).

Whitworth, A. (2009). *Information Obesity*. Oxford, UK: Chandos Publishing. doi:10.1533/9781780630045

Wurman, R. (1989). *Information Anxiety*. New York: Doubleday.

KEY TERMS AND DEFINITIONS

Attention Economy: A term coined by Michael H. Goldhaber in 1997 to refer to the transition from a material-based economy, where money is the currency, to a situation in which, due to the abundance of information, the currency is attention, understood as a scarce resource.

Content Curation: The process of finding, filtering, ordering and making sense of information coming from different sources.

Digital Disconnection: A period of time, whether one-off or repeated, in which the user voluntarily abstains from using information technology, particularly the Internet.

Hyperconnectivity: A state of continuous connection via digital devices, facilitated by the mass adoption and ubiquity of information and communication technology.

Information Overload: The effect caused by receiving a quantity of information that exceeds our capacity to process, leading to cognitive reduction and a drop in the quality of appreciation in the decision-making process.

Media Consumption: The information and entertainment acquired by users or groups of users via the media and the habits and patterns of use associated with it.

Second Screening: Use of a device (usually a cellphone or tablet) while watching television, either to search for additional information or to interact on social networks regarding the content of the television program, or as a source of distraction from this content.

Chapter 10
Shared and Distributed Team Cognition and Information Overload:
Evidence and Approaches for Team Adaptation

Thomas Ellwart
Trier University, Germany

Conny Herbert Antoni
Trier University, Germany

ABSTRACT

This chapter discusses information overload (IO) from a team level perspective. Organizational team research underlines the importance of emergent knowledge structures in work groups, so-called team cognition. Two types of team cognition are introduced that are closely related to IO, namely shared team mental models and transactive memory systems. After a brief introduction of the concepts, empirical evidence about the impact of team cognition on dysfunctional IO as well as functional information exchange are presented. In the second part of the chapter, strategies and tools for adapting team cognition in high IO situations are introduced. The focus on team level constructs in IO research complements individual, technical, and organizational approaches to IO by underlining the importance of team knowledge structures in social systems.

DOI: 10.4018/978-1-5225-2061-0.ch010

INTRODUCTION

Team Level Perspective on Information Overload (IO)

In modern organizational settings, many tasks and projects are performed by teams. Due to technical developments, collaboration over spatial, temporal, and even organizational boundaries becomes normality (e.g., virtual teams; Hertel & Konradt, 2007). Although organizational psychology has focused on the facilitation of information exchange within teams (cf. Mesmer-Magnus & DeChurch, 2009), many teams report dysfunctional information exchange or information overload (IO) on account of too much and irrelevant information (cf. Eppler & Mengis, 2004). In this chapter, information overload (IO) is considered a dysfunctional team process occurring at the team level. Regarding information sharing in teams, several authors have suggested that electronic media can overload team members with information (Ellwart, Happ, Gurtner, & Rack, 2015; Miranda & Saunders, 2003). Especially simultaneity or fast and immediate answers in electronic communication settings facilitate the experience of IO (Thorngate, 1997), mainly in association with e-mails (Bawden, 2001; Speier, Valacich, & Vessey, 1999). Social media, such as Facebook or WhatsApp (which are based on pushing information), did not even exist when these early studies were conducted, and this might add to IO. Thus, IO in teams can be described on a quantitative dimension as too much information obtained and on a qualitative dimension if the information exchanged within the teams lacks novelty, is low in accuracy, is ambiguous, complex, or uncertain (cf. Evaristo, 1993).

There are manifold consequences of quantitative and qualitative IO in teams and organizations. Research discusses emotional and motivational consequences (stress, anxiety, or tiredness; Bawden & Robinson, 2009; Edmunds & Morris, 2000), as well as effects on performance and team efficiency (Ayyagari, Grover, & Purvis, 2011; Rutkowski & Saunders, 2010) which can lead to increasing organizational cost. Eppler and Mengis (2004) differentiate four main symptoms/effects of IO in their review: (1) limited information search and retrieval strategies (e.g. lower systematic search strategies, limited search directions), (2) arbitrary information analysis and organization (e.g. overlapping and inconsistent information categories, highly selective information disregard), (3) suboptimal decisions (e.g. loss of control over information, higher time requirements for information handling, lower decision accuracy) and (4) strenuous personal situations (e.g. inefficient work, demotivation, lowered job satisfaction, potential paralysis and delay of decisions). Especially in team decision making, efficiency decreases as the amount of information increases (e.g., Bawden, 2001). In their explorative interview study analyzing the main barriers and enablers of organizational virtual teamwork in multinational organizations, Rack, Tschaut, Giesser, and Clases (2011) found that virtual teams often exchange

(a) too much information in an (b) unfiltered and (c) inaccurate way. Subsequently, IO led to detrimental effects, like delays in decision making and the subjective experience of strain.

How can teams successfully adapt to IO situations, avoid IO, and support functional information exchange? Most research on the causes of IO has focused on individual factors such as the handling of electronic correspondence and on task-related factors such as time, organization, or technical support (Eppler & Mengis, 2004). In a review of the relevant literature, Eppler and Mengis distinguished five antecedents that cause experience of IO: (1) individual factors (e.g., attitudes, motivation, age, experience), (2) information characteristics (e.g., quantity, uncertainty, and complexity of information), (3) task and process parameters (e.g., time pressure, interruptions, and interdependencies), (4) information technologies (e.g., push systems and access speed) as well as (5) organizational and team structural variables (e.g., group heterogeneity). Thus, it becomes apparent that most of these focus on structure, task, or technical variables. However, organizational team research underlines the importance of team cognitions on functional and dysfunctional processes in teams (DeChurch & Mesmer-Magnus, 2010a; Ellwart, 2011).

Thus, this chapter will introduce emergent team knowledge structures (team cognition) within teams as relevant mediators for explaining IO and adapting team processes to a more functional information exchange. Two concepts of shared and distributed team cognition are introduced: (1) Team Mental Models (TMM) and (2) Transactive Memory Systems (TMS) (see Figure 1). Empirical data will show the importance of both shared and distributed cognitions for effective information exchange and, in turn, for less IO. In the second section of this chapter, the processes and support tools for IO adaptation that have been tested in research and practice are introduced. It will become apparent that teams need a third type of shared team cognition, so-called Team Situation Awareness (TSA) to foster the recognition of IO in the team. Stepwise adaptation will help the team members to plan and execute efficient communication strategies by synchronizing and updating TMM and TMS. At the end, adaptation will guide teams in future interactions in order to reduce quantitative and qualitative IO.

BACKGROUND

The concepts and definitions of team cognition, IO-relevant processes, and adaptation presented in this chapter are grounded on theoretical frameworks of so-called input-process-output models (IPO) (Hackman, 1987; McGrath, 1984) or more recently of input-mediator-output-input models (IMOI) (Ilgen, Hollenbeck, Johnson,

& Jundt, 2005). These models from organizational team research offer a systematic overview and understanding of

1. Core input variables that influence team processes from an individual level (e.g., personality of team members), team level (e.g., leadership, diversity), and organizational level (e.g., structure, culture).
2. The mediator variables are cognitive states (i.e., team cognition), emotional states (e.g., shared moods), or behavioral processes like functional information exchange and coordination as well as dysfunctional communication processes related to IO.
3. The output variables classify different effects of teamwork, such as performance, learning, or adaptation. Different from the single-circle path of previous IPO models (from inputs to outputs), the IMOI concept underlines the importance of feedback loops and a temporal view on team processes (Ilgen et al., 2005; Marks, Zaccaro, & Mathieu, 2000).

Especially in team adaptation and team learning processes, output from one work phase can be treated as input or a cue for the subsequent work phase that can signal the team to change its behavior (Oertel & Antoni, 2015).

In this chapter, team cognition, dysfunctional and functional IO-relevant processes as well as team adaptation are all considered parts of an IMOI model. TMS and TMM are cognitive states that are considered the most relevant mediators for explaining the inefficient IO-related performance in teams. Moreover, team cognitions also trigger subsequent adaptation of team communication and planning by representing a shared awareness of the IO situation (Ellwart et al., 2015) and, in

Figure 1. Overview: Effects and adaptation of team cognition in information overload situations

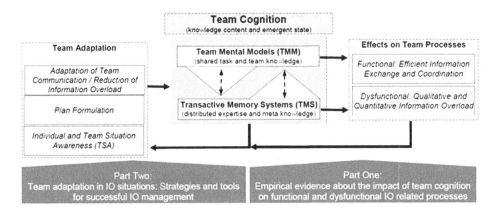

the next step, to the synchronization of TMM and TMS in order to interact more efficiently (Oertel & Antoni, 2014). Behavioral team processes like ineffective information exchange, e-mail overload, and low coordination are indicators of dysfunctional IO-related behavior in teams. This chapter introduces strategies and tools to adapt this dysfunctional behavior in IO situations and to ensure functional information exchange and successful coordination.

TEAM COGNITION AND ADAPTATION: EFFECTS ON FUNCTIONAL AND DYSFUNCTIONAL PROCESSES

The Concept of Team Cognition

Team cognition represents an emergent state that facilitates and triggers effective team performance (DeChurch & Mesmer-Magnus, 2010a; Kozlowski & Illgen, 2006). Specifically, team cognition "refers to the manner in which knowledge important to team functioning is mentally organized, represented, and distributed within the team and allows team members to anticipate and execute actions" (DeChurch & Mesmer-Magnus, 2010a, p. 33). Team cognition, as an emergent state, can be conceptualized as (1) compilation-based team knowledge or (2) composition-based team knowledge (Kozlowski, Chao, Grand, Braun, & Kuljanin, 2013). Compilation-based team knowledge refers to a memory network or TMS (Ellwart, Konradt, & Rack, 2014; Zajac, Gregory, Bedwell, Kramer, & Salas, 2014), in which individual experts have to hold specific divergent knowledge, and team members can access this knowledge by knowing who knows what (Kozlowski et al., 2013). While TMS emphasizes the distribution of knowledge across team members (i.e., compilation), composition-based team knowledge underlines the sharedness of mental representations or TMM across different team members. In the following sections, the empirical evidence of TMM and TMS on dysfunctional IO as well as on functional and efficient coordination are reviewed and discussed.

Team Mental Models (TMM): Effects on Information Overload

The concept of TMM (DeChurch & Mesmer-Magnus, 2010a, 2010b; Mohammed, Ferzandi, & Hamilton, 2010) describes the shared, organized understanding of knowledge relevant to key elements of the team and its task(s). While taskwork related TMM refer to characteristics of the team's work, major task duties, equipment, and resources, teamwork related TMM include features of how team members interact and about their roles, responsibilities, and knowledge domains which facilitate team interactions to accomplish team goals (Marks et al., 2000; Mathieu, Heffner, Goodwin, Salas, & Cannon-Bowers, 2000). Beyond having a shared understanding of what team members do and how they do it, it is important for effective team coordination to have congruence about when they have to do it (Mohammed & Harrison, 2013). Temporal TMM describe "the agreement among group members concerning deadlines for task completion, the pacing or speed of activities, and the sequencing of tasks (Mohammed, Hamilton, Tesler, Mancuso & McNeese, 2015, p. 696).

There is some empirical data showing that a high quality of task, team as well as temporal related TMM will result in effective communication and coordination patterns in teams (functional outcome that avoids IO, see Table 1). Meta analytic studies by DeChurch and Messmer-Magnus (2010a, 2010b) analyzed team studies and found positive relationships between shared and accurate TMM with functional team processes such as coordination. With values between $\rho = .22$ and $\rho = .29$, the mean correlations indicated medium effects. For example, Stout, Cannon-Bowers, Salas, and Milanovich (1999) demonstrated that teams with high planning activities also developed shared taskwork and teamwork knowledge (e.g., clarifying roles and information to be exchanged), communicated more efficiently, and showed higher performance. Specifically for virtual teams, Fiore, Salas, Cuevas, and Bowers (2003) postulate a close and high impact relationship between TMM and successful team coordination processes because of the team's opacity arising from distributed interaction.

In a recent experimental simulation study, Mohammed et al. (2015) investigated the impact of temporal TMM on performance and found correlations of $r = .31$ between temporal TMM and performance, indicating the usefulness of these constructs for functional team performance. Similarly, in a longitudinal study of 48 student project teams, Gevers, Van Eerde, and Rutte (2009) showed, after controlling for team size and familiarity, that high levels of temporal consensus in early project phases and the increase in temporal consensus significantly predicted meeting project deadlines, and that this effect was mediated by coordinated team action, explaining 24 percent of the variance in meeting project deadlines. Although the focus of both studies was not on the effects of IO, however, the constructs of temporal TMM are nevertheless closely related to causes of IO in teams. For example, the shared knowledge about deadlines allows team members to prioritize their time as well as to communicate their actions. Similar perceptions about the pacing speed may avoid coordination problems and dysfunctional communication. Pacing styles reflect how team members distribute their effort over time (Mohammed et al., 2015). Gevers, Mohammed, and Baytalskaya (2015) differ between steady action style, where activities are spread out across time compared to early and deadline action style, where work is completed within a clearly defined period. One can assume that dysfunctional IO will occur if team members have unshared perceptions about the temporal TMM because their communication will not be synchronized.

Table 1. Selected evidence of TMM and functional/dysfunctional team processes

	Process	Type of TMM	Type of Study	Result
DeChurch & Messmer-Magnus (2010a, 2010b)	Functional	TMM behavioral processes (e.g., coordination)	meta-analyses of 15/17 studies	TMM is positively related (ρ = .29/.22) to team processes (e.g., coordination)
Mohammed; Hamilton, Tesler, Mancuso, & McNeese (2015)	Functional	TMM task, team, and temporal	experiment	Temporal TMM are related to team performance ($r = .31$)
Gevers, Van Eerde, & Rutte (2009)	Functional	TMM temporal	field	Temporal TMM predict meeting deadlines because of high coordination
Ellwart, Happ, Gurtner, & Rack (2015)	Dysfunctional	TMM task, team, and situation awareness	experiment	Unshared TMM predict high subjective and objective IO (emails)
Ellis (2006)	Dysfunctional	TMM roles, responsibilities, interaction pattern	experiment	TMM are negatively affected by team stress, which explains low performance

TMM research with a focus on dysfunctional IO is sparse compared to the functional side of information exchange. In a recent review of 259 studies since 2000, Coultas, Driskell, Burke, and Salas (2014) recommend that "researchers and practitioners should pay close attention to the type of task(s) and the level of task interdependence under investigation because this can serve as a decision aid when selecting emergent state measures" (p. 8). This calls for IO specific determinations of TMM measures that are theoretically linked to dysfunctional processes. For example, Ellwart et al. (2015) applied a TMM measure that included IO related processes in an experimental team task. They found significant relationships between TMM and subjective as well as objective IO (i.e., e-mails). The TMM measure captured IO related task and team knowledge for each team member after a first working phase (i.e., task strategy, responsibilities, interaction pattern, goal clarity, roles) and included two items of IO awareness in the scale. The TMM index included the degree of knowledge and sharedness. IO was measured subjectively ("I have received too much information from my colleagues") and objectively by counting all e-mails in the inbox of the participants. Regarding subjective IO, teams with better TMM (more knowledge and higher sharedness) experienced less IO ($b = -0.33$, $p < .01$). A similar result was found for objective IO.

Other studies address the relationship between TMM and dysfunctional team processes indirectly. Ellis (2006) underlined the negative role of stressful situations for the development of good team cognitions (such as TMM and TMS). In this study, stress was induced by time pressure which resulted in lower TMM similarity and accuracy (partial $\eta^2 = -.22/-.28$) which in turn decreased team performance. For IO research, the results indicate that unshared TMM will not only affect IO (which is a stressful situation); moreover, this environment may serve as a stressor or as input hindering TMM development in subsequent phases of performance.

Transactive Memory Systems (TMS): Effects on Information Overload

TMS, proposed by Wegner, Giuliano, and Hertel (1985), is a memory system distributed across team members – a team-level construct that reflects encoding, storing, and retrieving information that is distributed across team members (Wegner, 1986). When each team member is aware of what other team members know, the team can draw on the knowledge distributed across members, with each member keeping track of each other's expertise, directing new information to the matching member, and using this knowledge to access relevant information (Mohammed & Dumville, 2001; Wegner 1986). Two important dimensions of TMS are relevant for IO. The first dimension is specialization of team members. Given the distribution of specialized memories across team members, teams with TMS should be more efficient due to the reduced cognitive load on each team member (Hollingshead, 1998). This is one relevant effect of TMS on functional outcomes. There is empirical evidence that the specification in functional roles will lead to a reduction of cognitive load within this expertise system (cf. Hollingshead, Gupta, Yoon, & Brandon, 2012). In turn, high cognitive capacity allows team members to process more information before IO occurs. Thus, information load and processing capabilities are inseparably linked (Schultze & Vandenbosch, 1998).

The second dimension is the shared knowledge about expertise location (metaknowledge) in TMS. Only if team members actually "know who knows what" are they able to use the specialization within the team efficiently: they can ask the "right" people for information or can distribute new information accordingly, and can avoid asking or disseminating information to all team members, for example, in the "cc" of e-mails. Thus, TMS also relate to functional and dysfunctional team processes. In meta-analyses by DeChurch and Messmer-Magnus (2010a, 2010b), compilational emergence (i.e., TMS) is strongly related to functional outcomes such as coordination and behavioral processes ($\rho = .62$). Compared to compositional emergence of TMM, the relationship is much stronger thus underlining the importance of TMS. For example, Lewis (2003) investigated the relationship between specialization in TMS and functional communication in experimental and field settings. Functional communication was determined as the extent to which team member communication is relevant, positive, precise, consistent, truthful, and fosters teamwork (Lewis, 2003). In an experimental setting (study 1), participants assembled telephone-kits in three-person teams with high and low specialization. In the applied setting of study 2, students worked in a management project and differed in the degree of specialization. In a third study, Lewis (2003) surveyed managers and team members of 11 high-technology companies. The measurement of specialization was based on a field-ready rating scale (sample item: "Each team member has specialized knowledge of some aspect of our project."). The results were consistent. High specialization (high TMS) was related to functional communication (study 1: $r = .33$; study 2: $r = .58$; study 3: .48). Similarly, Ellwart, Bündgens, and Rack (2013) measured knowledge about expertise location (metaknowledge in TMS) in 73 organizational teams using a rating scale approach following Faraj and Sproull (2000) (sample item: "The team has a good map of each other's talents and skills"). Results showed that a clear understanding of expertise roles (high TMS) is associated with functional knowledge exchange ($r = .39$). More recently, Lin,

Table 2. Selected evidence of TMS and functional/dysfunctional team processes

	Process	Type of TMS	Type of Study	Result
DeChurch & Messmer-Magnus (2010a)	Functional	TMS behavioral processes (e.g., coordination)	meta-analysis of 10 studies	TMS is positively related ($\rho = .62$) to team processes (e.g., coordination)
Lewis (2003)	Functional	TMS specialization	experiment and field	Specialization is strongly related to functional communication
Ellwart, Bündgens, & Rack (2013)	Functional	TMS knowledge expertise location	field	Knowledge of experts in diverse teams predicts knowledge exchange ($r = .39$)
Lin, Cheng, & Wu (2014)	Functional	TMS specialization, coordination, credibility	field	TMS are related to heedful interrelation of actions among team members ($r = .62$)
Hollingshead & Brandon (2003) Hollingshead, Gupta, Yoon, & Brandon (2012)	Functional	TMS knowledge about expert roles and accuracy	review	TMS is related to reduced cognitive load, better communication and team processes
Whelan & Teigland (2013)	Dysfunctional	TMS directory updating, information allocation, retrieval coordination	field	TMS as a collective filter for reducing IO in digitally enabled organizational groups
Ellwart, Konradt, & Rack (2014)	Dysfunctional	TMS knowledge of expertise location	field and experiment	low TMS (low agreement and knowledge) of expertise roles leads to high number of e-mails ($r = -.46$)

Cheng, and Wu (2014) reported similar results. Specifically, they applied Lewis's (2003) TMS measurement approach in a field student sample and showed that TMS is related to knowledge integration ($r = .62$), another functional process of successfully integrating existing and acquired knowledge within a team.

Two studies investigated the effect of TMS on dysfunctional processes. In a field study, Whelan and Teigland (2013) demonstrated that TMS serve as a collective filter for mitigating IO in digitally enabled organizational groups. In their paper, the authors underline the importance of TMS and subsequent collective behavior as a social solution for the IO in organizations. In their cases studies, Whelan and Teigland (2013) applied social network analysis and qualitative interviews. They showed that specialized roles in R&D divisions in the medical devices industry developed filters for external and internal information exchange. For example, some individuals specialize in filtering external information into the team while others specialize in filtering information for internal use. Whelan and Teiglan (2013) state that "each individual in the network then has his/her own directory that is used to filter information from others and that is constantly updated" (p. 190). Therefore, collective filters in TMS reduce IO and therefore should be considered in combination with technical solutions.

In an experimental study, Ellwart, Konradt, and Rack (2014) manipulated the amount of TMS metaknowledge between teams. The experimental teams consisted of three participants, who were assigned to solve a decision-making task. In the task, the teams were told that they worked for a company that analyzes weather information to provide recommendations to customers regarding the best of three potential travel routes. Each member received a specific customer request regarding the three possible routes. Based on weather criteria given by the customers, each team member had to decide which of the three routes was best suited to the customer wishes. The team members decided on weather information that was shared among specific weather experts within the team. Thus, a TMS was implemented with with specialization of weather domain experts (e.g., expert for wind, temperature, or rain). In order to receive missing information from the other experts, participants had to write e-mails to the team members asking for the missing information. However, teams differed in the degree of TMS metaknowledge. In the high metaknowledge condition, quantitative IO (number of e-mails each team member received) was much lower than in the low metaknowledge condition ($r = -.46, p < .001$). Moreover, teams with good metaknowledge and fewer e-mails reported better performance than the other conditions ($r = .32, p < .01$). Ellwart et al. (2014) assessed similar variables in field settings and replicated the findings. High metaknowledge (knowledge about the expertise location in the team) was related to better coordination ($r = .46; p < .001$) and higher performance evaluated by an external judge ($r = .31; p < .05$).

In sum, TMS are team cognition structures that can be characterized by a certain degree of specialization and metaknowledge, indicating the location of specific expertise as well as functional processes such as information exchange and coordination. Dysfunctional IO, such as quantitative and qualitative overload, are associated with a low degree of specialization and metaknowledge.

Managing Information Overload through Team Cognition Updating and Team Adaptation

In this section, strategies and tools to support teams when experiencing IO are introduced. The core mechanism is team adaptation in which teams will adjust their communication behavior to establish a functional information exchange with low dysfunctional IO. In this regard, successful management of IO can be understood as adaptive team performance that "emerges from a series of cognitive and behavioral actions carried out by team members" (Burke, Stagl, Salas, Pierce, & Kendall, 2006, p. 1192). Major theoretical lines of team adaptation research have contributed to the development of models of team adaptation processes or interventions that link between team cognition and adaptation including:

1. Team adaptation models (Burke et al., 2006),
2. Cross-training interventions (e.g., Cannon-Bowers, Salas, Blickensderfer, & Bowers, 1998; Cooke et al., 2003; Marks, Sabella, Burke, & Zaccaro, 2002; Volpe, Cannon-Bowers, Salas, & Spector, 1996),
3. Team reflexivity interventions (e.g., Gurtner, Tschan, Semmer, & Nägele, 2007),
4. Team coordination trainings (e.g., Salas, Nichols, & Driskell, 2007), and
5. Heuristics (e.g., Frese & Zapf, 1994; Hacker, 2005).

Looking at the sequential phases of team adaptation, recent models describe a circular process over time (Burke et al., 2006; Maynard, Kennedy, & Sommer, 2015) that can be adjusted to the management of dysfunctional IO. In this regard, Ellwart et al. (2015) developed STROTA, a structured online team adaptation intervention that supports teams to become aware of IO, to understand the causes of IO, and to develop strategies to reduce IO. In three subsequent phases of STROTA, the team members are guided through an assigned and moderated process of individual and team situation assessment (1a/1b), plan formulation (2), and subsequent adaptation (3) of dysfunctional information exchange behavior during the following action phase (see Figure 1, left side). The three stages of adaptation are implemented by means of a highly structured procedure. Phases (1) and (2) are based on the concept of heuristics (Frese & Zapf, 1994), also referred to as question-answering techniques

(Winkelmann & Hacker, 2010) or heuristic rules (Hacker, 2005). Heuristics are an assembly or hierarchy of questions that provide hints and guidance for reflection and development of plans. According to Daudelin (1996), such questions can stimulate the description of the situation (cf. situation assessment and awareness), the analysis of the task, and the development of new perspectives (cf. planning and adaptation). Thus, team adaptation stimulates TMM and TMS development and the implementation of functional strategies of information exchange in later actions.

The first phase of STROTA, individual and team situation assessment, refers to the individual process of scanning, identifying, and processing the information that indicates the need for change (Burke et al., 2006). First, there must be an individual awareness that IO is a problem within the team and that team members experience too much and low quality information. Burke and colleagues (2006) proposed an initial situation assessment, in which team members scan the current environment for success-relevant cues and ascribe meaning to them. This individual enhancement of awareness turned out to be highly important for later collective team situation awareness, plan formulation, and subsequent adaption. However, in order to change the cognitive representations of IO-relevant aspects (i.e., strategies, roles, responsibilities, goals, interaction patterns), the team needs to have a collective up-to-date awareness of the current status and knowledge (i.e., Team Situational Awareness, TSA). Team members need the shared perception of whether there is IO within the team, whether responsibilities are clear, and whether member roles are transparent. To support individual and team situational awareness in this phase, Ellwart, Peiffer, Matheis, and Happ (in press) developed an online team awareness tool (OnTEAM) for application in STROTA that gives the team feedback about the perceived IO and the quality of TMM. Within a given task, members rate the perception of task and team relevant knowledge domains on a 7-item online scale (assessing e.g., clarity of task roles, responsibilities, interaction patterns). Additional items reflect the situational perception of IO by asking if team members have received too much information (IO quantity). A PHP based script immediately transforms each individual rating into a team chart. This is a color-based graphical feedback displaying level (critical vs. noncritical perception) and sharedness (shared vs. unshared) of IO-relevant TMM contents for the specific team. Figure 2 displays an example of team feedback to three team members. The first five items refer to task and team specific knowledge whereas items 6 and 7 focus on the awareness of IO. For each of the seven items, the level of the individual ratings is displayed and coded by a color (green = noncritical IO/high knowledge, yellow = medium critical IO/medium knowledge, red = critical IO/low knowledge). Perceived sharedness of the ratings among the team members is displayed by different colors within the team for each specific item (e.g., item 2 in Figure 2: person A perceives that responsibilities are clear (green), person B and C do not share this perception (red)). The typical traffic signal colors (red, yellow, green) facilitate the cognitive elaboration of the feedback, because red signals critical knowledge/IO situations compared to green and yellow (Elliot, Maier, Moller, Friedman & Meinhardt, 2007).

In this phase of STROTA (1a), each team member receives the OnTEAM feedback individually. Each member is asked to express his personal perception: "Based on this feedback chart, how do you perceive the perceptions of the other team members on potential problems or ambiguities?" (Ellwart et al., 2015). Subsequently, the team members are asked individually to write down the problems and IO-relevant phenomena they view in this feedback.

In order to support the development of a shared understanding in team cognitions (TSA, TMM, and TMS), the team members need to discuss the OnTEAM feedback collectively (phase 1b in STROTA). In cross-training approaches (Marks et al., 2002) and team coordination training programs (Salas, Burke, & Cannon-Bowers, 2002), this collective clarification of team members' roles and responsibilities has been shown to be an effective intervention to increase team members' understanding of each other's team knowledge (Cannon-Bowers et al., 1998; Cooke et al., 2003; Volpe et al., 1996). In the STROTA application, team member come together in this phase (1b) and discuss the feedback chart utilizing questions such as like: "What are the reasons for unshared and inhomogeneous perceptions in the visual feedback?" Next, the external moderator summarizes the ideas of the team members. In their study, Ellwart et al. (2015) administered this phase online for virtual teams, with a moderated discussion via Skype© instant messenger service.

Subsequently, plan formulation is the next phase of team adaptation. In STROTA this phase (2) is also moderated in a face-to-face or online team meeting. The guiding heuristic question is "What should be done differently in your team? What are the specific plans/consequences for the upcoming action phase?" Guided by the external moderator, the team members now develop commonly shared rules and guidelines in order to reduce IO in the next action phase.

Figure 2. Hypothetical OnTEAM feedback in the STROTA adaptation intervention

Items evaluated by the team members	Responses in the team		
	Person A	Person B	Person C
1. The strategies to work on the task are unclear to me.			
2. The responsibilities of the team members are not clear.			
3. I do not know who I should forward the information to.			
4. I am unsure about what task to do first.			
5. I am not sure how to integrate the results of the team members.			
6. I am often disturbed by unimportant messages.			
7. I receive too much irrelevant information.			

Finally, team members are debriefed and return to their tasks. Guided by their TMM and the plans they formulated during STROTA, functional processes should increase whereas dysfunctional IO should decrease. Empirical evidence supports the functionality of STROTA in IO environments. Ellwart and colleagues (2015) investigated 120 experimental teams working on an interdependent decision-making task while completely relying on e-mail communication. After a first action phase with high IO induced by numerous external and within team e-mails, teams in the intervention condition received STROTA as an experimental manipulation compared to controls without STROTA. Subsequently, the teams returned to a second task phase. During all phases, TMM as well as IO was measured. Overall, the results of multilevel analyses showed that STROTA led to an improvement of TMM. In addition, good quality and shared TMM related to reduced IO during the second task phase (objective assessment: number of e-mails, subjective: individual rating). Finally, also a direct effect of STROTA on IO was found for subjective and objective IO. Mediation analyses showed that TMM are able to explain the effects of STROTA on IO, therefore underlining the importance of team cognition for adaptation.

In sum, experimental data provides evidence that STROTA in combination with the team awareness tool, OnTEAM, support a modification of information exchange processes leading to reduced IO.

PERSPECTIVES FOR RESEARCH AND PRACTITIONERS

This chapter underlined the importance of team cognition (TMM, TMS, TSA) for functional information exchanges as well as for dysfunctional information overload. Specifically, team cognition as a "social solution" to manage IO (Whelan & Teigland, 2013) complements the existing individual, technical, and task-oriented approaches (Eppler & Mengis, 2004). Consequently, there are multiple factors for research and practice in order to explain and modify IO in modern work processes. Following the notion of IMOI models (Ilgen et al., 2005), even more variables of influence move into the focus of future research that may directly or indirectly affect team cognition and subsequently IO. For example, leadership behavior like explaining job responsibilities and task objectives (Yukl, Gordon, & Taber, 2002) will affect TMM and TMS and reduce IO by facilitating functional processes and performance (cf. Mohammed & Nadkarni, 2011). With respect to a practitioner perspective, the present research shows that supporting team awareness about IO as well as about task and team contents will help the team to identify unshared perceptions or critical situations. Support tools like OnTEAM may be helpful, but even "simple" team phases of reflection and adaptation may have similar effects (Wiedow, Konradt, Ellwart & Steenfatt, 2013). However, modern work designs often depend on electronic communication and virtual team structures that are less suited for face-to-face reflection. However, STROTA, as an online-based approach for team adaptation, offers a useful tool for dispersed teams.

Despite this positive perspective, it is necessary to mention some limitations. First, team reflection—either online or face-to-face—will utilize resources for planning, administering, and meeting which may hinder its implementation in daily busy routines. Moreover, STROTA and OnTEAM are interventions that uncover and visualize possible problems, individual misunderstandings, or leadership deficits in front of the whole team. Individual team members may perceive themselves as a low performer (or having low knowledge) which may lead to withdrawal or reactivity behaviors. From research on team learning we know that a positive climate or psychological safety within the team is necessary for an open and task-oriented development (Edmondson, 1999; Oertel & Antoni, 2014). Thus, effective IO modification depends on team environments that offer the space, culture, and personalities to analyze and optimize deficits. Second, the concepts of team cognition focus on a closed team structure with team members that belong unmistakably to this team. However, from an organizational perspective, modern workers belong to more than one team (multiple team membership, MTM) (O'Leary, Mortenson, & Woolley, 2011) and teams are acting in dynamic and complex multiple team systems (MTS) (Zaccaro, Marks, & DeChurch, 2012). Strategies based on the notion of team cognition to overcome IO will be limited if the overload also has origins in MTS/MTM organizational structures and processes.

FUTURE RESEARCH DIRECTIONS

Future research should provide more evidence about the functional and, most importantly, the dysfunctional effects of team cognitions. Compared to functional outcomes such as coordination and efficient information exchange, the dysfunctional outcomes of team cognitions are seldom investigated. One path of future research should directly address the negative process and outcome variables of teamwork. Another path of future research could transfer the concepts of TMM and TMS into organizational structures. For example, team research has shown that specialization or team expertise systems reduced IO and that more cognitive capacity was available when expert roles were distributed in TMS (cf. Hollingshead et al., 2012). Could this notion be implemented in complex expertise structures on the organizational level? There is little empirical research on the effects of complex and dynamic organizational structures on dysfunctional IO or cognitive capacity (e.g., organizational structure and memory; Fiedler & Welpe, 2010). One reason may be the lack of suitable methods for modeling the dynamic nature of MTM and MTS in organizations (Zaccaro et al., 2012). Rich data designs, event history analysis, or simulation studies may provide interdisciplinary perspectives for future research (Coen & Schnackenberg, 2012).

CONCLUSION

Emergent knowledge structures in teams represent the shared understanding of task, team, and temporal contents (team mental models, TMM) or the distributed expertise and knowledge about the expertise location (transactive memory system, TMS). Complementing other approaches, both concepts from organizational team research yield effective factors on functional information exchange as well as on dysfunctional information overload. The successful synchronization and adaptation of team cognition offers a "social solution" for IO (Whelan & Teigland, 2013) that is theoretically founded, empirically investigated, and practically applicable for virtual and face-to-face teams. Future research should address both functional and dysfunctional processes and outcomes of complex expertise structures in MTS and organizations.

REFERENCES

Ayyagari, R., Grover, V., & Purvis, R. (2011). Technostress: Technological antecedents and implications. *Management Information Systems Quarterly, 35,* 831–858.

Bawden, D. (2001). Information and digital literacies: A review of concepts. *The Journal of Documentation, 57*(2), 218–259. doi:10.1108/EUM0000000007083

Bawden, D., & Robinson, L. (2009). The dark side of information: Overload, anxiety and other pathologies. *Journal of Information Science, 35*(2), 180–191. doi:10.1177/0165551508095781

Burke, C. S., Stagl, K. C., Salas, E., Pierce, L., & Kendall, D. (2006). Understanding team adaptation: A conceptual analysis and model. *The Journal of Applied Psychology, 91*(6), 1189–1207. doi:10.1037/0021-9010.91.6.1189 PMID:17100478

Cannon-Bowers, J. A., Salas, E., Blickensderfer, E., & Bowers, C. A. (1998). The impact of cross-training and workload on team functioning: A replication and extension of initial findings. *Human Factors: The Journal of the Human Factors and Ergonomics Society, 40*(1), 92–101. doi:10.1518/001872098779480550

Coen, C. A., & Schnackenberg, A. (2012). Complex systems methods for studying multiteam systems. In S. J. Zaccaro, M. A. Marks, & L. A. DeChurch (Eds.), *Multiteam systems: An organization form for dynamic and complex environments* (pp. 459–486). New York: Routledge.

Cooke, N. J., Kiekel, P. A., Salas, E., Stout, R. J., Bowers, C., & Cannon-Bowers, J. A. (2003). Measuring team knowledge: A window to the cognitive underpinnings of team performance. *Group Dynamics, 7*(3), 179–199. doi:10.1037/1089-2699.7.3.179

Coultas, C. W., Driskell, T., Burke, C. S., & Salas, E. (2014). A conceptual review of emergent state measurement: Current problems, future solutions. *Small Group Research, 45*(6), 671-703. doi:1046496414552285

Daudelin, M. W. (1996). Learning from experience through reflection. *Organizational Dynamics, 24*(3), 36–48. doi:10.1016/S0090-2616(96)90004-2

DeChurch, L. A., & Mesmer-Magnus, J. R. (2010a). The cognitive underpinnings of effective teamwork: A meta-analysis. *The Journal of Applied Psychology, 95*(1), 32–53. doi:10.1037/a0017328 PMID:20085405

DeChurch, L. A., & Mesmer-Magnus, J. R. (2010b). Measuring shared team mental models: A meta-analysis. *Group Dynamics, 14*(1), 1–14. doi:10.1037/a0017455

Edmondson, A. (1999). Psychological safety and learning behavior in work teams. *Administrative Science Quarterly, 44*(2), 350–383. doi:10.2307/2666999

Edmunds, A., & Morris, A. (2000). The problem of information overload in business organisations: A review of the literature. *International Journal of Information Management, 20*(1), 17–28. doi:10.1016/S0268-4012(99)00051-1

Elliot, A. J., Maier, M. A., Moller, A. C., Friedman, R., & Meinhardt, J. (2007). Color and psychological functioning. *Current Directions in Psychological Science, 16*(5), 250–254. doi:10.1111/j.1467-8721.2007.00514.x PMID:17324089

Ellis, A. P. (2006). System breakdown: The role of mental models and transactive memory in the relationship between acute stress and team performance. *Academy of Management Journal, 49*(3), 576–589. doi:10.5465/AMJ.2006.21794674

Ellwart, T. (2011). Assessing coordination in human groups: Concepts and methods. In M. Boos, M. Kolbe, P. Kappeler, & T. Ellwart (Eds.), *Coordination in human and primate groups* (pp. 119–135). Heidelberg, Germany: Springer. doi:10.1007/978-3-642-15355-6_7

Ellwart, T., Bündgens, S., & Rack, O. (2013). Managing knowledge exchange and identification in age diverse teams. *Journal of Managerial Psychology, 28*(7/8), 950–972. doi:10.1108/JMP-06-2013-0181

Ellwart, T., Happ, C., Gurtner, A., & Rack, O. (2015). Managing information overload in virtual teams: Effects of a structured online team adaptation on cognition and performance. *European Journal of Work and Organizational Psychology, 24*(5), 812–826. doi:10.1080/1359432X.2014.1000873

Ellwart, T., Konradt, U., & Rack, O. (2014). Team mental models of expertise location: Validation of a field survey measure. *Small Group Research, 45*(2), 119–153. doi:10.1177/1046496414521303

Ellwart, T., Peiffer, H., Matheis, G., & Happ, C. (in press). Möglichkeiten und Grenzen eines Online Team Awareness Tools (OnTEAM) in Adaptationsprozess en[Opportunities and limitations of an online team awareness tool (OnTEAM) in adaptation processes]. *Wirtschaftspsychologie.*

Eppler, M. J., & Mengis, J. (2004). The concept of information overload: A review of literature from organization science, accounting, marketing, MIS, and related disciplines. *The Information Society, 20*(5), 325–344. doi:10.1080/01972240490507974

Evaristo, J. R. B. (1993). *An empirical investigation of the impact of information characteristics and information technology on individual information load* (Unpublished doctoral thesis). Carlson School of Management, University of Minnesota, Minneapolis, MN.

Faraj, S., & Sproull, L. (2000). Coordinating expertise in software development teams. *Management Science, 46*(12), 1554–1568. doi:10.1287/mnsc.46.12.1554.12072

Fiedler, L., & Welpe, I. (2010). How do organizations remember? The influence of organizational structure on organizational memory. *Organization Studies, 31*(4), 381–407. doi:10.1177/0170840609347052

Fiore, S. M., Salas, E., Cuevas, H. M., & Bowers, C. A. (2003). Distributed coordination space: Toward a theory of distributed team process and performance. *Theoretical Issues in Ergonomics Science, 4*(3-4), 340–364. doi:10.1080/1463922021000049971

Frese, M., & Zapf, D. (1994). Action as the core of work psychology: A German approach. In H. C. Triandis, M. D. Dunnette, & L. M. Hough (Eds.), *Handbook of industrial and organizational psychology* (pp. 271–340). Palo Alto, CA: Consulting Psychologists Press.

Gevers, J. M. P., Mohammed, S., & Baytalskaya, N. (2015). The conceptualization and measurement of pacing style. *Applied Psychology, 64*(3), 499–540. doi:10.1111/apps.12016

Gevers, J. M. P., Van Eerde, W., & Rutte, C. G. (2009). Team self-regulation and meeting deadlines in project teams: Antecedents and effects of temporal consensus. *European Journal of Work and Organizational Psychology, 18*(3), 295–321. doi:10.1080/13594320701693217

Gurtner, A., Tschan, F., Semmer, N. K., & Nägele, C. (2007). Getting groups to develop good strategies: Effects of reflexivity interventions on team process, team performance, and shared mental models. *Organizational Behavior and Human Decision Processes, 102*(2), 127–142. doi:10.1016/j.obhdp.2006.05.002

Hacker, W. (2005). Allgemeine Arbeitspsychologie: Psychische Regulation von Wissens-, Denk- und körperlicher Arbeit [General industrial psychology. Mental regulation of knowledge work, mental work and physical work] (2nd ed.). Bern: Huber.

Hackman, J. R. (1987). The design of work teams. In J. W. Lorsch (Ed.), *Handbook of organizational behavior* (pp. 315–342). Englewood Cliffs, NJ: Prentice-Hall.

Hertel, G., & Konradt, U. (2007). *Telekooperation und virtuelle Teamarbeit* [Telecooperation and virtual team work]. München: Oldenbourg. doi:10.1524/9783486594898

Hollingshead, A. B. (1998). Distributed knowledge and transactive processes in decision-making groups. In M. A. Neal, E. A. Mannix, & D. H. Gruenfeld (Eds.), *Research on managing groups and teams* (pp. 103–123). Stanford, CA: JAI Press.

Hollingshead, A. B., & Brandon, D. P. (2003). Potential benefits of communication in transactive memory systems. *Human Communication Research, 29*(4), 607–615. doi:10.1111/j.1468-2958.2003.tb00859.x

Hollingshead, A. B., Gupta, N., Yoon, K., & Brandon, D. P. (2012). Transactive memory theory and teams: Past, present and future. In E. Salas, S. M. Fiore, & M. P. Letsky (Eds.), *Theories of team cognition: Cross-disciplinary perspectives* (pp. 421–455). New York, NY: Routledge.

Ilgen, D. R., Hollenbeck, J. R., Johnson, M., & Jundt, D. (2005). Teams in organizations: From input-process-output models to IMOI models. *Annual Review of Psychology, 56*(1), 517–543. doi:10.1146/annurev.psych.56.091103.070250 PMID:15709945

Kozlowski, S. W. J., Chao, G. T., Grand, J. A., Braun, M. T., & Kuljanin, G. (2013). Advancing multilevel research design – Capturing the dynamics of emergence. *Organizational Research Methods, 16*(4), 581–615. doi:10.1177/1094428113493119

Kozlowski, S. W. J., & Ilgen, D. R. (2006). Enhancing the effectiveness of work groups and teams. *Psychological Science in the Public Interest, 7,* 77–124. doi:10.1111/j.1529-1006.2006.00030.x PMID:26158912

Lewis, K. (2003). Measuring transactive memory systems in the field: Scale development and validation. *The Journal of Applied Psychology, 88*(4), 587–604. doi:10.1037/0021-9010.88.4.587 PMID:12940401

Lin, T.-C., Cheng, K.-T., & Wu, S. (2014). Knowledge integration in ISD project teams: A transactive memory perspective. *Open Journal of Business and Management, 2*(04), 360–371. doi:10.4236/ojbm.2014.24042

Marks, M. A., Sabella, M. J., Burke, C. S., & Zaccaro, S. J. (2002). The impact of cross-training on team effectiveness. *The Journal of Applied Psychology, 87*(1), 3–13. doi:10.1037/0021-9010.87.1.3 PMID:11916213

Marks, M. A., Zaccaro, S. J., & Mathieu, J. E. (2000). Performance implications of leader briefings and team-interaction training for team adaptation to novel environments. *The Journal of Applied Psychology, 85*(6), 971–986. doi:10.1037/0021-9010.85.6.971 PMID:11125660

Mathieu, J. E., Heffner, T. S., Goodwin, G. F., Salas, E., & Cannon-Bowers, J. A. (2000). The influence of shared mental models on team process and performance. *The Journal of Applied Psychology, 85*(2), 273–283. doi:10.1037/0021-9010.85.2.273 PMID:10783543

Maynard, M. T., Kennedy, D. M., & Sommer, S. A. (2015). Team adaptation: A fifteen-year synthesis (1998–2013) and framework for how this literature needs to adapt going forward. *European Journal of Work and Organizational Psychology, 24*(5), 652–677. doi:10.1080/1359432X.2014.1001376

McGrath, J. E. (1984). *Groups: Interaction and performance.* Englewood Cliffs, NJ: Prentice-Hall.

Mesmer-Magnus, J. R., & DeChurch, L. A. (2009). Information sharing and team performance: A meta-analysis. *The Journal of Applied Psychology, 94*(2), 535–546. doi:10.1037/a0013773 PMID:19271807

Miranda, S. M., & Saunders, C. S. (2003). The social construction of meaning: An alternative perspective on information sharing. *Information Systems Research, 14*(1), 87–106. doi:10.1287/isre.14.1.87.14765

Mohammed, S., & Dumville, B. C. (2001). Team mental models in a team knowledge framework: Expanding theory and measurement across disciplinary boundaries. *Journal of Organizational Behavior*, *22*(2), 89–106. doi:10.1002/job.86

Mohammed, S., Ferzandi, L., & Hamilton, K. (2010). Metaphor no more: A 15-year review of the team mental model construct. *Journal of Management*, *36*(4), 876–910. doi:10.1177/0149206309356804

Mohammed, S., Hamilton, K., Tesler, R., Mancuso, V., & McNeese, M. (2015). Time for temporal team mental models: Expanding between what and how to incorporate when. *European Journal of Work and Organizational Psychology*, *24*(5), 693–709. doi:10.1080/1359432X.2015.1024664

Mohammed, S., & Harrison, D. (2013). The clocks that time us are not the same: A theory of temporal diversity, task characteristics, and performance in teams. *Organizational Behavior and Human Decision Processes*, *122*(2), 244–256. doi:10.1016/j.obhdp.2013.08.004

Mohammed, S., & Nadkarni, S. (2011). Temporal diversity and team performance: The moderating role of team temporal leadership. *Academy of Management Journal*, *54*(3), 489–508. doi:10.5465/AMJ.2011.61967991

O'Leary, M. B., Mortensen, M., & Woolley, A. W. (2011). Multiple team membership: A theoretical model of its effects on productivity and learning for individuals and teams. *Academy of Management Review*, *36*(3), 461–478. doi:10.5465/amr.2009.0275

Oertel, R., & Antoni, C. H. (2014). Reflective team learning: Linking interfering events and team adaptation. *Team Performance Management*, *20*(7/8), 328–342. doi:10.1108/TPM-03-2014-0027

Oertel, R., & Antoni, C. H. (2015). Phase-specific relationships between team learning processes and transactive memory development. *European Journal of Work and Organizational Psychology*, *24*(5), 726–741. doi:10.1080/1359432X.2014.1000872

Rack, O., Tschaut, A., Giesser, C., & Clases, C. (2011). Collective Information Management - Ein Ansatzpunkt zum Umgang mit Informationsflut in virtueller Kooperation[Collective information management - A starting point for handling information overload in virtual cooperation]. *Wirtschaftspsychologie*, *13*(3), 41–51.

Rutkowski, A. F., & Saunders, C. S. (2010). Growing pains with information overload. *Computer*, *43*(6), 94–96. doi:10.1109/MC.2010.171

Salas, E., Nichols, D. R., & Driskell, J. E. (2007). Testing three team training strategies in intact teams: A meta-analysis. *Small Group Research*, *38*(4), 471–488. doi:10.1177/1046496407304332

Schultze, U., & Vandenbosch, B. (1998). Information overload in a groupware environment: Now you see it, now you dont. *Journal of Organizational Computing and Electronic Commerce*, *8*(2), 127–148. doi:10.1207/s15327744joce0802_3

Speier, C., Valacich, J. S., & Vessey, I. (1999). Information overload through interruptions: An empirical examination of decision making. *Decision Sciences*, *30*(2), 337–360. doi:10.1111/j.1540-5915.1999.tb01613.x

Stout, R. J., Cannon-Bowers, J. A., Salas, E., & Milanovich, D. M. (1999). Planning, shared mental models, and coordinated performance: An empirical link is established. *Human Factors*, *41*(1), 61–71. doi:10.1518/0018720099779577273

Thorngate, W. (1997). More than we can know: The attentional economics of Internet use. In S. Kiesler (Ed.), *Culture of the Internet* (pp. 296–297). Mahwah, NJ: Lawrence Erlbaum Associates.

Volpe, C. E., Cannon-Bowers, J. A., Salas, E., & Spector, P. E. (1996). The impact of cross-training on team functioning: An empirical investigation. *Human Factors: The Journal of the Human Factors and Ergonomics Society*, *38*(1), 87–100. doi:10.1518/001872096778940741 PMID:8682521

Wegner, D. M. (1986). Transactive memory: A contemporary analysis of the group mind. In B. Mullen & G. R. Goethals (Eds.), *Theories of group behavior* (pp. 185–205). New York: Springer-Verlag.

Wegner, D. M., Giuliano, T., & Hertel, P. (1985). Cognitive interdependence in close relationships. In W. J. Ickes (Ed.), *Compatible and incompatible relationships* (pp. 253–276). New York: Springer-Verlag. doi:10.1007/978-1-4612-5044-9_12

Whelan, E., & Teigland, R. (2013). Transactive memory systems as a collective filter for mitigating information overload in digitally enabled organizational groups. *Information and Organization*, *23*(3), 177–197. doi:10.1016/j.infoandorg.2013.06.001

Wiedow, A., Konradt, U., Ellwart, T., & Steenfatt, C. (2013). Direct and indirect effects of team learning on team outcomes: A multiple mediator analysis. *Group Dynamics*, *17*(4), 232–251. doi:10.1037/a0034149

Winkelmann, C., & Hacker, W. (2010). Question-answering-technique to support freshman and senior engineers in processes of engineering design. *International Journal of Technology and Design Education, 20*(3), 305–315. doi:10.1007/s10798-009-9086-8

Yukl, G., Gordon, A., & Taber, T. (2002). A hierarchical taxonomy of leadership behavior: Integrating a half century of behavior research. *Journal of Leadership & Organizational Studies, 9*(1), 15–32. doi:10.1177/107179190200900102

Zaccaro, S. J., Marks, M. A., & DeChurch, L. A. (Eds.). (2012). *Multiteam systems: An organization form for dynamic and complex environments.* New York: Routledge.

Zajac, S., Gregory, M. E., Bedwell, W. L., Kramer, W. S., & Salas, E. (2014). The cognitive underpinnings of adaptive team performance in ill-defined task situations: A closer look at team cognition. *Organizational Psychology Review, 4*(1), 49–73. doi:10.1177/2041386613492787

KEY TERMS AND DEFINITIONS

Information Overload: A team process variable that addresses too much information within the team (quantitative IO) and information of low novelty, accuracy, or uncertainty (qualitative IO).

Team Adaptation: The process of changing team behaviors. It consists of the phase of individual and eam situation awareness, plan formulation, and behavioral adaptation in the subsequent work phase.

Team Cognition: Emergent knowledge structure of team members that can differ in structure (shared vs. unshared) and content (task, team, situation).

Team Mental Models (TMM): A specific type of team cognition that emphasizes the collectively shared contents of task and team knowledge.

Team Processes: Observable behavior within the team that can be either dysfunctional (qualitative and quantitative IO) or functional (good coordination, efficient information exchange).

Team Situational Awareness (TSA): A specific type of team cognition that emphasizes collectively shared attentiveness to situational signals that are relevant for the team.

Transactive Memory Systems (TMS): A specific type of team cognition that emphasizes unshared expertise roles within a team. However, shared metaknowledge (knowing who knows what) is also necessary for effective TMS.

Chapter 11
Information Management in Fab Labs:
Avoiding Information and Communication Overload in Digital Manufacturing

Sérgio Maravilhas
UNIFACS Salvador University, Brazil

Joberto S. B. Martins
UNIFACS Salvador University, Brazil

ABSTRACT

Information is managed avoiding overload in Fab Labs, digital manufacturing environments. Collaborative spaces like Maker Spaces, Hacker Spaces, Tech Shops and Fab Labs are intended to stimulate innovation, through the exchange and sharing of information, knowledge, and experience among its members. They leverage innovation stimulating the creativity of its participants and enabling the creation of products and solutions based on personal projects, developed communally. With the motto "Learn, Make, Share," these spaces aim to empower its members for the realization of local and community-based sustainable solutions, using open source tools and equipment's, to allow every member the possibility of creating low cost products, with the ability to very quickly show the viability of these ideas through the acceptance by the community, that will make these solutions evolve collaboratively. It will be analyzed and described how Fab Labs manage their information to avoid information overload, maximizing the networking amongst its members.

DOI: 10.4018/978-1-5225-2061-0.ch011

INTRODUCTION

Information, along with natural and economic resources, proves to be an unprecedented social and strategic expedient (McGee & Prusak, 1995; Beuren, 1998).

Therefore, the importance of information for organizations is now universally accepted, being, if not the most important, at least one of the resources whose management influences the success of organizations (Ward & Griffiths, 1996).

Information management relates to the organizational ability to make the right information available for use in decision making (Davenport, 1997; Rascão, 2008), transforming the informational chaos into useful and practical knowledge application, leading to benefits for the organizations (Maravilhas, 2014b).

Maker Spaces, Hacker Spaces, Tech Shops and Fab Labs are collaborative spaces for stimulating innovation, through the exchange and sharing of information, knowledge, and experience among its members.

They leverage innovation through the use of technological resources available in the space, stimulating the creativity of its participants and enabling the development of products and solutions based on personal projects from ideation, or the construction supported on knowledge developed by other Makers, collaboratively, enhancing the final result (Gershenfeld, 2005, 2012).

With the motto[1] "Learn, Make, Share", these spaces aim to empower its members for the realization of sustainable solutions, local and community-based, using open source tools and equipment's whenever possible (open software, open hardware, open design, open learning), to allow all the possibility of creating low cost products, with the ability to very quickly show the viability of these ideas through the acceptance by the community, leveraging improvements that will make these solutions evolve collaboratively (Anderson, 2010, 2012).

In these collaborative spaces the participation of all community members is nurtured, promoting equality of race and gender, benefiting from cross-knowledge, shared by every culture and subculture, which will enrich the final result.

Teachers, researchers and students, young and more experienced, men and women of all races and religions, small business owners, inventors and entrepreneurs, members of the local community, all in a horizontal relationship, without titles or awards, just competence and mutual respect, working and learning from each other in a common space.

The purpose is to enhance the entry of women in technical fields and Engineering, but also to attract students and professionals of Arts and Humanities, Design and Architecture, allowing them to materialize their ideas based on available and affordable technology, supporting creative inventions and aesthetic processes that will enrich the research and development results (R&D) (Blikstein, 2014; Troxler, 2014).

It will be analyzed and described how Fab Labs, which are laboratories of digital fabrication, with broad educational, social and economic advantages, manage their information to avoid information and communication overload. A simple model will be suggested, to be used worldwide.

The methodology used for the successful development of the project consisted, to begin with, on bibliographic analysis from monographs, journal articles, websites, theses and reports, allowing understanding of the topic, its stakeholders and participating entities. Afterwards, an inquiry with 10 open questions was realized by e-mail to deepen the knowledge gathered in the previous instances.

The analysis of other existing Fab Labs makes possible to propose the introduction of best practices in the collaborative space, through benchmarking, avoiding mistakes and leaping steps for best performance.

BACKGROUND AND LITERATURE REVIEW

Like the inventors and entrepreneurs of the nineteenth and early twentieth century, who worked in their spare time in a shed, basement or, more recently, garage, creating prototypes of what later would become a successful product in a given market (Rifkin, 2011), Maker Spaces provide access to technologically advanced tools and machines, inserted in a network of participants, called Makers or Tinkerers, that can help answering questions and overcoming obstacles, faster than occurred with the lone inventor (Anderson, 2010, 2012).

A collaborative space for stimulating innovation is a place of learning through the exchange and sharing of knowledge and experience (Piscione, 2014) among its members, the Makers.

At the same time, allows to leverage innovation through the use of technological resources available in the space, stimulating the creativity of its participants and enabling the development of products and solutions based on personal projects from ideation, or the construction supported on knowledge developed by other users, together, collaboratively, enhancing the final result.

These spaces have several designations and typologies, like Makerspaces, Hackerspaces, Techshops and Fab Labs. In this project we focus in a model, widely tested and in use in several places of the world, the Fab Lab, or fabulous laboratory (Gershenfeld, 2005, 2012), which is a laboratory of digital fabrication, serving as a prototyping platform of physical objects (Eychenne & Neves, 2013), with broad educational (Mandavilli, 2006; Blikstein, 2014) social and economic advantages (Anderson, 2010, 2012; Troxler, 2014).

These Labs are used by everybody to enrich their projects, in a creative manner, inducing the creation of prototypes to leverage innovation, giving wings to their imagination and develop sustainable, social, local, economic innovative solutions to solve real problems.

Created in 2001 in the Massachussets Institute of Technology (MIT) Center for Bits and Atoms (CBA), directed by Neil Gershenfeld, linked to the famous MIT Media Lab, created by Nicholas Negroponte in 1985, the first Fab Lab was funded by the National Science Foundation (NSF) from the United States of America (USA), and begins based on the success of the course taught by Gershenfeld himself titled "How to Make (Almost) Anything" (Gershenfeld, 2012).

Eychenne and Neves mention that these Fab Labs are the "educational component of awareness to digital and personal fabrication, democratizing the conception of techniques and technologies and not just the consumption" (2013, p.10).

To quickly realize the viability of the solution, the machines and tools available in the space will allow developing a prototype that, if it's not feasible, will lead to the search for new solutions[2].

Fail early, fail cheap, fail always, continuing to learn and evolve so that entrepreneurship is encouraged and emulated by others[3].

Students are encouraged to be producers of knowledge and not mere passive recipients[4].

Fab Labs build bridges between the engineers and fabrication of high-tech products, and other actors usually more averse to technical and manual manufacturing.

The typology of academic Fab Lab, created in universities or research centers, aims to develop a culture of learning by doing, giving students, teachers, independent inventors and entrepreneurs the opportunity to learn by doing, creating a multidisciplinary space open to the outside to receive different insights and inputs[5].

In such cases, funding depends on the university or research center where they are installed, as well as the purchase of equipment and materials necessary for their operation, having its educational aspect assured by teachers and Postdoctoral Fellows (Eychenne & Neves, 2013, p.18) that support the management and maintenance of the space and its dynamics[6].

Working in a network, like the Internet supporting them, there are currently 678 Fab Labs worldwide[7], facilitating the sharing of information and knowledge, connecting people and organizations and, thus, enabling the collaborative innovation (Hatch, 2013; Troxler, 2014).

These spaces aim to develop access to knowledge of science and engineering, democratizing the practice of using the technic on the proposed projects (Blikstein, 2014), providing training courses to the community on the use of the equipment available in the space[8], allowing the use of machines to carry out participants own projects or to participate in collaborative projects of the Fab Lab network (Walter-Herrmann & Büching, (Eds.), 2014).

CONDITIONS TO START A FAB LAB

For the opening of such a space, the initial investment is around USD$100.000, according to the inventory required and proposed by the CBA, plus the monthly cost of salaries and maintenance of the machinery and location.

Usually, the university or research center provides the space and buys the machines, accessories and consumables, trains the responsible team and pays their salaries, and can provide scholars who collaborate in the organization of the space and scheduling times, while taking their projects and internships.

All Fab Labs must function according to the Fab Charter that sets the rules for the maintenance of the spaces, with its guidelines and policy[9].

On the website of Fab Foundation[10] instructions can be found of how a Fab Lab could be implemented in relation to its size, organization and necessary equipment.

Eychenne and Neves (2013, p.27), after visiting several spaces in different countries, found some common points, such as: an area between 100 and 250m[2]; at least one separate and closed room for the use of the large computer numeric control (CNC) milling machine; a large open central area with side stands containing on one side the less noisy machines and in the other the potentially dangerous machines or the ones who generate dust; computer equipment for work and conference or meeting tables; space for quick meals equipped with coffee machine and refrigerator; exhibition space for the completed projects and a place to store materials and tools.

Regarding the machinery and equipment to start the space, five CNC machines make up its base: a vinyl cutter, a laser cutter, a 3D printer, a precision milling machine, and a large format milling machine.

Being its concept based on the philosophies of open software and open hardware (Troxler, 2014), this reduces its cost, as there are several machines that can be built by themselves, allowing to replicate the equipment at a very low cost (Gershenfeld, 2005, 2012; Troxler, 2014).

The open software and other open source projects like Arduíno – a printed circuit having a microcontroller that allows you to control chips and sensors – also enable the realization of several low-cost projects (Walter-Herrmann & Büching (Eds.), 2014).

Fab Foundation[11] also lists the necessary staff for the proper functioning of the space, and the pattern is constituted of: a Director, a Fab Manager, a Guru and three Interns (Eychenne & Neves, 2013, p. 37).

KNOWLEDGE CREATION AND TRANSFER

Currently, innovative products are developed based on rapid prototyping in universities R&D departments and research institutes, and in some larger companies.

Only a small group of experts has the possibility of making prototypes in a short period of time and using simple means and resources (Anderson, 2010, 2012). In a Fab Lab this process is democratized and any new technologies are taught so that everyone can enjoy the space and equipment's.

My view is that people are creative animals and will figure out clever new ways to use tools that the inventor never imagined (Steve Jobs in Isaacson, 2011, p. 241).

In relation to its effectiveness, since 2001 at MIT and since 2005, when the first Fab Lab was created outside of MIT, the model has proved to be a facilitator for the creation of regional innovation, building bridges and relationships between experts in technology, design, education, small business owners and entrepreneurs, architects, artists, non-profit organizations, etc.

The idea of a Fab Lab rests on social interaction, in projects involving both academics and craftsmen, the handyman and garage skilled inventors, bringing to the manual and practical learning the ones that in recent years have distanced themselves from the technology and have chosen a more intellectual and less physical training, less hands-on.

The interaction between people with such diverse skills and features, along with the acquired training on the use of the available equipment's, will create a creative and stimulating environment thanks to the power of intellectual and cultural diversity[12].

As for the potential of transfer of the generated knowledge, the Fab Lab benefits from an extensive worldwide network which promotes the adoption of knowledge created in several laboratories spread across several continents, allowing to test the acceptance of a huge number of potential users and adapt, improve or complement the initial versions with the return, the feedback, obtained in this way.

Regarding the interdisciplinary collaboration, this is enhanced, as mentioned above, by the number of technical, academic and skillful handy men that will cross the space and contribute with tips, advices, warnings and suggestions.

Several areas of knowledge are present in these spaces, such as: electronics, mechanics, computer science, design, chemistry, administration, fine arts, and humanities.

This mix turns the space into a melting pot of cultures and sciences that will enable all to teach and to learn, enriching each of the worldviews involved and profiting all with the multiplicity of the knowledge obtained[13].

Several examples demonstrate the importance of these places for science and technology education, like learning concepts of Engineering and Mathematics (Blikstein, 2014), stimulating creativity and the development of inventions that allow to solve local problems of the communities where these Labs are located, promoting innovation and social economy, empowering people who are part of these networks allowing them an autonomy never imagined before (Mandavilli, 2006; Troxler, 2014).

Because all materials from the projects are made available to the entire network, the potential of dissemination of information allows building on prior knowledge, leveraging innovation and maximizing the previous research (Nonaka, & Takeushi, 1997). That way, the open innovation and the ascent innovation are privileged (Eychenne & Neves, 2013, pp. 45, 61), transforming the Do It Yourself (DIY) model in Do It With Others (DIWO), or Do It Together (DIT)[14], maximizing the educational and research function, with social and local impacts.

With a markedly educational and research side, interdisciplinary, multidisciplinary and intradisciplinary (Blikstein, 2014; Troxler, 2014), it will allow to develop innovative projects of high scientific quality and high social relevance, following the model "faster, higher, better, more precise", determined by the Fab Lab network. This will be achieved by following the criteria of effectiveness, transfer of knowledge potential, originality and interdisciplinary collaboration[15].

The advantage of being based on an international model that has been tested, offers a place with an innovative atmosphere that will make possible the exchange of knowledge based in fortuitous but fruitful encounters among its members[16], similar to what happens in the more innovative companies like Google, IDEO, Idealab, Pixar, Apple, among others (Dodgson & Gann, 2014; Isaacson, 2011, 2014; Kahney, 2009, 2013; Majaro, 1990).

A Fab Lab attracts more actors from companies than the university itself can do. With its innovative DIY concept, opens up innumerous possibilities for universities and ensures a productivity index that will be relevant to the increased volume of innovations in the state, and the consequent creation of wealth resulting from it[17].

Economic and Financial Return

The big challenge is to find industrial partners who want to use the space, financially maximizing the continued acquisition of materials and the maintenance of the equipment.

This solution allows a very quick and effective market research with the possibility of increasing the ultimate solution based on acceptance and criticism received.

Technology transfer between Fab Lab and industry can also be enhanced globally as a product developed in one Lab can solve a problem or need in another place in the world where the network is present.

It's important to remember that in a collaborative space with a conducive environment for innovation, the most important are not the machines and equipment, but people and their ideas (Dodgson & Gann, 2014), that should be encouraged and cherished for the production of new solutions that can be used to solve local community problems and empower its creator and the ones benefiting with the solution. Technology is only an enabler for this purpose.

If successful, the practices introduced can be replicated, creating a new model of innovation support, which will have a significant impact on the social and economic development of countries.

INFORMATION

A new vision must be considered in relation to information and the role it plays in the organization.

The efficient exploitation of information as an economic resource and one of the production sectors has become a factor of strategic, economic, social and political importance (Best, 1996b).

If, on the one hand, an organization cannot function without information, on the other it is important to know how to use this resource in order to improve its functioning.

Thus, the faster the identification of the relevant information to the organizations and the quicker the access to this information more easily their goals will be achieved.

Information is an intuitive, indefinable principle, such as energy, whose precise definition always seems to escape through the fingers like a shadow (Gleick, 2011; Jorge, 1995; Morin, 1996).

But, most important is that information plays a key role in business since this affects the competition at three levels:

1. Modifies the industrial structure and, therefore, changes the rules of the competition;
2. Creates competitive advantage for organizations offering new ways to overcome their rivals;
3. Create new business opportunities, most often from the organization's internal processes (Porter, 1985; Porter & Millar, 1985).

It is important to remember that the primary function of information is to try to eliminate uncertainty (Wilson, 1985, 2001), a problem that plagues any area of activity.

Organizations should follow some recommendations in order to successfully achieve their goals, such as:

1. Value information as a resource so or more important than any other that it needs to function (Maravilhas, 2013b);

2. Give the employees the relevant and necessary information to the excellent performance of their function minimizing, where possible, the overhead with unnecessary information (information overload);

3. Pay attention not only to the internal information generated within the organization, necessary to carry out the organizational tasks it undertakes, but also external information, from various points of interest to the sector in order to maintain their activity profitable.

Effective managers and decision-makers should not ask about the cost of obtaining the information needed. They should ask instead how much will be the loss if they don't have it (Maravilhas, 2013a).

Information Management

Information management is usually defined as a comprehensive organizational capacity to create, maintain, retrieve and make available the right information, at the right place, at the right time and in the hands of the right person, at the lowest cost, in the best support for its use in decision making (Choo, 2003; Davenport, 1997; Earl, 1998; Hinton, 2006; Maravilhas, 2013d).

Information management must be based on developing a strategy that involves the entire organization, taking into account mainly the users, information resources and appropriate technology available (Hinton, 2006; Wilson, 1985, p. 65).

It is also an economic coordination of the efficient and effective production, control, storage, retrieval and dissemination of information from internal and external sources, in order to improve the performance of a given organization (Best, 1996a; Beuren, 1998; Choo, 2003; Davenport, Marchand, & Dickson, 2004; Prusak & McGee, 1995).

The important role of information management and its integration into the organizational strategy must be emphasized, revealing itself as a key factor in creating added value for the company, as it helps to detect new opportunities and create competitive advantages and enables to defend them from the competitors (Maravilhas, 2013c; 2013d; 2015c).

Information management is an activity that aims to regulate the information, the information and communication technologies (ICT) and their respective users, through the application of management techniques to process and provide updated and relevant information, using electronic means or not, depending on the user's needs.

Information management is much more than the ability to obtain information from computer form (the computer will be just a tool here). Managing information means information processing so that, whoever needs it, can then get some help to achieve their goals (Maravilhas, 2013a; 2013c; 2013d).

Armed with relevant information, at the appropriate time, at the lowest possible cost, the organization will be better prepared to face the adversities and profit from the opportunities of its environment.

Information Overload

If information is not delivered with the right quality, proportion and measure it can originate "information overload", also called "infoxication", which occurs when excess of information suffocates businesses and causes employees to suffer mental anguish and physical illness, exacerbated nowadays by the huge amount of information from Web 2.0 and Social Media (Maravilhas, 2015b; 2016).

The effects of the information glut are procrastination and time wasting, leading to the delaying of important decisions, distraction from main job responsibilities, tension between colleagues and loss of job satisfaction. Information overload causes high levels of stress that can result in illness and the breakdown of individuals' personal relationships (Dearlove, 1998).

The amount of information available on the Internet is gigantic, so, professionals are constantly facing the problem of information overload. Information overload is a real phenomenon, increased by Social Media (Maravilhas, 2013b; 2015a).

Much time and effort is required for professionals to search for relevant information on the Internet and then analyze the information collected in the correct context.

Internet search engines have been useful in helping people search for information on the Internet. Nevertheless, the exponential growth of information sources on the Internet and the unregulated and dynamic nature of many Web sites are making it increasingly difficult to locate useful information using these search engines (Maravilhas, 2014c).

Due to the amount of information exchanged in these platforms, companies can look at Web 2.0 tools like Wikis, Blogs, Social Networking sites and so forth, to check for some pieces of information that come in first hand to these communication tools (Maravilhas, 2014a).

This leads to another problem that should be seriously considered, and with regard to the issue of excess of information, or information overload[18]. If, on the one hand, an organization cannot function without information, on the other it is important to know how to use this resource in order to improve its functioning. Since we live in an era of abundance of information, it is necessary to distinguish the useful, relevant and necessary information from the surplus. Thus, the faster the identification of the relevant information to the organization, and the faster the access to this information, more easily their goals will be achieved (Edmunds, & Morris, 2000).

Since people and organizations, similarly, have a peak in the information processing capacity, there is a saturation point from which an increase of the available information does not correspond to an increase in its use, but rather corresponds to its contraction (Wilson, 2001).

It is considered information overload, in personal terms, when someone has the perception (either the user or an observer) that the information associated with the tasks to perform in the workplace is in greater quantity than can be managed efficiently and effectively. Also involves the perception that this excess creates a degree of stress in the attempt to adapt to the strategies defined that proves itself ineffective (Dearlove, 1998).

Excess of information is considered, then, in organizational terms, when the situation in which the extent of perceived individual information is sufficiently dispersed in the organization, thus reducing the effectiveness of all operations management[19].

The impact of information overload causes bad time management, delaying decision-making, allowing distractions of the main tasks, causing stress and consequent lack of job satisfaction, reduced social activity, fatigue, and, in more severe cases, effective disease[20].

Although not a new or recent phenomenon, it tends to worsen with the advent of IT, Social Media and the Internet being a risk factor in terms of organizational control, and also the health of the employees[21].

All this is aggravated by multitasking, the attempt of performing several tasks with the quality that each one deserves, with the fake impression that technology will help us doing more in less time, when several research studies show that it's really the opposite[22]. Seems that we are doing more, but the time consumed in reworking what has been done without quality, and the personal losses it implies, suggest that we should do things differently[23].

We should use the information for our benefit, without incurring in the error described above of an eventual excess of irrelevant information that could interfere with our personal performance[24].

Information in Fab Labs

In Fab Labs the use of digital devices that can cause distractions are discouraged, because the bad use of electric equipment's and heavy machinery can cause harm if not properly used and maintained. Also, the price of the equipment's, raw materials, and the safety of the Lab users are always taken into consideration, making it not socially accepted that someone could be using sources of distraction while operating the digital machines. Everybody is well aware of the rules and regulations of the place because the Fab Charter is always visible in the entrance and in some other visible places. Everybody can use the smartphone or tablet to see instructions about the task been done or an educational video, but posting and checking Social Media sites while doing the job is not advisable. In the end, everyone can take photos and post in their Social Network sites, but when the equipment's and tools are off and saved in their proper places.

People learn by observing and imitating the accepted behaviors inside the Lab, and any wrong acting will be called to the attention as a warning and a form of learning the right way of behave to be accepted by the Lab community. Anyone inside the Lab will prevent a wrong or damaging behavior that could put everybody in danger. In case of insistence, in the wrong way of acting, the user will be invited to leave.

Fab Labs are now a world phenomenon. With 1077 existing Labs in the world, managing information and avoiding overload is not an easy task. Considering that almost all the projects are shared amongst all the Labs, so anyone can learn and improve on them, is a gigantic and epic endeavor.

It's not easy to manage all this information because not every member is aware of this sensitive situation. Every 'open day' anyone can use Fab Labs for free but in exchange, all the data and information from the project done must be shared with everyone through the network. This way, the free use of the resources encourages the sharing of details that can be used by other users, anywhere in the world, to learn or improve their own projects.

A massive amount of data is generated this way, and some people just don't know how to save it for further easy recovery and use.

The Fab Manager or the Fab Guru should train every user on the best ways to save their information, making it easily retrievable, so they can find it and other users too.

RESEARCH METHODOLOGY AND RESULTS

Researching for a second Postdoctoral, directed to the implementation of a Fab Lab in a private University in Brazil, the topic of managing information and minimizing information overload come about as very important to maximize creative results that could conduct to innovative outputs. This research is derived from that finding.

From the 678 Fab Labs in the world, operating at the time that the research was done, 68, about 10%, were chosen in a random, probabilistic, cluster sample, using a process that consisted in picking a number from one to ten (1 - 10) in a raffle (number 7 came out), and then from the list of all the Labs in alphabetical order, starting with number seven, and counting from seven to seven in the list until gather 68. Questionnaires by e-mail were sent to the addresses in the Labs web pages, whenever possible. In total, 62 e-mails were sent, because six (6) didn´t had an active web page or e-mail address. The distribution covered all the continents on the planet.

The rate of response was 35,4% of the sample, because 22 Labs answered our questionnaire.

The answers obtained were as follows:

- Two (2) from Spain;
- Three (3) from Brazil;
- Two (2) from China;
- One (1) from Italy;
- Five (5) from the United States of America (USA);
- Three (3) from France;
- Two (2) from The Netherlands;
- One (1) from South Africa
- One (1) from Portugal
- Two (2) from England.

The distribution resulted as follows:

- Eleven (11) from Europe;
- Five (5) from North America (NAm);
- Two (2) from Asia;
- Three (3) from South America (SAm);
- One (1) from Africa.

Figure 1. Number of answers per Fab Lab/Country
(Source: Author)

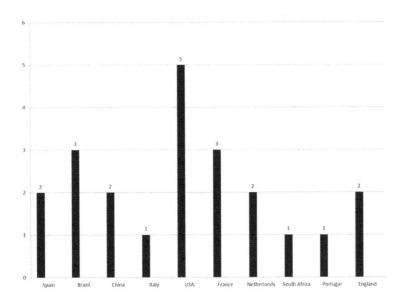

Figure 2. Number of answers per Region
(Source: Author)

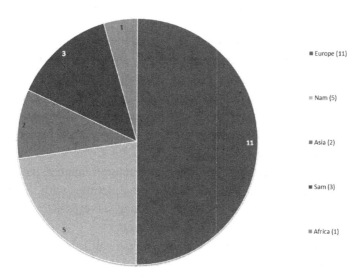

The e-mail consisted in 10 open questions, so it would be easy to answer and improve the rate of response. It was written in English for every e-mail address sent. The privacy of the respondents was guaranteed in the e-mail sent with the questions.

The answers were analyzed through content analysis, placing each one in an Excel sheet for easy comparison of the results.

From the answers received, there is a big concern about the subject of information overload, because almost all of them had already problems dealing with the amount of data and information generated in their Labs. Even the users – the Makers – sometimes complain that there is too much information to absorb. Not only they have to know how to operate all the machines safely, but they also have to register their project advances and search for other Makers projects, for inspiration. Not everybody is obliged to register their projects, just the Makers who use the Labs on open days without paying for the use of the equipment's.

Nevertheless, they don't seem to be very worried with that, focusing instead in the financial survival of the Lab, their first priority. Their biggest concern relates to the payment of the rent, the leasing of the equipment's, and raw materials to be processed in the Lab. Information overload is important but not so much as keeping the business running and paying the bills.

It's consensual that the Fab Manager should have that responsibility of managing the information to an optimal level, and that seems to be the real case in the USA, France and The Netherlands. In Spain it is the Fab Director that tries to keep information managed for easy use of other interested Makers, helping and directing everyone to save the projects the right way for easy retrieval, whenever needed. Asia, South America, and Africa don't seem to be as concerned about that subject as the other Labs do.

They all keep a computer (PC) for the registration and record of the projects, but the users, normally, try to avoid that responsibility and sometimes the Fab Manager must intervene so that mandatory task on open days is fulfilled. Operating in a network will have more value if everybody participates and contributes to augment the collective knowledge of the Labs. There are projects involving several different Labs and without the exchange of the details of the project it'll be very difficult to achieve a reasonable output.

Files are saved in the Lab PC but in an unstructured manner, usually in a File with the name of the author, or its nickname, or sometimes with the name of the project, that anyone can search and consult. A Cloud server is also available for the users of almost all the Labs to register their projects.

Almost all the Labs reported that other users check Files for inspiration, but usually just in the Files from their own Lab. Only in bigger projects, conducted by more experienced users, and involving several Labs, the Files from other Labs are retrieved for the purpose of getting insights for the new project at hand or for problem solving. In the South African Lab there is no habit of doing so, letting creativity flow only from the participants of the projects, without inspiration from their peers' previous projects.

Usually, users record their projects in their own language for easiness of the task (English, Dutch, Spanish, French, Afrikaans, Tsonga, Xhosa, Portuguese, Italian, and several Chinese dialects). This makes very difficult the retrieval of information, because the linguistic differences will make very hard to analyze and interpret the information gathered by other interested Makers from other countries. Photos, designs, videos, and schemes, will be very helpful and should be included.

All the Labs that answered had examples of Makers that had benefited from the information sharing in the Lab, but especially in oral form. The written documentation is not as valued as the oral transmission and the observation experience.

The privileged form of information and knowledge exchange goes to videoconference solutions available in all the Labs. Seems to be easier for Makers to watch and debate with their peers, than to read what has been done previously.

It is consensual that, if possible in financial terms, an information management specialist should help in organizing the information in each Lab to avoid overload and make the retrieval easy for the users. Although a lot of computer specialists frequent the Labs, their core business is not managing information. They are more concerned in developing new products or solutions, than in maintaining data and information in optimal levels avoiding information overload. Nevertheless, they all try to help with it.

Model for the Organization of Information, Minimizing Overload

The model for saving the information, allowing easy retrieval for everybody, everywhere, should be in a sequence as follows:

File "Country" > File "City" > File "Fab Lab Name" > File "Subject Area" > File "Name of the User" OR "Codename of the User" > File "Finished Projects" AND File "Projects in Progress" > File "Project Name" > Text File "Description of the Project and Results" containing an English Abstract AND Photo Files AND CAD Files (if needed). Other relevant Files, when complimentary, should be included for illustration, like diagrams, schemes, drawings, videos, instructions, etc.

All this information should be in English for the use of other Makers in other countries or, at least, have an English Abstract for international user's aid. The Abstract can be done with the Fab Director or Fab Guru help, or using a web translator. A Lab colleague can help performing this task.

Figure 3. Simplified Model for information management for the Makers in Fab Labs. Repeat the same process in each of the Labs/Country
(Source: Author)

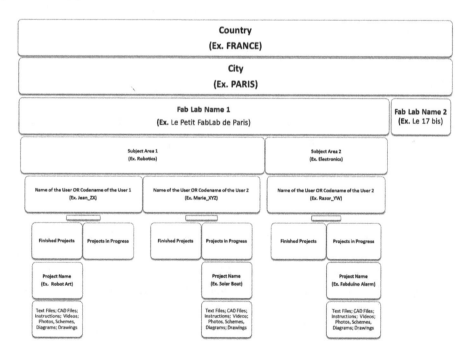

This information can be made available in a Cloud Server maintained by the Fab Foundation, allowing the access to everyone involved to improve results and knowledge sharing.

Extensible Markup Language (XML) and databases can be used to assist in the information visualization and finding from all the Labs, along with other technology solutions that allow to search by keyword, subject, title, name or codename of the Makers, subject area, country, city, etc., mixing them all to filter the results. That way, the information retrieval will be easier and the overload kept to a minimum.

FURTHER RESEARCH DIRECTIONS

Further research should be performed to analyze other information solutions in place in other Fab Labs around the world, covering a biggest number of Labs, in order to adopt those best practices in all the Labs to improve their management and sustainability.

Also, if the Model suggested here is to be adopted, measures should be done to verify the benefits of it for the users. If it's beneficial for the search and retrieval of useful information and allows the Makers to find solutions to solve their problems and give them insights for new projects, then it should be suggested to all the Labs as a way of reducing the overload of information, until a better solution is implemented. All the help is welcome and the network can think of it collaboratively to find new ways to support their work.

CONCLUSION

The Fab Lab aims to develop a culture of learning by doing, giving students, teachers, independent inventors and entrepreneurs the opportunity to learn by doing it themselves (DIY), and learn together (DIWO or DIT) with other Makers from their Lab or another from the network, creating a multidisciplinary space, open to the outside, to receive different insights and inputs (Gershenfeld, 2005, 2012).

Avoiding information overload is an individual responsibility. Everybody should be responsible to avoid information overload for him and others. If properly managed, information is a helpful resource that can support faster decision making and the creative process of individuals (Maravilhas, 2014a). If overload occurs, everybody will have a prejudice, losing momentum for the entire Lab and not only the irresponsible user.

Information from projects, collective and individual, and from the courses to learn how to operate all the machines and equipment's in the Lab, together with rules and regulations about the use of the space, can be a daunting task.

To avoid all these problems, Fab Labs manage the information to improve their performance while avoiding that its users get paralyzed with excess of information, being it in terms of rules and regulations, being it in terms of the use of the information generated internally or gathered externally.

All this internal and external influxes of information needs to be managed, to avoid a surplus of information that can have the opposite result (Wilson, 2001).

Information management is usually defined as a comprehensive organizational capacity to create, maintain, retrieve and make available the right information, at the right place, at the right time and in the hands of the right person, at the lowest cost, in the best support for its use in decision making (Maravilhas, 2013c; 2013d).

Information management must be based on developing a strategy that involves the entire organization (Maravilhas, 2015b), taking into account mainly the users, information resources and appropriate technology available (Wilson, 2002).

It is also an economic coordination of the efficient and effective production, control, storage, retrieval and dissemination of information from internal and external sources, in order to improve the performance of a given organization (Petit, 2001).

Information management is an activity that aims to regulate the information, the information and communication technologies (ICT) and their respective users, through the application of management techniques to process and provide updated and relevant information, using electronic means or not, depending on the user's needs.

The role of the information management professional should be to focus on optimization, as well as in service personalization (Maravilhas, 2013d).

Technology should be used to assist the Makers in finding the needed resources, without overwhelming them with unnecessary data and information.

Although, without a general strategy implemented in all Labs, small steps adequate to the Labs public and technology competence are being taken, being a starting point for a future best practice to be implemented in all the Fab Lab network.

REFERENCES

Anderson, C. (2010). In the Next Industrial Revolution, Atoms are the New Bits. *Wired Magazine, 1*(25).

Anderson, C. (2012). *Makers: The New Industrial Revolution* (1st ed.). New York: Crown Business.

Best, D. (1996a). Business process and information management. In Best (Ed.), The fourth resource: Information and its management. Hampshire, UK: Aslib/Gower.

Best, D. (1996b). *The fourth resource: Information and its management.* Hampshire, UK: Aslib/Gower.

Beuren, I. (1998). *Gerenciamento da informação: um recurso estratégico no processo de gestão empresarial.* São Paulo: Atlas.

Blikstein, P. (2014). Digital Fabrication and 'Making' in Education: The Democratization of Invention. In J. Walter-Herrmann & C. Büching (Eds.), *FabLabs: Of Machines, Makers and Inventors.* Bielefeld: Transcript-Verlag.

Choo, C. (2003). *Gestão de informação para a organização inteligente: A arte de explorar o meio ambiente.* Lisboa: Editorial Caminho.

Davenport, T. (1997). *Information ecology: Mastering the information and knowledge environment.* New York: Oxford University Press.

Davenport, T., Marchand, D., & Dickson, T. (2004). *Dominando a gestão da informação.* Porto Alegre: Bookmann.

Dearlove, D. (1998). *Key management decisions: Tools and techniques of the executive decision-maker* (1st ed.). Wiltshire: Financial Times/Pitman.

Dodgson, M., & Gann, D. (2014). *Inovação* (1st ed.). Porto Alegre: L&PM Pocket Encyclopaedia.

Earl, M. (1998). *Information management: The organizational dimension.* New York: Oxford University Press.

Edmunds, A., & Morris, A. (2000). The problem of information overload in business organizations: A review of the literature. *International Journal of Information Management, 20*(1), 17–28. doi:10.1016/S0268-4012(99)00051-1

Eychenne, F., & Neves, H. (2013). *Fab Lab: A Vanguarda da Nova Revolução Industrial.* Associação Fab Lab Brasil.

Gershenfeld, N. (2005). *Fab: The Coming Revolution on Your Desktop: from Personal Computers to Personal Fabrication.* New York: Basic Books.

Gershenfeld, N. (2012). How to Make Almost Anything: The Digital Fabrication Revolution. *Foreign Affairs, 91*(6).

Gleick, J. (2011). The information: A history, a theory, a flood (1st ed.). St. Ives: 4th Estate.

Hatch, M. (2013). *The Maker Movement Manifesto: Rules for Innovation in the New World of Crafters, Hackers, and Tinkerers* (1st ed.). McGraw-Hill Education.

Hinton, M. (2006). *Introducing information management: The business approach* (1st ed.). Burlington: Elsevier Butterworth-Heinemann.

Isaacson, W. (2011). *Steve Jobs* (1st ed.). New York: Simon & Schuster.

Isaacson, W. (2014). Os Inovadores: Uma biografia da revolução digital (1st ed.). S. Paulo: Companhia das Letras.

Jorge, M. (1995). *Biologia, informação e conhecimento*. Lisboa: F. C. Gulbenkian.

Kahney, L. (2009). *A cabeça de Steve Jobs* (2nd ed.). Rio de Janeiro: Agir.

Kahney, L. (2013). Jony Ive: O gênio por trás dos grandes produtos da Apple (1st ed.). S. Paulo: Portfolio-Penguin.

Majaro, S. (1990). *Criatividade: Um passo para o sucesso*. Lisboa: Europa-América.

Mandavilli, A. (2006). Make Anything, Anywhere. *Nature, 442*(8). PMID:16929273

Maravilhas, S. (2013a). A web 2.0 como ferramenta de análise de tendências e monitorização do ambiente externo e sua relação com a cultura de convergência dos media. *Perspectivas em Ciência da Informação, 18*(1), 126–137. doi:10.1590/S1413-99362013000100009

Maravilhas, S. (2013b). Social media tools for quality business information. In Information quality and governance for business intelligence. Hershey, PA: IGI Global.

Maravilhas, S. (2013c). A gestão da informação na análise de Foucault sobre as relações poder-saber. *Biblios – Revista de Bibliotecología y Ciencias de la Información, 51,* 70-77.

Maravilhas, S. (2013d). A importância dos profissionais da gestão da informação para as organizações. *Biblios – Revista de Bibliotecología y Ciencias de la Información, 51,* 91-98.

Maravilhas, S. (2014a). Competitive Intelligence from Social Media, Web 2.0, and the Internet. In Khosrow-Pour (Ed.). Encyclopedia of Information Science and Technology (3rd ed.). Hershey, PA: IGI Global.

Maravilhas, S. (2014b). Information Quality and Value. In Khosrow-Pour (Ed.), Encyclopedia of Information Science and Technology (3rd ed.). Hershey, PA: IGI Global.

Maravilhas, S. (2014c). Challenges for Education in the Information Society. In Khosrow-Pour (Ed.), Encyclopedia of Information Science and Technology (3rd ed.). Hershey, PA: IGI Global.

Maravilhas, S. (2015a). Social Media Tools for Quality Business Information. In *Social Media and Networking: Concepts, Methodologies, Tools, and Applications* (Vol. 2, pp. 636–662). Hershey, PA: IGI Global.

Maravilhas, S. (2015b). Managing an information strategy project: The case of a real estate broker organization. In *Handbook of Research on Effective Project Management through the Integration of Knowledge and Innovation* (pp. 19–43). Hershey, PA: IGI Global. doi:10.4018/978-1-4666-7536-0.ch002

Maravilhas, S. (2015c). Vantagens Competitivas da Informação de Patentes. In Estratégias Defensivas: Assegurando Vantagens Competitivas já Conquistadas. Rio de Janeiro: NovaTerra.

Maravilhas, S. (2016). Social Media Intelligence for Business. *International Journal of Organizational and Collective Intelligence*, 6(4), 100–125. doi:10.4018/IJOCI.2016100102

McGee, J., & Prusak, L. (1995). *Gerenciamento estratégico da informação: Aumente a competitividade e a eficiência de sua empresa utilizando a informação como uma ferramenta estratégica*. Rio de Janeiro: Campus.

Nonaka, I., & Takeushi, H. (1997). *Criação de Conhecimento na Empresa: Como as Empresas Japonesas geram a dinâmica da Inovação*. Rio de Janeiro: Campus.

Petit, P. (2001). *Economics and information*. Dordrecht: Kluwer. doi:10.1007/978-1-4757-3367-9

Piscione, D. (2014). Os Segredos do Vale do Silício: O que Você Pode Aprender com a Capital Mundial da Inovação (1ª ed.). São Paulo: HSM.

Porter, M. (1985). *Competitive advantage: creating and sustaining superior performance*. New York: Free Press.

Porter, M., & Millar, V. (1985, July-August). How information gives you competitive advantage. *Harvard Business Review*, 75–98.

Rascão, J. (2008). *Novos desafios da gestão da informação* (1st ed.). Lisboa: Sílabo.

Rifkin, J. (2011). *The Third Industrial Revolution: How Lateral Power is Transforming Energy, the Economy, and the World*. New York: Palgrave Macmillan.

Troxler, P. (2014). Making the 3rd Industrial Revolution: The Struggle for Polycentric Structures and a New Peer-Production Commons in the Fab Lab Community. In J. Walter-Herrmann & C. Büching (Eds.), *FabLabs: Of Machines, Makers and Inventors*. Bielefeld: Transcript-Verlag.

Walter-Herrmann, J., & Büching, C. (Eds.). (2014). *FabLab: Of Machines, Makers, and Inventors*. Bielefeld: Transcript-Verlag.

Ward, J., & Griffiths, P. (1996). *Strategic planning for information systems* (2nd ed.). Wiley.

Wilson, D. (2002). *Managing information: IT for business processes* (3rd ed.). Woburn: Butterworth-Heinemann.

Wilson, T. (1985). Information management. *The Electronic Library*, *3*(1), 62–66. doi:10.1108/eb044644 PMID:2498741

Wilson, T. (2001). *Information overload: Myth, reality and implications for health care*. International Symposium on Health Information Management Research, Halkidiki, Greece.

ADDITIONAL READING

Cleveland, H. (1983). A informação como um recurso. Diálogo. Rio de Janeiro, 16, 7-11.

Davenport, T. (2007). *Profissão: Trabalhador do conhecimento: Como ser mais produtivo e eficaz no desempenho das suas funções*. Amadora: Exame.

Davenport, T. (s/dat.). *Information management: A broader approach*. http://www.unisys.com/execmag/1997-09/journal/conversation.htm

Davenport, T., & Prusak, L. (1998). *Working knowledge: How organizations manage what they know*. Boston: Harvard Business School Press.

Davenport, T., Prusak, L., & Wilson, J. (2003). *What's the big idea: Creating and capitalizing on the best management thinking. Boston: Harvard Business School Instituto de Altos Estudos Militares. (2000). A gestão da informação e a tomada de decisão*. Sintra: Atena.

Hampton, D. (1992). *Administração contemporânea* (3rd ed.). São Paulo: Makron Books.

Introna, L. (1997). Management, information and power (1ª ed.). London: MacMillan.

Jamil, G., Maravilhas, S., Malheiro, A., & Ribeiro, F. (Eds.). (2015). *Handbook of Research on Effective Project Management through the Integration of Knowledge and Innovation*. Hershey: IGI Global. doi:10.4018/978-1-4666-7536-0

Johannessen, J., & Olaisen, J. (1993). The information intensive organization. In J. Olaisen (Ed.), *Information management: A Scandinavian approach*. Oslo: Scandinavian University Press.

Penzias, A. (1989). *Ideas and information: Managing in a high-tech world*. New York: W. W. Norton.

Penzias, A. (1995). *Harmony: Business, technology & life after paperwork*. Harper Collins.

Rascão, J. (2012). *Novas realidades na gestão e na gestão da informação* (1st ed.). Lisboa: Sílabo.

Ward, J., & Peppard, J. (2002). *Strategic planning for information systems* (3rd ed.). Chichester: Wiley.

Webster, F. (2000). *Theories of the information society*. Cornwall: Routledge.

KEY TERMS AND DEFINITIONS

Fab Lab: A laboratory of digital fabrication, serving as a prototyping platform of physical objects, with broad educational, social and economic advantages. These spaces aim to empower its members for the realization of sustainable solutions, using open source tools and equipment's, to allow all the possibility of creating low cost products which meet the need for one, one hundred, or a thousand people.

Innovation: The application of new knowledge, resulting in new products, processes or services or significant improvements in some of its attributes. A new solution brought to the market to solve a problem in a new or better way than the existent solutions.

Invention: The creation or discovery of a new idea, including the concept, design, model creation or improvement of a particular piece, product or system. Even though an invention may allow a patent application, in most cases it will not give rise to an innovation.

Information: A set of data arranged in a certain order and form, useful to people to whom it is addressed. Reduces uncertainty and supports decision-making. Information is considered to support human knowledge and communication in the technical, economic and social domains. Results from the structuring of data in a given context and particular purpose.

Information Management: Usually defined as a comprehensive organizational capacity to create, maintain, retrieve and make available the right information, at the right place, at the right time and in the hands of the right person, at the lowest cost, in the best support for its use in decision making.

Information Overload: Also called "infoxication", occurs when excess of information suffocates organizations and causes employees to suffer mental anguish and physical illness, exacerbated nowadays by the huge amount of information from Social Media. The effects of this information glut are procrastination and time wasting, leading to the delaying of important decisions, distraction from main job responsibilities, tension between colleagues and loss of job satisfaction. It causes high levels of stress that can result in illness and the breakdown of individuals' personal relationships.

Knowledge: Is a fluid composed of experiences, values, context information and apprehension about their own field of action that provides a cognitive apparatus for evaluating and incorporating new experiences and information.

ENDNOTES

[1]   http://www.forbes.com/2008/08/13/diy-innovation-gershenfeld-tech-egang08-cx_ag_0813gershenfeld.html

[2]   http://www.makerinnovation.cc ; http://wefab.cc/

[3]   http://www.instructables.com/id/FabYearBook-2010/

[4]   http://studentasproducer.lincoln.ac.uk/

[5]   http://fab.cba.mit.edu/about/faq/

[6]   http://www.fabfoundation.org

[7]   http://www.fabfoundation.org/fab-labs/ ; https://www.fablabs.io/labs

[8]   http://makercity.wpengine.com/docs/makercity-preview-chapter.pdf

[9]   http://fab.cba.mit.edu/about/charter/

[10] http://www.fabfoundation.org/fab-labs/setting-up-a-fab-lab/ideal-lab-layout/

[11] http://www.fabfoundation.org

[12] http://www.thefreelibrary.com/Fabricating+dreams+in+3D%3A+FabLab+Luzern.-a0336489127

[13] http://www.instructables.com/id/FabYearBook-2010/

[14] http://makercity.wpengine.com/docs/makercity-preview-chapter.pdf , p. 6

[15] http://fablab-luzern.ch/

[16] http://www.thefreelibrary.com/Fabricating+dreams+in+3D%3A+FabLab+Luzern.-a0336489127

[17] http://www.instructables.com/id/FabYearBook-2010/

[18] https://hbr.org/2009/09/how-much-is-information-overlo

19 https://hbr.org/2010/05/on-managing-information-overlo

20 https://hbr.org/2009/12/why-we-dont-care-about-informa

21 https://hbr.org/2009/09/death-by-information-overload

22 http://www.inc.com/jessica-stillman/multitasking-is-making-you-stupid.html

23 https://hbr.org/2010/05/how-and-why-to-stop-multitaski.html

24 https://hbr.org/2015/07/just-hearing-your-phone-buzz-hurts-your-productivity

Chapter 12

Information Overload in Augmented Reality:
The Outdoor Sports Environments

Rui Miguel Pascoal
Lusófona University, Portugal

Sérgio Luís Guerreiro
Lusófona University, Portugal

ABSTRACT

This chapter explores the benefits and challenges of using augmented reality (AR) technology in outdoor sports environments. Questions emerge about the presentation of information more appropriate to give a user without being excessive. The aim is to assess the problems related with information overload before implementing an AR system to be used in outdoors environments. Solutions are listed to manage and interact, the best way, with the information on the mobile device of AR, and achieve social acceptance. The Solutions and Recommendations answer through an empirical research about what data are more appropriate without information overload for outdoor sports. Finally, to better understand, an AR Mockup example frame AR components of information and possible features, which represent the ideal display for sportsman, without information and communication overload.

INTRODUCTION

This chapter presents the implications of using the augmented reality (AR) and identifies the benefits of this new media technology when applied to the sports outdoor environments. AR is receiving increased interest from industry, *e.g.*, the

DOI: 10.4018/978-1-5225-2061-0.ch012

new Samsung Galaxy 7, which offers the ability to use new AR applications for a richer end-user experience. However, the use of AR generates too much data, usually named as big data problem, which must be computed before presenting contextualized information to an outdoor sports end-user. If too much contextualized information is given, then, AR applications will lose its purpose. For instance, which practical value can be extracted from an advanced interface (Craig, 2013). Furthermore, issues arise about the presentation of information, and what are the most appropriate to give an user without being excessive? In addition, this paper presents an evaluation of the AR technology benefits, grounded in the following research question: *the dangers of information overload, and that should be considered before implementing a system specifically to use in outdoors* (Azuma, 1999; You, Neumann, & Azuma, 1999; Azuma el al., 2001). This research question is considered essential for sports and competition technology.

The AR mobile applications in mountain biking and trekking, or other outdoor sports such as athletics and tourism are very recent and didn't evolved very significantly yet, *e.g.*, to inform end-users about their health condition, weather state, geolocation, path distances and time measures, events and wise advices personalized. They can also need communicate and take a picture or film.

AR is technology, but *should not be categorized as mere technology*. Instead, AR is an *advanced computer interface* (Craig, 2013) being developed more than forty years ago. Still, has not been implemented in a significant way in society and is increasingly closer to its overall improvement, *e.g.*, there is a *strong requirement to be adopted to people, being required usability of technology* (Sawyer, Finomore, Calvo, & Hancock, 2014; Chi, Kang, & Wang, 2013), in various areas of society. Therefore, to be socially acceptable, it is essential to balance the amount of information without neglecting the quality that is displayed to an AR user.

Specifically, AR is an user interface to interact with the information displayed and perform tasks more intuitively and efficiently. It increases the user's perception about the real world by adding virtual information to it. The AR images are generated by devices and can be designed in transparent glasses, most suitable in the case of outdoor sports or using a monitor, in the indoor case. AR is a specific example of what Fred Brooks[1] calls *"Amplification Intelligence" (AI): use the computer as a tool to perform human tasks in an easier way.* Or like Alan D. Craig has defined on his book, *augmented reality is a medium in which digital information is overlaid on the physical world that is in both spatial and temporal registration with the physical world and that is interactive in real time* (Craig, 2013).

Thus, AR can be defined as a combination of a real environment with the virtual environment, creating a mixed reality. According to Paul Milgram[2]*augmented*

Figure 1. Continuum Reality-Virtuality
Adapted from the Milgram's Reality-Virtuality continuum. Visual Taxonomy of Mixed Reality (Milgram, Takemura, Utsumi, & Kishino, 1995).

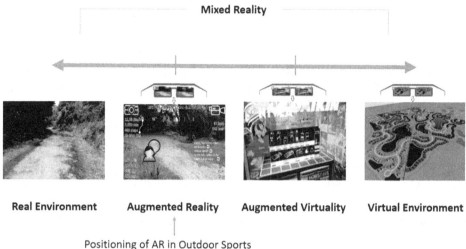

reality is a subclass of a larger class of technologies, the "Mixed Reality" (MR), a continuum between the real and virtual environments, cf. Figure 1.

This is a *dimensional taxonomy framework*, in other words a taxonomy for classifying different types of environments within the mixed reality between the real and the virtual. AR is the second category, just after the real-world environment. This taxonomy was proposed in 1995 by Paul Milgram, or *the mixture of real and virtual worlds* (Milgram, Takemura, Utsumi, & Kishino, 1995).

This continuum reality-virtuality was not defined until 1994 by Paul Milgram and Fumio Kishino[3] as a continuum that extends from the real environment to the virtual environment (Furht, 2011). Since the AR systems can be divided into five categories:

1. Indoor fixed system
2. Outdoor fixed system
3. Indoor system
4. Outdoor mobile system
5. Indoor and outdoor mobile system

Therefore, in this chapter, under the outdoor sports focus is only in the fourth category, in outdoor mobile systems.

Key Concepts and Limitations

By analyzing the various systems of AR developed in recent years, anyone can identify that the software and hardware architecture adopted between them differs widely. Since the medicine, sports, games, science, engineering, design, leisure and so on.

Therefore, advances in mobile AR technology were essential because although the concept dates to the 1960s, Ronald T. Azuma[4] explained that *not made a search field until the 1990s* initially was used for a wide range of applications, from flight training simulators and military training, even for science fiction films. However, *the most recent application was Google Glass* (Ross & Harrison, 2016). Although the first version of the equipment has been withdrawn from the market, *this innovation has been described as one of the most interesting developments in "wearable" technology or truly mobile in the last four years*. What helped were the advances in mobile computing systems, especially *the inclusion of cameras in mobile phones, which did accelerate the development of innovative applications of AR* (Ross & Harrison, 2016). That's why this chapter is limited to the outdoor sports of mountain biking and trekking. It's circumscribed the use of AR in mobile devices, whose output is only in transparent glasses, and the calculation and storage of information data, is done by mobile device sensors. Here a Big Data Server could be used to bring significant benefits, and in the case of AR outdoor sports environments, will return intelligent information, also understood as added value, to complement the communication of intelligent data. As such, the data source and data aggregator of AR glasses can be a Server, installed remotely, but in such a way that operating the mobile AR equipment does not require constant communication with the server, to prevent the overload and dependence of communication between the server and the equipment.

Finally, the mission is to contribute to the implementation of a mobile AR system, which has the aim of being used outside, overcoming the constraints and limitations of current mobile AR applications. Moreover, requirements faced by the application developers were identified, *e.g.*, to overcome the technological and environmental limitations, because they are clearly interrelated. In addition, to the human limitations in understanding due to information overload, restrictions also often relate to the limited capabilities of mobile devices, and the fact that *AR equipment should be usable in a wide range of environmental conditions* (You & Azuma, 1999).

QUESTIONS AND METHODOLOGY

The specific questions in the context of AR information overload in outdoor sports environments, including mountain biking and trekking are:

1. Is the user's attention dispersed, by information overload in mobile AR glasses and may cause accidents, *e.g.*, riding a bike? The answer is necessary to explain that, although there are risks, *i.e.*, loss of concentration. However, there are many advantages to using an AR system. The process for finding this response may be to investigate the results of tests performed, *e.g.*, with the Google Glass and with an AR prototype for interactive end-user testing.

2. What is the most appropriate data, to be shown and how to present in output, an outdoor sportsman, particularly for biking and trekking? To answer this, it's crucial to know what a sportsman practicing mountain biking and trekking, needs, *e.g.*, if he's in a group, or if he's competing with other athletes, if he is alone and lost on the ground, or if he has a high heart rate.

3. How to ensure social acceptance of an AR application to be used in outdoors? The answer is related to knowing what happened, *e.g.*, regarding the social rejection of Google Glass, and find an optimal solution. To solve this issue, we'll also need to look at the end-users' reactions when exposed to different kinds of information.

4. What are the alternatives for AR equipment regarding outdoor mobile communication when there is no internet access, to minimize the need to being dependent on that? It's mandatory to answer this question, because outdoor communications may not exit, or if communications are overloaded and the internet connection is too slow, then, it is essential to have alternatives in order to provide information to an user in outdoor environments.

In this context, the virtual AR elements are almost non-existents, except for representative icons, it'll be proved that they aren't appropriate to display to an user for outdoor sports, to avoid information overload and increased physical hazards inherent to these types of sports.

STUDY SCOPE

Gartner predicts that, *after a long period of technological development and refinement, the implementation of AR applications for the general public are achieving its peak.* And in the year 2016, AR solutions, are poised for rapid growth, empowered by the Internet of Things (IoT), digital business, and next-generation smartphones [Market Guide for Augmented Reality for 2016 (gartner.com)].

In Solutions and Recommendations, it's initially shown an empirical research with a quantitative and qualitative approach. The authors observed during interaction tests with twelve real end-users that had some difficulties to execute solicited tasks. Finally, an abstraction through a frame mockup is displayed, used to represent and exemplify the ideal information layout for the user to *support communication with mobile augmented reality system* (Furht, 2011). This information which can be communicated to the user, is the climate data, the health condition, location and time, paths measurement, recording, telecommunications, events and intelligent data cleverly suggested, *e.g.*, the mobile use of AR in outdoor sports mountain bike and trekking, which serves to inform the athlete of temperature, atmospheric pressure, altitude, and relative humidity; heart rate and caloric expenditure; GPS, compass and chronometer; speed rate and count steps, initial and final position; photos and video; telephone communication, radio communication, sms or mms messages and social networks; current event, future events, news, landmarks, support places and vital advices; has the potential to have an intelligent agent that informs and guides users.

The component that enriches could be the information about events and intelligent data, like current and future events, news, landmarks, supported places, and vital advices, that are nearby according to the preferences of each user. Based on vital advices are included measuring the heart rate, and caloric expenditure. But the display of information should always be balanced. One way, of reduce some complexity, is to present the information in the hearing form, rather than in writing form, for which can overload the user with too much information in glasses' display. Because, AR can be applied in every sense, not only visually. The researchers focused on mixing images and graphics real and virtual. However, *AR can be extended to include sound. Users can use headsets equipped with microphones* (Azuma, 1997).

This AR system outdoors can also perform tasks to *display the traffic areas, or tracks and milestones directly on your point of view of the surrounding area without a high cognitive load*. Example, Ronald Azuma said *soldiers could even see the enemy sites and dangerous areas such as minefields that could not be easily noticeable to the naked eye* (Azuma, 1999), or places where friends, or in this case, the companions of the biking or trekking group. Thus, this AR system for outdoor is also useful for groups of users working or entertains together.

The Information and Communication Overload of AR

To build a mobile AR system to be used in outdoor sports is needed to understand and identify what are the causes of information and communication overload of this AR technology today. Should be identified hazards, and thus, know what are the solutions, to adapt information for present context, with the intent has not be ambiguity or information overload. Are assessed the *dangers of information overload and should be considered before implementing a system specifically for use outdoors*, because they are essential for the technology to be used for sport or competition (Bawden & Robinson, 2009; Azuma, Hoff, Neely, & Sarfaty, 1999).

People are increasingly interested in outdoor sports, especially trekking and mountain biking, for a variety of reasons, *e.g.*, to improve health and combat sedentary lifestyle, to go out with friends, reduce weight, or just to "catch some air", and in this context should be used the new information and communication technologies in a wise and balanced way, but have to be sensible because there are social and political dimensions to assess when they arrive new technologies such as AR, and *are intended to be put in the hands of real users* (Azuma, 1997).

Some *examples of information and communication overloaded* (Bawden & Robinson, 2009) and that can be created with AR technology, are *"Information anxiety"*, a term coined by Saul Wurman[5], is usually taken to be *a condition of stress caused by the inability to access, understand, or make use of, necessary information. The cause of this may be either information overload or insufficient information; it may equally be due to poorly organized or presented information, or a variety of other causes, including a lack of understanding of the information environment in which one is working. The rather similar condition of library anxiety was recognized and named as far back as 1986, and has been analyzed further since. This is a type of anxiety which leads to a sense of powerlessness when beginning an information search in a library, and in feelings of being lost, unable to find one's way around, and afraid to approach the library staff* (Bawden & Robinson, 2009). According to statistics of the Journal of Information Science of 2008, it would take over 200.000 years to 'read all the Internet', allowing 30 minutes per document, and more information has been created in the past 30 years than in the previous 5.000 years. Increasing diversity of information can also lead to overload, partly by a consequent increase in the volume of information on a given topic, which may come from varying perspectives, but also because of an intellectual difficulty in fitting it within a cognitive framework, appropriate for use and for users. *Diversity may occur both in the nature of the information itself, and in the format in which it appears, with a typical business user having to deal with paper, e-mail, voicemail, traditional websites, and so on* (Bawden & Robinson, 2009). It's crucial for an AR application, organized display, simplified and direct information, especially for competition sports and outdoor environments. Even in a simple walk of relaxation, with an AR system outdoors, an user wants to relax, and has no logic if overload him with too much information, which causes rejection and discourage using of AR in outdoor sports.

Can be seen the height of information overload at *"Keiichi Matsuda's film, augmented (hyper) Reality: Domestic Robocop"*, *offers a glimpse of an alternate universe, with augmented reality cranked up to the next level.* Matsuda studied at London's Bartlett School of Architecture, where students have used animation and motion graphics to investigate new architectural possibilities.

Figure 2. Augmented (hyper) Reality - Domestic Robocop
Source: Keiichi Matsuda

"The latter half of the 20th century saw the built environment merged with media space, and architecture taking on new roles related to branding, image and consumerism", wrote Matsuda on his Vimeo page. AR may re-contextualize the functions of consumerism and architecture, and change in the way in which operate within it. A film produced for final year masters in architecture, part of a larger project about the social and architectural consequences of new media and AR. Keiichi has also commented on some of the issues he was attempting address: media intrusion, tech-dependence, and so on. "It is", he wrote, "like most sci-fi, a critique of the present rather than the future".

Another example, are psychological studies show that due to short-term memory limits, humans have a very limited capacity for processing information. This is estimated to be "the magical number seven, plus or minus two concepts" simultaneously (Miller, 1956). If the amount of information received exceeds these limits, followed by an information overload and understanding by the user degrades quickly.

A series of experiments using a range of different experimental stimuli - tones, flavors, colors, points, numbers and words, a striking resemblance of "channel capacity of the human" in all these experiments was observed, with an average of 6.5 concepts, and a standard deviation, including 4 to 10 concepts. This has been described as the "inelastic limit of human capacity" or "cognitive ability", and is one of the most enduring laws of human cognition. The main mechanism used by the human mind to handle large amounts of information is to organize it into "chunks" of manageable size (Miller, 1956). The ability to develop recursively chunks saturated information is key to the ability of people to deal with the complexity every day.

Ann M. Barry[6] in his famous book *"Visual Intelligence"* said that

even when we watch television, we do not understand about 30 percent of what we are shown. Our emotional state, the mentality at the time, and previous experiences, all seem to conspire against the vision of things and how they really are.

The movement is essential for vision because our eyes function is to observe and record changes. *Without motion, the eyes just not anything they recorded* (Barry, 1997).

Generally, is considered the activity of memory has a limited capacity. The oldest quantifications capacity limit associated with short-term memory was the "magical number seven" introduced by Miller (1956). What became known as the Miller's Law. George A. Miller[7] noted that *the ability of young adults' memory was about seven elements, called "chunks" (bits), regardless of whether the elements were digits, letters, words, or other units.* A subsequent research revealed that capacity depends on the category of used chunks, *i.e.*, the capacity is about seven for digits, about six to letters and about five to words, and even the characteristic of chunks within a category. Example, the ability for long words is smaller than for short words. In general, the memory capacity for verbal contexts - digits, letters, words, and so on, strongly depends on the time it takes to speak aloud content and lexical function of the content, *i.e.*, if the contents are known words person or not. Several other factors also affect the measure of a person's memory and so it is difficult to establish the capacity of short-term memory by several chunks. However, in 2001 Nelson Cowan[8] proposed that *the activity of memory has a capacity of about four chunks in young adults (and lower in older children and adults).*

Thus, the user's information in outdoor sports, cannot be in excess, must be structured in transparent glasses, *e.g.*, a wise suggestion, till a set of seven elements displayed from right to left with a degree of decreasing importance. As follows, according to Figure 3.

But how is the information can be managed? The following subtopic will answer.

Information Management Given the Outdoor Sportsman

Based on earlier subtopics, and the point of view of a sportsman user, the main question is how to get all relevant information with minimal effort and how to minimize information overload on the AR glasses, *e.g.*, riding a bicycle or to take a walk.

What a sportsman wants? Example, what is his geographical position? The local weather state, and his health condition? Has possibility of communicating with other

Figure 3. Output of AR for mountain biking and trekking

users? Measurement paths and the possibility of recording, meaning to take a photo or film? Finally, knows automatic events, appropriate and useful information to his location, what are his preferences? In this case are talking about seven informative data, to be within the limits of human ability to digest the information volume.

Next are described in detail the seven groups of informative data elements to be submitted to the sportsman outdoor mountain biking and trekking. These elements could fit their needs:

1. **Weather State:** Involves temperature, atmospheric pressure, altitude and relative humidity. This data serves, not only to inform, but also to intelligently calculate together with the sportsman's health status data, with or without the help of internet.
2. **Health Condition:** Involves the heart rate and calorie expenditure. These are important data to calculate and provide vital advices. Without this sensor, it will not be possible to deliver alerts, which could make the difference.
3. **Location and Time:** Involves the global position system (GPS), compass and stopwatch. Geolocation serves not only to inform but also to index the server database, events and points of interest. Can be a good tracker of an user in motion, and what their cadence or rhythm is.
4. **Measurement Paths:** Involves speed, measure steps and distances, initial and final positions.

5.   **Recording:** Involves audio and video recording. Can be used expressions like: "Ok photo" or "Ok film". Followed by the final execution command "Ok" to take a picture or film.

6.   **Telecommunications:** Involves mobile telecommunications through Telephone Company - phone calls and sending messages or by radio - free communications with other members of the group. The Call communication icons and SMS or MMS messages can be displayed intermittently whenever is received a phone call and/or a written message. If user wants to make a call should run the command: "Ok phone" or "Ok radio". If wants to send a message with the command: "Ok message" and then the name or contact number, followed by audio message, transformed in the written form, and to send the message, must run the command "Ok send".

7.   **Events:** Involves news, events, interest places and vital advices, information can be displayed in audio and write form. Relevant information can be "the heart rate is too high", or alerts about a near water supply point. Events are data that have support for advertising information, *e.g.*, sporting news or corporate sponsors. But, spamming, sending and posting advertisement and unwanted information in mass, will not be tolerated. It is easy to imagine that spam could overwhelm the AR with unwanted advertising or information overload of any kind.

As the authors speak of AR, there is still the possibility for another element that may be present in display of a sportsman user. It's the presence of virtual objects overlaid on the real environment, *e.g.*, a virtual walker who follows the user's path and gives vital information, guide them, and a mentor in specific landmarks or supported places. This hypothesis of technological functionality in AR equipment is quite possible in the current era. This virtual element is basically an artificial intelligence[9] that needs access to the internet, due to the computational requirement. Therefore, the server support is necessary to address this intelligent component that will interact and follow AR user abroad. Without access to the network, and with the current autonomy of mobile devices is very difficult, but not impossible, to have computing power to handle this volume of data.

Finally, comes the need of quality criteria of information provided to AR end-user, which also includes providing the suitable and useful amount of information in order not to complicate the use of an AR device, and thus, have greater social acceptance to adopt this technology, let's see next subtopic.

Social Acceptance of New AR Technologies

After being identified the information and communication overload problems, *e.g.*, from study results and interactions with AR prototype, authors have defined the appropriate and useful information to give to AR users. Also, is need to define quality criteria of information provided. That is, with the aim of having a greater social acceptance to adopt AR technology.

First must be used effective ways to convince users of the benefits of this emerging AR technology, and its use as well as gather the best way to convince them to achieve the possible and better social acceptance. To show the best way for potential market, the needs and possibilities, this *technology must be present in consumer education* (Ross & Harrison, 2016).

In addition, some doubts about whether the technology is socially acceptable and their interaction is as natural as possible to enjoy the best of this technology abroad and convince users, *e.g.* it was observed a simple interaction with microphone performs better in outdoor operations by end-users, around one second. When win the trust, is essential doesn't disappoint them. Social acceptance in the field of AR is directly related to the information overload. Because, if the mobile device is overload users, they will get tired, and cannot deal with complexity, and finally they'll stop using this equipment.

Mobile systems such as AR in outdoor environments, are constantly faced with problems of social acceptance to go from laboratory to industry, *e.g.* what happened to the Google Glass. There was clearly a lack of social acceptance, especially originated with concerns about privacy and security, which saw the product withdrawn from the market after less than a year, and suffered social rejection. It's what many new devices must overcome in their quest for widespread adoption. In this case, it not only involved the attitude to use experienced user of Google Glass, but also included negative reactions, the early adopters, ones who begin using a product or technology as soon as it becomes available, and demonstrated by others in society in general. However, *the "Glass" was one of the most interesting developments in "wearable technology" the past four years* (Ross & Harrison, 2016). Wearable technology is a new approach to computing, redefining human-machine interaction, where technological equipment is directly connected to user.

Strategies to minimize social rejection are still evolving. The need for such strategies was highlighted by research that Heather F. Ross[10] who undertook a study on the knowledge and acceptance of AR by a group of people with 20, 30, 40, 50, 60 and over 60 years for survey of your emotional reactions, cognitive, and behavioral in relation to AR. The result was that *while the AR is "technically impressive" participants demonstrate a total lack of knowledge of this technology. There was a group feeling that they should know better, but they were not aware of what the brands were doing to inform them about the benefits to be gained* (Ross & Harrison, 2016). The authors saw, from their empirical tests, that is some interaction advantage if users had some knowledge and continued use or habituation and accumulated experience.

Thus, for systems succeed in the market that is placed in the hands of real users, developers need to consider that *the device needs to be a socially acceptable interface, natural to interact and be an acceptable fashion* (Azuma, 1999).

To achieve social acceptance, *e.g.*, the researchers can use a qualitative methodology and technology acceptance model (TAM) as introduced by Fred Davis[11] in 1986 in his doctoral thesis. This his research aimed to provide the theoretical basis for a practical methodology *"user acceptance test" that allows creators and implementers of information systems know how to improve acceptance prior to their implementation* (Ross & Harrison, 2016). Example, what is the perception that consumers have of the usefulness and ease of use of AR? What is your attitude to AR? Or what are behavioral intentions?

In the book "Visual Intelligence" Ann Marie Barry examined the role that *various media play in the creation of images that impact our lives: how visual images that create a language with deep psychological meaning, and as the press, television and movie manipulate images to create desired emotional effect* (Barry, 1997). The close-ups explore the visual subtleties in areas such as digital manipulation, the attitudes of camera and contextual framework and the social image as an abstract concept expressed in concrete visual terms.

Defines the process by which the technology is introduced and diffuses through the company to gain acceptance. The new technology emerges in the field of technologists and those who are "early adopters". Your potential begins to engage innovators who explore pioneering ways to connect to the target audience. This later technology brings to the mainstream, main chain, since it becomes adopted as the standard. During this process, individuals must be aware, accept and learn to use the new technology. To explain this process, Fred Davis developed the *Technology Acceptance Model (TAM)*. See Figure 4.

According to Figure 4, a user's attitude toward using a system is a function of two major beliefs: perceived usefulness and perceived ease of use. Perceived ease of use has a causal effect on perceived usefulness. Design features directly influence perceived usefulness and perceived ease of use.

Many research groups have raised the problem of socially acceptable technology. The mobile systems are constantly faced with problems to go from laboratory to industry. For systems succeed or be introduced to the market, developers must consider that *device needs to be socially acceptable to have a neutral interaction and acceptable fashion* (Furht, 2011).

Mobile phones, tablets, messages, calls, and so on, were judged as distractions and are often considered as not socially acceptable, in the sense that not only inter-

Figure 4. The Technology Acceptance Model (TAM)
Adapted of Fred D. Davis – A technology acceptance model for empirically testing new end-user information systems: Theory and results.

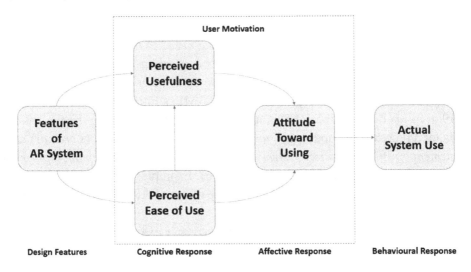

rupt the person whose phone or tablet is receiving a message or remember its most owner or less important information, but also other people present in the same room, if they are having a conversation or are in a public place such as a bus. Thus, research groups, decided that the interaction with the AR systems implemented in mobile applications need to be subtle, discreet and gentle, so as not to disturb the user if they are under a high workload and disruption is not priority. A system that is subtle, discreet and moderate becomes socially acceptable. In fact, the main problem with social acceptance comes the level of disturbance created portable devices in public places and during conversations. *The researchers studied the peripheral vision and adapted the mobile devices, for eyes, so it does not obstruct the field of foveal vision*, responsible for sharp central vision, which is necessary for activities where visual detail is of primary importance, such as reading and driving, which is *the focus in the human field of vision* (Furht, 2011).

After field tests using Google Glass, Ben Sawyer case study of the University of Central Florida, concluded that when using AR glasses to receive or send messages when are driving, *lanes become less and less visible depending on the concentration and level of user workload*, making it *a natural adaptation to the cognitive workload and stress of users* (Sawyer, 2014). Since the signs are visible only to the user, which can be considered socially acceptable, it will only disturb the user, depending on your level of concentration and it can choose not to respond to stimuli. Furthermore, multimodal interfaces are crucial to greater acceptance of fuzzy systems in public places as they offer the user the freedom to choose from a variety of modes of interaction. Thus, users are presented with the freedom to choose the most appropriate and socially acceptable communication with their devices. The challenge is to convince people to use the AR technology. It's a revolution, this because, to participate in this revolution, *the consumer must engage with innovative technological advances, and which often involve downloading appropriate applications that allow AR to each individual technology company have its own specification* (Ross & Harrison, 2016).

Another important factor of socially acceptable devices is that the user must be able to interact with them in a natural way. If the interaction between the user and the device is not natural, its use will appear awkward in public places.

Mobile AR systems that wish to spend the laboratories for the industry are also focused on fashion issues, as users may not want to use a head mounted display (HMD) or other visible devices. Example, some AR devices seem to turn a human into a robot, therefore, *should be light with optical* (Azuma el al., 2001). Thus, developers of mobile systems should consider fashion trends, and this can be a major obstacle to overcome. In recent past, groups like the MIT Media Lab, constantly trying to reduce the amount of unwanted visible devices or arrange them in different ways to design. They also are *searching for a way to replace the need to use colored markers at your fingertips. Although these may not look much for fashion* (Furht, 2011), they are an excellent step towards acceptable fashion mobile AR systems.

Mobile applications also need to be subtle and discreet. Should not make random noise at inopportune moments for the user. No matter how is used the phones, but in our society, it's still considered to be unpleasant when someone is on the phone in a public place; when a person's phone is ringing in public, and the first such person is searching for the phone to turn off the sound and then check who was calling or reminder, or message received.

Potential Distraction with Glasses

The road is a known danger, *e.g.*, see text messages while driving has been targeted legislation and is widely prohibited. But *the supporters of Google Glass claim the wearable computer mounted on the head to be designed to provide information without being distracted* (Sawyer, Finomore, Calvo, & Hancock, 2014).

Critics of the Google Glass are concerned with the ease of access to distractions by drivers. In the early discussions of potential legislative efforts, dangers were presented. *Proponents of "Glass" say the interface is designed to provide information simultaneously, without increasing the risks* (Sawyer, Finomore, Calvo, & Hancock, 2014). Similarly, a sportsman riding a bike can risk an accident by distract the eyes to read messages while guiding a bicycle, originated by information overload, and has no time to dodge an obstacle.

Ben D. Sawyer[12] of University of Central Florida worked in cooperation with the Air Force's 771st Human Performance Wing, about a study of "Google Glass: A Driver Distraction Cause or Cure?" (Study at MIT Laboratory). *The objective was evaluating the driving distraction potential of texting with "Glass" and the method was asked drivers in a simulator to drive and use "Glass" or a smartphone based messaging interface, then interrupted them with an emergency brake event. Both the response event and subsequent recovery were analyzed.* The results were, delivered messages served to moderate, but didn't eliminate distracting cognitive demands. *A potential passive cost to drivers merely wearing Glass was also observed. Messaging using either device impaired driving as compared to driving without multitasking* (Sawyer, Finomore, Calvo, & Hancock, 2014).

What happens most often is that, in the case of a cyclist when overloaded with distractions moves more slowly, and cannot keep in proper lane of the road correctly, but to compensate the risk of collision, experienced athletes psychologically maintain, or safeguard, for maintaining a greater distance of other cyclists and other obstacles there is ahead. It is a self-protection to reduce accidents. Another option is to reduce some information presented in AR glasses, on the other hand has better results if two formats of information are displayed - written format and audio format.

Another recent driving study of National Highway Traffic Safety Administration *showed that messaging-related interaction with smartphones more than doubled crash risk* (Fitch et al., 2013)[13].

Figure 5. Head Up Display (HUD) is a tool originally developed for use in aircraft aiming to provide visual information to the driver, without having to look away from the target in front of the aircraft, the Super Hercules Air Force C-130J
Courtesy of Wikipedia

These devices have been a feature of cockpits since before the Second World War. Research of aviation HUD has shown generally mixed benefits: although the technology to increase the performance, there are costs, *e.g., the detection of unexpected obstacles* (Sawyer, Finomore, Calvo, & Hancock, 2014). A strong proof that the displays are useful, is this tool installed in this kind of military aircraft, and everybody know that to pilot a plane of these, requires professional concentration.

The windshield HUD are available in cars production, for over 20 years. Driving with these technologies has also been closely investigated, revealing the benefits for HUD users in terms of vehicle control and detection of road events. However, there's evidence these benefits don't maintain under high workload and with unexpected events. In other words, watching the road doesn't mean a distracted driver will react to events that occur on the road.

About Figure 6, Jaguar Land Rover introduced the 360 Virtual Urban Windscreen, with heads-up technology and promised to safeguard against distractions whilst driving, but how safe is it really? Car manufacturers argue the heads-up displays are a safeguard against fumbling with smartphones and other distractions while driving, but these safety claims haven't been supported by any scientific research. Same can be said to ride a bike, but the key of success and without information overload is simplicity. This is what was said for several car manufacturers, Hyundai, Volvo and BMW are already offering colorful displays of warning signs and animated icons across windshields in selected models. While Mercedes-Benz began offering heads-up displays, touting high-definition readouts and special windshield

Figure 6. The Vehicle Jaguar Land Rover, introduced the windscreen 360 Urban Virtual
Source: Article "Heads-up Display - How safe is it really?" Website: autoglaze.co.uk

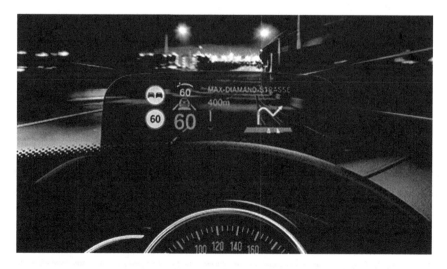

glass, which offers little more than a speedometer. Qualitatively they believe simplicity is the key to this technology, so it may not be a distraction.

Researchers say some simple displays of information in a driver's field of view can be helpful. But as the displays begin to include more complicated information, much of it far from necessary for keeping the car on track, some said they serve as more of a distraction, when they should otherwise pay attention to the road. Just because someone has their eyes straight ahead doesn't mean they're seeing everything in their line of sight, and so, some worry that the heads-up displays will lead to even more dangerous roads. As the technology becomes cheaper and easier to install, the displays could start appearing everywhere, even before any scientific study determines their safety on the road.

The conclusion is that glasses and head-up displays delivers moderately messages, but doesn't eliminate the distraction of cognitive demands while driving or riding a bike. Attention is higher when using the voice interface to send messages compared to text messages, though attention is higher than the conduction is also impaired, therefore, there is a cognitive interference previewing messages while driving. Authors saw from interaction tests that a voice interface is better for outdoor.

Technologic Overview for Location and Referencing of AR in Outdoor

The accuracy of the location method is critical for AR in outdoor sports, even more if there is no access to the Internet network. What location technologies may be required or are available for outdoor sportsman who use a mobile AR system? One question this chapter is: "What are the alternatives, for mobile communications with AR equipment in outdoor, if there is no internet access or not always be dependent on it?"

The location technologies are needed for AR. They are part of the core functionality of AR for outdoor, and are expected to significantly influence the future development of other AR applications. The accuracy of the location method places limitations on how AR applications can superimpose virtual information into the real world. The question of *determining the geometric properties of an user in an unfamiliar environment has been studied for several decades* (Chi, Kang, & Wang, 2013).

With the development of theories of research and GPS, people can identify their exact position, referring to points of control and enforcement of interpolation processes. Addition to GPS, there are other location technologies that combine various sensors and provide similar functionality, such as location identification (RFID), ultra-wide band (UWB), and barcode. In AR, the location has an important role in the algorithm used to determine where information from the virtual environment should be superimposed.

There is a relationship with AR and GPS, because GPS can, in fact, be used with AR. Currently, it is a support technology for AR. There is a dependence of spatial registration, many people equate it with anything having to do with maps. One of the most "pervasive technologies" that people equate with maps are the Geographic Information Systems, commonly referred as GIS, that provides the capability to analyze, store, manipulate, and display geographic information. With pervasive technologies, *are able to interact with web everywhere and at any time using mobile devices with speech, pen, and other tailored human-machine inter-faces. It goes beyond the realm of personal computers. Any device, from clothing to tools to appliances to cars to homes to the human body to your coffee mug, can be imbedded with chips to connect the device to an infinite network of other devices*[14].

Also hybrid location obtained from various sensors for stable location of results and consequently improve the performance of AR applications. For example, by combining the results obtained from GPS and Simultaneous Localization and Mapping (SLAM), can ensure the continuous detection of a location where one of the sensors fails, or the satellite signals are blocked in a dynamic environment such as a construction site. Moreover, the melting process can increase the speed and location, providing more information of geometric references.

With the development of the Internet, appeared the cloud computing environment and this technology has become powerful. Used as a platform for access to information, it has the potential to expand the use of AR applications, also for use in outdoor, because cloud computing is a service through the Internet, and the hardware and software on the data servers that provide these services. Cloud computing increases the freedom to use AR applications in Architecture, Engineering, Construction and Facilities Management (AEC/FM), which are also applications of AR for outdoor. Another factor that will lead to more widespread use of AR is that mobile devices are becoming smaller, more powerful, and less expensive. Cloud computing and mobile devices have the potential to influence the development of AR applications. Advances in location technologies will enable the deployment of AR in complex environments.

Appeared robust applications such as ARToolkit. This tool uses computer vision methods for detecting tags in the image captured by a camera. The optical tracking of this tag enables the adjustment of position and orientation to perform the rendering of a virtual object so that the object appears to be "pegged" tag, so the user can manipulate the virtual object using a real object. *Key Features of ARToolkit are complete access to the computer vision algorithm allows to modify the source code to fit a specific application. Developed for Smart Glasses* (Source: artoolkit.org/).

Because of the complexity of outdoor places, it's often difficult without the use of GPS, have references to identify places and trails where an outdoor setting sportsman crosses or passed. Another way is put there, regular markers, which are location technologies used by default bookmarks. However, new AR technologies detect unique characteristics of complex scenes and use them to determine virtual objects to overlap. These types of AR technologies are called "markerless".

Methods for Human-Computer Interaction AR

To improve usability and maintain functionality in outdoor, the hosting devices for AR applications are becoming ubiquitous and portable, *especially well-suited to ideas such as "ubiquitous learning" in which the plan is that every person learns all the time, wherever they are, when they need* (Craig, 2013). The human-computer interaction must be a natural interface, meaning the interfaces of AR applications must be intuitive for users and easily controlled using the natural human movements, or even with gestures and kinesthetic control. Bodily-kinesthetic intelligence is to use one's body in highly differentiated and skilled ways, for expressive and goal-directed purposes. Gives rise to athletes develop skills to the required coordination of precise movements needed to perform their techniques. But for hands-free, a good method could be with microphone interaction, by key words, like "Ok photo, Ok". The quantitative methods shown, in solutions and recommendations, is more fast and usable for end-users.

These kinds of human-computer interactions have been discussed in the International Symposium on Mixed and Augmented Reality (ISMAR) is the leading international academic conference in the field of Augmented Reality and Mixed Reality. The symposium is organized and supported by the IEEE Computer Society. Mixed Reality (MR) and Augmented Reality (AR) allow the creation of fascinating new types of user interfaces, and are beginning to show significant impact on industry and society. The field is highly interdisciplinary, bringing together signal processing, computer vision, computer graphics, user interfaces, human factors, wearable computing, mobile computing, computer networks, displays, sensors, and so on. The MR/AR concepts are suitable for a wide range of applications.

In ISMAR, researchers identified numerous opportunities for AR to improve practical applications. The natural user interfaces are intuitive control mechanisms that mimic human behavior and gestures. They can be used to communicate without the use of indirect input devices. Moreover, because they are lighter, are suitable for devices in the field of AR. Design and control of intuitive user interfaces of AR are currently a topic of popular search. Specifically, an increasing number of AR applications use gestures and kinesthetic control.

To create the best human-computer interaction, in other words, mobile human-device AR abroad with AR applications, that is, *to give the user the ability to walk around large environments, outdoor is essential good guidance tracking abroad* (Azuma, 1997; Craig, 2013; You, Neumann, & Azuma, 1999). Microphone of outdoor also be used to tracking, *e.g.*, can be used as sensor in acoustical tracking system. To detect ultrasounds - sounds of higher frequency. This has the advantage of not being affected by lighting conditions. It can function in the dark, as well as in bright sunlight. Another way is using GPS with help the internet wireless, as it will serve to make an index based on geolocation a sportsman user. Will contribute to the intelligent information and communication use, *good perception and "common sense" visual* (Barry, 1997) in outdoor sports. Thus, no information overload.

To show end-users' interactions with an AR system, is presented the following Use Case Diagram. It's an abstraction for outdoor sportsmen.

One of existing specializations of actor AR end-user, can be a mountain biker or a trekker, as shown in following diagram.

TESTING RESEARCH HYPOTHESES

With a quantitative and qualitative treatment of research hypotheses are implemented the user's information, as next Solutions and Recommendations, an AR prototype that simulates an outdoor sports environment to collect data, through observation of interaction tests with twelve end-users. Next will show reaction's results with

Figure 7. UML Use Case Diagram

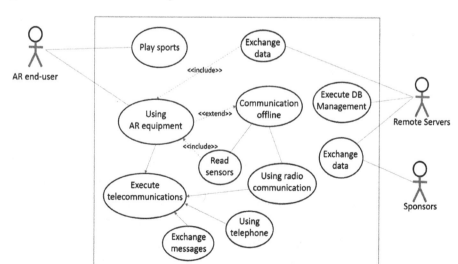

Figure 8. Specialization of Actor - User AR

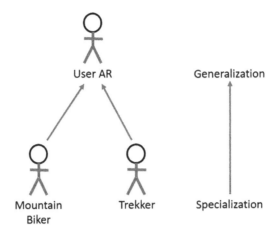

overload and better usability, then, a framed mockup, which helps to do conceptual testing the presentation of all data information and features for users. Thus, avoids giving unnecessary information isn't within the outdoor sports, that is, particularly for those who practice either biking or trekking.

Tests up through a practical implementation output, the provision of the information given to athletes, in which case the use is preferably a pair of AR glasses, because they are portable and mobile, and suitable for using to ride a bike, so there is no need to use their hands to operate, at the expense of using mobile phones or tablets, which also currently have the capacity to run AR applications, but more difficult to use a bicycle.

SOLUTIONS AND RECOMMENDATIONS

An AR prototype simulates an outdoor sports environment to collect data, through observation of interaction tests with twelve end-users. This empirical research was conducted to obtain a quantitative approach. Afterwards, a questionnaire was applied to have a qualitative evaluation of end-users. Finally, reviews were collected by structured interviews.

Data were collected for further analysis, from direct sources, *i.e.* outdoor sports AR experienced users. The objective was to gather facts and situations that caused differentiation in the understanding *versus* a significant increase leading to information overload. Moreover, this prototype assesses whether certain information is appropriate to be presented to a sportsman outdoor practicing biking or trekking.

Figure 9. Interaction tests of end-users with AR prototype

Reaction time was and the results are presented in in seconds. Figure 9 depicts an exemplification of an end-user interaction.

End-users performed tasks with five application features, which are the following voice commands: "Ok photo", "Ok films", "Ok communications", "Ok message" and "Ok agent". These commands are exemplifications of end-users' interactions by voice. The aim of this set of commands is to simulate the AR glasses setting, *e.g.*, google glasses, environment. Moreover, the end-users were requested to identify some sounds while performing their assigned tasks - named as audible operations.

From an usability point of view, the users were faster in the audible operations with an average value 1 to 2 seconds faster than in gestural form, mouse interaction. 58.33% reacted positively to the information presented, *e.g.*, climate information, biometrics, geographic and orientation. Figure 10 depicts the time differences of interactions.

Below of graphic lines are the habituation/education data, and below is environment/distractions data, next below are age, sex and the name of individual users. The approach followed mainly the quantitative method to give more weight to scientific research findings. The collected sample was heterogeneous, *i.e.*, users have ages 14, 17, 20, 27, 32, 36, 37, 45, 48, 52, and 67 years. Framed in various activities, like students, medical assistants, lawyers, teachers, insurance professionals, computer technicians and retired people.

Another relevant execution is the last task – "Ok agent", immediately after the task "Ok message", there was a 50% task execution degradation have not complied

Figure 10. Interaction with functionality "Ok photo"

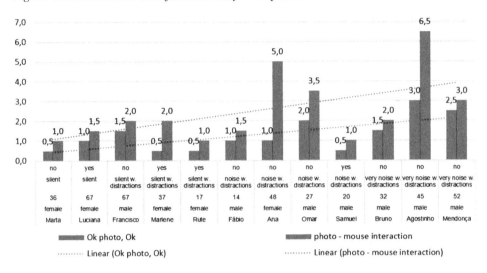

with expectations, but the previous 100% task performed successfully. See next these time differences.

Seven users are sportsmen, whereas four are accustomed, had previous education/habituation of closer AR prototype, but eight, had no experience with that, and it was the first time they experienced. All users were exposed in different environments/distractions as it makes sense in an external environment, uncontrolled sonically speaking, *i.e.*, silent, silent with distractions, noise with distractions and very noise with distractions.

Figure 11. Interaction with functionality "Ok message" versus "Ok agent"

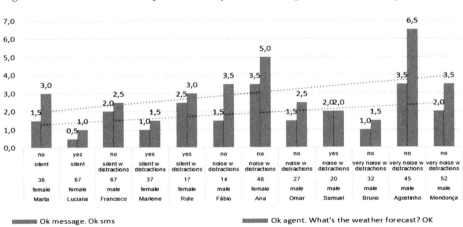

End-users were clustered through the most significant variables like education/ habituation, and others were differences of environments, with or without distractions that influenced their performance. Four accustomed users executed all features, 100% successfully. They also reacted better to all information provided.

The first task "Ok photo" had the best execution, users were more focused, but the last task "Ok agent" had the worst execution, users were more distracted.

In the qualitative approach with personal opinions of each user, found users' preference for version 2, which are presented only representative icons of different types of information without numerical information, and comparing to the quantitative results, numbers may be irrelevant for some users. There have been several qualitative opinions in that sense, *e.g.*, request a numerical specific information by functionality "Ok agent", or the transition from versions can be dependent of sportsman speed.

Finally, various opinions with free text through interviews have been met, the national and international personalities associated with information technology and human cognition, where was found by their opinions and among other things, considered the most appropriate data to be presented in outdoor sports biking and trekking. Some examples:

1. Pedro Pinto, a PhD student in Research Interests: Mobile and ubiquitous computing and Master in Networks and Multimedia from the University of Beira Interior, Portugal said:

The best information to be presented will be the one be useful to your walk and monuments you can see and hear stories of the area where you are. Something more cultural. In BTT information only about the difficulty of trails and pathways that are also such as weather information.

2. Christiane Perey is executive director of the AR for Business Alliance, participated in the conference "Challenges and Opportunities of Augmented Reality in Organizations" in Lusófona University, December 11, 2015:

The development of an AR system/solution must always begin with studies of the user requirements. The user requirements then will define which date is most relevant. Frequently the solution is designed for use by many people who have similar, but not the same requirements. In these cases, the user shouldn't be able to configure the system with settings. Also, the device can detect the user's environment and conditions and adjust.

In addition, the most controlled environments, silent with or without distractions were submitted 5 users and showed a very good performance, 60% performed all features. On the other hand, 7 users were submitted to a noise and very noise environment, and half felt overloaded with information and 6 had no reaction to the information shown, although 5 users have performed successfully full application functionalities. So, the presence of environmental noise and distractions affected negatively users' performance in outdoor environment. However, if there is a previous AR education and habituation will mitigate and positively influence their performance. Also, observed, most users had difficulties to react to the last functionality "Ok agent" because there is greater amount of information before and after, which indicates information overload and cause slower users.

Authors concluded that equilibrium and simplicity is the key and the best response to combat some information overload, as well as reducing risks of potential loss of concentration.

Based on researchers' work in the fields of AR, and human-computer interaction, the data most appropriated, to present and how to display in output, an outdoor sportsman, and how can it be applied to the "mountain biking and trekking", will show next. Data most appropriate to the users could be, such as climatic data, health condition, location and time, paths measurement, recording, telecommunications, events and intelligent data, and virtual objects.

Next, the AR mockup is a suggested example serves of component arrangement.

Figure 12. Practical View of the Information Given to Athletes

FUTURE RESEARCH DIRECTIONS

The future of AR in the everyday life of people will be more and more present. New technologies must pass by largest progressive acceptance of AR. The researchers found that the tendency imposed passes through the portability, mobility and simplicity. The use of information systems is transversal of every area of society, and will be increasingly present in the use of this advanced interface.

The research done by the authors concerning the paradigms of information overload and social acceptance, opens the doors to an effective implementation of a mobile AR system that would have better chances of being successful to be introduced and accepted by real end-users in outdoor sports environments. As well as being able to get the best possible benefit of this advanced technology.

CONCLUSION

This chapter identified the issues of information and communication overload of AR in outdoor sports environments and demonstrated several solutions, such as the need for balance and simplicity in the display of data, and has mobility with the aim of social acceptance, as well as usability, because if AR information is natural and organized, end-users better understand all features and most important real benefits for them.

Solutions and recommendations showed results of interactions with twelve end-users. Their reactions indicated that voice operations are better than gestural operations in outdoor, as well as some information are irrelevant to users, so were presented through a set of appropriate data to mountain biking and trekking ever as a framed mockup for understanding the relationship between sport users and AR data components. This mockup is a demonstration, or a hypothetical example design for future construction of an AR system.

Strengthened the foundations, which should take into account before implementing in practice a mobile AR system, like simplicity, previous education and previous collection of user requirements. It serves to encourage authors and other researchers, disseminate good practices, like simplicity, natural and organized information for future implementations of applications and interfaces in this field.

REFERENCES

Azuma, R., Baillot, Y., Behringer, R., Feiner, S., Julier, S., & MacIntyre, B. (2001). Recent advances in augmented reality. *Computer Graphics and Applications, IEEE, 21*(6), 34–47. doi:10.1109/38.963459

Azuma, R., Hoff, B., Neely, H., III, & Sarfaty, R. (1999, March). A motion-stabilized outdoor augmented reality system. In Virtual Reality, 1999. Proceedings., IEEE (pp. 252-259). IEEE. doi:10.1109/VR.1999.756959

Azuma, R. T. (1997). A survey of augmented reality. *Presence (Cambridge, Mass.), 6*(4), 355–385. doi:10.1162/pres.1997.6.4.355

Azuma, R. T. (1999). The challenge of making augmented reality work outdoors. *Mixed reality: Merging real and virtual worlds*, 379-390.

Barry, A. M. (1997). *Visual intelligence: Perception, image, and manipulation in visual communication*. SUNY Press.

Bawden, D., & Robinson, L. (2009). The dark side of information: Overload, anxiety and other paradoxes and pathologies. *Journal of Information Science, 35*(2), 180–191. doi:10.1177/0165551508095781

Chi, H. L., Kang, S. C., & Wang, X. (2013). Research trends and opportunities of augmented reality applications in architecture, engineering, and construction. *Automation in Construction, 33*, 116–122. doi:10.1016/j.autcon.2012.12.017

Craig, A. B. (2013). *Understanding augmented reality: Concepts and applications*. Newnes.

Davis, F. D., Jr. (1986). *A technology acceptance model for empirically testing new end-user information systems: Theory and results* (Doctoral dissertation). Massachusetts Institute of Technology.

Furht, B. (Ed.). (2011). *Handbook of augmented reality*. Springer Science & Business Media. doi:10.1007/978-1-4614-0064-6

Milgram, P., Takemura, H., Utsumi, A., & Kishino, F. (1995, December). Augmented reality: A class of displays on the reality-virtuality continuum. In *Photonics for industrial applications* (pp. 282–292). International Society for Optics and Photonics.

Miller, G. A. (1956). The magical number seven, plus or minus two: Some limits on our capacity for processing information. *Psychological Review, 63*(2), 81–97. doi:10.1037/h0043158 PMID:13310704

Ross, H. F., & Harrison, T. (2016). Augmented Reality Apparel: an Appraisal of Consumer Knowledge, Attitude and Behavioral Intentions. *2016 49th Hawaii International Conference on System Sciences*. University of Edinburgh, Business School.

Sawyer, B. D., Finomore, V. S., Calvo, A. A., & Hancock, P. A. (2014). Google Glass A Driver Distraction Cause or Cure?. *Human Factors: The Journal of the Human Factors and Ergonomics Society*.

You, S., Neumann, U., & Azuma, R. (1999, March). Hybrid inertial and vision tracking for augmented reality registration. In Virtual Reality, 1999. Proceedings., IEEE (pp. 260-267). IEEE.

You, S., Neumann, U., & Azuma, R. (1999). Orientation tracking for outdoor augmented reality registration. *Computer Graphics and Applications, IEEE, 19*(6), 36–42. doi:10.1109/38.799738

KEY TERMS AND DEFINITIONS

ARToolkit: Open source library, enables the development of interfaces for augmented reality.

Close-Ups: Widely used expression in the photography industry and recording videos that mean a plane where the camera is very close to the person or object in question, allowing a close and detailed view.

Internet of Things: Is an integration of several technologies and communications solutions. Identification and tracking technologies, wired and wireless sensor and actuator networks, enhanced communication protocols, and distributed intelligence for smart objects.

Relative Humidity: Normally expressed as a percentage; a higher percentage means the air-water mixture is more humid. Humans are sensitive to humidity because the human body uses evaporative cooling, enabled by perspiration, as the primary mechanism to rid itself of waste heat. Perspiration evaporates from the skin more slowly under humid conditions than under arid conditions.

Simultaneous Localization and Mapping: Technique used by robots and autonomous vehicles to build a map of an environment while it is located.

ENDNOTES

[1]   Frederick Phillips Brooks, software engineer and computer. Known by the project OS/360 operating system developed by IBM for the System/360 mainframe. Wrote book The Mythical Man-Month.

[2]   Paul Milgram, PhD. Professor of Mechanical and Industrial Engineering, University of Toronto. Fields of studies in human factors, man-machine interfaces, remote operation and augmented reality.

[3]   Fumio Kishino, professor in the engineering lab and Human Interface. Osaka University.

[4]   Ronald T. Azuma, known as pioneer in the field of augmented reality and generally contributor in the definition of AR and guiding of new developments. University of North Carolina.

[5]   Saul Wurman talked of information anxiety. Source: R.A. Wurman, *Information Anxiety 2* (New Riders Publishers, New York, 2001).

[6]   Ann Marie Barry, PhD. Interdisciplinary scholar whose main interest lies in neurological dynamic visual communication, visual perception, aesthetic and ethical practice.

[7]   George Armitage Miller, one of the creators of modern cognitive science. Performed studies on language and are among the first in psycholinguistics.

[8]   Nelson Cowan, works at the University of Missouri in cognitive psychology.

[9]   AI is the simulation of human intelligence, *e.g.*, through software. Where an intelligent agent is a system that perceives its environment and makes decisions to reach the goal or succeed. That has similar capacity of the human being to solve problems.

[10]   Heather F. Ross, doctoral student with research topics in corporate social responsibility and sustainability: the influence of communication ethics initiatives in the knowledge of those concerned, perception and behavior.

[11]   Fred D. Davis, PhD. Professor of Information Systems at the University of Arkansas. Developed work on acceptance of the technology.

[12]   Ben D. Sawyer, PhD, a strong researcher, team leader, looking for opportunities to understand and solve difficult man-machine problems using their own experience in psychology, neuroscience and engineering.

[13]   Fitch, G. A., Soccolich, S. A., Guo, F., McClafferty, J., Fang, Y., Olson, R. L., Perez, M. A., Hanowski, R. J., Hankey, J. M., & Dingus, T. A. (2013). The impact of hand-held and hands-free cell smartphone use on driving performance and safety-critical event risk (Report No. DOT HS 811 757). Washington, DC: National Highway Traffic Safety Administration.

[14]   Burkhardt, J., Schaeck, T., Henn, H., Hepper, S., & Rindtorff, K. (2001). *Pervasive computing: technology and architecture of mobile internet applications*. Addison-Wesley Longman Publishing Co., Inc.

Chapter 13

Information Overload as a Challenge and Changing Point for Educational Media Literacies

Sonja Ganguin
Leipzig University, Germany

Johannes Gemkow
Leipzig University, Germany

Rebekka Haubold
Leipzig University, Germany

ABSTRACT

This article deals with the concept of information overload as a crucial element of the changing information environment. Against this background, the authors discuss an alternative process for the conceptualisation of educational media literacy. By combining two nationally-based concepts on media literacy (German and Anglo-American), the yield of such a transnational approach will be demonstrated. The first section is dedicated to a historical overview. Based on the observation that humanity is currently dealing and always has dealt with information overload, leads to the necessity of coping with said overload. To this end, the second section will present and didactically reduce both discourses to their essentials. The third section provides a possible conceptualisation of both concepts and practical application of the combined approach for scholastic learning. The aim of this paper is to stimulate an international exchange on media literacy.

DOI: 10.4018/978-1-5225-2061-0.ch013

THE CHALLENGE OF INFORMATION OVERLOAD

Clay Shirky, media professor at New York University, said at the Web 2.0 Expo in New York in 2008, "It's not information overload. It's filter failure" (Shirky, 2008). This paper aims at demonstrating, that humanity is and always has been dealing with information overload. From an educational standpoint, the solution to so called information overload "revolve[s] around the principle of taking control on one's information environment" (Bawden & Robinson 2009, p. 187). Digital media change the information environment. This is due to many factors, including the changing places of knowledge and their authorities or simply the technological basis of digital media. It is the responsibility of education media literacies to tackle these factors and to give adequate recommendations for action related to information appropriation with digital media. This understanding of information overload leads directly to the discussion about information literacy.

The present chapter outlines the possibilities to cope with information overload by bolstering the competencies of media users. Therefore, the authors will discuss an approach to face the changing information environment for educational media literacies without abandoning originally educational ideals. The first section is dedicated to a historical overview of the said information overload. The approach points out the theoretical foundation of the German theorem of competence as well as Anglo-American literacy research. To this end, the second section will present and didactically reduce both discourses to their essentials. By using the information landscape in digital media, the possibilities of a mutual complement of both specific nationally-characterised approaches will be demonstrated in the third section. Furthermore, this section provides practical application of the combined approach for scholastic learning. The authors assume that combining both concepts will result in an important contribution to the research field. Combining the German literacy approach with the Anglo-American one means integrating subject-orientated ideals into a concept which is naturally based on users' activities in the media environment. The subject-orientated ideals refer to the confident and independent handling of digital media, which implies a reflexive distance to the way information is generated by digital media. This distance enables the use of digitised information in relation to subjective demands and living environments. This criterion of literacy is called media critique (Ganguin, 2004, 2006, 2014). The pragmatical approach can be used to identify specific "top-down"-challenges caused by the way digital media have changed the manner of generating and presenting digitised information. The management of information will continue to prefer pragmatic solutions. But for an educational approach on information literacy, which tries to implant idealistic values on education, the scope of digitised information should extend to looking for possibilities to use the current state of the information landscape.

Information Overload History

People have been discussing communication or information overload since and during the rise of each new media. The authorities, who foster or inhibit information overload, are changing, with it, and so the structures and challenges for the users do. Therefore, the chapter is dedicated to emerging challenges for media literacy because it is not just necessary what or which, but also *how* digital media are and how they are dealt with by people.

People have been exposed to an overload of information, from which they need to make selections, since the dawn of humanity. Whether the invention of letterpress printing, the telephone, or photography, people have faced a "regretted inability to read" (Bawden & Robinson, 2009, p. 182), listen or watch. The rise of digital media, where watching, listening and reading are familiar practices and especially with the implementation of the social web as a user-generated database, gives the impression that this 'regretted inability' is growing immeasurably to an information overload. Stimulus satiation as sensory overload does not necessarily depend on media, but media visualise them and improve their transparency, making the information quantifiable, showing them "in cold print". For this, media are reproductions of reality as well as they are part of reality throughout their possibilities to act with them, both technically and content-related (including trading). With media, empirical reality becomes a cultural encoded continuum, which could be seen when the brothers Grimm wrote down oral fairy-tales for instance, or also since the point where it has been possible to take photographs of single elusive situations. Media "are constructed complexes of habits, beliefs, and procedures embedded in elaborate codes of communication" (Anderson & Curtin, 2002, p. 24) and concerning, places of information-collection such as libraries are obtaining "bodies of knowledge and per se published science" (Schanze, 2001, p. 234).

The rise of each new media is driving the process of information overload forward. Developing graphic characters, in addition to oral tradition, information was collected through several media. With the invention of Gutenberg's movable-type printing, a media system and cultural practice was rising around 1440 upon which today's mass media is based. With the Protestant Reformation, people started to address and reach a broad audience with their written information. When the "press" was reacting to public-orientated current incidents, the information increased further. Distribution of newspapers via post led to a wider dissemination of information. Broadcasting enabled the reception of cross-border channels. In the advent of the First World War, the appeal was extended to the entire population, who became interesting as voters (Stöber, 2003a, p. 150). Already Otto von Bismarck (1869) sharpened his statement about the various sources of information, saying that in the past there was the proverb "He is lying as if it were printed. In the future, it will perhaps come to the saying: He is lying as if it were telegraphed." (Stöber, 2003b, p. 240).

By looking at the past, it can be noted that such gatekeepers who were lying as if it were printed or telegraphed were always present, fostering or – sometimes unintentionally – inhibiting information overload. One of the first medial information overloads in the Gutenberg age was inhibited by religious authorities. The clergy started controlling the new mass media early on, which preserves unity of faith (for both Protestants and Catholics alike). Pope Innocence VIII established a prior censorship in 1487. It was needed to make clear that instances like this always have influenced information and thoughts but it was not as visible as censorship is today; it was not "in cold print". Furthermore, economic motivations are on display in "Postdebits", which inhibit information overload in newspapers, leading to the high prices of media, e.g. so that broadcasting or telegrams do not "overwhelm" the people or their material availability (Stöber, 2003b, 140). For this, on the one hand, censorship inhibits information overload and on the other hand, it ensures that the 'right' information are overloading.

Later, the influence of the church decreased and politics gained the upper hand over moral, ethical or aesthetic censorship. In contrast to print media, films were *ab inicio* established in and classified as commercial law; in Anglo-America as well as in Germany. In Prussia, the local Berlin police were responsible for film-censorship until 1906, whereby they used the General Land-Law from 1794 as a foundation for their actions. Also in the USA, the state – especially the local Chicago police – protected the moral order for films starting in 1907 (Stöber, 2003b, p. 64). The states collected taxes and started to educate journalists and moviemakers as gatekeepers on a subordinate level. During the Second World War in Germany, the transition of the National Socialist German Workers' Party (NSDAP) led to convictions and expropriations to an all-embracing centralization and nationalization of media and with it to censorship. It could therefore be said that the information overload controlled and inhibited thinking about the radical handling of mass media. The burning of books on 10th May 1933, where socialist, Jewish or other not system-compatible media were destroyed symbolically and materially, the unification of mass media under the Reich's Ministry of Public Enlightenment and Propaganda, or the punishments for receiving foreign broadcasts (Kohl & Hasse, 2001, p. 174) are some examples of establishing an ideological information overload.

The beginning of governmental influence also simultaneously strengthened media as an economic product. Nevertheless, what was regarded as improper by the church, was continued by governmental power, as well as the economic system that carried on governmental functions such as youth media protection and taxes.

All those gatekeepers have in common that they are using their power in a culturally pessimistic way. The main focus is on moral and ethical aspects along with law and order, which are important factors for the retention of the power of the authorities. Societal values need to protect, which means protecting people who cannot protect themselves. In the past these were women, the youth and children as well as the lower class(es), who needed to be kept separated from media, at least from the authorities' perspective (Barth, 2002, p. 82). They had a deep concern for information overload (already the rising use of the telephone caused immediate excitement) (Stöber, 2003b, 62). On the assumption that behaviour patterns are copied one-to-one by these groups, fear increases with each new media. Youth media protection was and is an overload inhibit factor because the youth need not select what already has been filtered. In Switzerland, censorship of films forbids young people (until the age of 18), from visiting the cinema until the middle of the 1960s. In the United States, youth media protection was more advanced in 1930 because media censors in the U.S. attached conditions to parental support. The control measures were compiled as a non-governmental department in 1922, and served as an early encapsulation of non-governmental censorship. In Germany youth media protection was orientated on the model of the U.S., but instead of accompanying the action of the children, their information overload should be inhibited through age-limits. The linear cause-effect assumptions are typical for views of new media (from the "Werther-Effect" up to "killer games"). Besides too much information, the authorities' concerns were also shifted to the concept of aesthetic habits such as "wrong" or "false" content. This moral assessment goes in hand with economic worries of how the old media will continue. Since governmental influence is decreasing because of the developments during the Second World War – where propaganda and nearly total control of media emanated from the states – the economy has become more powerful and thus technical and "false" appropriation are in the focus of information and information overload. The view on information overload is changing due to society facing worse consequences of controlled media and connecting with new developments in digital media.

Digital Information Overload Regarding History

Digital adventages and, especially the rise of the user-generated internet, foster information overload. Digital information overload means now, for example, participation because no licences, privileges, permission to print or publish, limit people. No index of opinions restricts creating information. Fewer barriers (except technical obstacles) such as profession access-control or frequency allocation prevent publication. Wikipedia as non-commercial could be called a digital world library. Information are arranged and managed, linked and stored there for usage; the reader pass is an internet connection.

Apparently it seems like, censorship currently does not inhibit access to and the flow of information. The economy presents the power structure which determines aesthetic, moral, as well as technical standards, "wrong-and-right" use or marginalised people. The power of censorships has changed from the Catholic point of view to market logic. Gatekeepers are neither popes nor ministries. Alphabeth Inc., Microsoft Cooperation, Oracle Cooperation, IBM, Apple Inc., Facebook Inc., Electronic Arts, Sony or Vodafone Group Plc are some of the new commercial information "overloaders" and overload inhibiters. They develop and filter, code and decode, buy and sell publishing, organise and manage information or companies, software or management systems, like the clergy or governments did in the past.

Nevertheless, who has the power and where information comes from, is not as necessary as it is to confront who is pulling the strings and for which purpose. Culturally pessimistic ways of thinking are repeated with the rise of digital media. The telephone disrupted and violated privacy in 1902 like smartphones do today. This, however, seems more like a question of politeness and conventions than of overload. In telephone books, the telephone book authors react to this deficit with recommendations for action (Stöber, 2003a, 198); nowadays an equivalent concept is internet "netiquettes". The accusations that media make people stupid and violent occured with the rise of books for women and youth. These books are/were often scolded as trashy and smut literature (Scholz, 2004, p. 17). Today videogames or smartphones run this same gauntlet. At least early propaganda papers were used to spread the word to opponents of reformation (Stöber, 2003a, 140). They had a similar structure and aim as the present filter-bubbles generated by algorithms e.g. from Google Analytics.

Nowadays, the thought of information overload through books is greeted with smiles and smirks. This has probably come to be due to the well organised and developed structures of administration and management for written texts such as libraries, archives or museums. Furthermore, the fact that censorship or youth media protection for books is not a point of discussion, shows how times and opinions about media can change. This could also be the fate of the supposed problem called information overload: it is not just the mass of information (quantity), but more the way the information is handled (quality), and organised. In the case of digital media, filtering and selecting as well as digital media's authority/reliability become high priorities. Furthermore, these issues demand innovative skills, abilities, attitudes and know-how of the users themselves; the aim is for users to *participate* and not just *use* new media. While neither information overload nor structures of power are new concepts, media make the structures visible and offer the possibility to conceptually grasp power structures if users are able to cope with media challenges. To find out *how* digital media are dealt with by people, media appropriation needs to be in the central focus. Media literacy is thus the path for a participated, self-determined subject in a mediatised world.

THE CHANCE OF EDUCATIONAL MEDIA LITERACIES

The condition of a permanent possibility to engage with multiple information activities with media electronics is actually a brand new status. Considering the limited possibilities in the last centuries for lifelong learning, the current opportunities trend to a new approach to literacy. Apparently, this allows for the vision of the so-called overload as a chance for low-threshold access to a wide range of information.

Digital media is metaphorically not a library but an information supply service. Therefore, the question of how to handle information overload begins with the question of how to handle information and leads to the question of how information is distributed and presented. This section illustrates an approach to answer this question from the application of the German theorem of competence and the Anglo-American models of educational media literacies. The pointed outline follows methodically Gustav Grüner's concept of the vertical reduction (1967, pp. 414-421). The vertical reduction allows one to reduce the huge amount of contributions in both concepts and to simplify them "in a way that the crucial aspects of the concepts are still valid" (Futschek, 2013, p. 1).

The German Theorem of Competence

The German theorem of competence is very much based on the work of Dieter Baacke. Media competence[1] has to enable subjects to engage in reasonable decision making with media technologies (Baacke, 1980, p. 287). According to Baacke, the theorem of competence became integral to the social sciences in the 1970s. Baacke extended Chomsky's linguistic competence theorem and Habermas's communicative competence theorem to a very first media competence theorem. With his hypothesis that mass communication and personal communication stick together, the former influences media socialisation (Baacke, 1980, p. 333). On the basis of this principle, mass communication can foster or inhibit the yield of media competence. Baacke concluded that media competence enables people to reasonable solutions with the objective of an empowered citizen (1980, p. 287).

Due to the increasing proliferation of personal media in the 1990s, the boom of the term media competence had started. In particular, in educational policy context, the term was often used as a key qualification for the information age. As a consequence, more and more models and definitions of media competence appeared. This is to the detriment of a content-related specification of media competence. By means of a content analytical study in 1999, Harald Gapski identified 104 different definitions of media competence for the period from 1996 to 1999. His work highlighted the subject-orientated origin, with its idealistic and universal claim (2001, p. 208, 242).

The more widespread use of digital media and an increasing mediatisation of society has led in the past years to new challenges relating to the German discourse on media competence. The term "Web 2.0" is repeatedly used as a decisive argument for a renewal of media competence models (Gapski & Gräßer, 2007, p. 11; Süss, Lampert, & Wijnen, 2013, p. 131). Furthermore, other aspects have been mentioned: the technological base of personal computers (Zorn, 2011, pp. 176-183), the permanent availability of media via mobile devices, a converging digital media landscape, new processes of knowledge construction (Pscheida, 2010), new ways of presenting information, enhanced possibilities for producing content (Sutter, 2010, p. 47), the opportunity for "informational self-determination" (Gapski & Gräßer 2007, p. 25), questions regarding privacy issues and semioticised algorithms (Zorn, 2011). All these aspects were brought into the discourse on media competence only as fragments.

With this scale of new challenges, the question arises whether older models of media competence respond to the specific characteristics of digital media. At least to subsume the challenge caused by digital media under the established models is debatable. This point of discussion is traced back to the deductive approach of the German media competence models (Herzig & Grafe, 2012, p. 93). The established models are divided into several dimensions, which the respective author or authors claim to be appropriated. Those models are not based on empirical work, but on the theoretical position of the author(s). Thus, the media competences representing dimensions are not necessarily those required practically. This means that every deductive model inevitably has to subsume what are given by theoretical derived dimensions. With this in mind, it can be noted that the German media competence models operate strongly idealistically.[2] Hence, the theorem of competence, which was originally developed as a manner of acting with media (Baacke, 1998), appears in an idealistic, normative and theorised way. Consequently, the dimensions of media competence models appear to be abstract. If the theorem of competence intends to refer to human actions as central principle for solving tasks, the specific of digital media has to be identified. Especially the way digitised information is generated and presented plays a decisive role for the conceptualisation of media competence.

In this regard, the German discourse on media competence offers no pragmatic approach. In 1996, Dieter Baacke postulated that media competence comes up with an empirical emptiness that needs to be filled. About twenty years later, this is still an urgent demand. For an operationalization of media competence, the German theorem of competence is tainted with its idealistic theorized origin. Therefore, the following sector focuses on the Anglo-American models of educational media literacies, which is based on a pragmatic foundation. This enables educational media literacies to identify specific "top-down"-challenges caused by digitized information.

Anglo-American Models of Educational Media Literacies

In contrast to the German discourse of media-competence, the theoretical foundation of media literacy is based on the concept of pragmatism. But first of all, it has to be taken into account that there is not only one approach to or definite use of the term "literacy". On the one hand, there are several disciplines operating with the term, each of them in its own way. On the other hand, the term mostly relates to a specific application, for instance, library, computer, technology, visual, critical, new media or digital. Thus, every syntagma has its own scope.

In the German speaking discussion, Christian Swertz and Clemens Fessler came up with a proposal to sort out this matter. Swertz and Fessler discussed a "general distinction between information literacy and media literacy" (2010, p. 1). In this context, information literacies refer to technical skills whereas medial literacies are based on an educational understanding of a reflective and self-actualizing media reception and production (Swertz & Fessler, 2010, p. 27). This distinction seems to be comprehensible at first glance, but the interpretation of both concepts and their application in science are not clear. The connection between those two concepts is not disjointed. The following examples illustrate this point: Renee Hobbs, for instance, sees in digital and media literacy the ability to "create content in variety of forms, making use of language, images, sound, and new digital tools and technologies" (2010, p. VIII). Information literacy in turn, comes for the BIG6 Skills, developed by Eisenberg and Berkowitz, with a self-actualizing reception:

"The examination and assessment of the information problem-solving process" (1990, p. 9) is an integral component of this model. To pick up two more examples: The PLUS model by Herring (2004) contains "the ability to reflect on the process" (p. 74) whereas the 'Seven Pillars Model', developed by SCONUL (Society of College, National and University Libraries) defines a literate individual as able to, "critically appraise and evaluate their own findings and those of others" (2011, p. 9). By including the ability of critical evaluating, these understandings of information literacy go beyond the technical skill definition by Swertz and Fessler. Thus, the general distinction between information and media literacy might not be able to represent the English speaking discourse of literacies. This analysis leads to the conclusion, to search for common grounds within the discourse on information literacy.

The BIG6 and PLUS models mentioned above are divided into six and four stages respectively. Beside those popular stage models, there is another point of view which Daniel Bawden pointed out: "This viewpoint [sees] information literacy less as a series of competences to be mastered and more as a set of general knowledge and attitudes to be possessed" (2008, p. 22). Notable examples are the set of seven key characteristics by Bruce (1997), the definition of ALA (American Library Association) or the eight competencies by the CILIP model (2012) as well as the already mentioned SCONUL model (2011). The general distinction between the stage models and the set of competencies results reserved to the former is characterized by a process, meanwhile the latter is an interaction between the respective competencies. Such a distinction refers to the process that Lankshear and Knobel offered for digital literacies when they distinguished conceptual from standardised operational definitions (2006, p. 13). One example of conceptual definitions is provided by Paul Gilster. He identifies four key competencies: knowledge assembly, evaluating information content, searching the internet, and navigating hypertext (1997, p. 130). This is surely a fundamental difference. But at the substantive level, both approaches are very similar, and thus they include the abilities to identify a need for information, to locate, use, evaluate and organize these aspects. All of these abilities mentioned above refer to idealistic or operational standardised actions by the individuals.

The same approach can be seen within the media literacy discourse. One of the most cited definitions of media literacy is the following succinct sentence formulated in 1992 by the Aspen Media Literacy Institute: media literacy "is the ability to access, analyze, evaluate and create messages in variety of forms" (Livingstone, 2004, p. X). In 2003, this definition was supplemented by two more competencies named "reflect" and "act" (2003, p. 15). Another popular approach has been proposed by W. James Potter, who identified seven skills of media literacy and furthermore a summary of three tasks of information processing. To give a brief overview, the skills contain actions such as "breaking down the message", "judging the value", "using general principles" and the information process is divided in three actions, named "task", "goal" and "focus" (Potter, 2004, pp. 36-38). Besides these two elements, Potter's approach contains the subject perspective by adding to his media literacy model the personal locus.

The personal locus is composed of goals and drives. The goals shape the information-processing tasks by determining what gets filtered in and what gets ignored. The more you are aware of your goals, the more you can direct the process of information seeking. And the stronger your drives for information are, the more effort you will expend to attain your goals. (p. 35).

In this sense, the personal locus is a control mechanism of the information process operating with the knowledge structure in a person's memory.

Thus, both approaches of media literacy and those of information literacy mentioned above operate with human actions. This, to break it down, is due to the theoretical foundation of the literacy discourse, which is based on the concept of pragmatism.[3] The philosophical concept of pragmatism understands the principle of acting as the decisive factor for solutions of life tasks. The literacy discourse and so, as this section has shown, most of the media or information literacy approaches are highly influenced by idealistic or operational standardised actions by individuals. Of course, there is a general distinction in the focus of every approach between technological skills and critical understandings. But also the critical abilities tend to appear in idealistic or operational standardised actions[4]. This concept can be traced back to the pioneering work for media literacy that has been done by Len Masterman. In one of his definitive works "Media Awareness Education: Eighteen Basic Principles" (1989) he claimed that "the central unifying concept of Media Education is that of representation. The media mediate. They do not reflect but re-present the world. The media, that is, are symbolic sign systems that must be decoded. Without this principle, no media education is possible. From it, all else flows" (Masterman, 1989). This is a fundamental distinction to the German discourse of media competence, where the core principles are based on an idealistic and subject focused perspective ("bottom-up").

The following section extends the descriptive manner of this article to an exemplary approach on a theory-based educational understanding of information literacy in the digital age. Therefore, the German perspective of media critique will be combined with a technical based perspective on the semiotisation of information, which is the crucial prerequisite for idealistic or operational standardised actions. Solving tasks by actions implies the situational context, which frames the actions. The pragmatic approach can be used to identify specific "top-down"-frames caused by the impact digital media has on the way digitised information are generated and presented.

THE CHANGE OF EDUCATIONAL LITERACIES

This section deals with the conceptualisation and practical application of both concepts presented in the previous section. As exemplary for the German discourse, the difficulties in operationalisation of the subject-orientated, idealistic and abstract theorem of competence will be shown by the concept of media critique. By including the digital characteristic of semiotised information, the mutual combination of both concepts is going to become accessible. The section ends with the practical application of the combined concepts in scholastic learning.

Media Critique

This section on media critique aims to outline the necessary inclusion of digital characteristics. The ability to engage in media critique demonstrates a cognitive process that centres on evaluating media based on certain criteria (Ganguin, 2004). This process requires knowledge of both the process of understanding and decoding media language as well as analytical ability in order to even be able to criticize media. These requirements are stipulated firstly in relation to one's self in the form of reflection, for example of media influences.

One problem with the empirical investigation of media critique is the fact that, theoretically, if a person is critical of media, he is not only critical of one medium but generally critical of all media. Thus it is truly a hallmark of competence that competence depicts a meta-trait that provokes situationally adequate action where the situational should be the medium itself. However, the phrase 'should be' implies that this is not in line with reality. It cannot be deduced that only because someone can critically appropriate newspaper content that this same person can simultaneously approach other media critically. This thus poses the question of whether the ability to carry out media critique is a generalized ability that can ideally more or less be applied to all media equally or whether there are certain requirements that lead to differing competencies depending on the medium, i.e. are media specific.

In this context, when dealing with the socialization process of young people, it is centrally important when dealing with communications media for them to learn how to understand language, symbols and develop the ability to interpret images. According to Piaget, this ability refers to the preoperational stage, the stage of thought in symbols that runs from the second to the seventh year of life. In this case, the ability to decode information requires a thought process that plays a major role in the semantic development of language and thus also of media language. Since a person has to be able to decode information and media symbols in order to understand media language since these symbols can take various forms, this process of information is collected under the heading of coding or 'symbol system'. For this reason, this text will use the term decoding ability.

Symbol systems can, for example, be verbal, pictorial or numerical. This can lead to the thesis that, for example, a book with its language, which I naturally have to decode, addresses very different senses and abilities than a film. In a textual decoding process, a person has to translate symbols into words, words into sentences and sentences into concepts and information. For this reason, one could postulate that it is 'easier' to watch T.V. than to read a book since a book requires at least the abilities of reading, text comprehension and interpretation. Thus the path to different information processing systems has to be different for different media and therefore the decoding ability is dependent on the decoding level of a particular medium.

Additionally, many media use certain symbols or metaphors. The identification of the patterns among them is a challenge in many cases. Since some codes are not obvious but rather are frequently hidden within the dramaturgy, one first has to discover them as codes and then identify them. Many media also invoke particular symbols that are often references to other medial codes. Additionally, every culture and society has certain symbols and signs that are integrated encrypted within medial depictions in order to, for example, underline and clarify certain issues. We often always associate the same particular meaning or interpretation with certain symbols (for examples flags) so that frequently a verbal explanation of the symbols is no longer necessary since we already know what they mean. We have, however, gained this knowledge through experience in the socialization process. In this manner, a previous cultural understanding is needed when dealing with the decoding of symbols. Otherwise, one cannot recognize and decode them.

Digital media thus work with digital codes and are especially distinguished by their increased richness of information such as, for example, multimedia or virtual reality. The increasingly blurred division between sender and receiver plays an important role here. This leads to new challenges in the implementation of media critique since frequently the offers that are on hand in, for instance, the internet, are produced unfiltered and with a greater diversity. With television there is usually a long production and certification process involving many parties that eventually culminates in broadcast publication. In the internet, each and every individual person can publish whatever he/she wants, whenever he/she wants. Therefore, due to a lack of publication monitoring, it could be ascertained that every claim becomes information and thus the power of publication becomes decentralized. In this regard, Ramonet talks of a "democratic censorship":

As opposed to autocratic censorship, it [democratic censorship] is no longer based on the oppression and curtailment of data, on their abridgement or the prohibition to publish them but rather to the contrary on their accumulation, on the oversaturation and on the excess of information (Ramonet, 1999, p. 35).

One result of a lacking supervisory body in the internet therefore is an excess of information since anyone can publish anything. This excess of information that a medium has to offer can represent a reason for selectivity. Due to the diversity of offerings, people have to differentiate and select among them and must decide more on their own; this is the case if they cannot subsume them under a prescribed generalization. The increasing relevance of media-specific critique thus arises from the circumstance that digital media exhibit increasingly stronger media characteristics that stand in contrast to the familiar world of most users and demand an increasing, independent competence for assessment from their users.

Therefore, in this sense, it can be verified that media dependence is one problem related to the ability to decode information in the sense of media critique. This is the case since different media use different systems of symbols and encoding and play with quantitatively as well as qualitatively different signs and symbols that are often hidden, although especially digital media, due to their excess of information, display a high level of decoding as well.

The Semiotisation of Information

In the previous section, it has been already explained that media competencies depend directly on the symbolic system of media technology. This statement refers directly to Len Masterman's conclusion about what distinguishes media education from other disciplines: "The media, that is, are symbolic sign systems that must be decoded." (1989, para. 2). Obviously, information overload is a repeatedly used term related to new media technology such as the transformation of oral to literate culture, the rise of printed books or, as we can see, the digital age. The focus on the information landscape needs to be much more than identifying main issues or potential problems. Trying to understand specific characteristics of the current essence of information has to face the question, "how is information scattered and presented?".

This topic refers to a wide range of scientific discourses. To name only a few: psychology, corporate communication, health communication, library science, information studies, science and technology studies, empirical educational research and communication and media studies. The fact that information overload appears as a crucial object of investigation is based on the mediatisation of all social areas. The mediatisation is characterised by an advancement from analog to digital technology. Tackling the root of information overload as a phenomenon in the digital age leads to the influence of digital technology on the way information emerges nowadays. As already mentioned, this article focuses on a media educational perspective on the mass of information media users encounter in modern society. As there is a myriad of possible approaches to the digital information landscape, this section takes one particular point into consideration. This will be the semiotisation of information in the digital age. On the basis of this aspect, the chance for educational literacies to combine media-specific aspects with subject-related ideals can be illustrated.

Information presented by digital media is totally semioticised. This is not necessarily something new in communication and media studies. Printed words semioticised oral words and radio or television engineering use electromagnetic waves for semioticised information transfer. But what is the special issue with digitised information? The digital code is not only exclusively a representation of information (Masterman, 1989), but also an interpretation through an algorithmic language. The algorithmic language is the basic feature of digital media, as already Lev Manovich pointed out: "New media may look like media, but this is only the surface" (2001, p. 48). All media reduce objects into syntactical characters, which is indeed a first step of semiotisation. Furthermore, and in contrast to print, radio or television, digital media operate automatically through algorithmic language. Thus, every representation (the surface) is based on machine-interpreted data and so on an abstraction of the interface from the algorithmic language. This process can easily be demonstrated by the adaption of a website related to the user. For example, while searching for a specific article someone intends to buy, the algorithmic language interprets personalised data and offers a customised output of information. Computers perform operations through a programming language. Thus, every process of information emergence and presentation has to be reduced to an operationalised form.

If educational media literacies, especially information literacy, orient themselves towards the specific features of digital media, they need to face those challenges. To find these potential features, this chapter recommends identifying them through empirical investigation rather than theoretical investigation.

How the digital technology influences the information process through algorithmic language has been exemplarily pointed out by Andrea Kohlhase's (2008) work. Kohlhase has shown that the user's benefit from information presented by semantic technologies tends to be more voluminous as the designer of the relating algorithmic code intended them to be. This is due to semantic data extending ordinary data by including the kinds of relationships between the various data elements. Information generates new information, which is one reason for the impression of an information overload. "If the machine is thus empowered, a new set of questions arise naturally, e.g. the semantic currencies" (2008, p. 37). Such currencies can easily be seen as part of the new information environment. Among others, Kohlhase summarises in this aspect the following two currencies (pp. 7-8):

1. **Handover of Semantics (HoS):** A discrepancy between potential and reality of content collaboration. Formalising knowledge down to a machine's level offers no direct or indirect, but just potential value.
2. **Formalisation of Knowledge (FoK):** Capturing knowledge from a Knowledge Management standpoint not only means obtaining any representations but formalised, contextualised representations. Thus the problem of formalising knowledge is transformed into a knowledge representation problem in which the modification of representation is in focus, particularly the translation into semantic data formats.

Now, both of these criteria can be assigned to either stages or sets of educational media literacy models. For this purpose, the above mentioned information literacy models are listed and compared in Table 1.

Table 1. Anglo-American models on information literacy with the assigned competence criteria

ALA (2000)	SCONUL (2011)	Bruce (1997)	PLUS (2004)	BIG6 (1990)	CILIP (2012)
Determine the extent of information needed	Identify (FoK)		Purpose (FoK)	Task definition	A need for information
Evaluate information and its sources critically (HoS, FoK)	Scope (HoS, FoK)	Information technology conception (HoS)	Purpose (FoK)	Information seeking (FoK)	The resources available (HoS, FoK)
Access the needed information (FoK)	Plan	Information sources conception (FoK)	Location	Location and access (FoK)	How to find information (FoK)
Use information	Gather (HoS)	Information process conception (HoS)	Use (HoS)	Use of Information	Ethics and responsibility of use
	Manage, Present	Information control conception		Synthesis	• Work with or exploit results • Communicate or share findings • Manage findings
Understand issues surrounding the use and access, and use of information ethically and legally (HoS)	Manage, Evaluate (HoS, FoK)	Knowledge construction conception	Self-evaluation	Evaluation (HoS, FoK)	Evaluate results (HoS, FoK)
Incorporate selected information into one's knowledge base		• Knowledge extension conception • Wisdom conception			

Both criteria, the Handover of Semantics (HoS) and the Formalisation of Knowledge (FoK), can be assigned multiple times. Those "top-down"-issues have to be known by the users and therefore they are central criteria of information literacy. This procedure allows for the combination of specific features of digital media with educational ideals. Moreover, it constructs an operationalised model of information literacy.

Summary of the Description Mentioned Above

1. Digital media are semioticised
2. Semioticised digital media operate with automatic algorithms
3. Digital media represent machine-interpreted data
4. Specific features of digital media should be adopted by educational media literacies
5. Operationalised model of information literacy can be constructed

The strategy and necessity of combining specific features of media with educational ideals also take place in formal learning processes. How they are addressed to pupils in an application-related way is described in the following section.

Source Criticism as Scholastic Scope against Information Overload

Bringing both perspectives of media literacy and media competence together is just the first step needed in an approach about participating subjects and thus dealing with a supposed information overload. To give an example, the focus of this section deals with the challenges of selecting medial information nowadays. Thereby media criticism and particularly source criticism is a desirable ability, which should be reconsidered to avoid the idea of information overload through digital media. Especially turning the gaze towards schools and their responsibility (and theoretical aim) raising self-determined subjects.

An advantage of medial information – caused by the fact that media are mediators and cultural content – is that structures (of power) are "in cold print" and thus indicated visually. They can be analysed and criticised. With the invention of script and later book print, educational institutions established and cultivated the praxis of medial information. Especially schools feel and take responsibility for passing on this culture to the next generation and aiding in their appropriation. Pupils learn to write and read letters – as semiotic symbols of languages – followed by reading and understanding texts as well as interpreting poems or prose texts during their school careers. But analysing movies, games or radio features are not included in the curriculum; neither of student teachers nor pupils. In the 1920s attempts were made to integrate telephony in scholastic learning because it was seen as a "culturally basic ability" (Stöber, 2003a, p. 202). This attempt failed because the usage was told as a matter of course, regardless of whether that not just technical, but also changes of communicative frames and skills such as nonverbal communication or protection of privacy. During the rise of the medium of film, scholastic learning integrated film as a mediator as well as their content became an object of criticism which was formed and established in the "educational film movement" in the 1920s. Meanwhile the praxis of criticism disappeared in the curricula, and media (as film) are more used as mediators than issue of debate, a destination, which has been attributed to each new rising medium. However, it would be even better to integrate media and their content culturally critically into each school subject, which has been demanded strongly since 1992. In regard to information overload, one criteria of literacy should be media criticism, especially criticism of sources because in an information overwhelmed situation it is needed to select for participation.

One access could be adapting source criticism from historical source criticism, like history teachers let students evaluate pictures or texts. A common approach for this practice orientates itself on Borowsky, Vogel, & Wunder (1989) and divides historical critique of sources into source criticism on the one hand with description of source, outer and inner critique and on the other hand interpretation of sources, including analysis of content, context and solution.

Adding Digital Sources, This Procedure Changes

1. **Own Purpose:**
   a. At first – referring to media literacy –, a step before the first step needs to be added, where the pupil must determine the purpose of searching for and criticising information as well as the extent of the information. To achieve this, it is necessary to have an overview about where, how and what can be looked for and to understand what is needed.
2. **Source Criticism:**
   b. **Description of Source:** The second step resembles the evaluation of information and its sources. It is important to know which sources are how and where available, which is followed by the question if the content is the same and everything depends on whether using the internet is possible or not. Usability and the ability to analyse are important in order to distinguish information. Usability itself presents a structure where power can be manifested.
   c. **Outer Critique:** Decoding plays a decisive role for outer critique. Describing the source in its connection with the seeker, the asked questions, which locate the pupil in time, space and into society and in relation to the sources, could be which sources are serious, how are the sources connected or which structures of power refer to them. An aspect for digital media which had never existed before appears: searching in books or libraries, in picture books or encyclopaedias, does not leave any traces behind. Looking up information in digital media, so called digital fingerprints can be easily collected through cookies or personalised settings.

Therefore, it is important to know who is collecting what information and who works together with whom. Not just data protection, but also copyrights are a more diverse topic to know about.

d.   **Inner Critique:** Multimodality describes well what traditional source criticism applies to a source's content. Digital information offers diverse modalities which can be – depending on usability – opened. To choose a source targeted, media appropriation skills and abilities are necessary. For digital information this means decoding as well as technical equipping. For example, it is impossible to listen to an audio-track in a very noisy environment similar to the way it is impossible to listen to an audio-file without headphones or the ability to push a play-button. Moreover, it is important to know where it is possible to find which kind of mode of the same content. In a library, books are arranged by content; all library books with similar topics are grouped together. This is not possible in digital sources like it is in traditional print media libraries. In digital sources, due to the unlimited content available, it is possible that the same topics are on completely different sites without any links.

3.   **Interpretation of Source:**

e.   **Content:** The passing on of semantics is crucial for digital content. As described above, reading and understanding texts is learned in school from the first year onwards, whereas understanding and interpreting a picture or the content of films, games or apps needs to be tapped autodidactically.

f.   **Area of Statement and Embedded Context:** Understanding digital content should lead to literacy programming language, editing images, cutting audios and visual material, filtering or search engine optimisation. Through learning by doing, structures and symbols can be seen, reflected upon and understood. Encoding allows a view on structures of power. Discovering contexts and understatements, knowledge about economy, market and media history as well as source history could be instructive.

g.   **Solution and Summary:** The best source with the best information is useless if the pupil is not able to manage and present it. Therefore, passing on semantics, decoding reflection skills, and the critical power of judgement are required. A written or audio text can be read out, if it is not possible to present it, but a picture or film is useless if the pupil does not know how to integrate it into his/her presentation.

4.   **Subject-Related Solution:**

h.   A critical reflection on one's personal standing regarding media, its sources or more generally, to the society in which media is embedded, produces results additional to the media-centred approach. A question could be, how media appropriation has changed within the information seeking process, how can it be adapted further, or how it has changed values, skills and abilities. Regarding digital media, changes of a filter-bubble and whether one's own presentation and reproduction of the information is clarified in its licence could be reflected upon. This approach could be developed further and concretely applied for every teaching subject and each medial device. For example, the reflection of each source a teacher is using, and how it has been found – beyond history lessons – would provide grounds for media criticism.

Some General Issues can Already be Combined

Issue 1: In a mediatised world, media need to be regarded as cultural practice, which demands an integrated media-education within each school subject.

Issue 2: Digital media information occurs in diverse forms such as texts, graphics, diagrams, pictures, films, banners, sound, audio, vibration, and so on. How to read a picture or react to a sound needs to be appropriated, in the same manner reading and understanding a text is. Therefore, scholastic education needs to expand the portfolio from books and texts to multimedia, which requires diverse strategies for each medial device and each medial content.

Issue 3: Criticising medial information, requires understanding of it. For digital media, more challenges are added through their semiotic structure of content, where understanding means decoding as well as encoding.

Issue 4: With digital semiotic, topics such as protection of data and privacy are accompanied.

Issue 5: Critique can refer to aesthetical or moral aspects or regard power structures such as censorship or filtering methods.

Media critique is understood as a complex multidimensional construct, consisting of the abilities to perceive, to decode, to analyse, to reflect and to judge medial content in its specific presentation (Ganguin, 2004, p. 4). For this, objective criteria are as essential as subjective ones, which results in subjective norms and values of a single person. Therefore, experience, observation and theoretical exploration are required to form media-specific knowledge. Knowledge about digital media is simultaneously consequence and precondition for learning processes and with it the basis to live and act independently in a mediatised world. Informal knowledge cannot be sufficiently achieved, e.g. about objectives and means of global media companies, if the information about it must be critically questioned; first the motivation is needed and secondly the ability of source criticism is necessary. For this reason, media criticism should take its place in formal learning processes, according to reading, writing, counting and interpreting. Establishing media criticism in schools is necessary because self-organisation and self-determination substitute the need of a 'digital-media-librarian' who arranges the information. On the pragmatical side, the media literacy/media-competence of criticism also prevents and avoids existing filtering and selecting systems from remaining undisputed and exercises their power.

CONCLUSION

Every change of the information environment has (re-)emerged new problems with regard to media behaviour. One driving force for that is certainly the wide-spread distribution and popularity of digital media. The discourse on educational media literacy has always been in response to the latest new media technologies. After a phase of irritation, anxiety and pedagogical prevention, follows a phase in which the possibilities of self-determined activities with media are highlighted. (Hüther & Podehl, 2010, p. 116). This paper interpreted the information overload as a crucial element of the changing information environment. Instead of spreading fear, this chapter applies a cultural-critical approach. It is then possible to reflect upon an adequate conceptualisation of educational media literacies for the new information environment.

The approach presented here is based on a transnational procedure. Due the global impact of digital media, the authors believe in the yield of an international exchange related to the discourse on media literacy. As the chapter has shown, both approaches presented on media literacy have their own characteristics. The German-speaking discourse on media competence is especially dominated by a subject-orientated and idealistic theorem of competences according to Habermas and Baacke. Important as the orientation on pedagogical ideals may be, German media education has not yet been able to conceptualise a media (or information) literacy model suitable for the digital age. The section on media critique has outlined the necessarily inclusion of digital characteristics.

In contrast, the Anglo-American discourse on media literacy follows the tradition of American pragmatism. The action model of pragmatism follows a problem-solving approach implying the definition of the situation and thus the information environment. Almost all models in the Anglo-American discourse operate with media activities by their users. There is, however, a lack of the specific characteristics of digitised information in those models. How easily they can be assigned to the models proposed, has also been showed.

It can accordingly be concluded that a possible conceptualisation of information literacy based on a pragmatical approach might be useful to identify specific feature of digital media. This "top-down" approach, can be added later on with educational ideals ("bottom-up"). Beginning the conceptualisation of media literacy from the actual requirements of media users is an unusual approach for the German media literacy discourse. Identifying specific features of digital media with Anglo-American media literacy models and adding them later on with educational ideals may be an alternative approach for educational media literacy and a contribution for the transnational exchange of media literacy.

REFERENCES

American Library Association. (2000). *Information literacy competency standards for higher education*. Retrieved May 8, 2016, from http://www.ala.org/acrl/sites/ala.org.acrl/files/content/standards/standards.pdf

Anderson, C., & Curtin, M. (2002). Writing cultural history. The challenge of radio and television. In N. Brügger & S. Kolstrup (Eds.), *Media history. Theories, methods, analysis* (pp. 15–32). Aarhus: University Press.

Aspen Media Literacy Institute. (2003). *Literacy for the 21ᵗʰ century. An overview & orientation guide to media literacy education*. Retrieved May 24, 2016, from http://www.medialit.org/sites/default/files/mlk/01_MLKorientation.pdf

Baacke, D. (1980). *Kommunikation und Kompetenz. Grundlegung einer Didaktik der Kommunikation und ihrer Medien* (3rd ed.). München: Juventa.

Baacke, D. (1998). *Zum Konzept der Operationalisierung von Medienkompetenz*. Retrieved May, 6, 2016, from http://www.produktive-medienarbeit.de/ressourcen/bibliothek/fachartikel/baacke_operationalisierung.shtml

Barth, S. (2002). *Mädchenlektüren: Lesediskurse im 18. und 19. Jahrhundert*. New York, NY: Campus Verlag.

Bawden, D. (2008). Origins and concepts of digital literacy. In C. Lankshear & M. Knobel (Eds.), *Digital Literacies: Concepts, Policies and Practices* (pp. 17–32). New York, NY: Peter Lang.

Bawden, D., & Robinson, L. (2009). The dark side of information: Overload, anxiety and other paradoxes and pathologies. *Journal of Information Science, 35*(2), 180–191. doi:10.1177/0165551508095781

Borowsky, P., Vogel, B., & Wunder, H. (1989). Einführung in die Geschichtswissenschaft I. Grundprobleme, Arbeitsorganisation, Hilfsmittel (6th ed.). Opladen: Leske + Budrich.

Bruce, C. (1997). *The seven faces of information literacy*. Adelaide: Auslib Press.

CILIP. (2012). *Information literacy skills*. Retrieved May 8, 2016, from http://www. cilip.org.uk/sites/default/files/documents/Information%20literacy%20skills.pdf

Dewey, J. (1997). *Democracy and education. An introduction to the philosophy of education*. New York, NY: The Free Press.

Eisenberg, M. B., & Berkowitz, R. E. (1990). *Information problem-solving. The big six skills approach to library & information skills instruction*. Norwood, NJ: Ablex Pub. Corp.

Futschek, G. (2013). *Extreme didactic reduction in computational thinking education*. Paper presented at the 10th World Conference on Computers in Education, Toruń.

Ganguin, S. (2004). *Medienkritik - Kernkompetenz unserer Gesellschaft. Ludwigsburger Beiträge zur Medienkritik*. Retrieved March 4, 2016, from http://www. ph-ludwigsburg.de/fileadmin/subsites/1b-mpxx-t-01/user_files/Online-Magazin/ Ausgabe6/Ganguin6.pdf

Ganguin, S. (2006). Vom Kritikbegriff zur Medienkritik. In H. Niesyto, M. Rath & H. Sowa (Eds.), Medienkritik heute. Grundlagen, Beispiele, Praxisfelder (pp. 71-86). München: kopaed.

Ganguin, S., & Sander, U. (2014). Zur Entwicklung von Medienkritik. In F. von Gross, D. M. Meister, & U. Sander (Eds.), *EEO. Enzyklopädie Erziehungswissenschaft Online*. Weinheim: Juventa Verlag.

Gapski, H. (2001). *Medienkompetenz. Eine Bestandsaufnahme und Vorüberlegungen zu einem systemtheoretischen Rahmenkonzept*. Wiesbaden: Westdt. Verl.

Gapski, H., & Gräßer, L. (2007). Medienkompetenz im Web 2.0 – Lebensqualität als Zielperspektive. In L. Gräßer & M. Pohlschmidt (Eds.), Praxis Web 2.0. Potentiale für die Entwicklung von Medienkompetenz (pp. 11-34). Düsseldorf: kopaed.

Gilster, P. (1997). *Digital literacy*. New York, NY: Wiley Computer Publications.

Grüner, G. (1967). Die didaktische Reduktion als Kernstück der Didaktik. *Die deutsche Schule, 59*(7/8), 414-430.

Herring, J. E. (2004). *The internet and information skills*. London: Facet Publishing.

Herzig, B., & Grafe, S. (2012). Medienkompetenz – Grundbegriffe, Kompetenzmodelle und Standards. In K. Eilerts, A. H. Hilligus, G. Kaiser, & P. Bender (Eds.), *Kompetenzorientierung in Schule und Lehrerbildung. Perspektiven der bildungspolitischen Diskussion, der Bildungsforschung und der Mathematik-Didaktik*. Berlin: LIT Verlag.

Hobbs, R. (2010). *Digital and media literacy: A plan of action*. Retrieved May 7, 2016, from http://www.knightcomm.org/wp-content/uploads/2010/12/Digital_and_Media_Literacy_A_Plan_of_Action.pdf

Hüther, J., & Podehl, B. (2005). Geschichte der Medienpädagogik. In J. Hüther & B. Schorb (Eds.), Grundbegriffe Medienpädagogik (pp. 116-127). München: kopaed.

Kohl, H., & Hasse, A. (2001). Medienrecht. In H. Schanze (Ed.), *Handbuch der Mediengeschichte* (pp. 165–185). Stuttgart: Kröner.

Kohlhase, A. (2008). *Semantic interaction design: Composing knowledge with CPoint*. Retrieved May 13, 2006, from http://citeseerx.ist.psu.edu/viewdoc/download?doi=10.1.1.472.3571&rep=rep1&type=pdf

Lankshear, C., & Knobel, M. (2006). Digital literacies: Policy, pedagogy and research considerations for education. *Nordic Journal of Digital Literacy*, *1*, 12–24.

Livingstone, S. (2004). *Media literacy and the challenge of new information and communication technologies*. Retrieved May, 11, 2016, from http://eprints.lse.ac.uk/1017/1/MEDIALITERACY.pdf

Manovich, L. (2001). *The language of new media*. Cambridge, MA: MIT Press.

Masterman, L. (1989). *Media awareness education: Eighteen basic principles*. Retrieved May, 10, 2016, from http://medialit.org/reading-room/media-awareness-education-eighteen-basic-principles

Potter, W. J. (2004). *The media literacy model*. Retrieved May 14, 2016, from http://www.sagepub.com/sites/default/files/upm-binaries/4889_Potter_Chapter_3_Media_Literacy_Model.pdf

Pscheida, D. (2010). *Das Wikipedia-Universum. Wie das Internet unsere Wissenskultur verändert*. Bielefeld: transcript.

Ramonet, I. (1999). *Die Kommunikationsfalle. Macht und Mythen der Medien*. Zurich: Rotpunktverlag.

Schanze, H. (2001). Integrale Mediengeschichte. In H. Schanze (Ed.), *Handbuch der Mediengeschichte* (pp. 207–280). Stuttgart: Kröner.

Scholz, L. (2004). Die Industrie des Buchdrucks. In A. Kümmel, L. Scholz, & E. Schumacher (Eds.), *Einführung in die Geschichte der Medien* (pp. 11–33). Paderborn: Fink.

SCONUL. (2011). *The SCONUL seven pillars of information literacy. Core model for higher education*. Retrieved May 9, 2016, from http://www.sconul.ac.uk/sites/default/files/documents/coremodel.pdf

Shirky, C. (2008, September 18). It's not information overload. It's filter failure. *Web 2.0 Expo New York*. Retrieved May 12, 2016, from https://www.youtube.com/watch?v=LabqeJEOQyI

Six, U., & Gimmler, R. (2013). Medienkompetenz im schulischen Kontext. In I. C. Vogel (Ed.), Kommunikation in der Schule (pp. 96-117). Bad Heilbrunn: Klinkhardt.

Stöber, R. (2003a). *Mediengeschichte. Die Evolution "Neuer" Medien von Gutenberg bis Gates. Eine Einführung. Presse – Telekommunikation* (Vol. 1). Wiesbaden: Westdeutscher Verlag.

Stöber, R. (2003b). *Mediengeschichte. Die Evolution "Neuer" Medien von Gutenberg bis Gates. Eine Einführung. Film – Rundfunk – Multimedia* (Vol. 2). Wiesbaden: Westdeutscher Verlag.

Süss, D., Lampert, C., & Wijnen, C. W. (2013). *Medienpädagogik. Ein Studienbuch zur Einführung* (2nd ed.). Wiesbaden: VS Verlag.

Sutter, T. (2010). Medienkompetenz und Selbstsozialisation im Kontext Web 2.0. In B. Herzig, D. M. Meister, H. Moser, & H. Niesyto (Eds.), *Jahrbuch Medienpädagogik 8. Medienkompetenz und Web 2.0* (pp. 41–58). Wiesbaden: VS Verlag.

Swertz, C., & Fessler, C. (2010). *Literacy – Facetten eines heterogenen Begriffs*. Retrieved May, 5, 2016, from http://homepage.univie.ac.at/christian.swertz/texte/2010_literacy/2010_literacy.pdf

Tulodziecki, G., & Grafe, S. (2012). *Approaches to Learning with Media and Media Literacy Education – Trends and Current Situation in Germany*. Retrieved May, 14, 2016, from http://digitalcommons.uri.edu/cgi/viewcontent.cgi?article=1082&context=jmle

Zorn, I. (2011). Medienkompetenz und Medienbildung mit Fokus auf Digitale Medien. In H. Moser, P. Grell, & H. Niesyto (Eds.), Medienbildung und Medienkompetenz. Beiträge zu Schlüsselbegriffen der Medienpädagogik (pp. 175-209). München: kopaed.

KEY TERMS AND DEFINITIONS

Discourse: A discourse combines all relevant factors the topic of the discourse is dealing with. Amongst others, this may consist of the historical background, cultural and power characteristics, communicative practices, the constellations of actors or the disciplinary orientation. The discourse shapes and forms all topics included with its own characteristics. Thus, every interpretation reveals the discourse and depends on it.

Information Literacy: Information literacy describes the handling of information in and facilitated by media with educational values. This includes self-determined, reflective and purposive activities. Moreover, all factors relevant to handling the information (the information environment) are taken in account. Approaches to information literacy can be assigned to either library science, empirical educational research or holistic approaches to research.

Media Critique: The ability to engage in media critique demonstrates a cognitive process that centres on evaluating media based on certain criteria. This process requires knowledge of both the process of understanding and decoding media language as well as analytical ability in order to even be able to critique media. The general competence of media critique then has to be implemented through performance in concrete, media-critical action in which there are media-specific requirements so that the required level of media critique can differ from one medium to the next.

Media Literacy: Media literacy describes the handling in and with media through educational values. This includes self-determined, reflective and purposive activities. Moreover, all relevant factors for media activity (the media environment) are taken into account.

Pragmatism: Pragmatism is a philosophical paradigm focusing on specific acts. Through the problem-solving processes, thinking results and can be expressed with language. Pragmatical approaches integrate the definition of the situation and contextual factors. Thus, pragmatism stands aloof from the rationalistic paradigm.

Semiotisation: Semiotisation describes the process of a syntactical reduction and semantical abstraction of sensual perceptions through media. Every media technology (e.g. print, radio, television, digital media) semioticise sensual perceptions (e.g. noises, colours, movements, touches) to mediatise them. Media technologies work with the use of syntactical reduction. Furthermore, digital media operates with semantical data, containing semioticised information about the syntactical data. This enables digital media to interpret and abstract data to new information.

Theorem of Competence: The theorem of competence is the foundation of German media competence discourse. It has been brought into media education by the work of Dieter Baacke and refers to enlightenment ideals, such as autonomy, emancipation, critical ability and self-determined activities.

ENDNOTES

1 Media competence is literally translated from the German term "Medienkompetenz". This is not comparable with the term "competence" used in the Anglo-American discourse on media literacy.

2 For example, Baacke (1996): media critique, media knowledge, media use and media creativity; Pöttinger (1997): perception competence, use competence and action competence; Schorb (1997): assessment, knowledge, acting (translated by the authors).

3 Gerhard Tulodziecki already pointed out the relation between literacy and pragmatism: "the understanding of literacy is based for example on insights of cultural studies or on the concept of pragmatism and is a modern concept of education in an information and knowledge society." (2012, p. 50).

4 One Exception is the approach by Bruce (1997), who constructed an evidence-based model that abstracts the action to higher categories.

Compilation of References

Bundy, A. (Ed.). (2004). Australian and New Zealand Information Literacy Framework. Adelaide: Australian and New Zeeland Institute for Information Literacy. Retrieved from http://www.caul.edu.au/content/upload/files/info-literacy/InfoLiteracyFramework.pdf

Abdel-Kader, K. (2006). The Impact of information and communication technology on economic growth in MENA countries. *EUI Working Papers, 2006/31*, 1-29.

Abolfazli, S., Sanaei, Z., Gani, A., Xia, F., & Yang, L. T. (2014). Rich mobile applications: Genesis, taxonomy, and open issues. *Journal of Network and Computer Applications, 40*, 345–362. doi:10.1016/j.jnca.2013.09.009

Abouserie, R. (1994). Sources and levels of stress in relation to locus of control and self-esteem in university students. *Educational Psychology, 14*(3), 323–330. doi:10.1080/0144341940140306

Acaso, M. (2007). *Esto no son las torres gemelas: cómo aprender a leer la televisión y otras imágenes*. Madrid: Catarata.

Ala-Mutka, K. (2011). *Mapping digital competence: Towards a conceptual understanding*. Sevilha: JRC-IPTS.

Alexanderson, P. (2004). Peripheral awareness and smooth notification: the use of natural sounds in process control work. In *Proceedings of the third Nordic conference on Human-computer interaction* (pp. 281-284). New York: ACM. doi:10.1145/1028014.1028057

Alleman, J., Hunt, C., Michaels, D., Mueller, D., Rappaport, P., & Taylor, L. (1994). *Telecommunications and economic development: empirical evidence from Southern Africa*. Paper presented at 10th Biennial International Telecommunications Society Meeting. Sydney.

Allen, D. K., & Shoard, M. (2005). Spreading the load: mobile information and communications technologies and their effect on information overload. *Information Research, 10*(2).

American Library Association. (2000). *Information literacy competency standards for higher education*. Retrieved May 8, 2016, from http://www.ala.org/acrl/sites/ala.org.acrl/files/content/standards/standards.pdf

Amin, M. A., Bakar, K. B. A., & Al-Hashimi, H. (2013). A review of mobile cloud computing architecture and challenges to enterprise users. In *GCC Conference and Exhibition (GCC), 2013 7th IEEE* (pp. 240-244). Piscataway, NJ: IEEE. doi:10.1109/IEEEGCC.2013.6705783

Anderson, C. (2010). In the Next Industrial Revolution, Atoms are the New Bits. *Wired Magazine, 1*(25).

Anderson, C. (2012). *Makers: The New Industrial Revolution* (1st ed.). New York: Crown Business.

Anderson, C., & Curtin, M. (2002). Writing cultural history. The challenge of radio and television. In N. Brügger & S. Kolstrup (Eds.), *Media history. Theories, methods, analysis* (pp. 15–32). Aarhus: University Press.

Andrejevic, M. (2013). *Infoglut: How Too Much Information Is Changing the Way We Think and Know*. London: Routledge.

Andrews, P., Paniagua, J., & Torsi, S. (2013). Katies Swiss Trip: A Study of Personal Event Models for Photo Sharing. *International Journal on Semantic Web and Information Systems, 9*(3), 42–56. doi:10.4018/ijswis.2013070103

Area, M., & Ribeiro, M. T. (2012). From Solid to Liquid: New Literacies to the Cultural Changes of Web 2.0. *Comunicar, 38*(38), 13–20. doi:10.3916/C38-2012-02-01

Ash, J. (2015). Sensation, Network, and the GIF: Toward an Allotropic Account of Affect. In K. Hillis, S. Paasonen, & M. Petit (Eds.), *Networked Affect* (pp. 119–113). Cambridge, MA: The MIT Press.

Aspen Media Literacy Institute. (2003). *Literacy for the 21ᵗʰ century. An overview & orientation guide to media literacy education*. Retrieved May 24, 2016, from http://www.medialit.org/sites/default/files/mlk/01_MLKorientation.pdf

Avrahami, D., Fussel, S. R., & Hudson, S. E. (2008, November 8-12). IM Waiting: Timing and Responsiveness in Semi-Synchronous Communication. *Proceeding of the CSCW'08*, San Diego, California, USA (pp. 285-294).

Ayyagari, R., Grover, V., & Purvis, R. (2011). Technostress: Technological antecedents and implications. *Management Information Systems Quarterly, 35*(4), 831–858.

Azuma, R. T. (1999). The challenge of making augmented reality work outdoors. *Mixed reality: Merging real and virtual worlds*, 379-390.

Azuma, R., Hoff, B., Neely, H., III, & Sarfaty, R. (1999, March). A motion-stabilized outdoor augmented reality system. In Virtual Reality, 1999. Proceedings., IEEE (pp. 252-259). IEEE. doi:10.1109/VR.1999.756959

Azuma, R. T. (1997). A survey of augmented reality. *Presence (Cambridge, Mass.), 6*(4), 355–385. doi:10.1162/pres.1997.6.4.355

Azuma, R., Baillot, Y., Behringer, R., Feiner, S., Julier, S., & MacIntyre, B. (2001). Recent advances in augmented reality. *Computer Graphics and Applications, IEEE, 21*(6), 34–47. doi:10.1109/38.963459

Baacke, D. (1998). *Zum Konzept der Operationalisierung von Medienkompetenz.* Retrieved May, 6, 2016, from http://www.produktive-medienarbeit.de/ressourcen/bibliothek/fachartikel/baacke_operationalisierung.shtml

Baacke, D. (1980). *Kommunikation und Kompetenz. Grundlegung einer Didaktik der Kommunikation und ihrer Medien* (3rd ed.). München: Juventa.

Bailey, B. P., & Konstan, J. A. (2006). On the need for attention-aware systems: Measuring effects of interruption on task performance, error rate, and affective state. *Computers in Human Behavior, 22*(4), 685–708. doi:10.1016/j.chb.2005.12.009

Bakker, S., van den Hoven, E., & Eggen, B. (2010). Design for the Periphery. *EuroHaptics, 2010,* 71.

Baliamoune-Lutz, M. (2003). An analysis of the determinants and effects of ICT diffusion in developing countries. *Information Technology for Development, 10*(3), 151–169. doi:10.1002/itdj.1590100303

Baltagi, B. H. (2008). *Econometric analysis of panel data* (4th ed.). West Sussex, UK: John Wiley.

Barley, S. R., Meyerson, D. E., & Grodal, S. (2011). E-mail as a source and symbol of stress. *Organization Science, 22*(4), 887–906. doi:10.1287/orsc.1100.0573

Baron, N. S. (2008). *Always On: Language in an Online and Mobile World.* New York: Oxford University Press. doi:10.1093/acprof:oso/9780195313055.001.0001

Barranquero-Carretero, A. (2013). *Slow media.* Comunicación, cambio social y sostenibilidad en la era del torrente mediático. *Palabra Clave, 16*(2), 419–448. doi:10.5294/pacla.2013.16.2.6

Barry, A. M. (1997). *Visual intelligence: Perception, image, and manipulation in visual communication.* SUNY Press.

Barthes, R. (1992). *La cámara lúcida, Nota sobre la fotografía.* Barcelona: Paidós Comunicación.

Barth, S. (2002). *Mädchenlektüren: Lesediskurse im 18. und 19. Jahrhundert.* New York, NY: Campus Verlag.

Bates, M. J. (2010). Information behavior. In *Encyclopedia of Library and Information Sciences* (pp. 2381–2391). New York: CRC Press.

Bauman, Z. (2012). *Modernidad Líquida,* Madrid: Fondo de cultura Económica de España.

Bauman, Z. (2004). *Identity. Conversations with Benedetto Vecchi.* Cambridge, UK: Polity Press.

Bauman, Z. (2007). *Liquid Times: Living in an age of uncertainty.* Cambridge, UK: Polity Press.

Baumeister, R. F., & Leary, M. R. (1995). The need to belong: Desire of interpersonal attachments as a fundamental human motivation. *Psychological Bulletin, 3*(3), 497–529. doi:10.1037/0033-2909.117.3.497 PMID:7777651

Baumer, E. P. S., Adams, P., Khovanskaya, V. D., Liao, T. C., Smith, M. E., Sosik, V. S., & Williams, K. (2013). Limiting, leaving, and (re)lapsing: An exploration of Facebook non-use practices and experiences.*Proceedings of the SIGCHI Conference on Human Factors in Computing Systems* (pp. 3257-3266). New York: ACM. doi:10.1145/2470654.2466446

Bawden, D. (2001). Information and digital literacies: A review of concepts. *The Journal of Documentation, 57*(2), 218–259. doi:10.1108/EUM0000000007083

Bawden, D. (2008). Origins and concepts of digital literacy. In C. Lankshear & M. Knobel (Eds.), *Digital Literacies: Concepts, Policies & Practices* (pp. 17–32). New York, NY: Peter Lang Publishing, Inc.

Bawden, D. (2008). Origins and concepts of digital literacy. In C. Lankshear & M. Knobel (Eds.), *Digital Literacies: Concepts, Policies and Practices* (pp. 17–32). New York, NY: Peter Lang.

Bawden, D., Holtham, C., & Courtney, N. (1999). Perspectives on information overload. *Aslib Proceedings, 51*(8), 249–255. doi:10.1108/EUM0000000006984

Bawden, D., & Robinson, L. (2009). The dark side of information: Overload, anxiety and other paradoxes and pathologies. *Journal of Information Science, 35*(2), 180–191. doi:10.1177/0165551508095781

Baym, N. K. (2010). *Personal connections in the digital age.* Cambridge, UK: Polity Press.

Bazin, A. (1990). *Qué es el cine, cap. Ontología de la imagen Fotográfica.* Madrid: RIALP.

Benselin, J. C., & Ragsdell, G. (2016). Information overload: The differences that age makes. *Journal of Librarianship and Information Science, 48*(3), 1–14. doi:10.1177/0961000614566341

Bergamaschi, S., & Leiba, B. (2010). Information overload. *IEEE Internet Computing, 14*(6), 10–13. doi:10.1109/MIC.2010.140

Bernstein, R., & Madlener, R. (2008). The impact of disaggregated ICT capital on electricity intensity of production: econometric analysis of major European industries. *FCN Working Paper, 4/2008,* 1-31.

Best, D. (1996a). Business process and information management. In Best (Ed.), The fourth resource: Information and its management. Hampshire, UK: Aslib/Gower.

Best, D. (1996b). *The fourth resource: Information and its management.* Hampshire, UK: Aslib/Gower.

Beuren, I. (1998). *Gerenciamento da informação: um recurso estratégico no processo de gestão empresarial.* São Paulo: Atlas.

Compilation of References

Bilandzic, M., & Foth, M. (2012). A review of locative media, mobile and embodied spatial interaction. *International Journal of Human-Computer Studies*, *70*(1), 66–71. doi:10.1016/j.ijhcs.2011.08.004

Birnholtz, J., Guillory, J., Hancock, J. T., & Bazarova, N. (2010, Feb. 6-10). "on my way": Deceptive Texting and Interpersonal Awareness Narratives. *Proceedings of the 2010 ACM conference on Computer supported cooperative work*, Savannah, Georgia, USA, 1-4. doi:10.1145/1718918.1718920

Birnholtz, J., Reynolds, L., Smith, M., & Hancock, J. (2013). Everyone Has To Do It: A joint action approach to managing social inattention. *Computers in Human Behavior*, *29*(6), 2230–2238. doi:10.1016/j.chb.2013.05.004

Blikstein, P. (2014). Digital Fabrication and 'Making' in Education: The Democratization of Invention. In J. Walter-Herrmann & C. Büching (Eds.), *FabLabs: Of Machines, Makers and Inventors*. Bielefeld: Transcript-Verlag.

Borowsky, P., Vogel, B., & Wunder, H. (1989). Einführung in die Geschichtswissenschaft I. Grundprobleme, Arbeitsorganisation, Hilfsmittel (6th ed.). Opladen: Leske + Budrich.

Bowen, S., & Petrelli, D. (2011). Remembering today tomorrow: Exploring the human-centred design of digital mementos. *International Journal of Human-Computer Studies*, *69*(5), 324–337. doi:10.1016/j.ijhcs.2010.12.005

Brandimonte, M., Einstein, G. O., & McDaniel, M. A. (1996). Prospective Memory. Theory and Applications. Mahwah, NJ: Lawrence Erlbaum Associates.

Bray, D. A. (2008, June). *Information Pollution, Knowledge Overload, Limited Attention Spans, and Our Responsibilities as IS Professionals*. Paper presented at the Global Information Technology Management Association (GITMA) World Conference, Atlanta, GA.

Brazil, E., & Fernstrom, M. (2007). *Investigating ambient auditory information systems*. Academic Press.

Breitenbach, M., Aderibigbe, O., & Muzungu, D. (2005). *The Impact of information and communication technology (ICT) on economic growth in South Africa: Analysis of evidence*. Retrieved from http://www.essa.org.za/download/2005Conference/Breitenbach.pdf

Brewster, S. A., & Brown, L. M. (2004a). Non-visual information display using tactons. In CHI'04 extended abstracts on Human factors in computing systems (787-788). New York: ACM. doi:10.1145/985921.985936

Brewster, S., & Brown, L. M. (2004b). Tactons: structured tactile messages for non-visual information display. In *Proceedings of the fifth conference on Australasian user interface* (vol. 28, pp. 15-23). Australian Computer Society, Inc.

Brewster, S., & Constantin, A. (2010). Tactile feedback for ambient awareness in mobile interactions. In *Proceedings of the 24th BCS Interaction Specialist Group Conference* (pp. 412-417). British Computer Society.

British Educational Communications and Technology Agency (BECTA). (2010). *Harnessing Technology Schools Survey 2010.*

Brock, G., & Sutherland, E. (2000). Telecommunications and economic growth in the former USSR. *East European Quarterly, 34*(3), 319–335.

Brod, C. (1984). *Technostress: The Human Cost of the Computer Revolution.* Reading: Addison Wesley.

Brown, S. (2012). Coping with information obesity: A diet for information professionals. *Business Information Review, 29*(3), 168–173. doi:10.1177/0266382112454355

Bruce, C. (1997). *The seven faces of information literacy.* Adelaide: Auslib Press.

Bruner, J. (1987). Life as narrative. *Social Research,* 11–32.

Bruner, J. (1991). The narrative construction of reality. *Critical Inquiry, 18*(1), 1–21. doi:10.1086/448619

Burgess, A., Jackson, T., & Edwards, J. (2005). Email training significantly reduces email defects. *International Journal of Information Management, 25*(1), 71–83. doi:10.1016/j.ijinfomgt.2004.10.004

Burke, C. S., Stagl, K. C., Salas, E., Pierce, L., & Kendall, D. (2006). Understanding team adaptation: A conceptual analysis and model. *The Journal of Applied Psychology, 91*(6), 1189–1207. doi:10.1037/0021-9010.91.6.1189 PMID:17100478

Butcher, H. (1995). Information overload in management and business. In *IEE Colloquium Digest.* London: IEE. Doi:10.1049/ic:19951426

Buttfield-Addison, P., Lueg, C., Ellis, L., & Manning, J. (2012). Everything goes into or out of the iPad: the iPad, information scraps and personal information management. In *Proceedings of the 24th Australian Computer-Human Interaction Conference* (pp. 61-67). New York: ACM. doi:10.1145/2414536.2414546

Calvo, R. A., & Peters, D. (2013). The irony and re-interpretation of our quantified self. In *Proceedings of the 25th Australian Computer-Human Interaction Conference: Augmentation, Application, Innovation, Collaboration* (pp. 367-370). New York: ACM. doi:10.1145/2541016.2541070

Camden, C., Motley, M. T., & Wilson, A. (1984). White Lies in Interpersonal Communication: A Taxonomy and Preliminary Investigation of Social Motivations. *Western Journal of Speech Communication, 48*(4), 309–325. doi:10.1080/10570318409374167

Cannon-Bowers, J. A., Salas, E., Blickensderfer, E., & Bowers, C. A. (1998). The impact of cross-training and workload on team functioning: A replication and extension of initial findings. *Human Factors: The Journal of the Human Factors and Ergonomics Society, 40*(1), 92–101. doi:10.1518/001872098779480550

Compilation of References

Caragliu, A., Del Bo, C., & Nijkamp, P. (2011). Smart cities in Europe. *Journal of Urban Technology*, *18*(2), 65–82. doi:10.1080/10630732.2011.601117

Carr, N. (2010). *The Shallows: What the Internet Is Doing to Our Brains*. New York: W. W. Norton & Company.

Castells, M. (1996). The Information Age: Economy. In *The Rise of the Network Society*. Malden, MA: Blackwell.

Cecchinato, M. E., Bird, J., & Cox, A. L. (2014). Personalised Email Tools: A Solution to Email Overload? In *CHI'14 Workshop on Personalised Behaviour Change Technologies* (pp. 1–4). ACM.

Chalfen, R. (1987). *Snapshot versions of life*. Madison, WI: University of Wisconsin Press.

Chan, M. (2014, August). Multimodal Connectedness and Quality of Life: Examining the Influences of Technology Adoption and Interpersonal Communication on Well-Being Across the Life Span. *Journal of Computer-Mediated Communication. Online First, 12*. doi:10.1111/jcc4.12089

Cheever, N. A., Rosen, L. D., Carrier, L. M., & Chavez, A. (2014). Out of sight is not out of mind: The impact of restricting wireless mobile device use on anxiety levels among low, moderate and high users. *Computers in Human Behavior*, *37*, 290–297. doi:10.1016/j.chb.2014.05.002

Chen, L. (2015). Mobile Technostress. In Y. Zheng, (Ed.), Encyclopedia of Mobile Phone Behavior (pp. 732-744). Hershey, PA, USA: IGI Global.

Chen, H. T., & Kuo, E. C. Y. (1985). Telecommunications and economic development in Singapore. *Telecommunications Policy*, *9*(3), 240–244. doi:10.1016/0308-5961(85)90055-2

Chenu-Abente, R., Zaihrayeu, I., & Giunchiglia, F. (2013). A Semantic-Enabled Engine for Mobile Social Networks. In ESWC (Satellite Events) (pp. 298-299). doi:10.1007/978-3-642-41242-4_50

Chen, W., & Lee, K. (2013). Sharing, liking, commenting, and distressed? The pathway between Facebook interaction and psychological distress. *Cyberpsychology, Behavior, and Social Networking*, *16*(10), 728–734. doi:10.1089/cyber.2012.0272 PMID:23745614

Chi, H. L., Kang, S. C., & Wang, X. (2013). Research trends and opportunities of augmented reality applications in architecture, engineering, and construction. *Automation in Construction*, *33*, 116–122. doi:10.1016/j.autcon.2012.12.017

Cho, J., Ramgolam, D. I., Schaefer, K. M., & Sandlin, A. N. (2011). The Rate and Delay in Overload: An Investigation of Communication Overload and Channel Synchronicity on Identification and Job Satisfaction. *Journal of Applied Communication Research*, *39*(1), 38–54. doi: 10.1080/00909882.2010.536847

Chomsky, N. (2003). *Sobre la naturaleza y el lenguaje*. Madrid: Cambridge University Press.

Choo, C. (2003). *Gestão de informação para a organização inteligente: A arte de explorar o meio ambiente*. Lisboa: Editorial Caminho.

Choo, C. W., Bergeron, P., Deltor, B., & Heaton, L. (2008). Information culture and information use : An exploratory study of three organizations. *Journal of the American Society for Information Science and Technology*, *59*(5), 792–804. doi:10.1002/asi.20797

Cho, Y., Lee, J., & Kim, T. Y. (2007). The Impact of ICT investment and energy price on industrial electricity demand: Dynamic growth model approach. *Energy Policy*, *35*(9), 4730–4738. doi:10.1016/j.enpol.2007.03.030

Church, K., & de Oliveira, R. (2013, August 27-30). *What's up with WhatsApp?Comparing Mobile Instant Messaging* Behaviors with Traditional SMS. Proceeding of the *Mobile HCI '13*, Munich, Germany (pp. 352-361). doi:10.1145/2493190.2493225

CILIP. (2012). *Information literacy skills*. Retrieved May 8, 2016, from http://www.cilip.org.uk/sites/default/files/documents/Information%20literacy%20skills.pdf

Coclar, A. N., & Sahin, Y. L. (2011). Technostress levels of social network site users based on ICTs in Turkey. *European Journal of Soil Science*, *23*(2), 171–182.

Coen, C. A., & Schnackenberg, A. (2012). Complex systems methods for studying multiteam systems. In S. J. Zaccaro, M. A. Marks, & L. A. DeChurch (Eds.), *Multiteam systems: An organization form for dynamic and complex environments* (pp. 459–486). New York: Routledge.

Colecchia, A., & Schreyer, P. (2002). ICT investment and economic growth in the 1990s: Is the United States a unique case? A comparative study of nine OECD countries. *Review of Economic Dynamics*, *5*(2), 408–442. doi:10.1006/redy.2002.0170

Collard, F., Feve, P., & Portier, P. (2005). Electricity consumption and ICT in the French service sector. *Energy Economics*, *27*(3), 541–550. doi:10.1016/j.eneco.2004.12.002

Conroy, D. E., Yang, C. H., & Maher, J. P. (2014). Behavior change techniques in top-ranked mobile apps for physical activity. *American Journal of Preventive Medicine*, *46*(6), 649–652. doi:10.1016/j.amepre.2014.01.010 PMID:24842742

Consolvo, S., Klasnja, P., McDonald, D. W., Avrahami, D., Froehlich, J., LeGrand, L., & Landay, J. A. et al. (2008). Flowers or a robot army? encouraging awareness & activity with personal, mobile displays. In *Proceedings of the 10th international conference on Ubiquitous computing* (pp. 54-63). New York: ACM.

Cooke, N. J., Kiekel, P. A., Salas, E., Stout, R. J., Bowers, C., & Cannon-Bowers, J. A. (2003). Measuring team knowledge: A window to the cognitive underpinnings of team performance. *Group Dynamics*, *7*(3), 179–199. doi:10.1037/1089-2699.7.3.179

Cornella, A. (2008). Principio de la intoxicación. In J. J. Fernández García (Ed.), *Más allá de Google* (pp. 19–22). Barcelona: Infonomía.

Costa, J. (1991). *La fotografía entre sumisión y subversión*. México: ed. Trillas.

Compilation of References

Coultas, C. W., Driskell, T., Burke, C. S., & Salas, E. (2014). A conceptual review of emergent state measurement: Current problems, future solutions. *Small Group Research, 45*(6), 671-703. doi:1046496414552285

Craig, A. B. (2013). *Understanding augmented reality: Concepts and applications*. Newnes.

Crenshaw, D. (2008). *The Myth of Multitasking: How "Doing It All" Gets Nothing Done*. San Francisco: Jossey-Bass.

Cronin, F., Parker, E., Colleran, E., & Gold, M. (1991). Telecommunications infrastructure and economic growth: An analysis of causality. *Telecommunications Policy, 15*(6), 529–535. doi:10.1016/0308-5961(91)90007-X

Cronin, F., Parker, E., Colleran, E., & Gold, M. (1993). Telecommunications infrastructure investment and economic development. *Telecommunications Policy, 17*(6), 415–430. doi:10.1016/0308-5961(93)90013-S

Csikszentmihalyi, M. (2013). *Flow: The psychology of happiness*. New York: Random House.

Cunningham, M., Harris, S., Kerr, K., & McEune, R. (2003). *New technologies supporting teaching and learning*. Slough: National Foundation for Educational Research.

Dabbish, L. A., & Kraut, R. E. (2006). Email overload at work: an analysis of factors associated with email strain. *Proceedings of the 2006 20th anniversary conference on Computer Supported Cooperative Work ICSCW '06* (pp. 431–440). New York: ACM. doi:10.1145/1180875.1180941

Dafonte, A. (2014). The Key Elements of Viral Advertising. From Motivation to Emotion in the Most Shared Videos. *Comunicar, 43*, 199–207. doi:10.3916/C43-2014-20

Damasio, A. (2012). *Self comes to mind: Constructing the conscious brain*. New York: Vintage.

Datta, A., & Agarwal, S. (2004). Telecommunications and economic growth: A panel data approach. *Applied Economics, 36*(15), 1649–1654. doi:10.1080/0003684042000218552

Daudelin, M. W. (1996). Learning from experience through reflection. *Organizational Dynamics, 24*(3), 36–48. doi:10.1016/S0090-2616(96)90004-2

Davenport, T. (1997). *Information ecology: Mastering the information and knowledge environment*. New York: Oxford University Press.

Davenport, T. H., & Beck, J. C. (2001). *The Attention Economy: Understanding the New Currency of Business*. Cambridge, MA: Harvard Business School Press.

Davenport, T., Marchand, D., & Dickson, T. (2004). *Dominando a gestão da informação*. Porto Alegre: Bookmann.

Davis, F. D., Jr. (1986). *A technology acceptance model for empirically testing new end-user information systems: Theory and results* (Doctoral dissertation). Massachusetts Institute of Technology.

de Souza e Silva, A. (2006). From Cyber to Hybrid: Mobile Technologies as Interfaces of Hybrid Spaces. *Space and Culture*, *9*(3), 261–278. doi:10.1177/1206331206289022

Dearlove, D. (1998). *Key management decisions: Tools and techniques of the executive decision-maker* (1st ed.). Wiltshire: Financial Times/Pitman.

DeChurch, L. A., & Mesmer-Magnus, J. R. (2010a). The cognitive underpinnings of effective teamwork: A meta-analysis. *The Journal of Applied Psychology*, *95*(1), 32–53. doi:10.1037/a0017328 PMID:20085405

DeChurch, L. A., & Mesmer-Magnus, J. R. (2010b). Measuring shared team mental models: A meta-analysis. *Group Dynamics*, *14*(1), 1–14. doi:10.1037/a0017455

Desmet, P., & Hassenzahl, M. (2012). Towards happiness: Possibility-driven design. In *Human-computer interaction: The agency perspective* (pp. 3–27). Berlin: Springer. doi:10.1007/978-3-642-25691-2_1

Deuze, M. (2012). *Media Life*. Cambridge, UK: Polity Press.

Dewan, S., & Kraemer, K. L. (2000). Information technology and productivity: Evidence from country-level data. *Management Science*, *46*(4), 548–562. doi:10.1287/mnsc.46.4.548.12057

Dewey, J. (1997). *Democracy and education. An introduction to the philosophy of education.* New York, NY: The Free Press.

Dewey, J. (2005). *Art as experience*. London: Penguin.

Dholakia, R., & Harlam, B. (1994). Telecommunications and economic development: Econometric analyses of the US experience. *Telecommunications Policy*, *18*(6), 470–477. doi:10.1016/0308-5961(94)90015-9

Di Loreto, I., & Gouaich, A. (2011). Facebook Games: The Point Where Tribes And Casual Games Meet. *GET'10: International Conference Game and Entertainment Technologies*.

Días, P., & Teixeira-Botelho, I. (2014). Is the Second Screen becoming the First? An exploratory study of emerging multi-screening practices.*Proceedings of the International Conference on Computer Graphics, Visualization, Computer Vision and Image Processing*. Lisbon: IADIS.

Díaz Arias, R. (2015). Curaduría periodística, una forma de reconstruir el espacio público. *Estudios sobre el Mensaje Periodístico, 21*, 61-80.

Díaz-Nosty, B. (2013). *La prensa en el nuevo ecosistema informativo. ¡Que paren las rotativas!* Barcelona: Ariel-Fundación Telefónica.

Dielman, T. E., Campanelli, P. C., Shope, J. T., & Butchart, A. T. (1987). Susceptibility to peer pressure, self-esteem, and health locus of control as correlates of adolescent substance abuse. *Health Education Quarterly*, *14*(2), 207–221. doi:10.1177/109019818701400207 PMID:3597110

Doctorow, C. (2009). Writing in the Age of Distraction. *Locus Magazine*, *62*(1), 29-35.

Compilation of References

Dodgson, M., & Gann, D. (2014). *Inovação* (1st ed.). Porto Alegre: L&PM Pocket Encyclopaedia.

Doughty, M., Rowland, D., & Lawson, S. (2012). Who is on your sofa? TV audience communities and second screening social networks. In *Proceedings of the 10th European conference on Interactive TV and video—EuroiTV* (pp. 79–86). New York: Association for Computing Machinery. doi:10.1145/2325616.2325635

Dourish, P. (2006, November). Re-space-ing place: place and space ten years on. In *Proceedings of the 2006 20th anniversary conference on Computer supported cooperative work* (pp. 299-308). New York: ACM. doi:10.1145/1180875.1180921

Doval, M. (2012). Por una dieta informativa más variada y sana. *Aceprensa*. Retrieved from http://www.aceprensa.com/articles/por-una-dieta-informativa-mas-variada-y-sana/

Driscoll, J. C., & Kraay, A. C. (1998). Consistent covariance matrix estimation with spatially dependent panel data. *The Review of Economics and Statistics*, *80*(4), 549–560. doi:10.1162/003465398557825

Dubois, P. (1994). *El acto fotográfico, De la representación a la recepción*. Barcelona: Paidós Comunicación.

Ducheneaut, N., & Bellotti, V. (2001). Email as habitat: An exploration of embedded personal information management. *Interaction*, *8*(5), 30–38. doi:10.1145/382899.383305

Duncheon, J. C., & Tierney, W. G. (2013). Changing conceptions of time implications for educational research and practice. *Review of Educational Research*.

Earl, M. (1998). *Information management: The organizational dimension*. New York: Oxford University Press.

Eckler, P., & Bolls, P. (2011). Spreading the Virus: Emotional Tone of Viral Advertising and its Effect on Forwarding Intention and Attitudes. *Journal of Interactive Advertising*, *11*(2), 1–11. doi:10.1080/15252019.2011.10722180

Eco, U. (1990). *Drift and Unlimited Semiosis* (Vol. 1). Indiana University.

Edmondson, A. (1999). Psychological safety and learning behavior in work teams. *Administrative Science Quarterly*, *44*(2), 350–383. doi:10.2307/2666999

Edmunds, A., & Morris, A. (2000). The Problem of Information Overload in Business Organisations: A Review of the Literature. *International Journal of Information Management*, *20*(1), 17–28. doi:10.1016/S0268-4012(99)00051-1

Eisenberg, M. B., & Berkowitz, R. E. (1990). *Information problem-solving. The big six skills approach to library & information skills instruction*. Norwood, NJ: Ablex Pub. Corp.

Elliot, A. J., Maier, M. A., Moller, A. C., Friedman, R., & Meinhardt, J. (2007). Color and psychological functioning. *Current Directions in Psychological Science*, *16*(5), 250–254. doi:10.1111/j.1467-8721.2007.00514.x PMID:17324089

Ellis, A. P. (2006). System breakdown: The role of mental models and transactive memory in the relationship between acute stress and team performance. *Academy of Management Journal, 49*(3), 576–589. doi:10.5465/AMJ.2006.21794674

Ellwart, T. (2011). Assessing coordination in human groups: Concepts and methods. In M. Boos, M. Kolbe, P. Kappeler, & T. Ellwart (Eds.), *Coordination in human and primate groups* (pp. 119–135). Heidelberg, Germany: Springer. doi:10.1007/978-3-642-15355-6_7

Ellwart, T., Bündgens, S., & Rack, O. (2013). Managing knowledge exchange and identification in age diverse teams. *Journal of Managerial Psychology, 28*(7/8), 950–972. doi:10.1108/JMP-06-2013-0181

Ellwart, T., Happ, C., Gurtner, A., & Rack, O. (2015, July). Managing information overload in virtual teams: Effects of a structured online team adaptation on cognition and performance. *European Journal of Work and Organizational Psychology, 5*(5), 812–826. doi:10.1080/13594 32X.2014.1000873

Ellwart, T., Konradt, U., & Rack, O. (2014). Team mental models of expertise location: Validation of a field survey measure. *Small Group Research, 45*(2), 119–153. doi:10.1177/1046496414521303

Ellwart, T., Peiffer, H., Matheis, G., & Happ, C. (in press). Möglichkeiten und Grenzen eines Online Team Awareness Tools (OnTEAM) in Adaptationsprozessen[Opportunities and limitations of an online team awareness tool (OnTEAM) in adaptation processes]. *Wirtschaftspsychologie*.

Elmqvist, N., Moere, A. V., Jetter, H. C., Cernea, D., Reiterer, H., & Jankun-Kelly, T. J. (2011). Fluid interaction for information visualization. *Information Visualization*.

EMC, & IDC. (2014). The digital universe of opportunities: rich data and the increasing value of the internet of things. Retrieved from http://www.emc.com/leadership/digital-universe/2014iview/index.htm

Eppler, M. J. (2015). Information quality and information overload: The promises and perils of the information age. In L. Cantoni & J. A. Danowski (Eds.), *Communication and Technology* (pp. 215–232). Berlin, Boston: De Gruyter; doi:10.1515/9783110271355-013

Eppler, M. J., & Mengis, J. (2004). The Concept of Information Overload: A Review of Literature from Organization Science, Marketing, Accounting, MIS, and related Disciplines. *The Information Society, 20*(5), 325–344. doi:10.1080/01972240490507974

Eshet-Alkalai, Y. (2004). Digital Literacy. A Conceptual Framework for Survival Skills in the Digital Era. *Journal of Educational Multimedia and Hypermedia, 13*(1), 93–106.

European Parliament and the Council. (2006). Recommendation of the European Parliament and of the Council of 18 December 2006 on key competences for lifelong learning. *Official Journal of the European Union, L, 394*(310).

Compilation of References

Evangelinos, G., & Holley, D. (2014a). Developing a Digital Competence Self-Assessment Toolkit for Nursing Students. In A.M. Teixeira, A. Szűcs & I. Mázár (Eds.), *E-learning at Work and the Workplace. From Education to Employment and Meaningful Work with ICT E-learning at Work and the Workplace*, (pp.206–212). European Distance and E-Learning Network (EDEN), Annual Conference, Zagreb.

Evangelinos, G., & Holley, D. (2014b). A Qualitative Exploration of the EU Digital Competence (DIGCOMP) Framework: A Case Study within Healthcare Education. In G. Vincenti, A. Bucciero & C. Vaz de Carvalho (Eds.), *E-Learning, E-Education, and Online-Training (ELEOT) First International Conference, Lecture Notes of the Institute for Computer Sciences, Social Informatics and Telecommunications Engineering*, (pp.85–92). Cham: Springer International Publishing. doi:10.1007/978-3-319-13293-8_11

Evangelinos, G., & Holley, D. (2015). Embedding digital competences in the curriculum: a case study on student-experience of an online technology-enhanced, activity-based learning design. *Proceedings of the European Distance and E-Learning Network 2015 Annual Conference*. Retrieved 6 October 2016 from http://arro.anglia.ac.uk/577015/

Evaristo, J. R. B. (1993). *An empirical investigation of the impact of information characteristics and information technology on individual information load* (Unpublished doctoral thesis). Carlson School of Management, University of Minnesota, Minneapolis, MN.

Eychenne, F., & Neves, H. (2013). *Fab Lab: A Vanguarda da Nova Revolução Industrial*. Associação Fab Lab Brasil.

Falloon, G. (2014). What's going on behind the screens? Researching young students learning pathways using iPads. *Journal of Computer Assisted Learning*, *30*(4), 318–336. doi:10.1111/jcal.12044

Faraj, S., & Sproull, L. (2000). Coordinating expertise in software development teams. *Management Science*, *46*(12), 1554–1568. doi:10.1287/mnsc.46.12.1554.12072

Ferguson, R., Wilkinson, W., & Hill, R. (2000). Electricity use and economic development. *Energy Policy*, *28*(13), 923–934. doi:10.1016/S0301-4215(00)00081-1

Ferrari, A. (2012). *Digital Competence in practice: An analysis of frameworks*. Seville: JRC-IPTS.

Ferrari, A. (2013). *DIGCOMP: A framework for developing and understanding digital competence in Europe*. Seville: JRC-IPTS.

Fiedler, L., & Welpe, I. (2010). How do organizations remember? The influence of organizational structure on organizational memory. *Organization Studies*, *31*(4), 381–407. doi:10.1177/0170840609347052

Filos, E., & Banahan, E. P. (2001). Will the organisation disappear? The challenges of the new economy and future perspectives. In L. M. Camarinha-Matos, H. Afsharmanesh, & R. J. Rabelo (Eds.), *E-business and virtual enterprises: managing business-to-business cooperation* (pp. 3–20). Dordrecht: Kluwer Academic Publishers. doi:10.1007/978-0-387-35399-9_1

Fiore, S. M., Salas, E., Cuevas, H. M., & Bowers, C. A. (2003). Distributed coordination space: Toward a theory of distributed team process and performance. *Theoretical Issues in Ergonomics Science, 4*(3-4), 340–364. doi:10.1080/1463922021000049971

Flusser, V. (2001). *Hacia Una filosofía de la Fotografía*. Madrid: Editorial Síntesis.

Fogg, B. J. (2003). *Persuasive Technology: Using Computers to Change What We Think and Do*. San Francisco, CA: Morgan Kauffman.

Fontcuberta, J. (2011). Por un manifiesto postfotográfico. *Lavanguardia*. Retrieved from http://www.lavanguardia.com/cultura/20110511/54152218372/por-un-manifiesto-posfotografico.html

Fontcuberta, J. (2010). *La cámara de Pandora, la fotografía después de la fotografía*. Barcelona: Gustavo Gili.

Foote, N. (2004). *"Los Anti-fotógrafos"*. In D. Fogle (Ed.), *The last picture show: artistas que usan la fotografía. Tendencias conceptuales de 1960 a 1982. Catálogo de exposición*. Vigo: Fundación MARCO.

Freeman, J. (2009). Manifesto for a Slow Communication Movement. In *The Tyranny of E-mail: The Four-Thousand-Year Journey to Your Inbox* (pp. 190–203). New York: Simon & Schuster.

Frese, M., & Zapf, D. (1994). Action as the core of work psychology: A German approach. In H. C. Triandis, M. D. Dunnette, & L. M. Hough (Eds.), *Handbook of industrial and organizational psychology* (pp. 271–340). Palo Alto, CA: Consulting Psychologists Press.

Fu, J. S. (2013). ICT in Education: A Critical Literature Review and Its Implications. *International Journal of Education and Development using Information and Communication Technology, 9*(1), 112-125.

Fuglseth, A. M., & Sørebø, Ø. (2014). The effects of technostress within the context of employee use of ICT. *Computers in Human Behavior, 40*, 161–170. doi:10.1016/j.chb.2014.07.040

Furht, B. (Ed.). (2011). *Handbook of augmented reality*. Springer Science & Business Media. doi:10.1007/978-1-4614-0064-6

Furuhata, M., Dessouky, M., Ordóñez, F., Brunet, M. E., Wang, X., & Koenig, S. (2013). Ridesharing: The state-of-the-art and future directions. *Transportation Research Part B: Methodological, 57*, 28–46. doi:10.1016/j.trb.2013.08.012

Futschek, G. (2013). *Extreme didactic reduction in computational thinking education*. Paper presented at the 10th World Conference on Computers in Education, Toruń.

Gadamer, H. G. (1977). *Verdad y método I*. Salamanca: Sígueme.

Gallagher, W. (2009). *Rapt. Attention and the Focused Life*. New York: The Penguin Press.

Ganguin, S. (2004). *Medienkritik - Kernkompetenz unserer Gesellschaft. Ludwigsburger Beiträge zur Medienkritik*. Retrieved March 4, 2016, from http://www.ph-ludwigsburg.de/fileadmin/subsites/1b-mpxx-t-01/user_files/Online-Magazin/Ausgabe6/Ganguin6.pdf

Compilation of References

Ganguin, S. (2006). Vom Kritikbegriff zur Medienkritik. In H. Niesyto, M. Rath & H. Sowa (Eds.), Medienkritik heute. Grundlagen, Beispiele, Praxisfelder (pp. 71-86). München: kopaed.

Ganguin, S., & Sander, U. (2014). Zur Entwicklung von Medienkritik. In F. von Gross, D. M. Meister, & U. Sander (Eds.), *EEO. Enzyklopädie Erziehungswissenschaft Online*. Weinheim: Juventa Verlag.

Gapski, H., & Gräßer, L. (2007). Medienkompetenz im Web 2.0 – Lebensqualität als Zielperspektive. In L. Gräßer & M. Pohlschmidt (Eds.), Praxis Web 2.0. Potentiale für die Entwicklung von Medienkompetenz (pp. 11-34). Düsseldorf: kopaed.

Gapski, H. (2001). *Medienkompetenz. Eine Bestandsaufnahme und Vorüberlegungen zu einem systemtheoretischen Rahmenkonzept*. Wiesbaden: Westdt. Verl.

Gartner, G., & Ortag, F. (2012). *Advances in location-based services*. New York: Springer. doi:10.1007/978-3-642-24198-7

Garzonis, S., Jones, S., Jay, T., & O'Neill, E. (2009, April). Auditory icon and earcon mobile service notifications: intuitiveness, learnability, memorability and preference. In *Proceedings of the SIGCHI Conference on Human Factors in Computing Systems* (pp. 1513-1522). New York: ACM. doi:10.1145/1518701.1518932

Geldard, F. A. (1957). Adventures in tactile literacy. *The American Psychologist, 12*(3), 115–124. doi:10.1037/h0040416

Gentile, M. (2012). The importance of managing iPads in the classroom. *The Education Digest. Essential Readings Condensed for Quick Review, 78*(3), 11–13.

Gergen, K. J. (2002). The Challenge of Absent Presence. In J. Katz & M. Aakhus (Eds.), *Perpetual Contact: Mobile Communication, Private Talk, Public Performance* (pp. 227–241). Cambridge: Cambridge University Press. doi:10.1017/CBO9780511489471.018

Gershenfeld, N. (2005). *Fab: The Coming Revolution on Your Desktop: from Personal Computers to Personal Fabrication*. New York: Basic Books.

Gershenfeld, N. (2012). How to Make Almost Anything: The Digital Fabrication Revolution. *Foreign Affairs, 91*(6).

Gevers, J. M. P., Mohammed, S., & Baytalskaya, N. (2015). The conceptualization and measurement of pacing style. *Applied Psychology, 64*(3), 499–540. doi:10.1111/apps.12016

Gevers, J. M. P., Van Eerde, W., & Rutte, C. G. (2009). Team self-regulation and meeting deadlines in project teams: Antecedents and effects of temporal consensus. *European Journal of Work and Organizational Psychology, 18*(3), 295–321. doi:10.1080/13594320701693217

Giaccardi, E. (2003). *Principles of metadesign: Processes and levels of co-creation in the new design space* (Dissertation). University of Plymouth.

Gibson, J. J. (1966). *The senses considered as perceptual systems*. Boston: Houghton Mifflin Company.

Giglietto, F., & Selva, D. (2014). Second Screen and Participation: A Content Analysis on a Full Season Dataset of Tweets. *Journal of Communication, 64*(2), 260–277. doi:10.1111/jcom.12085

Gilster, P. (1997). *Digital literacy*. New York, NY: Wiley Computer Publications.

Gitlin, T. (2003). *Media Unlimited: How the Torrent of Images and Sounds Overwhelms Our Lives*. New York: Henry Holt and Company.

Giunchiglia, F., & Hume, A. (2013). A distributed entity directory. In *Extended Semantic Web Conference* (pp. 291-292). Berlin: Springer.

Glanz, K., Rimer, B., & Viswanath, K. (2002). *Health Behavior and Health Education*. San Francisco, USA: Wiley.

Gleick, J. (2011). The information: A history, a theory, a flood (1st ed.). St. Ives: 4th Estate.

Gleick, J. (2011). *The Information: A History, A Theory, A Flood*. London: Harper Collins.

Goldhaber, M. (1997). The Attention Economy and the Net. *First Monday, 2*(4). Retrieved from: http://firstmonday.org/article/view/519/440

Goleman, D. (2013). *Focus: The Hidden Driver of Excellence*. New York: Harper Collins.

González, A. M. (2013). Introducción: emociones y análisis social. In L. Flamarique & M. D'Oliveira-Martins (Eds.), Emociones y estilos de vida: radiografía de nuestro tiempo (pp. 9-24). Madrid: Biblioteca Nueva.

Gordon-Beckford, A. (2015). *Clinical Benefits of Aquarium Design*. Retrieved from http://www.sbid.org/2013/09/clinical-benefits-of-aquarium-design/

Graham, K. (2011). TechMatters: Happily "Evernote" After: Storing and Sharing Research in the Cloud. *LOEX Quarterly, 38*(1), 4.

Grandhi, S., & Jones, Q. (2010). Technology-mediated interruption management. *International Journal of Human-Computer Studies, 68*(5), 288–306. doi:10.1016/j.ijhcs.2009.12.005

Grintner, R. E., & Eldridge, M. (2001, September 16–20). y do tngrs luv 2 txt msg? *Proceedings of the 7thEuropean Conference on Computer-Supported Cooperative Work (ECSCW)*, Bonn, Germany (pp. 219–238).

Grintner, R. E., Palen, L., & Eldridge, M. (2006). Chatting with Teenagers: Considering the Place of Chat Technologies in Teen Life. *ACM Transactions on Computer-Human Interaction, 13*(4), 423–447. doi:10.1145/1188816.1188817

Grüner, G. (1967). Die didaktische Reduktion als Kernstück der Didaktik. *Die deutsche Schule, 59*(7/8), 414-430.

Compilation of References

Gupta, A., Sharda, R., & Greve, R. A. (2011). Youve got email! Does it really matter to process emails now or later? *Information Systems Frontiers, 13*(5), 637–653. doi:10.1007/s10796-010-9242-4

Gurtner, A., Tschan, F., Semmer, N. K., & Nägele, C. (2007). Getting groups to develop good strategies: Effects of reflexivity interventions on team process, team performance, and shared mental models. *Organizational Behavior and Human Decision Processes, 102*(2), 127–142. doi:10.1016/j.obhdp.2006.05.002

Gutiérrez, A., & Tyner, K. (2012). Media Education, Media Literacy and Digital Competence. *Comunicar, 38,* 31–39. doi:10.3916/C38-2012-02-03

Gwizdka, J. (2004, April 24-29). Email task management styles: the cleaners and the keepers. *Proceedings of theConference on Human Factors in Computing Systems,* Vienna, Austria (pp. 1235–1238). doi:10.1145/985921.986032

Haase, R. F., Ferreira, J. A., Fernandes, R. I., Santos, E. J. R., & Jome, L. M. (2015). Development and Validation of a Revised Measure of Individual Capacities for Tolerating Information Overload in Occupational Settings. *Journal of Career Assessment, 24*(1), 130–144. doi:10.1177/1069072714565615

Haase, R. F., Jome, L. M., Ferreira, J., Santos, E. J. R., Connacher, C. C., & Sendrowitz, K. (2014). Individual Differences in Capacity for Tolerating Information Overload Are Related to Differences in Culture and Temperament. *Journal of Cross-Cultural Psychology, 45*(5), 728–751. doi:10.1177/0022022113519852

Hacker, W. (2005). Allgemeine Arbeitspsychologie: Psychische Regulation von Wissens-, Denk- und körperlicher Arbeit [General industrial psychology. Mental regulation of knowledge work, mental work and physical work] (2nd ed.). Bern: Huber.

Hackman, J. R. (1987). The design of work teams. In J. W. Lorsch (Ed.), *Handbook of organizational behavior* (pp. 315–342). Englewood Cliffs, NJ: Prentice-Hall.

Hall, J. A., & Baym, N. K. (2012). Calling and texting (too much): Mobile maintenance expectations,(over)dependence, entrapment, and friendship satisfaction. *New Media & Society, 14*(2), 316–331. doi:10.1177/1461444811415047

Halskov, K., & Dalsgård, P. (2006). Inspiration card workshops. In *Proceedings of the 6th conference on Designing Interactive systems* (pp. 2-11). New York: ACM. doi:10.1145/1142405.1142409

Hammond, M. (2014). Introducing ICT in schools in England: Rationale and consequences. *British Journal of Educational Technology, 45*(2), 191–201. doi:10.1111/bjet.12033

Han, B.-C. (2015). *El aroma del tiempo: un ensayo filosófico sobre el arte de demorarse.* Barcelona: Herder.

Hancock, J., Birnholtz, J., Bazarova, N., Guillory, J., Perlin, J., & Amos, B. (2009, April 4-9). Butler Lies: Awareness, Deception, and Design. Proceedings of the *CHI '09,* Boston, MA, USA (pp. 517-526).

Hanrahan, B. V., Pérez-Quiñones, M. A., & Martin, D. (2014). Attending to Email. In *Interacting with Computers*.

Hardy, A. (1980). The role of the telephone in economic development. *Telecommunications Policy*, 4(4), 278–286. doi:10.1016/0308-5961(80)90044-0

Harris, C. (2013). Less is more. *School Library Journal*, 59(6), 7–8. PMID:23312511

Harris, K. J., Harris, R. B., Carlson, J. R., & Carlson, D. S. (2015). Resource loss from technology overload and its impact on work-family conflict: Can leaders help? *Computers in Human Behavior*, 50, 411–417. doi:10.1016/j.chb.2015.04.023

Harvey, D. (1989). *The Condition of Postmodernity. An Enquiry into the Origins of Cultural Change*. Blackwell.

Harvey, D. (1989). *The condition of postmodernity*. Oxford, UK: Blackwell.

Hassard, J. (2002). Essai: Organizational time; modern, symbolic and postmodern reflections. *Organization Studies*, 23(6), 885–894. doi:10.1177/0170840602236010

Hatch, M. (2013). *The Maker Movement Manifesto: Rules for Innovation in the New World of Crafters, Hackers, and Tinkerers* (1st ed.). McGraw-Hill Education.

Hefner, D., & Vorderer, P. (2016). Digital Stress. Permanent Connectedness and Multitasking. In L. Reinecke & M. B. Oliver (Eds.), *The Routledge Handbook of Media Use and Well-Being: International Perspective on Theory and Research on Positive Media Effects* (pp. 237–249). New York: Routledge.

Hemmert, F. (2008). Ambient Life: Permanent Tactile Life-like Actuation as a Status Display in Mobile Phones. Proc. of the 21st annual NEW YORK: ACM symposium on User Interface Software and Technology (UIST).

Henderson, A., & Mapp, K. (2002). *A new wave of evidence: The impact of school, family, and community connections on student achievement*. Austin: Southwest Educational Development Laboratory.

Herring, J. E. (2004). *The internet and information skills*. London: Facet Publishing.

Hertel, G., & Konradt, U. (2007). *Telekooperation und virtuelle Teamarbeit* [Telecooperation and virtual team work]. München: Oldenbourg. doi:10.1524/9783486594898

Herzig, B., & Grafe, S. (2012). Medienkompetenz – Grundbegriffe, Kompetenzmodelle und Standards. In K. Eilerts, A. H. Hilligus, G. Kaiser, & P. Bender (Eds.), *Kompetenzorientierung in Schule und Lehrerbildung. Perspektiven der bildungspolitischen Diskussion, der Bildungsforschung und der Mathematik-Didaktik*. Berlin: LIT Verlag.

Hilbert, M. (2014). What is the content of the worlds technologically mediated information and communication capacity: How much text, image, audio, and video? *The Information Society: An International Journal*, 30(2), 127–143. doi:10.1080/01972243.2013.873748

Compilation of References

Hiltz, S. R., & Turoff, M. (1985). Structuring computer-mediated communication systems to avoid information overload. *Communications of the ACM, 28*(7), 680–689. doi:10.1145/3894.3895

Hinrichs, U., & Carpendale, S. (2011). Gestures in the wild: studying multi-touch gesture sequences on interactive tabletop exhibits. In *Proceedings of the SIGCHI Conference on Human Factors in Computing Systems* (pp. 3023-3032). New York: ACM. doi:10.1145/1978942.1979391

Hinton, M. (2006). *Introducing information management: The business approach* (1st ed.). Burlington: Elsevier Butterworth-Heinemann.

Hobbs, R. (2010). *Digital and media literacy: A plan of action.* Retrieved May 7, 2016, from http://www.knightcomm.org/wp-content/uploads/2010/12/Digital_and_Media_Literacy_A_Plan_of_Action.pdf

Hochman, N., & Manovich, L. (2013). Zooming into an Instagram City: Reading the local through social media. *First Monday, 18*(7). doi:10.5210/fm.v18i7.4711

Hochman, N., & Schwartz, R. (2012, June). Visualizing instagram: Tracing cultural visual rhythms. *Proceedings of the Workshop on Social Media Visualization (SocMedVis) in conjunction with the Sixth International AAAI Conference on Weblogs and Social Media (ICWSM–12)*, 6-9.

Hodges, M. (2008). Rethinking times arrow Bergson, Deleuze and the anthropology of time. *Anthropological Theory, 8*(4), 399–429. doi:10.1177/1463499608096646

Hoggan, E., Raisamo, R., & Brewster, S. A. (2009, November). Mapping information to audio and tactile icons. In *Proceedings of the 2009 international conference on Multimodal interfaces* (pp. 327-334). New York: ACM. doi:10.1145/1647314.1647382

Hollingshead, A. B. (1998). Distributed knowledge and transactive processes in decision-making groups. In M. A. Neal, E. A. Mannix, & D. H. Gruenfeld (Eds.), *Research on managing groups and teams* (pp. 103–123). Stanford, CA: JAI Press.

Hollingshead, A. B., & Brandon, D. P. (2003). Potential benefits of communication in transactive memory systems. *Human Communication Research, 29*(4), 607–615. doi:10.1111/j.1468-2958.2003.tb00859.x

Hollingshead, A. B., Gupta, N., Yoon, K., & Brandon, D. P. (2012). Transactive memory theory and teams: Past, present and future. In E. Salas, S. M. Fiore, & M. P. Letsky (Eds.), *Theories of team cognition: Cross-disciplinary perspectives* (pp. 421–455). New York, NY: Routledge.

Honoré, C. (2004). *In praise of slowness.* New York: Harper Collins.

Horkheimer, M. (2002). *Crítica de la razón instrumental.* Madrid: Trotta.

Hosman, E., Fife, E., & Armey, L. (2008). The case for a multi-methodological, cross-disciplinary approach to the analysis of ICT investment and projects in the developing world. *Information Technology for Development, 14*(4), 308–327. doi:10.1002/itdj.20109

Hung, Y. H., Hu, P. C., & Lee, W. T. (2013, August). Improving the design and adoption of travel websites: An user experience study on travel information recommender systems.*5th IASDR International Conference*.

Hurst, M. (2007). *Bit Literacy: Productivity in the Age of Information and E-mail Overload*. New York: Good Experience.

Hüther, J., & Podehl, B. (2005). Geschichte der Medienpädagogik. In J. Hüther & B. Schorb (Eds.), Grundbegriffe Medienpädagogik (pp. 116-127). München: kopaed.

Ilgen, D. R., Hollenbeck, J. R., Johnson, M., & Jundt, D. (2005). Teams in organizations: From input-process-output models to IMOI models. *Annual Review of Psychology, 56*(1), 517–543. doi:10.1146/annurev.psych.56.091103.070250 PMID:15709945

Ingham, J. (2003). E-mail overload in the UK workplace. *Aslib Proceedings, 55*(3), 166–180. doi:10.1108/00012530310472651

Isaacs, E., Szymanski, P., Yamauchi, Y., Glasnapp, J., & Iwamoto, K. (2012, February 11-15). Integrating Local and Remote Worlds Through Channel Blending. *Proceeding of the CSCW'12*, Seattle, Washington, USA. doi:10.1145/2145204.2145299

Isaacson, W. (2014). Os Inovadores: Uma biografia da revolução digital (1st ed.). S. Paulo: Companhia das Letras.

Isaacson, W. (2011). *Steve Jobs* (1st ed.). New York: Simon & Schuster.

Ishii, H., Lakatos, D., Bonanni, L., & Labrune, J. B. (2012). Radical atoms: Beyond tangible bits, toward transformable materials. *Interactions, 19*(1), 38-51.

Jackson, T. W., & Farzaneh, P. (2012). Theory-Based Models of Factors Affecting Information Overload. *International Journal of Information Management, 32*(6), 523–532. doi:10.1016/j.ijinfomgt.2012.04.006

Jacob, R. J., Girouard, A., Hirshfield, L. M., Horn, M. S., Shaer, O., Solovey, E. T., & Zigelbaum, J. (2008). Reality-based interaction: a framework for post-WIMP interfaces. In *Proceedings of the SIGCHI conference on Human factors in computing systems* (pp. 201-210). New York: ACM. doi:10.1145/1357054.1357089

Jalava, J., & Pohloja, M. (2002). Economic growth in the new economy: Evidence from advanced economics. *Information Economics and Policy, 14*(2), 189–210. doi:10.1016/S0167-6245(01)00066-X

Jalava, J., & Pohloja, M. (2008). The roles of electricity and ICT in economic growth: Case Finland. *Explorations in Economic History, 45*(3), 270–287. doi:10.1016/j.eeh.2007.11.001

Janssen, J., & Stoyanov, S. (2012). *Online consultation on experts' views on digital competence*. Seville: JRC-IPTS.

Jipp. A (1963, July). Wealth of Nations and Telephone Density. *Telecommunications Journal,* 199-201.

Johnson, C. A. (2012). *The Information Diet: A Case for Conscious Consumption.* Cambridge, MA: O'Reilly Media.

Jorge, M. (1995). *Biologia, informação e conhecimento.* Lisboa: F. C. Gulbenkian.

Jorgenson, D. W. (2001). Information technology and the U.S. economy. *The American Economic Review, 91*(1), 1–32. doi:10.1257/aer.91.1.1

Jorgenson, D. W., & Vu, K. (2007). Information technology and the world growth resurgence. *German Economic Review, 8*(2), 125–145. doi:10.1111/j.1468-0475.2007.00401.x

Jorgenson, D., & Stiroh, K. J. (2000). U.S. economic growth in the new millennium. *Brookings Papers on Economic Activity, 1,* 125–211. doi:10.1353/eca.2000.0008

Kahney, L. (2013). Jony Ive: O gênio por trás dos grandes produtos da Apple (1st ed.). S. Paulo: Portfolio-Penguin.

Kahney, L. (2009). *A cabeça de Steve Jobs* (2nd ed.). Rio de Janeiro: Agir.

Kajtazi, M. (2011, September 27-28). Information Inadequacy: The Lack of Needed Information in Human, Social and Industrial Affairs. in DM., Hercheui, D., Whitehouse, W. McIver, Jr., & J. Phahlamohlaka, (Eds.) Proceedings of the 10th IFIP TC 9 International Conference on Human Choice and Computers, 2012, Amsterdam, The Netherlands. Retrieved from https://pdfs. semanticscholar.org/3c02/e75efec30abc5051e0fa9bb7905a3e9b6ad8.pdf

Kang, S., & Jung, J. (2014). Mobile communication for human needs: A comparison of smartphone use between the US and Korea. *Computers in Human Behavior, 35,* 376–387. doi:10.1016/j. chb.2014.03.024

Kan, V., Fujii, K., Amores, J., Zhu Jin, C. L., Maes, P., & Ishii, H. (2015). Social textiles: Social affordances and icebreaking interactions through wearable social messaging. In *Proceedings of the Ninth International Conference on Tangible, Embedded, and Embodied Interaction* (pp. 619-624). New York: ACM. doi:10.1145/2677199.2688816

Karahanoğlu, A., & Erbuğ, Ç. (2011). Perceived qualities of smart wearables: determinants of user acceptance. In *Proceedings of the 2011 Conference on Designing Pleasurable Products and Interfaces* (p. 26). New York: ACM. doi:10.1145/2347504.2347533

Katz, J. E., & Aakhus, M. (2002). *Perpetual Contact. Mobile Communication, Private Talk, Public Performance.* Cambridge: Cambridge University Press. doi:10.1017/CBO9780511489471

Kehr, F., Hassenzahl, M., Laschke, M., & Diefenbach, S. (2012). A transformational product to improve self-control strength: the chocolate machine. In *Proceedings of the SIGCHI Conference on Human Factors in Computing Systems* (pp. 689-694). New York: ACM. doi:10.1145/2207676.2207774

Kershaw, A. (2013, December 2). Tablets mean children 'struggle to use a pencil'. *The Scotsman.* Retrieved from http://www.scotsman.com/news/education/tablets-mean-children-struggle-to-use-a-pencil-1-3216500#ixzz4DickYPcS

Kim, P. H., & Giunchiglia, F. (2012). Life logging practice for human behavior modeling. In *2012 IEEE International Conference on Systems, Man, and Cybernetics (SMC)* (pp. 2873-2878). IEEE. doi:10.1109/ICSMC.2012.6378185

Kim, P. H., & Giunchiglia, F. (2013). The open platform for personal lifelogging: The elifelog architecture. In *CHI'13 Extended Abstracts on Human Factors in Computing Systems* (pp. 1677–1682). New York: ACM. doi:10.1145/2468356.2468656

Kirsch, D. (2000). A few thoughts on cognitive overload. *Intellectica, 30,* 19–51.

Kirsh, D. (2013). Embodied cognition and the magical future of interaction design.[TOCHI]. *ACM Transactions on Computer-Human Interaction, 20*(1), 3. doi:10.1145/2442106.2442109

Klapp, O. E. (1986). *Overload and boredom: Essays on the quality of life in the information society.* New York: Greenwood Press.

Klausegger, C., Sinkovics, R. R., & Zou, H. (2007). Information overload: A cross-national investigation of influence factors and effects. *Marketing Intelligence & Planning, 25*(7), 691–718. doi:10.1108/02634500710834179

Klingberg, T. (2009). *The Overflowing Brain: Information Overload and the Limits of Working Memory.* Oxford, UK: Oxford University Press.

Kohl, H., & Hasse, A. (2001). Medienrecht. In H. Schanze (Ed.), *Handbuch der Mediengeschichte* (pp. 165–185). Stuttgart: Kröner.

Kohlhase, A. (2008). *Semantic interaction design: Composing knowledge with CPoint.* Retrieved May 13, 2006, from http://citeseerx.ist.psu.edu/viewdoc/download?doi=10.1.1.472.3571&rep=rep1&type=pdf

Koprinska, I., Poon, J., Clark, J., & Chan, J. (2007). Learning to classify e-mail. *Information Sciences, 177*(10), 2167–2187. doi:10.1016/j.ins.2006.12.005

Koubek, T., Procházka, D., & Šťastný, J. (2013). Augmented reality services. *Acta Universitatis Agriculturae et Silviculturae Mendelianae Brunensis, 61*(7), 2337–2342. doi:10.11118/actaun201361072337

Kozlowski, S. W. J., Chao, G. T., Grand, J. A., Braun, M. T., & Kuljanin, G. (2013). Advancing multilevel research design – Capturing the dynamics of emergence. *Organizational Research Methods, 16*(4), 581–615. doi:10.1177/1094428113493119

Kozlowski, S. W. J., & Ilgen, D. R. (2006). Enhancing the effectiveness of work groups and teams. *Psychological Science in the Public Interest, 7,* 77–124. doi:10.1111/j.1529-1006.2006.00030.x PMID:26158912

Compilation of References

Krause, B. (2008). Anatomy of the soundscape: Evolving perspectives. *Journal of the Audio Engineering Society, 56*(1/2), 73–80.

Krueger, R. A., & Casey, M. A. (2009). *Focus Groups: A practical guide for applied research* (4th ed.). Los Angeles, CA: Sage.

Kuniavsky, M. (2003). *Observing the user experience: a practitioner's guide to user research.* Burlington, MA: Morgan kaufmann.

Lachman, R. W. (1997). *Animist interface: Experiments in mapping character animation to computer interface* (Doctoral dissertation). Massachusetts Institute of Technology.

Lam, P. L., & Shiu, A. (2010). Economic growth, telecommunications development and productivity growth of the telecommunications sector: Evidence around the world. *Telecommunications Policy, 34*(4), 185–199. doi:10.1016/j.telpol.2009.12.001

Lankshear, C., & Knobel, M. (2006). Digital literacies: Policy, pedagogy and research considerations for education. *Nordic Journal of Digital Literacy, 1*, 12–24.

Larose, R., Connolly, R., Lee, H., Li, K., & Hales, K. D. (2014). Connection Overload? A Cross Cultural Study of the Consequences of Social Media Connection. *Information Systems Management, 31*(1), 59–73. doi:10.1080/10580530.2014.854097

Lasén, A. (2014). Introducción. Las mediaciones digitales de la educación sentimental de los y las jóvenes. In I. Megía Quirós & E. Rodríguez San Julián (Eds.), Jóvenes y Comunicación: La impronta de lo virtual (pp. 7-16). Madrid: Fundación de Ayuda contra la Drogadicción.

Lazarus, R. S., & Cohen, J. B. (1977). Environmental Stress. In I. Altman & J. F. Wohlwill (Eds.), *Human Behavior and Environment* (Vol. 2, pp. 90–127). New York: Plenum. doi:10.1007/978-1-4684-0808-9_3

Lee, S., Jin, S., & Choi, B. (2012): The influences of technostress and antismart on continuous use of smartphones. *Paper presented atWorld Congress on Engineering and Computer Science,* San Francisco, CA, USA.

Lee, A. R., Son, S. M., & Kim, K. K. (2016). Information and communication technology overload and social networking service fatigue: A stress perspective. *Computers in Human Behavior, 55,* 51–61. doi:10.1016/j.chb.2015.08.011

Lee, S. B., Lee, S. C., & Suh, Y. S. (2016). *Technostress from mobile communication and its impact on quality of life and productivity.* Total Quality Management & Business Excellence; doi:10.1080/14783363.2016.1187998

Lee, S. H., Levendis, J., & Gutierrez, L. (2012). Telecommunications and economic growth: An empirical analysis of sub-Saharan Africa. *Applied Economics, 44*(4), 461–469. doi:10.1080/00036846.2010.508730

Lee, S. K., & Katz, J. E. (2014). Disconnect: A case study of short-term voluntary mobile phone non-use. *First Monday, 19*(12). doi:10.5210/fm.v19i12.4935

Lee, S., Gholami, R., & Tang, T. Y. (2005). Time series analysis in the assessment of ICT impact at the aggregate level-lessons and implications for the new economy. *Information & Management*, *42*(7), 1009–1022. doi:10.1016/j.im.2004.11.005

Lee, Y., Chang, C., Lin, Y., & Cheng, Z. (2014). The dark side of the smartphone usage: Psychological traits, compulsive behavior and technostress. *Computers in Human Behavior*, *31*, 373–383. doi:10.1016/j.chb.2013.10.047

Lerman, K., & Jones, L. (2006). *Social browsing on flickr.* arXiv preprint cs/0612047

Lewis, K. (2003). Measuring transactive memory systems in the field: Scale development and validation. *The Journal of Applied Psychology*, *88*(4), 587–604. doi:10.1037/0021-9010.88.4.587 PMID:12940401

Licoppe, C. (2004). "Connected Presence": The emergence of a new repertoire for managing social relationships in a changing communication technoscape. *Environment and Planning. D, Society & Space*, *22*(1), 135–156. doi:10.1068/d323t

Li, I., Dey, A. K., & Forlizzi, J. (2011). Understanding my data, myself: supporting self-reflection with ubicomp technologies. In *Proceedings of the 13th international conference on Ubiquitous computing* (pp. 405-414). New York: ACM. doi:10.1145/2030112.2030166

Li, K. A., Sohn, T. Y., Huang, S., & Griswold, W. G. (2008). Peopletones: a system for the detection and notification of buddy proximity on mobile phones. In *Proceedings of the 6th international conference on Mobile systems, applications, and services* (pp. 160-173). New York: ACM. doi:10.1145/1378600.1378619

Lim, C. P. (2007). Effective integration of ICT in Singapore schools: Pedagogical and policy implications. *Educational Technology Research and Development*, *55*(1), 83–116. doi:10.1007/s11423-006-9025-2

Lin, J. J., Mamykina, L., Lindtner, S., Delajoux, G., & Strub, H. B. (2006). Fish'n'Steps: Encouraging physical activity with an interactive computer game. In *International Conference on Ubiquitous Computing* (pp. 261-278). Berlin: Springer Berlin Heidelberg. doi:10.1007/11853565_16

Li, N., & Chen, G. (2010). Sharing location in online social networks. *IEEE Network*, *24*(5), 20–25. doi:10.1109/MNET.2010.5578914

Ling, R. (2004). *The Mobile Connection*. Germany: Elsevier.

Ling, R., & Yttri, B. (2002). Hyper-coordination via mobile phones in Norway. In J. Katz & M. Aakhus (Eds.), *Perpetual Contact: Mobile Communication, Private Talk, Public Performance* (pp. 139–169). Cambridge: Cambridge University Press. doi:10.1017/CBO9780511489471.013

Lin, T.-C., Cheng, K.-T., & Wu, S. (2014). Knowledge integration in ISD project teams: A transactive memory perspective. *Open Journal of Business and Management*, *2*(04), 360–371. doi:10.4236/ojbm.2014.24042

Compilation of References

Lipovetsky, G., & Serroy, J. (2009). *La pantalla global. Cultura mediática y cine en la era hipermoderna*. Barcelona: Anagrama.

Lister, M. (1997). *La imagen fotográfica en la cultura digital*. Barcelona: Paidós.

Livingstone, S. (2004). *Media literacy and the challenge of new information and communication technologies*. Retrieved May, 11, 2016, from http://eprints.lse.ac.uk/1017/1/MEDIALITERACY.pdf

Löwgren, J. (2007). Inspirational patterns for embodied interaction. *Knowledge, Technology & Policy, 20*(3), 165–177. doi:10.1007/s12130-007-9029-1

Lucchetti, S. (2010). *The Principle of Relevance. The Essential Strategy to Navigate Through the Information Age*. Hong Kong: RT Publishing.

Madden, G., & Savage, S. (2000). Telecommunications and economic growth. *International Journal of Social Economics, 27*(7/8/9/10), 893–906. doi:10.1108/03068290010336397

Mageau, T. (2012). Stop buying iPads, please. *Technological Horizons in Education Journal*. Retrieved from http://online.qmags.com/TJL0912/default.aspx?pg=2 &mode=1#pg2&mode1

Mai, L. M., Freudenthaler, R., Schneider, F. M., & Vorderer, P. (2015). I know youve seen it! Individual and social factors for users chatting behavior on Facebook. *Computers in Human Behavior, 49*, 296–302. doi:10.1016/j.chb.2015.01.074

Majaro, S. (1990). *Criatividade: Um passo para o sucesso*. Lisboa: Europa-América.

Mandavilli, A. (2006). Make Anything, Anywhere. *Nature, 442*(8). PMID:16929273

Manjunath, K. U. K. (2014). *Location Based Context-Aware Systems* (Doctoral dissertation). University of Birmingham.

Manovich, L. (2001). *The language of new media*. Cambridge, MA: MIT Press.

Manovich, L. (2005). *El lenguaje de los nuevos medios de comunicación: la imagen en la era digital*. Barcelona: Paidós.

Maravilhas, S. (2013b). Social media tools for quality business information. In Information quality and governance for business intelligence. Hershey, PA: IGI Global.

Maravilhas, S. (2013c). A gestão da informação na análise de Foucault sobre as relações poder-saber. *Biblios – Revista de Bibliotecología y Ciencias de la Información, 51*, 70-77.

Maravilhas, S. (2013d). A importância dos profissionais da gestão da informação para as organizações. *Biblios – Revista de Bibliotecología y Ciencias de la Información, 51*, 91-98.

Maravilhas, S. (2014a). Competitive Intelligence from Social Media, Web 2.0, and the Internet. In Khosrow-Pour (Ed.). Encyclopedia of Information Science and Technology (3rd ed.). Hershey, PA: IGI Global.

Maravilhas, S. (2014b). Information Quality and Value. In Khosrow-Pour (Ed.), Encyclopedia of Information Science and Technology (3rd ed.). Hershey, PA: IGI Global.

Maravilhas, S. (2014c). Challenges for Education in the Information Society. In Khosrow-Pour (Ed.), Encyclopedia of Information Science and Technology (3rd ed.). Hershey, PA: IGI Global.

Maravilhas, S. (2015c). Vantagens Competitivas da Informação de Patentes. In Estratégias Defensivas: Assegurando Vantagens Competitivas já Conquistadas. Rio de Janeiro: NovaTerra.

Maravilhas, S. (2013a). A web 2.0 como ferramenta de análise de tendências e monitorização do ambiente externo e sua relação com a cultura de convergência dos media. *Perspectivas em Ciência da Informação, 18*(1), 126–137. doi:10.1590/S1413-99362013000100009

Maravilhas, S. (2015a). Social Media Tools for Quality Business Information. In *Social Media and Networking: Concepts, Methodologies, Tools, and Applications* (Vol. 2, pp. 636–662). Hershey, PA: IGI Global.

Maravilhas, S. (2015b). Managing an information strategy project: The case of a real estate broker organization. In *Handbook of Research on Effective Project Management through the Integration of Knowledge and Innovation* (pp. 19–43). Hershey, PA: IGI Global. doi:10.4018/978-1-4666-7536-0.ch002

Maravilhas, S. (2016). Social Media Intelligence for Business. *International Journal of Organizational and Collective Intelligence, 6*(4), 100–125. doi:10.4018/IJOCI.2016100102

Marks, M. A., Sabella, M. J., Burke, C. S., & Zaccaro, S. J. (2002). The impact of cross-training on team effectiveness. *The Journal of Applied Psychology, 87*(1), 3–13. doi:10.1037/0021-9010.87.1.3 PMID:11916213

Marks, M. A., Zaccaro, S. J., & Mathieu, J. E. (2000). Performance implications of leader briefings and team-interaction training for team adaptation to novel environments. *The Journal of Applied Psychology, 85*(6), 971–986. doi:10.1037/0021-9010.85.6.971 PMID:11125660

Martín Algarra, M., Torregrosa, M., & Serrano-Puche, J. (2013). Un periodismo sin períodos: actualidad y tiempo en la era digital. In A. García (Ed.), Periodística y web 2.0: hacia la construcción de un nuevo modelo (pp. 73-83). Madrid: CEU Ediciones.

Martín Barbero, J. (2008). *Políticas de la comunicación y la cultura: Claves de la investigación. Documentos del CIDOB. Serie Dinámicas interculturales, 11*. Barcelona: Fundación CIDOB.

Masterman, L. (1989). *Media awareness education: Eighteen basic principles*. Retrieved May, 10, 2016, from http://medialit.org/reading-room/media-awareness-education-eighteen-basic-principles

Matei, S. A., Faiola, A., Wheatley, D. J., & Altom, T. (2012). The role of physical affordances in multifunctional mobile device design. *Models for Capitalizing on Web Engineering Advancements: Trends and Discoveries: Trends and Discoveries*, 306.

Compilation of References

Mathieu, J. E., Heffner, T. S., Goodwin, G. F., Salas, E., & Cannon-Bowers, J. A. (2000). The influence of shared mental models on team process and performance. *The Journal of Applied Psychology, 85*(2), 273–283. doi:10.1037/0021-9010.85.2.273 PMID:10783543

Maynard, M. T., Kennedy, D. M., & Sommer, S. A. (2015). Team adaptation: A fifteen-year synthesis (1998–2013) and framework for how this literature needs to adapt going forward. *European Journal of Work and Organizational Psychology, 24*(5), 652–677. doi:10.1080/1359 432X.2014.1001376

Mayring, P. (2008). *Die Praxis der qualitativen Inhaltsanalyse (2nd ed.).* Beltz.

McCullough, M. (2006). On the Urbanism of Locative Media [Media and the City]. *Places, 18*(2).

McCullough, M. (2007). New media urbanism: Grounding ambient information technology. *Environment and Planning. B, Planning & Design, 34*(3), 383–395. doi:10.1068/b32038

McDuff, D., Karlson, A., Kapoor, A., Roseway, A., & Czerwinski, M. (2012). AffectAura: an intelligent system for emotional memory. In *Proceedings of the SIGCHI Conference on Human Factors in Computing Systems* (pp. 849-858). New York: ACM. doi:10.1145/2207676.2208525

McGee, J., & Prusak, L. (1995). *Gerenciamento estratégico da informação: Aumente a competitividade e a eficiência de sua empresa utilizando a informação como uma ferramenta estratégica.* Rio de Janeiro: Campus.

McGrath, J. E. (1984). *Groups: Interaction and performance.* Englewood Cliffs, NJ: Prentice-Hall.

McGuckin, R. H., & Stiroh, K. J. (2001). Do computers make output harder to measure? *The Journal of Technology Transfer, 26*(4), 295–321. doi:10.1023/A:1011170416813

McMurty, K. (2014). Managing email overload in the workplace. *Performance Improvement, 53*(7), 31–37. doi:10.1002/pfi.21424

McNeil, E. (2016, June). Maine teachers trade iPads for laptops. *Education Week, 8,* 4.

Meadow, C. T., & Yuan, W. (1997). Measuring the impact of information: Defining the concepts. *Information Processing & Management, 33*(6), 697–714. doi:10.1016/S0306-4573(97)00042-3

Meier, R. L. (1963). Communications Overload - Proposals from the Study of a University Library. *Administrative Science Quarterly, 7*(4), 521–544. doi:10.2307/2390963

Mesmer-Magnus, J. R., & DeChurch, L. A. (2009). Information sharing and team performance: A meta-analysis. *The Journal of Applied Psychology, 94*(2), 535–546. doi:10.1037/a0013773 PMID:19271807

Milgram, P., Takemura, H., Utsumi, A., & Kishino, F. (1995, December). Augmented reality: A class of displays on the reality-virtuality continuum. In *Photonics for industrial applications* (pp. 282–292). International Society for Optics and Photonics.

Miller, G. A. (1956). The magical number seven, plus or minus two: Some limits on our capacity for processing information. *Psychological Review, 63*(2), 81–97. doi:10.1037/h0043158 PMID:13310704

Miller, K. (2004). *Surviving Information Overload.* Zondervan.

Miranda, S. M., & Saunders, C. S. (2003). The social construction of meaning: An alternative perspective on information sharing. *Information Systems Research, 14*(1), 87–106. doi:10.1287/isre.14.1.87.14765

Mishra, P., & Koehler, M. J. (2006). Technological Pedagogical Content Knowledge: A framework for teacher knowledge. *Teachers College Record, 108*(6), 1017–1054. doi:10.1111/j.1467-9620.2006.00684.x

Misra, S., & Stokols, D. (2012). Psychological and health outcomes of perceived information overload. *Environment and Behavior, 44*(6), 737–759. doi:10.1177/0013916511404408

Mittelstädt, V., Brauner, P., Blum, M., & Ziefle, M. (2015). On the Visual Design of ERP Systems The – Role of Information Complexity, Presentation and Human Factors. *Procedia Manufacturing, 3*, 448–455. doi:10.1016/j.promfg.2015.07.207

Moeller, S., Powers, E., & Roberts, J. (2012). The World Unplugged and 24 Hours without Media: Media Literacy to Develop Self-Awareness Regarding Media. *Comunicar, 39*, 45–52. doi:10.3916/C39-2012-02-04

Mohammed, S., & Dumville, B. C. (2001). Team mental models in a team knowledge framework: Expanding theory and measurement across disciplinary boundaries. *Journal of Organizational Behavior, 22*(2), 89–106. doi:10.1002/job.86

Mohammed, S., Ferzandi, L., & Hamilton, K. (2010). Metaphor no more: A 15-year review of the team mental model construct. *Journal of Management, 36*(4), 876–910. doi:10.1177/0149206309356804

Mohammed, S., Hamilton, K., Tesler, R., Mancuso, V., & McNeese, M. (2015). Time for temporal team mental models: Expanding between what and how to incorporate when. *European Journal of Work and Organizational Psychology, 24*(5), 693–709. doi:10.1080/1359432X.2015.1024664

Mohammed, S., & Harrison, D. (2013). The clocks that time us are not the same: A theory of temporal diversity, task characteristics, and performance in teams. *Organizational Behavior and Human Decision Processes, 122*(2), 244–256. doi:10.1016/j.obhdp.2013.08.004

Mohammed, S., & Nadkarni, S. (2011). Temporal diversity and team performance: The moderating role of team temporal leadership. *Academy of Management Journal, 54*(3), 489–508. doi:10.5465/AMJ.2011.61967991

Niada, M. (2010). *Il tempo breve. Nell'era della frenesia: la fine della memoria e la morte dell'attenzione.* Milano: Garzanti.

Nielsen. (2014). *The digital consumer.* Retrieved May 14th, 2014 from http://www.nielsen.com/us/en/insights/reports/2014/the-us-digital-consumer-report.html

Compilation of References

Nielsen, R. K. (2009). The Labors of Internet-Assisted Activism: Overcommunication, Miscommunication, and Communicative Overload. *Journal of Information Technology & Politics, 6*(3–4), 267–280. doi:10.1080/19331680903048840

Nivala, M. (2009). Simple answers for complex problems: Education and ICT in Finnish information society strategies. *Media, Culture & Society, 31*(3), 433–448. doi:10.1177/0163443709102715

Nonaka, I., & Takeushi, H. (1997). *Criação de Conhecimento na Empresa: Como as Empresas Japonesas geram a dinâmica da Inovação.* Rio de Janeiro: Campus.

O'Conaill, B., & Frohlich, D. (2012). *Timespace in the workplace: Dealing with interruptions. Proceedings of Human Factors in Computing Systems* (pp. 262–263). Denver, CO: ACM Press.

O'Hara, K., Massimi, M., Harper, R., Rubens, S., & Morris, J. (2014, February 15-19). Everyday Dwelling with WhatsApp. *Proceedings of the Mobile Apps for Enhancing Connectedness CSCW '14*, Baltimore, MD, USA (pp. 1131-1143). doi:10.1145/2531602.2531679

Oertel, R., & Antoni, C. H. (2014). Reflective team learning: Linking interfering events and team adaptation. *Team Performance Management, 20*(7/8), 328–342. doi:10.1108/TPM-03-2014-0027

Oertel, R., & Antoni, C. H. (2015). Phase-specific relationships between team learning processes and transactive memory development. *European Journal of Work and Organizational Psychology, 24*(5), 726–741. doi:10.1080/1359432X.2014.1000872

Oh, H. J., Ozkaya, E., & LaRose, R. (2014). How does online social networking enhance life satisfaction? The relationships among online supportive interaction, affect, perceived social support, sense of community, and life satisfaction. *Computers in Human Behavior, 30*, 69–78. doi:10.1016/j.chb.2013.07.053

O'Leary, M. B., Mortensen, M., & Woolley, A. W. (2011). Multiple team membership: A theoretical model of its effects on productivity and learning for individuals and teams. *Academy of Management Review, 36*(3), 461–478. doi:10.5465/amr.2009.0275

Oleksik, G., Frohlich, D., Brown, L. M., & Sellen, A. (2008). Sonic interventions: understanding and extending the domestic soundscape. In *Proceedings of the SIGCHI conference on Human Factors in computing systems* (pp. 1419-1428). New York: ACM. doi:10.1145/1357054.1357277

Oliner, S. D., & Sichel, D. E. (2000). The resurgence of growth in the late 1990s: Is information technology the story? *The Journal of Economic Perspectives, 14*(4), 3–22. doi:10.1257/jep.14.4.3

OMahony, M., & Vecchi, M. W. (2005). Quantifying the impact of ICT capital on output growth: A heterogeneous dynamic panel approach. *Economica, 72*(288), 615–633. doi:10.1111/j.1468-0335.2005.0435.x

Oulasvirta, A., Rattenbury, T., Ma, L., & Raita, E. (2012). Habits make smartphone use more pervasive. *Personal and Ubiquitous Computing, 16*(1), 105–114.

Oulton, N. (2002). ICT and productivity growth in the United Kingdom. *Oxford Review of Economic Policy, 18*(3), 363–379. doi:10.1093/oxrep/18.3.363

Overbeeke, K., Djajadiningrat, T., Hummels, C., Wensveen, S., & Prens, J. (2003). Let's make things engaging. In *Funology* (pp. 7–17). Dordrecht: Springer Netherlands. doi:10.1007/1-4020-2967-5_2

Palfrey, J., & Gasser, U. (2013). *Born digital: Understanding the first generation of digital natives*. New York: Basic Books.

Papacharissi, Z. (Ed.). (2011). A Networked Self: Identity, Community, and Culture on Social Network Sites. New York: Routledge.

Parisier, E. (2011). *The Filter Bubble: What The Internet Is Hiding From You*. New York: The Penguin Press.

Pérez Latre, F. (2012). The Paradoxes of Social Media: A Review of Theoretical Issues. In M. McCombs & M. Martín Algarra (Eds.), *Communication and social life* (pp. 257–274). Pamplona: Eunsa.

Petit, P. (2001). *Economics and information*. Dordrecht: Kluwer. doi:10.1007/978-1-4757-3367-9

Petrelli, D., Bowen, S., & Whittaker, S. (2014). Photo mementos: Designing digital media to represent ourselves at home. *International Journal of Human-Computer Studies*, *72*(3), 320–336. doi:10.1016/j.ijhcs.2013.09.009

Petrelli, D., & Whittaker, S. (2010). Family memories in the home: Contrasting physical and digital mementos. *Personal and Ubiquitous Computing*, *14*(2), 153–169. doi:10.1007/s00779-009-0279-7

Pielot, M., & Oliveira, R. D. (2013). Peripheral vibro-tactile displays. In *Proceedings of the 15th international conference on Human-computer interaction with mobile devices and services* (pp. 1-10). New York: ACM.

Piscione, D. (2014). Os Segredos do Vale do Silício: O que Você Pode Aprender com a Capital Mundial da Inovação (1ª ed.). São Paulo: HSM.

Plant, S. (2002). *On the mobile. The effects of mobile telephones on social and individual life*. Motorola.

Pohjola, M. (2000). *Information technology, productivity, and economic growth*. UNU World Institute for Development Economics Research Working Papers, No 173.

Porter, M. (1985). *Competitive advantage: creating and sustaining superior performance*. New York: Free Press.

Porter, M., & Millar, V. (1985, July-August). How information gives you competitive advantage. *Harvard Business Review*, 75–98.

Potter, W. J. (2004). *The media literacy model*. Retrieved May 14, 2016, from http://www.sagepub.com/sites/default/files/upm-binaries/4889_Potter_Chapter_3_Media_Literacy_Model.pdf

Powers, W. (2010). *Hamlet's Blackberry. A practical philosophy for building a good life in the digital age*. New York: Harper Collins.

Compilation of References

Pradhan, R. P., Bele, S., & Pandey, S. (2013). Internet-growth nexus: Evidence from cross-country panel data. *Applied Economics Letters, 20*(16), 1511–1515. doi:10.1080/13504851.2013.829170

Price, D. J. de S. (1963). Little Science, Big Science. Book, New York: Columbia University Press.

Pryzbylski, A. K., Muraryama, K., DeHaan, C. R., & Gladwell, V. (2013). Motivational, emotional, and behavioral correlates of fear of missing out. *Computers in Human Behavior, 29*(4), 1841–1848. doi:10.1016/j.chb.2013.02.014

Pscheida, D. (2010). *Das Wikipedia-Universum. Wie das Internet unsere Wissenskultur verändert.* Bielefeld: transcript.

Quah, D. (2002). Technology dissemination and economic growth: Some lessons for the new economy. In C. E. Bai & C. W. Yuen (Eds.), *Technology and the new economy* (pp. 95–156). Cambridge, MA: MIT Press.

Quan-Haase, A., & Collins, J. L. (2008). Im there, but I might not want to talk to you. *Information Communication and Society, 11*(4), 526–543. doi:10.1080/13691180801999043

Qureshi, S. S., Ahmad, T., & Rafique, K. (2011). Mobile cloud computing as future for mobile applications-Implementation methods and challenging issues. In *2011 IEEE International Conference on Cloud Computing and Intelligence Systems* (pp. 467-471). Piscataway, NJ: IEEE. doi:10.1109/CCIS.2011.6045111

Rack, O., Tschaut, A., Giesser, C., & Clases, C. (2011). Collective Information Management - Ein Ansatzpunkt zum Umgang mit Informationsflut in virtueller Kooperation[Collective information management - A starting point for handling information overload in virtual cooperation]. *Wirtschaftspsychologie, 13*(3), 41–51.

Radicati Group. (2015). Email statistics report 2015-2019. Retrieved from http://www.radicati.com/wp/wp-content/uploads/2015/02/Email-Statistics-Report-2015-2019-Executive-Summary.pdf

Radicati Group. (2016). Email market 2016-2020. Retrieved from http://www.radicati.com/wp/wp-content/uploads/2016/01/Email_Market_2016-2020_Executive Summary.pdf

Raghunath, M., Narayanaswami, C., & Pinhanez, C. (2003). Fostering a symbiotic handheld environment. *Computer, 36*(9), 56–65. doi:10.1109/MC.2003.1231195

Rainie, L., Smith, A., & Duggan, M. (2013). *Coming and going on Facebook.* Pew Research Center's Internet and American Life Project.

Rainie, L., & Wellman, B. (2012). *Networked. The New Social Operating System.* Cambridge, MA: The MIT Press.

Ramonet, I. (1999). *Die Kommunikationsfalle. Macht und Mythen der Medien.* Zurich: Rotpunktverlag.

Ramsay, J., Hair, M., & Renaud, K. V. (2008). Ubiquitous connectivity & work-related stress. In P. Zemliansky & K. St. Amant (Eds.), *Handbook of research on virtual workplaces and the new nature of business practices* (pp. 167–182). Hershey, PA, USA: IGI Global. doi:10.4018/978-1-59904-893-2.ch013

Rascão, J. (2008). *Novos desafios da gestão da informação* (1st ed.). Lisboa: Sílabo.

Reig, D., & Vílchez, L. (2013). *Los jóvenes en la era de la hiperconectividad: tendencias, claves y miradas*. Madrid: Fundación Telefónica.

Reinke, K., & Chamorro-Premuzic, T. (2014). When email use gets out of control: Understanding the relationship between personality and email overload and their impact on burnout and work engagement. *Computers in Human Behavior*, *36*, 502–509. doi:10.1016/j.chb.2014.03.075

Rennecker, J., & Derks, D. (2013). Email overload: Fine-tuning the research lens. In D. Derks & A. B. Bakker (Eds.), *The psychology of digital media at work*. New York, U.S.A.: Routledge.

Rettie, R. (2009). Mobile Phone Communication: Extending Goffman to Mediated Interaction. *Sociology*, *43*(3), 421–438. doi:10.1177/0038038509103197

Reuters Business Information. (1996). *Dying for information: an investigation into the effects of information overload in the UK and worldwide*. London: Reuters.

Ribble, M. (2001). *Digital Citizenship in Schools* (2nd ed.). Arlington, Virginia: International Society for Technology in Education.

Rifkin, J. (2011). *The Third Industrial Revolution: How Lateral Power is Transforming Energy, the Economy, and the World*. New York: Palgrave Macmillan.

Rim, H., Turner, B. M., Betz, N. E., & Nygren, T. E. (2011). Studies of the dimensionality, correlates, and meaning of measures of the maximizing tendency. *Judgment and Decision Making*, *6*, 656–579.

Ritchin, F. (2009). Awakening the Digital. *Foam Magazine*, 21, Winter.

Ritchin, F. (2009). *After Photography*. New York: Norton & Company.

Robertson, J. (2002). The ambiguous embrace: Twenty years of IT (ICT) in UK primary schools. *British Journal of Educational Technology*, *33*(4), 403–409. doi:10.1111/1467-8535.00277

Rodríguez, D. (2013). Memecracia. Los virales que nos gobiernan. Barcelona. *Gestion*, 2000.

Roeger, W. (2001). The Contribution of information and communication technologies to growth in Europe and the US: a macroeconomic analysis. *Economic Papers, European Commission Directorate-General for Economic and Financial Affairs*, 147.

Roginska, A. (2013). Auditory icons, earcons, and displays: Information and expression through sound. *The Psychology of Music in Multimedia*, 339.

Compilation of References

Röller, L., & Waverman, L. (2001). Telecommunications infrastructure and economic development: A simultaneous approach. *The American Economic Review, 91*(4), 909–923. doi:10.1257/aer.91.4.909

Romm, J. (2002). The internet and the new energy economy. *Resources, Conservation and Recycling, 36*(3), 197–210. doi:10.1016/S0921-3449(02)00084-8

Rooksby, J., Rost, M., Morrison, A., & Chalmers, M. C. (2014). Personal tracking as lived informatics. In *Proceedings of the 32nd Annual ACM Conference on Human Factors in Computing Systems* (pp. 1163-1172). New York: ACM.

Ropke, I., Christensen, T. H., & Jensen, J. O. (2010). Information and communication technologies-a new round of household electrification. *Energy Policy, 38*(4), 1767–1773. doi:10.1016/j.enpol.2009.11.052

Ross, H. F., & Harrison, T. (2016). Augmented Reality Apparel: an Appraisal of Consumer Knowledge, Attitude and Behavioral Intentions. *2016 49th Hawaii International Conference on System Sciences*. University of Edinburgh, Business School.

Rosson, M. B., & Carrol, J. M. (2008). Scenario-based Design. In A. Sears & J. A. Jacko (Eds.), *The Human-Computer Interaction Handbook. Fundamentals, Evolving Technologies and Emerging Applications*. Lawrence Erlbaum Associates.

Rubin, D. C. (1986). *Autobiographical memory*. New York: Cambridge University Press. doi:10.1017/CBO9780511558313

Ruff, J. (2002). Information Overload: Causes, Symptoms and Solutions. Harvard Graduate School of Education.

Ruiz, J., Li, Y., & Lank, E. (2011). User-defined motion gestures for mobile interaction. In *Proceedings of the SIGCHI Conference on Human Factors in Computing Systems* (pp. 197-206). New York: ACM.

Rushkoff, D. (2013). *Present Shock. When Everything Happens Now*. New York: The Penguin Group.

Rutkowski, A. F., & Saunders, C. S. (2010). Growing pains with information overload. *Computer, 43*(6), 94–96. doi:10.1109/MC.2010.171

Sadorsky, P. (2012). Information communication technology and electricity consumption in emerging economies. *Energy Policy, 48*, 130–136. doi:10.1016/j.enpol.2012.04.064

Salas, E., Nichols, D. R., & Driskell, J. E. (2007). Testing three team training strategies in intact teams: A meta-analysis. *Small Group Research, 38*(4), 471–488. doi:10.1177/1046496407304332

Sartori, G. (1998). *El Homo videns: la sociedad teledirigida*. Madrid: Taurus.

Satti, S. O., & Nour, M. (2002). ICT opportunities and challenges for development in the Arab world. *WIDER Discussion Paper, 2002/83*, 1-15.

Saunders, R., Warford, J., & Wellenius, R. (1983). *Telecommunications and economic development*. Baltimore, MD: John Hopkins University Press.

Savolainen, R. (2007). Filtering and withdrawing: Strategies for coping with information overload in everyday contexts. *Journal of Information Science, 33*(5), 611–621. doi:10.1177/0165551506077418

Sawyer, B. D., Finomore, V. S., Calvo, A. A., & Hancock, P. A. (2014). Google Glass A Driver Distraction Cause or Cure?. *Human Factors: The Journal of the Human Factors and Ergonomics Society*.

Scannell, P. (1996). *Radio, television and modern life: A phenomenological approach*. Oxford, UK: Blackwell.

Schaefer, C., Weber, C., & Voss, A. (2003). Energy usage of mobile telephone services in Germany. *Energy, 28*(5), 411–420. doi:10.1016/S0360-5442(02)00154-8

Schaeffer, J.M. (1990). *La imagen precaria: del dispositivo fotográfico*. Barcelona: Cátedra.

Schanze, H. (2001). Integrale Mediengeschichte. In H. Schanze (Ed.), *Handbuch der Mediengeschichte* (pp. 207–280). Stuttgart: Kröner.

Schoenebeck, S. (2014a). Developing Healthy Habits with Social Media: Theorizing the Cycle of Overuse and Taking Breaks. Workshop Refusing, Limiting, Departing: Why We Should Study Technology Non-Use, Toronto, Canada.

Schoenebeck, S. Y. (2014b). Giving up Twitter for Lent: How and Why We Take Breaks from Social Media. *Proceedings of the SIGCHI Conference on Human Factors in Computing Systems* (pp. 773-782). New York: ACM. doi:10.1145/2556288.2556983

Scholz, L. (2004). Die Industrie des Buchdrucks. In A. Kümmel, L. Scholz, & E. Schumacher (Eds.), *Einführung in die Geschichte der Medien* (pp. 11–33). Paderborn: Fink.

Schreyer, P. (2000). *The contribution of information and communication technology to output growth: a study of the G7 countries*. OECD, DSTI Working Paper, Paris.

Schroder, H. M., Driver, M. J., & Streufert, S. (1967). *Human information processing - Individuals and groups functioning in complex social situations*. New York, U.S.A.: Holt, Rinehart, & Winston.

Schroeder, R. (2010). Mobile phones and the inexorable advance of multimodal connectedness. *New Media & Society, 12*(1), 75–90. doi:10.1177/1461444809355114

Schuff, D., Turetken, O., & DArcy, J. (2006). A multi-attribute, multi-weight clustering approach to managing b e-mail overload. *Decision Support Systems, 42*(3), 1350–1365. doi:10.1016/j.dss.2005.11.003

Schultze, U., & Vandenbosch, B. (1998). Information overload in a groupware environment: Now you see it, now you dont. *Journal of Organizational Computing and Electronic Commerce, 8*(2), 127–148. doi:10.1207/s15327744joce0802_3

Schwartz, B., Ward, A., Monterosso, J., Lyubomirsky, S., White, K., & Lehman, D. R. (2002). Maximizing versus satisficing: Happiness is a matter of choice. *Personality and Social Psychology, 83*(5), 1178–1197. doi:10.1037/0022-3514.83.5.1178 PMID:12416921

Schwartz, R., & Halegoua, G. R. (2014). The spatial self: Location-based identity performance on social media. *New Media & Society*.

SCONSUL Working Group on Information Literacy. (2011). The SCONUL seven pillars of information literacy: core model for higher education. Retrieved from http://www.sconul.ac.uk/sites/default/files/documents/coremodel.pdf

SCONUL. (2011). *The SCONUL seven pillars of information literacy. Core model for higher education*. Retrieved May 9, 2016, from http://www.sconul.ac.uk/sites/default/files/documents/coremodel.pdf

Sellberg, C., & Susi, T. (2014). Technostress in the office: A distributed cognition perspective on human-technology interactions. *Cognition Technology and Work, 16*(2), 187–201. doi:10.1007/s10111-013-0256-9

Sellen, A. J., & Whittaker, S. (2010). Beyond total capture: A constructive critique of lifelogging. *Communications of the ACM, 53*(5), 70–77. doi:10.1145/1735223.1735243

Seo, H., & Lee, Y. (2006). Contribution of information and communication technology to total factor productivity and externalities effects. *Information Technology for Development, 12*(2), 159–173. doi:10.1002/itdj.20021

Serra, R. (Director). (1973). *Televisión Delivers People* [Film].

Serrano, P. (2013). *La comunicación jibarizada. Cómo la tecnología ha cambiado nuestras mentes*. Barcelona: Ediciones Península.

Serrano-Puche, J. (2014). Hacia una comunicación *slow*: El hábito de la desconexión digital periódica como elemento de alfabetización mediática. *Trípodos, 34*, 201–214.

Shahiduzzaman, M., & Atam, K. (2014). The long-run impact of information and communication technology on economic output: The case of Australia. *Telecommunications Policy, 38*(7), 623–633. doi:10.1016/j.telpol.2014.02.003

Shapiro, C., & Varian, H. R. (1999). *Information rules. A strategic guide to the network economy*. Boston: Harvard Business School Press.

Shenk, D. (1997). *Data Smog: surviving the information glut*. New York: Harper Collins.

Shifman, L. (2012). An anatomy of a YouTube meme. *New Media & Society, 14*(2), 187–203. doi:10.1177/1461444811412160

Shirky, C. (2008, September 18). It's not information overload. It's filter failure. *Web 2.0 Expo New York*. Retrieved May 12, 2016, from https://www.youtube.com/watch?v=LabqeJEOQyI

Shirky, C. (2010). It's not Information Overload. It's Filter Failure. *Mas Context*, (7), 76-85.

Shore, R. (2014). *Post-Photography: The Artist with a Camer*. London: Laurence King Publishing.

Sieberg, D. (2011). *Digital Diet: The 4-Step Plan to Break Your Addiction and Regain Balance in Your Life*. New York: Three River Press.

Siiman, L. A., Mäeots, M., Pedaste, M., Simons, R.-J., & Leijen, Ä. Rannikmäe, M., …, & Timm, M. (2016). An Instrument for Measuring Students' Perceived Digital Competence According to the DIGCOMP Framework. In P. Zaphiris & Ioannou, A. (Eds.), *Third International Conference, LCT 2016, Held as Part of HCI International 2016*, (pp. 233-244). Springer International Publishing. doi:10.1007/978-3-319-39483-1_22

Six, U., & Gimmler, R. (2013). Medienkompetenz im schulischen Kontext. In I. C. Vogel (Ed.), Kommunikation in der Schule (pp. 96-117). Bad Heilbrunn: Klinkhardt.

Snyder, C. (2003). *Paper prototyping: The fast and easy way to design and refine user interfaces*. Burlington, MA: Morgan Kaufmann.

Sobotta, N., & Hummel, M. (2015). A capacity perspective on e-mail overload: how E-mail use contributes to information overload. Proceedings of the 48th Hawaii International Conference on System Sciences (pp. 692–701). IEEE. doi:10.1109/HICSS.2015.89

Soucek, R., & Moser, K. (2010). Coping with information overload in email communication: Evaluation of a training intervention. *Computers in Human Behavior*, *26*(6), 1458–1466. doi:10.1016/j.chb.2010.04.024

Speier, C., Valacich, J. S., & Vessey, I. (1999). Information overload through interruptions: An empirical examination of decision making. *Decision Sciences*, *30*(2), 337–360. doi:10.1111/j.1540-5915.1999.tb01613.x

Spitzberg, B. H. (2014). Toward a Model of Meme Diffusion (M3D). *Communication Theory*, *24*(3), 311–339. doi:10.1111/comt.12042

Stewart, T. A. (1998). *Intellectual capital. The wealth of organisations*. London: Nicholas Brealey.

Stöber, R. (2003a). *Mediengeschichte. Die Evolution "Neuer" Medien von Gutenberg bis Gates. Eine Einführung. Presse – Telekommunikation* (Vol. 1). Wiesbaden: Westdeutscher Verlag.

Stöber, R. (2003b). *Mediengeschichte. Die Evolution "Neuer" Medien von Gutenberg bis Gates. Eine Einführung. Film – Rundfunk – Multimedia* (Vol. 2). Wiesbaden: Westdeutscher Verlag.

Stout, R. J., Cannon-Bowers, J. A., Salas, E., & Milanovich, D. M. (1999). Planning, shared mental models, and coordinated performance: An empirical link is established. *Human Factors*, *41*(1), 61–71. doi:10.1518/001872099779577273

Strother, J. B., Ulijn, J. M., & Fazal, Z. (Eds.). (2012). *Information overload: An international challenge for professional engineers and technical communicators*. Wiley-IEEE Press. doi:10.1002/9781118360491

Compilation of References

Sumecki, D., Chipulu, M., & Ojiako, U. (2011). Email overload: Exploring the moderating role of the perception of email as a business critical tool. *International Journal of Information Management, 31*(5), 407–414. doi:10.1016/j.ijinfomgt.2010.12.008

Süss, D., Lampert, C., & Wijnen, C. W. (2013). *Medienpädagogik. Ein Studienbuch zur Einführung* (2nd ed.). Wiesbaden: VS Verlag.

Sutter, T. (2010). Medienkompetenz und Selbstsozialisation im Kontext Web 2.0. In B. Herzig, D. M. Meister, H. Moser, & H. Niesyto (Eds.), *Jahrbuch Medienpädagogik 8. Medienkompetenz und Web 2.0* (pp. 41–58). Wiesbaden: VS Verlag.

Sutton, J. (2008). Material agency, skills and history: Distributed cognition and the archaeology of memory. In *Material agency* (pp. 37–55). New York: Springer US. doi:10.1007/978-0-387-74711-8_3

Sweetland, J. H. (1993). Information Poverty – Let Me Count the Ways. *Database, 16*(4), 8–10.

Swertz, C., & Fessler, C. (2010). *Literacy – Facetten eines heterogenen Begriffs*. Retrieved May, 5, 2016, from http://homepage.univie.ac.at/christian.swertz/texte/2010_literacy/2010_literacy.pdf

Szóstek, A. M. (2011). Dealing with my emails: Latent user needs in email management. *Computers in Human Behavior, 27*(2), 723–729. doi:10.1016/j.chb.2010.09.019

Takase, K., & Murota, Y. (2004). The impact of IT investment on energy: Japan and US comparison in 2010. *Energy Policy, 32*(11), 1291–1301. doi:10.1016/S0301-4215(03)00097-1

Tankoyeu, I., Stöttinger, J., Paniagua, J., & Giunchiglia, F. (2012). Personal photo indexing. In *Proceedings of the 20th ACM international conference on Multimedia* (pp. 1341-1342). New York: ACM. doi:10.1145/2393347.2396474

Tarafdar, M., Tu, Q., Ragu-Nathan, T. S., & Ragu-Nathan, B. S. (2007). The Impact of Technostress on Role Stress and Productivity. *Journal of Management Information Systems, 24*(1), 301–328. doi:10.2753/MIS0742-1222240109

Taylor, D. R. F., & Lauriault, T. (Eds.). (2006). *Cybercartography: Theory and practice* (Vol. 5). Amsterdam: Elsevier.

Tearle, P. (2005). ICT Implementation: What makes the difference? *British Journal of Educational Technology, 34*(5), 567–583. doi:10.1046/j.0007-1013.2003.00351.x

Thomée, S., Härenstam, A., & Hagberg, M. (2011). Mobile phone use and stress, sleep disturbances, and symptoms of depression among young adults-a prospective cohort study. *BMC Public Health, 11*(1), 66. doi:10.1186/1471-2458-11-66 PMID:21281471

Thorngate, W. (1997). More than we can know: The attentional economics of Internet use. In S. Kiesler (Ed.), *Culture of the Internet* (pp. 296–297). Mahwah, NJ: Lawrence Erlbaum Associates.

Tidline, T. J. (1999). The mythology of information overload. *Library Trends, 47*(3), 485–506.

Timmer, M. P., & Van Ark, B. (2005). Does information and communication technology drive EU-US productivity growth differentials? *Oxford Economic Papers*, *57*(4), 693–716. doi:10.1093/oep/gpi032

Tobak, S. (2010). Ten ways to stop communication overload. *CBS Moneywatch*. Retrieved June 16, 2016, from http://www.cbsnews.com/news/10-ways-to-stop-communication- overload/

Tolido, R. (2012). Cómo apaciguar la Tormenta de Información. El impacto de la abundancia de información y las posibilidades que ofrece la tecnología de la información al tratar esta cuestión. In J. Victoria Mas, A. Gómez Tinoco, & J. B. Arjona Martín (Eds.), Comunicación 'Slow' (y la Publicidad como excusa) (pp. 277-314). Madrid: Fragua.

Tolmie, P., Pycock, J., Diggins, T., MacLean, A., & Karsenty, A. (2002). Unremarkable computing. In *Proceedings of the SIGCHI conference on Human factors in computing systems* (pp. 399-406). New York: ACM.

Tomlinson, J. (2007). *The culture of speed: the coming of immediacy*. Los Angeles, CA: SAGE.

Torsi, S. (2015). Design for Consciousness in the Wild: Notes on Cognition and Space. *Analyzing Art, Culture, and Design in the Digital Age*, 279.

Torsi, S., & Giunchiglia, F. (2015). *Early prototyping for prospective memory, behavior change and self-biography*. ARTECH 2015. 7th International Conference on Digital Arts – Creating Digital e-Motions, Óbidos, Portugal.

Torsi, S., Wright, P., Mountain, G., Nasr, N., Mawson, S., & Rosser, B. (2010). The self-management of chronic illnesses: Theories and technologies. In *2010 4th International Conference on Pervasive Computing Technologies for Healthcare* (pp. 1-4). Piscataway, NJ: IEEE.

Torsi, S. (2013). Notification in Motion. Theoretical Frameworks and Design Guidelines. *JMMT: Journal of Man. Machine and Technology*, *2*(1), 1–11.

Trejo Delarbre, R. (2006). *Viviendo en el Aleph. La Sociedad de la Información y sus laberintos*. Barcelona: Gedisa.

Troxler, P. (2014). Making the 3rd Industrial Revolution: The Struggle for Polycentric Structures and a New Peer-Production Commons in the Fab Lab Community. In J. Walter-Herrmann & C. Büching (Eds.), *FabLabs: Of Machines, Makers and Inventors*. Bielefeld: Transcript-Verlag.

Tsur, O., & Rappoport, A. (2012). What's in a hashtag? Content based prediction of the spread of ideas in microblogging communities. In *Proceedings of the fifth ACM international conference on Web search and data mining* (pp. 643-652). New York: ACM.

Tulodziecki, G., & Grafe, S. (2012). *Approaches to Learning with Media and Media Literacy Education – Trends and Current Situation in Germany*. Retrieved May, 14, 2016, from http://digitalcommons.uri.edu/cgi/viewcontent.cgi?article=1082&context=jmle

Tu, Q., Wang, K., & Shu, Q. (2005). Computer-related technostress in China. *Communications of the ACM*, *48*(4), 77–81. doi:10.1145/1053291.1053323

Compilation of References

Turkle, S. (2008). Always-on/always-on-you: The tethered self. In J.E. Katz (Ed.), *Handbook of Mobile Communication Studies* (pp. 121–138). Cambridge, MA: MIT. doi:10.7551/mitpress/9780262113120.003.0010

Turkle, S. (2011). *Alone together. Why We Expect More from Technology and Less from Each Other*. New York: Basic Books.

UNESCO. (2013). *Global Media and Information Literacy Assessment Framework: Country Readiness and Competencies*. UNESCO.

United Nations. (2014). *World economic situation and prospects 2014*. New York: United Nations Publication.

Utz, S. (2015). The function of self-disclosure on social network sites: Not only intimate, but also positive and entertaining self-disclosures increase the feeling of connection. *Computers in Human Behavior*, *45*, 1–10. doi:10.1016/j.chb.2014.11.076

Vacek, M. (2014b). How to survive email. *Proceedings of the 9th IEEE International Symposium on Applied Computational Intelligence and Informatics* (pp. 49–54). IEEE.

Vacek, M. (2014a). Email Overload: Causes, Consequences and the Future. *International Journal of Computer Theory and Engineering*, *6*(2), 170–176. doi:10.7763/IJCTE.2014.V6.857

Valdes, C., Eastman, D., Grote, C., Thatte, S., Shaer, O., Mazalek, A., & Konkel, M. K. et al. (2014). Exploring the design space of gestural interaction with active tokens through user-defined gestures. In *Proceedings of the SIGCHI Conference on Human Factors in Computing Systems* (pp. 4107-4116). New York: ACM. doi:10.1145/2556288.2557373

Valkenburg, P. M., & Peter, J. (2011). Online communication among adolescents: An integrated model on its attraction, opportunities, and risks. *The Journal of Adolescent Health*, *48*(2), 121–127. doi:10.1016/j.jadohealth.2010.08.020 PMID:21257109

van Deursen, A. J. A. M. (2010). *Internet Skills. Vital assets in an information society* (Unpublished doctoral dissertation). University of Twente, Netherlands.

Vanderlinde, R., Dexter, S., & van Braak, J. (2012). School-based ICT policy plans in primary education: Elements, typologies and underlying processes. *British Journal of Educational Technology*, *43*(3), 505–519. doi:10.1111/j.1467-8535.2011.01191.x

Velicu, A., & Mitarca, M. (2016). *Young children (0-8) and digital technology: A qualitative exploratory study*. National Report Romania.

Vincent, J. (2005). Emotional Attachment to Mobile Phones: An Extraordinary Relationship. In L. Hamill & A. Lasen (Eds.), *Mobile World. Past, Present and Future* (pp. 95–104). London: Springer. doi:10.1007/1-84628-204-7_6

Virilio, P. (2012). The Administration of Fear. Los Angeles, CA: Semiotext(e).

Volpe, C. E., Cannon-Bowers, J. A., Salas, E., & Spector, P. E. (1996). The impact of cross-training on team functioning: An empirical investigation. *Human Factors: The Journal of the Human Factors and Ergonomics Society, 38*(1), 87–100. doi:10.1518/001872096778940741 PMID:8682521

Vu, K. M. (2011). ICT as a source of economic growth in the information age: Empirical evidence from the 1996–2005 period. *Telecommunications Policy, 35*(4), 357–372. doi:10.1016/j.telpol.2011.02.008

Vuorikari, R., Punie, Y., Carretero, S., & Van den Brande, L. (2016). *DigComp 2.0: The Digital Competence Framework for Citizens: Update Phase 1: The Conceptual Reference Model.* Sevilha: JRC-IPTS.

Wajcman, J. (2015). *Pressed for Time. The Acceleration of Life in Digital Capitalism.* Chicago: The University of Chicago Press.

Wajcman, J., Bittman, M., & Brown, J. E. (2008). Families without borders: Mobile phone connectedness and work-home divisions. *Sociology, 42*(4), 635–652. doi:10.1177/0038038508091620

Wallace, J. (2007). *Emotionally charged: A practice-centred enquiry of digital jewellery and personal emotional significance* (Doctoral dissertation). Sheffield Hallam University.

Walter-Herrmann, J., & Büching, C. (Eds.). (2014). *FabLab: Of Machines, Makers, and Inventors.* Bielefeld: Transcript-Verlag.

Waltz, E. (2012). How I quantified myself. *IEEE Spectrum, 49*(9), 42–47. doi:10.1109/MSPEC.2012.6281132

Walz, K. (2012): Stress Related Issues Due to Too Much Technology: Effects on Working Professionals. *MBA Student Scholarship.* Retrieved from http://scholarsarchive.jwu.edu/mba_student/12

Ward, J., & Griffiths, P. (1996). *Strategic planning for information systems* (2nd ed.). Wiley.

Warfield, K. (2014). *Making selfies/making self: Digital subjectivities in the selfie.* Academic Press.

Warm, J. S., Parasuraman, R., & Matthews, G. (2008). Vigilance requires hard mental work and is stressful. *Human Factors, 50*(3), 433–441. doi:10.1518/001872008X312152 PMID:18689050

Waters, J. K. (2010). Enter the iPad (or Not?). *Technological Horizons in Education Journal.* June 2010.

Webster, F. (2006). *Theories of the Information Society* (3rd ed.). Abingdon: Routledge.

Wegner, D. M. (1986). Transactive memory: A contemporary analysis of the group mind. In B. Mullen & G. R. Goethals (Eds.), *Theories of group behavior* (pp. 185–205). New York: Springer-Verlag.

Wegner, D. M., Giuliano, T., & Hertel, P. (1985). Cognitive interdependence in close relationships. In W. J. Ickes (Ed.), *Compatible and incompatible relationships* (pp. 253–276). New York: Springer-Verlag. doi:10.1007/978-1-4612-5044-9_12

Compilation of References

Weil, M. M., & Rosen, L. D. (1997). *Technostress: Coping with Technology @Work, @Home, @Play*. New York: Wiley.

Weinberger, D. (2012). *Too Big to Know: Rethinking Knowledge Now That the Facts Aren't the Facts, Experts Are Everywhere, and the Smartest Person in the Room Is the Room*. New York: Basic Books.

Wellman, B., Quan-Haase, A., Boase, J., Chen, W., Hampton, K., Díaz de Isla, I., & Miyata, K. (2003). The social affordances of the Internet for networked individualism. *Journal of Computer-Mediated Communication, 8*(3).

Whelan, E., & Teigland, R. (2013). Transactive memory systems as a collective filter for mitigating information overload in digitally enabled organizational groups. *Information and Organization, 23*(3), 177–197. doi:10.1016/j.infoandorg.2013.06.001

Whittaker, S., Kalnikaite, V., Petrelli, D., Sellen, A., Villar, N., Bergman, O., Clough, P., Brockmeier, J. (2012). Socio-technical lifelogging: Deriving design principles for a future proof digital past. *Human-Computer Interaction, 27*(1-2), 37-62.

Whittaker, S., & Sidner, C. (1996). Email overload: exploring personal information management of ernail.*Proceedings CHI '96* (pp. 276–283). doi:10.1145/238386.238530

Whitworth, A. (2009). *Information Obesity*. Oxford, UK: Chandos Publishing. doi:10.1533/9781780630045

Wiedow, A., Konradt, U., Ellwart, T., & Steenfatt, C. (2013). Direct and indirect effects of team learning on team outcomes: A multiple mediator analysis. *Group Dynamics, 17*(4), 232–251. doi:10.1037/a0034149

Wilson, T. (2001). *Information overload: Myth, reality and implications for health care*. International Symposium on Health Information Management Research, Halkidiki, Greece.

Wilson, D. (2002). *Managing information: IT for business processes* (3rd ed.). Woburn: Butterworth-Heinemann.

Wilson, M. W. (2012). Location-based services, conspicuous mobility, and the location-aware future. *Geoforum, 43*(6), 1266–1275. doi:10.1016/j.geoforum.2012.03.014

Wilson, T. (1985). Information management. *The Electronic Library, 3*(1), 62–66. doi:10.1108/eb044644 PMID:2498741

Winkelmann, C., & Hacker, W. (2010). Question-answering-technique to support freshman and senior engineers in processes of engineering design. *International Journal of Technology and Design Education, 20*(3), 305–315. doi:10.1007/s10798-009-9086-8

Wright, P. (2013, June 20). Why new technologies could never replace great teaching. *The Guardian*. Retrieved from https://www.theguardian.com/teacher-network/teacher-blog/2013/jun/20/technology-not-replace-teaching-learning

Wright, P., & McCarthy, J. (2004). *Technology as experience*. Cambridge, MA: The MIT Press.

Wurman, R. (1989). *Information Anxiety*. New York: Doubleday.

Yee, K. P. (2003). Peephole displays: pen interaction on spatially aware handheld computers. In *Proceedings of the SIGCHI conference on Human factors in computing systems* (pp. 1-8). New York: ACM. doi:10.1145/642611.642613

You, S., Neumann, U., & Azuma, R. (1999, March). Hybrid inertial and vision tracking for augmented reality registration. In Virtual Reality, 1999. Proceedings., IEEE (pp. 260-267). IEEE.

Young, J. R. (2005). Knowing When to Log Off. *The Chronicle of Higher Education, 51*(33), 1–5.

You, S., Neumann, U., & Azuma, R. (1999). Orientation tracking for outdoor augmented reality registration. *Computer Graphics and Applications, IEEE, 19*(6), 36–42. doi:10.1109/38.799738

Yousefi, A. (2011). The Impact of information and communication technology on economic growth: Evidence from developed and developing countries. *Economics of Innovation and New Technology, 20*(6), 581–596. doi:10.1080/10438599.2010.544470

Yukl, G., Gordon, A., & Taber, T. (2002). A hierarchical taxonomy of leadership behavior: Integrating a half century of behavior research. *Journal of Leadership & Organizational Studies, 9*(1), 15–32. doi:10.1177/107179190200900102

Yu, L. (2006). Understanding information inequality: Making sense of the literature of the information and digital divides. *Journal of Librarianship and Information Science, 38*(4), 229–252. doi:10.1177/0961000606070600

Zaccaro, S. J., Marks, M. A., & DeChurch, L. A. (Eds.). (2012). *Multiteam systems: An organization form for dynamic and complex environments*. New York: Routledge.

Zahra, K., Azim, P., & Mahmood, A. (2008). Telecommunication infrastructure development and economic growth: A panel data approach. *Pakistan Development Review, 47*(4), 711–726.

Zajac, S., Gregory, M. E., Bedwell, W. L., Kramer, W. S., & Salas, E. (2014). The cognitive underpinnings of adaptive team performance in ill-defined task situations: A closer look at team cognition. *Organizational Psychology Review, 4*(1), 49–73. doi:10.1177/2041386613492787

Zalaznick, M. (2013). Managing the move to mobile. *District Administration*, (December), 82–85.

Zeni, M., Zaihrayeu, I., & Giunchiglia, F. (2014). Multi-device activity logging. In *Proceedings of the 2014 ACM International Joint Conference on Pervasive and Ubiquitous Computing: Adjunct Publication* (pp. 299-302). New York: ACM.

Zorn, I. (2011). Medienkompetenz und Medienbildung mit Fokus auf Digitale Medien. In H. Moser, P. Grell, & H. Niesyto (Eds.), Medienbildung und Medienkompetenz. Beiträge zu Schlüsselbegriffen der Medienpädagogik (pp. 175-209). München: kopaed.

About the Contributors

Rui Pedro Figueiredo Marques received the PhD degree in Computer Science, in 2014, from the universities of Minho, Aveiro and Porto, three of the top universities in the north of Portugal. In 2008 he concluded his Masters degree in Electronics and Telecommunications Engineering, at the University of Aveiro, and in 2005 he graduated in the same area, also from the University of Aveiro. He is a researcher at the Algoritmi, a research unit of University of Minho, and his main research interests are on Organizational Information Systems and Information Systems Auditing. He has been lecturing Informatics classes since 2007 at the Higher Institute of Accounting and Administration, University of Aveiro.

Joao Batista received a PhD degree in Information and Communication in Digital Platforms, from the University of Aveiro, a Master degree in Science and Information Technology from the University of Coimbra and a first degree in Geographic Engineering from the University of Coimbra. He is a member of the Center for Research in Communication, Information and Digital Culture (CIC.Digital), where he works on the use of communication technologies in higher education and training contexts, and on information and communication overload as well. He has been lecturing Informatics courses at the Institute of Accounting and Administration (University of Aveiro, Portugal), since 1987. He has previous experience in academic management and as a private consultant as well.

* * *

Gülsüm Akarsu is research assistant at the Faculty of Economic and Administrative Sciences in Ondokuz Mayıs University, Samsun, Turkey. Dr. Akarsu teaches Mathematical Economics and Calculus for Economists courses. She received the B.S. degree in Economics, Ege University, Turkey in 2003 and PhD. Degree in Economics from Middle East Technical University, Turkey, in 2013. Her main areas of research interest are Energy Economics and Applied Econometrics.

Sameera T. Ahmed is currently an Assistant Professor in Mass Communication at the UAE University in the United Arab Emirates. She has been in the higher education sector and has worked extensively as a researcher for 20 years, including lecturing in Oman for 8 years and in the UK for 6 years. Issues about media, communication and technology form part of her research interests but they are also areas of concern relating to her children's education.

Conny Herbert Antoni is Professor for Work and Organizational Psychology at the University of Trier and President of the German Psychology Society. He is co-editor of the Zeitschrift für Arbeits- und Organisationspsychologie, consulting editor of the European Journal of Work and Organizational Psychology, and on the advisory board of Team Performance Management, and Zeitschrift für Angewandte Organisationspsychologie (GIO). His current research related to team work focuses on affective and cognitive processes in teams, team learning and team adaptation, as well as to leadership and coordination processes in IT mediated team work.

Burcu Berke is assistant professor at the faculty of Economic and Administrative Sciences in Omer Halisdemir University, Niğde, Turkey. Dr. Berke teaches International Economics and Development economics courses. She received the B.S. degree in Public Finance, Uludag University, Turkey in 2002; Master degree in Economics from Akdeniz University, Turkey, in 2004; and finally, she obtained PhD. Degree in Economics from Akdeniz University, Turkey, in 2011. Her main areas of research interest are Open Macroeconomics, International Economics and Applied Econometrics.

Enrique Corrales Crespo has a PhD in Arts obtaining extraordinary award mention. Universidad Complutense de Madrid (Spain) Cinematographer and fimlmaker. He studied in International School of Film and TV Escuela. San Antonio de los Baños. La Habana. Cuba 1997. Director of Mater PhotoEspaña and at present he is Proffesor at Universidad Europea de Madrid (Spain) 2008-2013. Visiting Lecturer in MA Design Program en el Royal College of Art, Londres, en BA Design Program de Goldsmith College, University of London, BA Interior Design Program, Geneve University of Art and Design, Ginebra, Suiza y Visiting Teacher en BA Photography Program de Santa Fe University of Art and Design, New Mexico, USA. Researcher in Zaunka Group (www.zaunka.com) and recieving several awards such as Comunidad de Madrid Award 2006, Montehermoso Creation 2006 or Premio Especial del Jurado al mejor documental Festival de cine Iberoamericano from Huelva 2005. His projects were projected in international competitions such as Les Reencontres Paris/Berlin/Madrid 08, Documenta Madrid 12 y 08, Docusur (Tenerife), European Independent Film Festival de Paris, Portobello FilmFestival (Londres), Poor film festival Gibara (Cuba), Digital Barcelona Film Festival de 2006, etc. Exhibitions: Marion Center for Photographic Art en Santa Fe, New Mexico, Centro de Creación Industrial Laboral de Gijón, Periferias 2008, Intermediae/Matadero, La Casa Encencida, Montehermoso... Off Limits Gallery (Madrid), The Aram Gallery (Londres), Galerie Klauss Braun (Berlin) y Universidades como Goldsmiths College, University of London.

Thomas Ellwart is full professor of business psychology at Trier University, Germany and works in the field of work, organizational and market psychology. He finished his PhD 2004 at Dresden University of Technology, and spent his postdoc at the University of Kiel, Germany. Between 2007 and 2010 he was professor at the University of Applied Sciences Northwestern Switzerland.

Sonja Ganguin has been a full professor for media education and further training research at the Institute of Communication and Media Studies as well as the director of the Center for Media and Communication (ZMK) at the University of Leipzig. Sonja Ganguin studied educational science at the University of Bielefeld from 1998 to 2003. After her studies she worked as a project coordinator for the DFG research project "Education through E-Learning and its Quality from the Perspective of the Subject". In 2009 Sonja Ganguin completed her PhD on Computer Games and Lifelong Learning. Thereafter she worked as an assistant professor at the University of Hagen as well as the University of Paderborn in the areas of educational theory, media pedagogy and empirical media research. Her main research areas are: media competence, media criticism, mobile media, digital games and empirical media research.

Johannes Gemkow is PhD student at the Institute of Communication and Media Studies. He studied communication and media science (BA) at the University of Leipzig and media anthropology (MA) at the University of Halle/Saale. Johannes Gemkow is a Member of European Communication Research and Education Association (ECREA) and of the German Educational Research Association (GERA). His current research focuses on media and information literacy. In his doctoral thesis he works on an international approach for the conceptualisation of information literacy. Currently, he is employed by the Department of Media Literacy and Media Appropriation (Leipzig University) as a research assistant.

Hernando Gómez Gómez is an Ex Graphic reporter, Photographer and Professor of Aesthetic and Photography at Universidad Europea de Madrid (Spain). PhD in Arts with European Mention in Photography and image construction (Universidad Complutense de Madrid). His speciality is focus on poetical image construction and photographic languages. He studied at Università Degli Studi di Torino and regular visiting proffesor in Universität der Künste Berlin, Università di Bologna, Università degli Studi di Torino, Coventry University… He covered Breaking news and Special Event news as camera operator for more than 14 years such as Political crisis, Natural Catastrophes, Terrorist Attacks, Champions Leagues, Rolland Garros, International Championship of Athletism, International Sports Events, FIFA World Cup France, Africa Cup of Nations… working with BBC, RAI, Al Jazeera, CNN, FRANCE tv, CANAL + France/Spain…and collaborator in GQ magazine, Lux Woman, Cosmopolitan, Maxima magazine, Salvatore Ferragamo.

Sérgio Guerreiro is an invited Assistant Professor at the Lusófona University, in Lisbon, Portugal, and a research member of CICANT/ULHT R&D unit. Concluded his Ph.D. degree in Information Systems and Computer Engineering at Instituto Superior Técnico / University of Lisbon (IST/UL) in 2012. Before that, he concluded the Ms.C. degree in 2003 and the engineering degree in 1999. Both degrees also in Information Systems and Computer Engineering at IST/UL. His research interests are Enterprise Ontology, Enterprise Architecture and Enterprise Governance, with a specific focus in developing and applying control systems that are able to support and deliver more information for the organizational actors involved in the decision-making processes. He has professional expertise in the mobile telecommunications field.

Rebekka Haubold is PhD student at the Institute of Communication and Media Studies at the University of Leipzig. She is employed by the Department of Media Literacy and Media Appropriation as a research assistant. Rebekka Haubold studied communication and media science (BA) and media education (MA) at the University of Leipzig. She is member of the German Educational Research Association (GERA) and project coordinator assistant of the intergenerational volunteering group "Medienclub Leipziger Löwen" of the GAM e.V. (Gesellschaft Altern Medien e.V.). In the past, she participated in several evaluation-teams of "Ein Netz für Kinder", an initiative by Federal Ministry for Family Affairs, Senior Citizens, Women and Youth. Her current research focuses on media competence for specific target groups; especially the elderly.

Bernadette Kneidinger-Müller is an Assistant Professor of Sociology at the University of Bamberg (Germany). Her research is focused on different fields of internet sociology, including mobile communication, social media research and computer-mediated communication.

Margarida Lucas holds PhD in Multimedia in Education from the University of Aveiro and is currently a Postdoctoral Researcher at the Research Centre "Didactics and Technology in Teacher Education."

Sérgio Maravilhas has two Post-Doctoral certificates. One about FAB LABS at UNIFACS in Brazil, where he teaches, and a second Post-Doc from UFBA in Patents and innovation, both with a PNPD/CAPES Grant. He has a PhD in Information and Communication in Digital Platforms (UA + UP), a Master in Information Management (FEUP and Sheffield University, UK), a Postgraduate Course in ICT (FEUP), a Specialization in Innovation and Technological Entrepreneurship (FEUP and North Carolina State University, USA) and a 5 years Degree in Philosophy, Educational Branch (FLUP). A Teacher and Trainer since 1998, worked at ESE - IPP as a Supervisor at the Internet@School project between 2002 and 2005, and a university teacher since 2005 at Aveiro University (DEGEI), and since 2010 at ULP and IESFF in Masters and MBA levels. Teaches Marketing, Research Methods, Creative Processes in Innovation, Intellectual and Industrial Property, Technology Watch, Information Management and Organizational Behaviour in universities and he's a trainer in ICT, Sales, Negotiation and Neuro-Linguistic Programming (NLP). Publishes and attends conferences mainly in the subjects of patent information, innovation, ICT, marketing, web 2.0, webradio and sustainability.

Joberto S. B. Martins has a PhD in Computer Science at Université Pierre et Marie Curie (Paris VI) - UPMC, Paris (1986), PosDoc at ICSI/ Berkeley University (1995) and Senior Visiting Researcher at Evry University – France (2016). Invited Professor at HTW - Hochschule für Techknik und Wirtschaft des Saarlandes (Germany)(since 2004) and Université d'Evry (France), teaching graduation and post-graduation courses in Computer Science and Engineering, Full Professor at Salvador University - UNIFACS on Computer Science, Head and Researcher at NUPERC (Computer Network Group) and IPQoS (IP QoS Group) research groups with research interests on Resource Allocation Models, Autonomic Computing, Software Defined Networking/ OpenFlow. Experimental Networks, Internet of Things (IoT), Smart Grid and Smart Cities. Publishing contributions in terms of book, book chapters and technical papers on journals, magazines and various congresses. Previously worked as Invited Professor at University Paris VI and Institut National des Télécommunications (INT) in France and as key speaker, teacher and invited lecturer in various international congresses and companies in Brazil, US and Europe. Active presence at R&D International Community with IFIP (International Federation for Information Process) as member of IFIP 3.6 (Distance Education) and IFIP 3.2 (Higher Education), President-Elect (2010 - 2011) of IEEE Bahia Section of IEEE (Institute of Electrical and Electronics Engineers), Higher Education Ad-hoc consultant for MEC-SESU, INEP, SEED, CAPES, computer science research projects Ad-hoc consultant for CNPq, FINEP, FAPESB and other research funding institutions and Member of Education Technical Chamber of FAPESB (Bahia State Research Funding Institution) (2005 - 2008).

António Moreira, former Director of the Department of Education, holds a PhD in Languages Teaching Methodologies and founded and directs the Doctoral Programme in Multimedia in Education at the University of Aveiro, where he also coordinated the ICT Competence Centre and the Digital Contents Laboratory up until 2011. He supervised 62 Masters dissertations and 32 PhD Theses, mainly in the integration of ICT into teaching. He is still supervising a Post-doctoral research project, having already completed 2. He was until recently the Chief Editor of the online Journal Indagatio Didactica, which he founded, and is a member of the Research Center on Didactics and Technology for the Training of Educators. He is currently a member of the University of Aveiro Doctoral School Council, and also a member of the Permanente Scientific Council of the CIDTFF R&D Center. He has profusely published both in national and international publishing contexts, and still acts as reviewer of nearly ten international journals, and also acts as an external evaluator of HEI courses in Portugal, also acting as consultant for European Projects and the Calouste Foundation.

Gökhan Obay is a master student at Institute of Social Sciences in Omer Halisdemir University, Nigde, Turkey. His main areas of research interest are Energy Economics and Macroeconomics.

Rui Miguel Simão Pascoal completed degree in Computer Engineering at the Autonomous University of Lisbon in 2014. Student of Master's degree in Computer Engineering and Information Systems at the Lusófona University of Humanities and Technologies, with the disciplinary component completed. He is finalizing the master's dissertation with title: "Augmented Reality in Outdoor Sports". In his professional activities, integrated teams in area of information technologies, particularly in 1998 at Hewlett Packard in Unix and NT servers configuration. In 2004 at IBM, operating Mainframes Z/OS and Critical Recovery. In 2011 the core technology of IBM, certification, distribution of software and fix identity management systems. In 2015 in the direction of Planning and Management Control of CTT in Business Intelligence and Executive Information System. In addition to the academic career, there are Electrotechnical professional education, in secondary education. An English course of 10th level, at the Institute of Oxford. Various professional certifications such as Unix courses, IBM Mainframes, Java language, in addition to several others.

Javier Serrano-Puche is a Senior Lecturer within the School of Communication and a research fellow for the Center for Internet Studies and Digital Life, both at the University of Navarra. He also collaborates with the Institute for Culture and Society (ICS). Professor Serrano-Puche has been a Visiting Fellow at the London School of Economics (LSE) and has published several papers and book chapters about the social impact of digital technologies. His articles has been published in journals such as Comunicar, Education in Knowledge Society, Observatorio (OBS*) or Communication & Society.

Ana Lúcia Terra is Adjunct Professor at Polytechnic Institute of Porto. She has a PhD in Information Science (2009) from University of Coimbra (Portugal). She holds a degree in History, a master degree in Modern History and has a Postgraduate Course in Libraries and Archives from the same university. Since 2002, she teaches Information Science topics in the degree of Library and Information Science and Technologies, in the Business Information master degree and in the Postgraduate Course in School Libraries Management. Her main research interests include information policies, information behavior, information management and knowledge organization.

Silvia Torsi has a five-year degree in Communication Sciences. Her first Ph.D. was in Cognitive Sciences; the second in Interaction Design, focusing on Healthcare Human-Computer Interaction. In 2006-07, she was a student at the University of Pittsburgh. In 2008-2010, she worked on a project to develop technologies for supporting the self-management of chronic illnesses. In 2010-2015 she was researcher at the University of Trento.

Index

Stay Current on the Latest Emerging Research Developments

Become an IGI Global Reviewer for Authored Book Projects

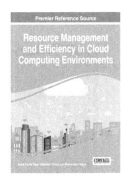

The overall success of an authored book project is dependent on quality and timely reviews.

In this competitive age of scholarly publishing, constructive and timely feedback significantly decreases the turnaround time of manuscripts from submission to acceptance, allowing the publication and discovery of progressive research at a much more expeditious rate. Several IGI Global authored book projects are currently seeking highly qualified experts in the field to fill vacancies on their respective editorial review boards:

Applications may be sent to:
development@igi-global.com

Applicants must have a doctorate (or an equivalent degree) as well as publishing and reviewing experience. Reviewers are asked to write reviews in a timely, collegial, and constructive manner. All reviewers will begin their role on an ad-hoc basis for a period of one year, and upon successful completion of this term can be considered for full editorial review board status, with the potential for a subsequent promotion to Associate Editor.

If you have a colleague that may be interested in this opportunity, we encourage you to share this information with them.

Printed in the United States
By Bookmasters